THE ANCIEN RÉGIME AND THE FRENCH REVOLUTION

THE ANCIEN RÉGIME AND THE FRENCH REVOLUTION

James B. Collins
Georgetown University

WADSWORTH
™
THOMSON LEARNING   Australia • Canada • Mexico • Singapore • Spain • United Kingdom • United States

WADSWORTH

✦
™

THOMSON LEARNING

Executive Editor: David Tatom
Development Editor: Rachel Pilcher
Marketing Manager: Steve Drummond
Project Editor: Rebecca Dodson and Cathy
 Townsend
Production Manager: Lois West
Print/Media Buyer: Lisa Kelley
Permissions Editor: Shirley Webster
Art Designer: Sue Hart

Photo Researcher: Lili Weiner
Copy Editor: Katherine Lincoln
Cover Designer: Sue Hart
Cover Image: Jacques David,
 Oath of the Horatii (1786)
Cover Printer: Transcontinental Gagne
Compositor: Thompson Type
Printer: Transcontinental Gagne

Printed in Canada

1 2 3 4 5 6 7 640 05 04 03 02 01

For more information about our products,
contact us at:
Thomson Learning Academic Resource Center
1-800-423-0563

For permission to use material from this text,
contact us by:
Phone: 1-800-730-2214
Fax: 1-800-730-2215
Web: http://www.thomsonrights.com

Library of Congress Cataloging-in-Publication
Data: 2001099210
ISBN: 0-15-507387-7

Asia

Thomson Learning
60 Albert Street, #15-01
Albert Complex
Singapore 189969

Australia

Nelson Thomson Learning
102 Dodds Street
South Melbourne, Victoria 3205
Australia

Canada

Nelson Thomson Learning
1120 Birchmount Road
Toronto, Ontario M1K 5G4
Canada

Europe/Middle East/Africa

Thomson Learning
Berkshire House
168-173 High Holborn
London WC1 V7AA
United Kingdom

Latin America

Thomson Learning
Seneca, 53
Colonia Polanco .
11560 Mexico D.F.
Mexico

Spain

Paraninfo Thomson Learning
Calle/Magallanes, 25
28015 Madrid, Spain

P R E F A C E

The historian writing about the French Revolution in 2001 faces an odd situation, because the long struggle of the Classicists and Revisionists has died down, in part because there are so few Classical historians of the French Revolution still active. That truce is puzzling in some ways, because the Revisionists, although they drove the Classicists from the field, never succeeded in creating a synthesis of their own. Now the old quarrel has moved to the wings; the new historiography of the French Revolution, both in the Francophone and Anglophone worlds, has shifted into cultural history, above all into studies of political culture's interaction with broader cultural evolution. *The Ancien Régime and the French Revolution* offers a synthesis of the events, but one that integrates material from these different historiographical schools with a careful look at many of the original documents.

For the last half century, historians of the Revolution have divided into two broad camps, called the Classicists and the Revisionists. The former see the triumph of the bourgeoisie over the aristocracy and view the French Revolution as the transition from one socioeconomic system, feudalism, to another, capitalism. The Revisionists reject this second position, focusing (like Alexis de Tocqueville) on the Revolution as a political event. Rejecting the broad perspective of transition from one socio-economic system to another, they naturally reject simplistic dichotomies such as bourgeoisie-aristocracy, too. Among the Revisionists, in recent years historians have argued vehemently when the key political and cultural shift took place: in the generation before the Revolution or in the white heat of Revolution itself, between 1787 and 1792. Much recent work has focused on political vocabulary, both in written documents and in symbolic presentations, such as festivals. Literary analysis, gender studies, and other methodologies from outside the traditional scope of historians have provided us with a much more nuanced and complex view of the Revolution.

This book seeks to provide a synthesis of the older and newer scholarship. The first synthesis combines the Classical and Revisionist positions. The book follows the Revisionist position that the Revolution was primarily a political event. It accepts the general premise of the Classical position that a fundamental socio-economic transformation underlay those events, but it argues that the transition had taken place long before the Revolution. The political events of the Revolution did provide important impetus to the transition to capitalism, above all in changed property laws, but the fundamental structures of French society and the French economy had been permanently altered by the creation of the Atlantic World economy, which was firmly in place by 1750 at the latest.

The second synthesis seeks to situate the shift in political discourse. In effect, the book agrees with both sets of historians. The book presents two shifts in political discourse, and in the larger cultural milieu of which they formed a part: the first shift sought to destroy, the second one to create. The first shift, between 1760 and 1787, rejected the Ancien Régime as a cultural and political construct. Paintings such as Jacques-Louis David's *Oath of the Horatii* (1786), on the cover, illustrate the extent to which loyalty to the fatherland, to what French people in the 1780s would have called the nation, had replaced loyalty to the King and the system for which he stood. Whether it is the legal briefs studied by David Bell or Beaumarchais's play *The Marriage of Figaro* or the paintings of David, the evidence everywhere shows that much of the French elite, particularly on its cutting edge, had abandoned the old cultural values by 1787.

The *cahiers de doléances* of the spring of 1789 provide irrefutable evidence of the shift: virtually every general *cahier* wanted three fundamental changes: 1) a representative assembly, not the king, would make the law (the *cahiers* accepted a role for the king in that process, but they disagreed about what it would be); 2) that same representative body, meeting at fixed intervals, would vote all taxes and loans, and would hold government ministers accountable for the spending of the revenue collected; and 3) the creation of civic equality for men. The great political events of 1789 concerned the destruction of the Ancien Régime. The central political issue, as the Revisionists have rightly argued, divided people by order, Third Estate versus nobility, that is, by socio-legal categories central to the Ancien Régime. The mneumonic device by which we remember that process, the fall of the Bastille, demonstrates the extent to which 1789 means the destruction of the Ancien Régime and of the political and cultural system for which it stood.

The Revolutionaries had to take two steps. First, they had to destroy the Ancien Régime. The political discourse of 1789 focused on that process, and so reflected the structure of Ancien Régime political life: opinion divided precisely on the issue of voting by order (one vote each for the clergy, nobles, and Third Estate) or voting by head (one vote per deputy). Once the Third Estate had eliminated voting by order, the new political system could begin.

The second step was the creation of that new political system, the foundations of modern political life, which, in the French case, began in earnest in August 1789. Modern political culture revolves quite often around economic interest, what some call class interest. That the French Revolution helped birth this modern political culture is made evident by the dramatically different divisions of 1791–1794 as against those of 1789–1790. In the first period, order (noble versus commoner) divided people. Many of the commoners who led the Third Estate (who were joined, let us remember, by a significant number of nobles) had exactly the same economic interests as those who opposed the Revolution. Virtually all prominent political figures of 1789 received the bulk of their income from the same source, land rent. Incrementally, that situation changed between 1789 and 1792; by 1792–1793, one could see a stark split between the landowning interests, heavily allied with the Girondin faction, and the merchant, manufacturing, and production interests, allied with the Jacobins. These two groups read different newspapers, insisted on the primacy of different levels of government (i.e., the levels they controlled), and soon engaged in a vicious, bloody fight for power. These two groups had initially formed an alliance on the political Left in 1791, but their very different economic interests, among other factors, drove them into conflict by 1793. That internecine warfare within the political Left destroyed it and paved the way for the return of a centralized government, led by Napoleon.

The Introduction examines some of the historiographical trends in French Revolution scholarship, while Chapter 1 presents the dying Ancien Régime. Chapter 2 covers its death, which took place between 1787 and August 1789. Chapter 3 shifts to the early stages of the Revolution and to the death of the monarchy, which fell in August 1792. Chapters 4 and 5 examine the First French Republic, in its Jacobin (Chapter 4) and post-Jacobin phases. Chapter 5 also examines the Revolution's social, economic, and cultural legacies. The Appendix includes a selection of documents, many of them specially translated for this volume, which allows readers to look at some of the most important primary sources from the Revolutionary period, beginning with the *cahiers* of 1789 and ending with important speeches by Robespierre and Danton. The special boxes offer brief looks at important events, such as the flight of the king, or at key personalities, like Danton and Robespierre.

Living in Washington, D.C., I have the extraordinary good fortune to be able to participate in the Washington-Baltimore area Old Regime study group. Some of the leading historians of Revolutionary period live in the area, so I have been able to draw upon the ideas of colleagues such as Christine Adams, Tom Adams, David Bell, Tom and Katherine Brennan, Jack Censer, Bob and Elborg Forster, Mack Holt, Sharon Kettering, Bob Kreiser, Orest Ranum, Robbie Schneider, Don Sutherland, and Zoë Schneider, as well as our frequent guests, people like Phil Hoffman, Tom Kaiser, Tim Le Goff, John Salmon, and Tim Tackett (a former head of our group, before his move to California). I did some of the research for this book in Paris, while staying at the house of Tim and his wife, Helen Chanut, whom I thank for allowing me the use of so unique a residence. I would like to offer a special thanks to the students in my French Revolution classes in the spring and summer of 2001, who read the manuscript and offered many valuable suggestions.

On the personal side, in addition to the support of my daughters, sisters, and mother, I want to recognize the contribution of my cousin, Tom Collins, and his wife, Sun Oak, who graciously allowed me to live in their home while writing part of the book. The larger tale of the writing is told in the acknowledgments to *From Tribes to Nation,* also published this year by Wadsworth/Thomson Learning.

At Thomson Learning, David Tatom, Glenna Stanfield, Rachel Pilcher, Cathy Townsend, and Becky Dodson have shown saintly patience. Above all, I want to thank David for assigning Stephen Wasserstein to be my editor. It has been a joy to work with such a true professional.

Acknowledgments

Wadsworth and the author would like to acknowledge the following for their support in reviewing this text:

Katherine Stern Brennan, Loyola College in Maryland; Jack R. Censer, George Mason University; Richard M. Golden, University of North Texas; James R. Lehning, University of Utah; Darline Gay Levy, New York University; Matthew Ramsey, Vanderbilt University; Alexander Sedgwick, University of Virginia (retired); Orest Ranum, Johns Hopkins University (retired).

INTRODUCTION

RETHINKING THE FRENCH REVOLUTION

Who says revolution, says violence, says subversion.[1]

Michel Vovelle, October 2001

"I was enjoying myself and watching my days go by when the French Revolution came suddenly and revived all our spirits. And the word liberty so often repeated had an almost supernatural effect and invigorated us all."[2] The Parisian glassmaker Jacques-Louis Ménétra's testimony bears ample witness to the confusion of everyone involved in the events of 1789, just as the dramatic power of the word liberty touches us more than two centuries later. We can think of the intoxicating effect of the words democracy and freedom on the peoples of Eastern and Central Europe in 1989, if we doubt the impact of the word liberty in the France of 1789.

The unexpectedness of the main events, combined with the climate of euphoric anticipation, gave revolutionary events an internal dynamic that pushed them forward in directions no one could have predicted, and which no person, nor group of people, could control. The French Revolution began as a response to the failure of the Ancien Régime. The broad-based support for the early goals of the Revolution, perhaps best demonstrated in the nearly universal jubilation on the Festival of the Federation (14 July 1790), focused on rejection of many of the Ancien Régime's fundamental attributes, above all its belief in the innate inequality of human beings. One constant—rejection of the old system—stood out from beginning to end, and its firmness meant that the more diffuse positive currents could not help but swirl around it. Once the king had turned his back on the Revolution by unsuccessfully fleeing Paris in June 1791, voices demanding complete rejection of everything related to the Ancien Régime became louder. The cacophony drowned out the softer tones of compromise. The darker urges of the human soul soon overwhelmed the better angels of our nature, sweeping all before them in a tidal wave of destruction. The bloodshed and horror of those terrible days provided the images for the nightmares of Europe's middle class and elite throughout the nineteenth century.

Yet the Revolution's excesses should not disguise its remarkable accomplishments, nor the extent to which its fundamental principles—liberty, equality, fraternity—undergird the modern struggle to achieve human rights for all. Posterity has long had an obsession with the unsavory aspect of the Revolution. Charles Dickens, relying heavily on the historian Thomas Carlisle and the political philosopher Edmund Burke, gave the English-speaking world its common cultural image of the Revolution as a bloodbath in *A Tale of Two Cities.* That image flourished in books, in films, such as the Ronald Colman version of Dickens' tale, the oft-remade *Scarlet Pimpernel,* or even D. W. Griffith's silent epic *Orphans of the Storm* (1921), and in popular culture. Textbooks continue to enshrine the dark Revolution in their visual presentation: illustrations invariably show Louis XVI or Marie Antoinette going to the guillotine, or the executioner displaying the severed head of the king to the crowd. In the bicentennial year of the Revolution, the *New York Times Book Review* ran a front-page review of Simon Schama's *Citizens* (itself a chronicle of blood and destruction), showing an open-mouthed Parisian sans-culotte with a guillotine taking the place of his teeth. The French, too, often focus on the violence: the most famous nineteenth-century attack was that of Hippolyte Taine, a conservative historian writing in the aftermath of the bloody uprising of the Paris Commune (1871). More recently, Pierre Chaunu has spearheaded a no-holds-barred attack on the radical legacy of the Revolution. In 1988, he wrote a bloodcurdling foreword to Reynald Secher's provocatively titled *La génocide franco-français: la Vendée-Vengé* (*The Franco-French Genocide*) and, in 1999, kept up the offensive in the foreword to Alain Géraud's book on the *Terror in the Vendée.*

Violent though it was, the Revolution should not and cannot be understood purely as negative, violent, and, by implication, senseless. Nor can we go to the other extreme, arguing that because the same socioeconomic group—large and medium-scale land owners—dominated the country in 1830 as well as in 1789, that nothing much had changed. Change was fundamental, irrevocable, and all-encompassing.

∾ IN SEARCH OF THE ORIGINS OF THE FRENCH REVOLUTION

What caused the French Revolution? Few questions in history have provoked such fierce debate. For specialists in other periods, the depth of feeling and the sense of engagement of specialists on the Revolution is astonishing. World-famous historians who differ in interpretation refuse to attend the same conferences, so closely do those interpretational divisions touch on personal identity. The celebrations of the bicentennial (1989), and the massive outpouring of material to which they gave rise, created further divisions; old friends stopped speaking to each other.[3] For historians of the Revolution, especially French historians, the Revolution is part of their identity. To give one's interpretation of the Revolution is to reveal one's position on contemporary politics: the Left has one interpretation, the Right another.

I do not think the search for "causes" is the right approach; we should look rather for preconditions. I believe that the French political and legal systems had lost touch with the socioeconomic reality, a process evident by the 1750s at the latest. Fundamental political and legal change had to happen in France; in that sense the Revolution was inevitable. By 1788, the Ancien Régime had tried every reform of which it was capable, and they had all failed. They failed not because individually they were bad ideas—quite the opposite was true, many of them were excellent ideas;

they failed because the fundamental intellectual underpinnings of the system had collapsed in response to socioeconomic and cultural change. As France moved toward a modern society and economy, and toward a culture consonant with that society and economy, it had to have the legal and political structures needed for its development. The Revolution made possible the creation of those structures.

Georges Lefebvre's masterpiece *The Coming of the French Revolution,* published in French in 1939, still appears frequently on American college reading lists about the Revolution, even though virtually no American specialist on the Revolution would agree with his interpretation. Lefebvre's book and interpretation survive because he offers a coherent view, focusing on the Revolution as the transition from feudalism to capitalism and on the bourgeoisie's conquest of a share of political power. The "Classical" position always stressed this transferral of political power from the aristocracy to the bourgeoisie; when the Marxists became its leading practitioners, they further emphasized class conflict as a driving motor of events.

The Revisionists, beginning with Alfred Cobban and George Taylor in the 1950s and continuing through François Furet, Donald Sutherland, William Doyle, Colin Lucas, and others in the 1980s, have blown enormous holes in the Classical interpretation. They have rejected a social or economic interpretation of the Revolution: their work shows clearly that easily defined economic classes did not take class positions in 1789, that a specific class—the bourgeoisie—did not "make" the Revolution, and that political considerations, rather than social and economic ones, usually drove the flow of events.

The Revisionists are surely right that the Revolution was, above all, a political event. That said, the hard-and-fast division of events into political, economic, and social (or cultural, etc.) does not make much sense to me. The Revolution brought French laws and political life into consonance with social and economic developments. It took place in a specific cultural moment, one which both had an impact on the Revolution and, in turn, was affected by it.

Some elements of the Classical interpretation of the Revolution survive because, at its core, it makes sense. The new social and economic order was that of capitalism: an economic order built on the free movement of capital. The laws created by the Revolution gave liberty to property (as well as to people), one of the fundamental preconditions of modern capitalism. The Revolution marked a clear break with the "feudal" past—"feudal" in the sense that much property did not have freedom of movement and did not convey a liberty of action to its "owner."

Be that as it may, in the past fifteen years, the old division between the Classical and Revisionist schools has become increasingly irrelevant. Pathbreaking scholars like Lynn Hunt and Mona Ozouf focused our attention, in the 1980s, on the symbolic life of the Revolution, examining its festivals and rhetoric. In the 1990s, specialists, influenced by cultural studies, have branched into more complex readings of the cultural structures of the Revolution. Here again, Hunt has been a leader, with her work, *The Family Romance of the French Revolution.*

In France, Antoine de Baecque's *The Body Politic* offers the best example of the impact of cultural studies on the staid historiography of the Revolution. Consider de Baecque's comments on the utility of examining the outlandish pamphlets produced during the Revolution (discussed in the text), precisely those that make the wildest charges:

> This universe created by the writing of pamphlets is like what could be called a "world of representation" where politics are exhibited as overt actions and at the same time reinvented in order to reveal to the reader the secret, inevitably hidden meaning of any event. In both cases, the narrative, overflowing with portraits, details, atmospheres, unfolds on a conventional political canvas: conspiracy, corruption of power, revolt, purification of public morality, France regenerated. These are the master fictions of narrative, the forms of representation, which are the "eyes" through which the reader is to understand this universe of alliances and rivalries knotted around power, the framework on which political events become fiction.
>
> Thus a paradox animates all these texts. How do these literally "unbelievable" narratives compel belief, constructed as they most often are out of excess, invented sources, and pretended confessions? What these pamphlets put into play is a very particular kind of accreditation of political narrative, close, in the forms of support used, to the caricature. Of course, recognizing the person or the power being portrayed is most important, but the distancing of falsity is absolutely necessary for these texts to be effective and to get read.[4]

Where is the historiography of the Revolution leading now? What, in 2001, is our French Revolution? The "New Wave" of French scholars, such as de Baecque, has reopened old questions, such as the politics of the Terror (Patrick Guinnefey), or posed new ones, like the definition of citizenship (Sophie Wahnich) or the meaning of popular sovereignty (Pierre Rosanvallon).[5] Anglophone scholars have returned to closer consideration of topics we have long thought we knew something about, but really did not: Timothy Tackett's look at the members of the National Constituent Assembly of 1789–91, the writings of Malcolm Crook and Mel Edelstein on electoral behavior, and the joint research of John Markoff and Gilbert Shapiro on the *cahiers* of 1789 offer the best examples of such iconoclasm. Their efforts have demolished long-standing myths about revolutionary France.[6]

Taking a cue from this new scholarship, I will begin by abandoning the notion of "causes" and look instead for preconditions. Moreover, as a specialist on sixteenth- and seventeenth-century France, one initially trained in the methodology of the Annales school and its emphasis on the long term (the French call it the "longue durée") I apply here the historian's craft of someone with a very different perspective than that of a specialist on the Revolution. I believe that the Classicists, the Revisionists, and the New Wave all take much too short a view of the preconditions to the French Revolution. I "read" the Revolution as part of the "longue durée" of French social, economic, political, and cultural history.[7]

To introduce the Revolution, I will first emulate the Classical historiography by focusing on the social and economic factors that made the Revolution possible, differing from much of that school's work in two fundamental ways: (1) I believe the social and economic transformation to an underlying (but not well elaborated)

capitalist system had taken place by the middle of the eighteenth century, long before the Revolution; (2) I am not seeking in social and economic factors some elusive determinative explanation. The second section will follow the Revisionists and the New Wave by analyzing the relationship between politics and culture. Again, my interpretation differs markedly from their analysis because I look for continuities in political culture that reach back hundreds of years. Most of the literature on the Revolution views the second half of the eighteenth century too much in isolation; even most of the "long-term" analyses rarely go back past Louis XIV. I will argue that key political concepts, such as citizen and nation, reached back to the political culture of the sixteenth century.

Social and Economic Preconditions of Revolution

The Classical interpretation of the Revolution rests on the fundamental assumption that a single class, the bourgeoisie, spearheaded it. For proponents of the Classical position, be they historians of Third Republic France, writing between the 1870s and the 1930s, or Marxist historians writing in the twentieth century, the French Revolution was *the* bourgeois revolution. The Marxist position provides a simple theoretical model: in the transition from feudal to capitalist society, the ruling class of the former, the nobility, had to be replaced by a new ruling class, the bourgeoisie.

This interpretation has some obvious flaws, most notable among them that the economic interests of those supporting and opposing the Revolution in 1789ñ90 were remarkably similar: wealthy and middling landowners (especially lawyers) dominated both sides, and neither mercantile nor industrial leaders played much of a role.[8] Many Revolutionary leaders of 1789, especially the famous Committee of Thirty, were nobles, and the coalitions of 1789 did not form along neat class lines. The nobility were an order (a group defined by sociolegal status), not a class, and the bourgeoisie as a coherent class (a group defined primarily in terms of the nature of their economic activity) cannot be identified. We must be extremely wary of seeing a class-based antagonism as the driving motor of the change: the great division of 1789, the question of whether the Estates General would vote by order (one each for clergy, nobles, and commoners) or by head (individual deputy) was not a class issue, but one of orders. Can we thus speak of a bourgeois revolution? How does that question get reformulated after 1791, when people from the mercantile and industrial worlds did get involved, particularly when we know that such people took a much more radical line than, say, lawyers and landlords? Moreover, the work of scholars like Guinnefey, Donald Sutherland, and Colin Lucas has shown that the Terror often pitted these two groups, initially allies, against one another, rather than pitting those in favor of the Revolution against the Counterrevolutionaries.

In the late nineteenth century, in isolated rural western Brittany, where the peasants still spoke Breton Gaelic rather than French, they called the days before 1789, "the time of the seigneurs." The folk memory recalled a time when one private individual had full rights of justice over another, when he (or she) could even condemn a neighbor to death. They remembered a time of codified legal inequality and associated that time with "feudalism." They associated the post-1789 world with fundamentally different principles: that only the state could judge individuals; that the law presumed all men to be equal to other men, and women equal to other women (although it did not presume women to be equal to men).[9]

Something like class antagonisms did exist in some parts of the countryside, where relations among the rural population grew more tense for primarily economic reasons. In most parts of France, however, these economic tensions did not crystallize along clearly definable "class" lines. Each little area, often each parish, had its own fault lines. Rich peasants fought one another for control of a lease or for control of the parish. People chose sides according to traditional clan rivalries; in the nineteenth and early twentieth centuries, many rural dwellers joined political "parties" for such purely family reasons. Class warfare does not offer a very good explanation of these conflicts, but the structural flaws of feudalism[10] inhibited everyone interested in agricultural modernization, so that the most powerful groups in rural society often wanted an abolition of the elements of this "feudal" order and the creation of what we might call a "capitalist" one.[11] This transition to a more modern form of property did not take place as a transition of absolutes: many forms of feudal property had weakened over the centuries, and capitalist forms, and practices, had long held sway in many sectors.

Fundamental economic change fostered a social confusion in late eighteenth-century France that cannot be ignored as a precondition of the Revolution. All social orders have value systems that most people accept, even if but tacitly. People share notions of accepted social hierarchy, share social myths, share values so evident to everyone that no one need ever discuss them. These shared myths, values, and principles of hierarchy had collapsed in France by the 1770s. The acceptance of God—of the God of the Catholic Church—remained universal among peasants in many regions, and even large numbers of urban dwellers stayed devoutly attached to the Church, but elites increasingly questioned the validity of this conception of God. By the 1780s, France had a distinctive split between believers and unbelievers: that split has divided France ever since, providing the driving motor for much of the country's internal politics for generations. The Revolution failed to navigate the straits between the Scylla of secularism and the Charybdis of Catholic conformity.

Social myths fell hard, as well. Perhaps the reading list of the "blue library" of Troyes gives us a hint: chivalric stories, a staple of popular literature until 1750, all but disappeared from the publication lists.[12] Upper-class readers, too, enjoyed a very different sort of literature; novels focused on enhanced sensibility and their locales shifted away from the Court and into the pastoral countryside so beloved by eighteenth-century French painters. In France, as in Germany or England, heroes and heroines in novels even came from the broad middle classes. The styles at Court—from the exaggerated hairpieces of the Queen and her circle to the punctilious, empty rituals of man and woman alike—increasingly drew ridicule more than emulation.

The Revolution brought with it an immediate, dramatic change in clothing styles. The superfluous luxury of Court fashion quickly gave way to the utilitarianism of middle-class costume (itself an adaptation of workers' clothes). Contemporaries called the workers of Paris the sans-culottes: those who wore trousers. Many of the Revolutionary leaders believed, like ordinary people, that real men wore trousers, not the contemptible culottes of the "aristos."[13]

The sudden and permanent change to trousers, and the concomitant simplification of women's everyday garments (among the well-to-do), indicates the profound distaste for old ways of dress and comportment: it shows that the middle and lower classes had decisively rejected many of the mores of the upper class well before 1789, but were simply in no position to do anything about it. Forms of speech show the same pattern: Monsieur and Madame shifted from terms reserved for the few, to ones automatically granted to all (at least in the city). These conventions eventually became foundation stones of everyday politeness in French society.

The Classical interpretation suggests that the economic dislocation in the 1770s and 1780s paved the way for a social and political revolution. Recent scholarship has, in my view, completely discredited this position. The key economic shifts had taken place a generation or two before the Revolution. That said, we still need to understand the economic situation in France during the 1780s, because short-term economic issues, above all the price of bread, often had an immediate effect on events. The confused French economy of the 1780s offers a microcosm of broader patterns in French life. Some sectors, such as the colonial trade, seemed to thrive, others (wine, in the early 1780s; cotton after 1786) to collapse, still others (grain) to fluctuate dangerously. Yet appearances could hide more fundamental realities: wine and cotton, in the throes of a typical capitalist shake-out in the 1780s, would rebound strongly in the nineteenth century, while the apparently flourishing colonial trade faced difficult days ahead.[14] The massive importation of slaves, averaging 40,000 Africans a year in the 1780s, put planters in a precarious economic position because of rising debts, and added fuel to the revolutionary fires soon to break out in Saint-Domingue (Haiti). Blacks organized and applied pressure to the slave system, creating profound unease among the colonial elite. The increased black agitation for freedom, and the rediscovery of human decency among some white French people, led to renewed demands for emancipation by groups such as the Society of the Friends of Blacks, founded in 1788. Its members included such important leaders of the Revolution as Brissot, Condorcet, Lafayette, La Rochefoucauld, and Mirabeau.

In the agricultural sector, two great myths have long sustained a completely misleading picture of the French countryside: (1) that the peasants owned a substantial portion (40 percent) of the land; and (2) that France had low, and comparatively stagnant productivity. The use of an overall statistic of land distribution grotesquely misrepresents the real land hunger of the peasants in 1789. True, French peasants owned about 40 percent of the land, including those areas held in common by their village communities (the nobility and the middle classes held about 25 percent each, the clergy 10 percent), but the overall figure disguises the peasants' ownership of fields. In village after village, in all but the wine-growing regions, the nobility, middle classes, and clergy owned virtually all the fields.[15] Although the French peasantry owned a considerable portion of the "land," therefore, they still suffered from a pronounced land hunger. They also wanted access to forests, which belonged overwhelmingly to the wealthy and to village communities. Complaints about lack of access to firewood and forest pasturage were endemic in the cahiers of 1789.

The productivity myth ignores historical reality. The work of historians such as Thomas Brennan, Philip Hoffman, Liana Vardi, Jean-Marc Moriceau, and

Jean-Laurent Rosenthal has shattered the low productivity myth. Some regions, such as Normandy or the area around Paris, had incontestable, measurable long-term growth in the eighteenth century, growth that matched that of eighteenth-century England. In backward regions, such as the Vannetais or the Massif Central, productivity did lag far behind that of more advanced regions. Even there, however, we should be careful: outlying regions seem to have had generalized yields of 4 to 1, which would be a 50 percent increase in the share of the harvest that did not have to go to next year's seed, when compared with the figures for the late seventeenth century.[16]

Overall, the French economy grew effectively through most of the eighteenth century. Evidence of that greater prosperity existed everywhere: extensive new building in major cities; much broader consumer spending; rapid expansion of markets for new goods; increased peasant ownership of house emplacements; larger livestock herds. Three crucial economic issues remained: (1) what to do about the growing numbers of those permanently displaced by economic change; (2) the land hunger of peasants for plots in the grain fields; and (3) the fundamental instability of the colonial sector.

These economic factors had two direct ties to the Revolution. First, the obvious change in the nature of the French economy between 1720 and 1770 had not led to a similar change in the political system. French law had become outmoded for the emerging capitalist economy of the eighteenth century. No example makes that more clear than the emergence of one of what would be a dominant industrial site of the nineteenth-century French economy, the iron mills of Le Creusot. The founders of the mill had great difficulty disciplining their workers. Unhappy with the interference of the bailiwick court of Montcenis in the internal affairs of the factory, the owners petitioned the king (1788) to make the iron mill into a fief, with rights of high, middle, and low justice! Nor did the Crown shrink from such actions: in 1783, the king had made the canal of the Charolais into a fief with full justice.[17] Any legal system that could find no other way to provide full authority to a business owner than to create a fief, was not long for this world in eighteenth-century northwestern Europe.

The government fully recognized its need to take into account these interests—that is one reason it refused to declare bankruptcy in 1787—but the existing system did not, could not, offer propertied elites sufficient protection or participation. These elites remained overwhelmingly landed ones, who derived by far the largest share of their income from simple land rent. As the example of Le Creusot suggests, the existing legal system could not provide legal guarantees for modern forms of property. Elites throughout the Atlantic world shared these concerns: such elites sought everywhere to define property as a natural right, one that, like liberty, deserved the complete protection of the law. Laws protecting property from everyone, especially from the government, were the first goal of these elites, especially in France. The fundamental question of 1789 was therefore quite simple: who would make such laws? Gouverneur Morris, an American representative in Paris at the time, stated it bluntly to a French friend in February 1789: "the great Question, shall we hereafter have a Constitution or shall Will continue to be Law, employs every mind and agitates every heart in France."

The second political effect appears obvious to anyone familiar with electoral politics in the contemporary world: holding elections in a climate of economic dislocation invariably produces a defeat for the government in power. The French elections of 1789 offer a textbook example of that political maxim.

Cultural and Intellectual Origins of the Revolution

Few propositions seem more self-evident than that of the ideas of the Enlightenment paved the way for the French Revolution, but the precise relationship has long proven difficult to pin down. The Enlightenment stressed the primacy of reason, the equality of individuals, the worth of the individual, and the need to reject received authority as a justification for anything—all ideas accepted by the Revolutionaries. Enlightenment ideas made the Revolution possible, but a directly causal relationship remains elusive. Philosophers like Montesquieu or Locke or Voltaire or Rousseau gave the French people a new political vocabulary, allowed them to live a new mental universe. Even the opponents of the Revolution had to live in that universe. The inventories after death of provincial notables who both supported and opposed the Revolution suggest that they read the same books (or rather had the same books in their libraries).

This new mental universe carried with it enormous dangers. Ménétra is certainly right that the word "liberty" had a supernatural effect, but what precisely did liberty mean? As events made clear, it did not mean the same thing to everyone, nor did words like citizen or *patrie* (fatherland) or people. Moreover, as the French historian François Furet and his followers have stressed, the Revolutionary triad—liberty, equality, fraternity—carried within it a fundamental conflict. Liberty and equality were not immediately reconcilable in the eyes of everyone. The founding document of the Revolution, *The Declaration of the Rights of Man and of the Citizen* (26 August 1789; see the Appendix), established the fundamental distinction between people ("man"), who shared civil rights, and citizens, who alone had civic rights.[18] The distinction between citizen and man (even if one accepts, as most Revolutionaries did not, that "man" should mean human, that is, should include women) created inequality. The radicals, like the Prussian baron Anacharsis Cloots, who sat as a deputy in the Convention, saw the problem at once. Cloots told the Convention, in April 1793: "Foreigner? barbarous expression that begins to make us blush and of which we leave the use to those ferocious hordes that the plough of civilized men will effortlessly make disappear."[19] Cloots's project for a "universal human republic" got as little acceptance as his rejection of the concept "foreigner": a year after he requested that the Convention ban the word "foreigner," they had him guillotined as a "foreign spy."

Just as the modern definitions of "citizen" and "nation," perhaps best embodied in the opening words of the Constitution of the United States (1787), "We the People," emerged embryonically in the fluid linguistic climate of the end of the eighteenth century, so, too, did many other modern political terms. The Revolutionaries borrowed ideas from a wide range of sources. Thus *The Declaration of the Rights of Man and of the Citizen* begins its main body with a quotation from Rousseau, "man is born free," but then rejects Rousseau's definition of natural rights, putting property on the same level as liberty and resistance to oppression.[20] They took ideas from Aristotle, Cicero, Locke, Montesquieu, Voltaire, and many others.

The explosion of 1789 makes sense only if we understand the depth to which new ideas had spread throughout French society. A painting like Jacques David's *Oath of the Horatii* (1786, on the cover), universally understood by his contemporaries to be an homage to the fatherland and patriotism, has obvious echoes in the *cahiers de doléances* (grievance lists) of the spring of 1789: they, too, think first of the *patrie* and only then of the king. Even the nobility used that ordering.

French culture also changed its understanding of the role of women in society. More and more French women had received an education; many of them (many in comparison to earlier times, not as a percentage of all women) received an outstanding education, sometimes provided by salons they themselves conducted. Women were becoming more and more independent: they ran more businesses; they more often chose their own marriage partners; they moved more readily. All of the factors that we now know lead to dramatic improvement in women's rights in our world—above all female literacy—were on the rise. French men feared this rising power of women. Women had long existed as powerful individuals within a patriarchal system: widows ran many a shop or farm, yet, by definition, powerful widows did not pose a threat to the patriarchal family.

In the eighteenth century, with the rise of individualism, male individuals had to wonder how they would create themselves as independent beings, breaking the collectivities' bonds on them, while simultaneously making sure that women did not break free. Individual women, sharing individual rights with all men, were one of men's worst nightmares. The more the Revolution moved toward rights for all men—moved, for example, toward the principle of universal male suffrage—the more it restricted the rights of women. I do not believe that relationship to be fortuitous. Men had to fight on two fronts to create themselves as independent entities: they had to defeat the old society of orders—their primary concern, as the debates of the National Constituent Assembly make quite clear—but they also had to defeat those who threatened their new independence. For all men, that meant restricting women; for middle-class men, it meant restricting lower-class men. For colonial whites, it meant restricting blacks.[21]

The Revolutionaries walked a tightrope in other ways. French culture had enormous tension between Puritanical and hedonist impulses. Writers used sexual imagery to make political points; some, like the Marquis de Sade, explored the limits of permitted sexual discussion in order to examine the boundaries of accepted discourse. Sade hardly stood alone in his use of sexual material. Once the Revolution broke out, political discourse turned heavily sexual, particularly the attacks on Marie Antoinette. Pamphlets offering explicit details of her supposed sexual life, complete with artists' impressions of what these acts must have looked like, circulated everywhere; these pamphlets left nothing to the imagination (see the illustration in Chapter 3).

Many of the Revolutionaries, like the Jacobin leader Maximilien Robespierre, known as "the Incorruptible," were Puritanical in their moral beliefs. They faithfully accepted a powerful image of popular culture: that of the corrupt, evil, decadent nobility sucking the blood of the nation to pay for its immoral hedonism. Starting in 1789, people read about these decadent nobles in every popular paper, but they had had access to such stories even under the Ancien Régime, by means of scandal sheets and other illicit publications. They read about sexual infidelity and unconventionality; they read about wild gambling and excessive parties; they read about poor girls corrupted by evil barons; they read about lecherous friars and promiscuous nuns. Robespierre and others easily tapped into this rich vein of anger, following a path well trodden by generations of Catholic preachers.

At the same time, artists and writers seized upon their new-found freedom to explore the limits of their imaginations. Another current of the Revolution encouraged this freedom of expression. In time, the two currents would clash, as we shall see. All of the personal accounts of the Revolution's early days emphasize the incredibly fluid nature of events. Political leaders rose and fell with bewildering speed. Citizens had to act in one way on Monday but then often in another later in the week. Leaders encouraged them to reject everything, and they often did. They changed the names they gave their children (a process already visible in some regions in the 1780s). They changed their patterns of speech. They decided they had an interest in politics, and had a right to be heard. Not everyone stood up, but politics became a popular concern in a way unimaginable to the Ancien Régime.

Individualism

The French Revolution gave concrete meaning to the word revolution, as we understand it: fundamental, all-encompassing, systemic change. Prior to 1789, the word, when used in a political sense, meant simply a sudden shift in government. Although the Revolution came to encompass every aspect of life, it began as a movement for political change and remained a political event above all else. The Revolution destroyed the monarchical system that had existed for centuries, putting in its place a political system based on three principles absolutely anathema to the Ancien Régime: (1) that all men (men only) were legally equal in every respect; (2) that the citizens of France had a right to a representative body that would approve laws, taxes, and all government policies; and (3) that the nation was the source of France's unified sovereignty. The Revolutionaries abandoned the Ancien Régime's society built on groups and created a society built around the individual.

Looking back on the outcome, historians have created a false narrative of these momentous changes; moreover, they have taken the "master fictions of narrative" from the Revolutionaries themselves. The ideal of citizenship becomes, in this fictional narrative, a bourgeois or middle-class value; the emphasis on equality arises, too, from the desire of the middle class to have "careers open to talent." Merit becomes, like citizenship, a middle-class imperative. In reality, in the France of 1789, the nobility were the one national source of an ethos of citizenship. The nobility long preserved the idea that they were the political nation, that is, in Aristotelian terms, the citizens. They further believed that all members of the political nation were fundamentally equal. Taking their Aristotelian idea one step further, they accept his principle of equality for equal things, and inequality for unequal things. Citizens were equal; non-citizens were not equal to citizens. The citizenship ideal persisted as well in the towns, but there it had focused for about two centuries on the local polity (the town itself) and not on France as a whole.

The Revolutionaries did not invent the vocabulary of citizenship, of the public good, of the republic; they simply stole it from the nobility, above all the provincial spokesmen of the old ideal of the commonwealth of noble citizens.[22] The fundamental change, of course, was that the political thinkers, pamphleteerists, and even public opinion of the second half of the eighteenth century rejected the premise that only nobles could be citizens. In fact, I would argue that the mounting vitriol against the nobility, whom the Revolutionaries rechristened the "aristocracy," stemmed precisely from this decisive conflict about the identity of the nation and the citizens. The militant wing of the Third Estate of 1789 argued that the nobles belonged to a different nation, to a noble commonwealth, of which they alone were citizens. The commoners belonged to the nation of France; they were its citizens. Nobles, by definition, were not. The Jacobin leader Saint-Just made the explicit connection noble-foreigner in his speeches of 1794. "We must make a *cité,* that is citizens who are friends, who will be Hospitallers [a Crusading order of knights]and brothers. . . . Forbid to all nobles, to all foreigners the right to remain in Paris and in fortified places." Ostracized from the political nation, nobles, like other foreigners, were "not to be admitted in popular societies [political clubs] and committees of surveillance, nor in communal or sectional assemblies."[23]

As de Baecque has shown, the Revolutionaries used the image of the body politic to insist that the nobles had to be cut out, as "privileged excrescences." Pamphlet after pamphlet, illustration after illustration, song after song called for the removal of the diseased nobility from the body politic. The "aristos" became a cancer that had to be cut out in order to restore the health of France. Abbé *Sièyes,* in the most famous pamphlet of 1789, "What is the Third Estate?", explicitly separated the nobility, and all the privileged, from the nation: "It is truly a people apart, but a false people that is unable, for lack of useful organs, to exist by itself and that attaches itself to a real nation, like those parasitic growths that cannot live except on the sap of plants that they exhaust and deplete."[24]

As for the movement to equality, that received its strongest push from below. Whether it was the peasants demanding equality of taxation or the artisans demanding equality of political rights, the push for equal rights for all (men) —on the grounds that all (men) were part of the nation—had little support from the middle classes. They sought throughout the Revolution to protect themselves from the dangers of "demagoguery" and the permanent sovereignty of the people. Condorcet, the day before the fall of the monarchy, warned that the people were about to assert their sovereignty: "One cannot be astonished to see citizens expecting their salvation only from themselves, and looking to the exercising of the inalienable sovereignty of the people—a right they hold from nature—as a last resource."[25] In France, as in the fledgling United States of America, the propertied middle classes believed in equal civil rights for a nation's inhabitants, but they certainly did not believe in equal civic rights. They tried to create polities that made a clear distinction between "men" and "citizens," and reserved political authority for the latter.

The middle classes tried to synthesize the ideals of citizenship, which they took from the nobility, and the principle of equality, demanded by the mass of the (male) population, into a system in which the representatives of the people would act as the political nation. Little wonder that the radical Jacobins turned to Jean-Jacques Rousseau, who denounced representative government as an odious sham, for their political vocabulary. Little wonder that their Constitution of 1793 (enacted, but suspended due to the "emergency"; it was abolished before it went into effect) enshrined many key principles of (male) equality, such as the right of all to education and subsistence. As soon as the middle classes, led by the substantial landowners and the lawyers, regained control of the Revolutionary government in the fall of 1794, they resolved the tension between representative government and democracy through a reassertion of a careful hierarchy of representative structures.

The changes begun in 1789 carried profound practical consequences; to cite only the most obvious, who should vote for the representatives? The Revolutionary governments, and subsequent ones, have answered that question in extremely different ways, ranging from the nearly universal adult suffrage of the 1990s to the roughly 10,000 electors of the Restoration (1815–30). Individual heads of government, such as Napoleon, have turned these representative assemblies into rubber stamps, but they have not gone back on the principle. French governments since the Revolution have also remained remarkably faithful to one element of the Rousseauian principle of popular (male) sovereignty. Again and again, the French people have been asked to vote in referenda for Constitutions or constitutional changes; even Napoleon submitted his laws changing France into a Consulate and, later, into an Empire, to the French people (men only) for a vote.

Because words like bourgeois and feudal now carry so much historiographical baggage, the idea that the French Revolution was a "bourgeois" revolution easily gets lost in semantic quarrels about what "bourgeois" means. Such quarrels distract us from the fundamental reality that the underlying basis of political society had changed completely. In its purest political sense, feudalism was the tie of one man to another: a vassal was his lord's man. Over time, however, that aspect of feudalism all but died out. In place of that individualist feudalism, the French had created a corporate society relying on what they themselves called feudal principles. The group or corporation—be it the Crown, the Church, a province, a town, a guild, a patriarchal family—was the basis of their society. By the seventeenth century, the monarchy rested on those privileged groups. The sixteenth-century ideal of the commonwealth headed by the king died during the Wars of Religion (1562–1598), but the ideal of the citizen lived on. The revival of the ideal of the "nation," not surprisingly set forth most clearly by the noble judges of the Parlements in the 1760s, led to the public reappearance of the citizen.

The new France of 1789 rejected a society based on the group; it rested on something else: the individual. Just as the monarchical state replaced the monarchical commonwealth at the end of the sixteenth century, so, too, the Revolution replaced that corporatist state with one built on the "nation." They reached back to the vocabulary of the old commonwealth (defined in its Aristotelian sense of the collective group of citizens) and made all male members of the nation into citizens. Their political entity was thus a nation-state. Each citizen had the right to contribute to the forming of the laws (himself or through a representative). The Revolution created a society built on these male individuals, on their liberty and their property.

The changed political system, and ethos, profoundly affected all elements of French life. The abolition of feudal property, the confiscation of the lands of the Catholic Church (on behalf of the nation), and the codification of private property as a natural right had important economic consequences. These developments mark a fundamental shift in the nature of the French economy, not because of any dramatic change in the nature of production, but because they created the legal framework for

but also hampered French development in 19th C.

modern economic development. The Revolution created in France a much more uni-fied legal definition of property; it abolished claims of economic and legal privilege owned by nobles, towns and communities, the Church, guilds, and many others.

French society became much more democratic. Quite apart from extending lin-guistic courtesies to a wide range of people, society's experiment with the Republi-can virtue of fraternity had permanent cultural effects. Although social distinctions returned with Napoleonic vengeance, beneath that surface of stratification lay a so-cial myth of equality—a myth, moreover, codified in law. Such myths can have im-portant practical implications, when the time is ripe. In the 1990s, riders of the Paris Metro witnessed a dramatic fraternal, egalitarian change. For many years, the Metro had first- and second-class cars, a sort of physical embodiment of Orwell's *Animal Farm* principle ("all of us are equal, but some of us are more equal than others"). The government provided mass transit for all—because all shared the need—but it provided nicer transportation (much smaller crowds) for those who could afford it—because some had greater wealth and "deserved" special treatment. Popular pres-sure—more and more people simply ignored the signs on the trains—has recently led to the abolition of the first-class cars. The Metro, after all, is too democratic for such things: Parisians believe they have a natural right to subsidized mass transit to and from work, just as their ancestors believed they had a right to subsidized bread. The radical Constitution of 1793, after all, made subsistence a legal right. The arti-sans who took part in the Prairial and Floréal uprisings of 1795 emphasized the con-nection in their basic demand, "Bread and the Constitution of 1793!"

The Revolution's emphasis on the individual did not extend to women. Quite the contrary: the Revolution stripped women of their individuality. The legal code to emerge from the Revolution, the Napoleonic Code, forced married women to take their husbands' last names, removed many property rights from women, virtually out-lawed divorce, and carried a specific clause stating that a wife "owes her husband obe-dience." Women emerged from the Revolution as non-citizens, as non-individuals. Men sacrificed female humanity on the altar of male individualism.

WAS THE FRENCH REVOLUTION INEVITABLE?

Did the specific events of the Revolution have to happen? No. Here we must distin-guish between the necessity of legal and political change and the serendipity of events. Circumstance—such as the bad harvest of 1788—played an important role in radicalizing the situation at various times. Individual people had a critical impact on events: royal ministers such as Brienne and Necker miscalculated; Louis XVI vac-illated constantly; individual leaders, like Mirabeau or Lafayette, Danton or Robe-spierre, made decisions that drove events in unexpected directions. Ordinary people took matters into their own hands, often in ways unanticipated by their so-called leaders. Important figures, like Mirabeau or Marat or Marshal Hoche, died young, in Marat's case, of course, due to assassination.

Yet we should not overestimate the role of individuals or chance. I believe French public opinion had reached an overwhelming consensus that the right to impose taxes on the people, and to make laws, belonged "to the nation assembled by means of deputies," as the Parlement of Paris put it in 1787. The French people enthusiastically welcomed the changes of 1789. Urban citizens rose up in town after town to overthrow the old order; peasants stopped paying feudal dues and tithes. The massive national outpouring of support for the Revolution on 14 July 1790 (the Feast of the Federation) reveals the extent to which the French people had sickened of the Ancien Régime and embraced the new order. David was right in 1785: the French Horatii were ready to take their Oath to the fatherland even before they dethroned their "father." The rapidity and totality of rejection of the Ancien Régime shows us how rotten it was at its core. The Revolution was not an accident.

Notes

1. From Professor Vovelle's remarks at the University of Maryland's conference on *The Terror and the French Revolution,* October 2001.

2. J. Ménétra, *Journal of My Life,* ed. D. Roche, trans. A. Goldhammer (New York: Columbia University Press, 1986), 217.

3. I had firsthand experience of the personal nature of these quarrels at the two main conferences in honor of the bicentennial, the meeting of the Society for French Historical Studies, held at Georgetown University in May 1989 (for which I was on the program and organizing committee), and the five-day celebration of "The Image of the French Revolution," held in Paris in July 1989 (at which I presented a paper). The great American specialist of late eighteenth-century France, Steven Kaplan, offers a fascinating in-depth look at these quarrels in *Farewell Revolution: The Historians' Feud, France, 1789/1989* (Ithaca and London: Cornell University Press, 1995).

4. A. de Baecque, *The Body Politic. Corporeal Metaphor in Revolutionary France, 1770–1800,* trans. C. Mandell (Stanford: Stanford University Press, 1997), 13.

5. S. Wahnich, *L'impossible citoyen. L'étranger dans le discours de la Révolution française* (Paris: Albin Michel, 1997); P. Rosanvallon, *La démocratie inachevée. Histoire de la souveraineté du peuple en France* (Paris: Gallimard, 2000).

6. The final frontier lies in economic and financial history. The Stygian darkness of our ignorance in these two areas is only rarely penetrated by the light offered in the works of people like Thomas Brennan, Philip Hoffman, and Liana Vardi, and in the superb articles jointly authored by Donald Sutherland and Timothy Le Goff. See the Bibliography for titles.

7. The Annales school, which takes its name from a leading French history journal, initially took three approaches to history: (1) the history of events, above all politics, which it de-emphasized; (2) the "conjuncture," medium-term factors such as economics; and (3) the "longue durée," long-term, slowly evolving factors such as climate and demography. In the past twenty years, some historiography, above all works on religion by scholars such as Jean Delumeau, has emphasized the slow, long-term evolution of systems of belief. I think political

culture must be examined from this same long-term perspective, so that a classic "history of events" moment like the French Revolution needs to be understood from the perspectives of the short-term (such as the influence of individual personalities), of the medium-term (economic changes in the century preceding 1789), and the long term (cultural continuities in the categories of political discourse).

8. H. Applewhite, *Political Alignment in the French National Assembly, 1789–1791* (Baton Rouge and London: Louisiana State University Press, 1993), offers extensive analysis of the backgrounds of the deputies and of their political coalition building.

9. French law had an ambiguous attitude toward male equality, too. The Jacobins abolished slavery in 1794, but Napoleon reinstated it. To cite another example, when France conquered Algeria (1830) and then incorporated it into metropolitan France, the law discriminated against the indigenous Algerian population to the end. Much of the literature simply ignores these elemental facts of French political life; Rosanvallon, *La démocratie inachevée,* offers a recent example of a book about the French path to democracy that makes no substantive mention of the denial of women's right to vote or of the racist voting rules in Algeria when it formed a legal part of metropolitan France.

10. Historians discussing these events disagree on a definition for feudalism. Conservative historians prefer the political definition—centered on the hierarchical system of fiefs, and thus believe feudalism had essentially died out long before in France. Marxist historians talk of a feudal mode of production, and of the transition to a capitalist mode of production. Each definition has its problems. Eighteenth-century French writers invented the term *féodalité* to describe the existing sociolegal system of their own day, not of that of the distant Middle Ages. I use feudalism to mean the social and legal system existing in France in the 1780s. The conservatives' alternative, manorialism, focuses too closely on the economic aspects of the fiefs, leaving out the very real importance of judicial and other rights. The Marxist usage ignores the fundamental shift from medieval feudalism, which revolved around the ties of one individual to another one, to the eighteenth-century variety, built on corporate groups, not on individuals. In that sense, Marx's comments in *The German Ideology,* that serfs could resist feudalism as individuals, by moving to towns, whereas proletarians had to assert themselves as individuals by acting collectively to overthrow the state, demonstrate his confusion about the bastard socioeconomic, and, by extension, political system of the eighteenth century. I would argue that eighteenth-century people asserted, and had to assert, their individuality by acting collectively to destroy what they themselves called feudalism. The sociolegal system placed significant limitations on enjoyment of property, particularly landed property, but it did not preclude the existence of sectors—manufacturing, commerce—essentially capitalist. More than 90 percent of the peasants in this eighteenth-century "feudalism" were free people: only two provinces, Burgundy and the Franche-Comté, had significant numbers of serfs.

11. By capitalist, I mean here two basic elements: rule of law equally applicable to all, particularly as it pertains to property; and a modern form of property, entailing the right of the owner to do what he wishes with his possessions. I use the pronoun he because the system created by the French Revolution did not give women full property rights. As in all systems, the state retained rights of eminent domain, providing for confiscation of private property for public purposes, with full compensation, legally determined and adjudicable, for those losing property.

12. The "blue library" of Troyes published cheap books such as almanacs, songbooks, and lives of saints for a mass audience; it took its name from the blue covers of the books.

13. Among the peasantry, well into the twentieth century, little boys wore skirts until age 5 or 6, when the family held a "trousering" ceremony, marking the boy's transition from infant to little man. The middle classes and others shared the use of the skirts for small boys, but there is little evidence they preserved the trousering ceremony.

14. In these shake-outs, visible in many sectors of the French economy since the late seventeenth century, rapidly increased demand leads to increases in production; over-production leads to consolidation (destruction of weak competitors, unemployment), followed by renewed growth led by fewer, but larger enterprises.

15. Where did the 40 percent come from? Many French peasants owned an "emplacement," a small cottage with a tiny plot attached; collectively these "emplacements" occupied a substantial portion of the village's land, but none of them were remotely large enough to support a family. Virtually no peasants in France owned the 20 acres of arable land necessary to support a family of four; the wealthiest peasants rented their large farms.

16. In a crop yield of 4 to 1, the farmer gets to keep three seeds for every one planted, as against only two in a 3 to 1 yield.

17. J. Bart, *La Révolution française en Bourgogne* (Dijon: La Française d'Édition et d'Imprimerie, 1996), 39–40.

18. Civil rights are those extended to all members of society, such as the protection afforded by the laws; civic rights pertain to political participation in the governing process. In the eighteenth century, French people would have used Aristotle's definition of the citizen as someone who has civic rights, that is, who participates, either directly or through his (men only) representative in the process of government. Noncitizens would not have the right to participate in civic life, but they would receive the same legal protections of their civil rights, such as security of their person and property.

19. Cited in Wahnich, *L'impossible citoyen*, 7.

20. Rousseau believed that society instituted property and that it was not a natural right; the men of 1789, like Locke, defined property as a natural right.

21. In places such as Saint-Domingue, those of mixed race faced the most confusing situation of all—some demanded rights equal to those of whites, ignoring the plight of blacks, whereas others joined with blacks to demand equal rights for all men.

22. The ties between the political vocabulary of the 1780s and that of the sixteenth century are very close. The concept of the "public good" (*bien public*) lay at the core of French political life from at least the middle of the fourteenth century until the late sixteenth century. It revived again after 1750, but in the dramatically different context of the emerging capitalist society. I have examined the issue of the public good in two recent articles, "Noble Political Ideology and the Estates General of Orléans and Pontoise: French Republicanism," *Historical Reflections/Reflexions Historiques* 27, n. 2 (2001): 219–240, and "La Guerre de la Ligue et le Bien Public," in *Le traité de Vervins,* ed. J.-F. Labourdette. (Paris: Presses Universitaires de France, 2000), 81–96.

23. Wahnich, *L'impossible citoyen,* 9–10. Saint-Just used the unusual French word for city or town, cité, rather than the usual ville, because he wanted listeners to make the direct association to the Greek concept of the polis and to the Roman one of the civitas, the urban community of citizens.

24. Cited in de Baecque, *The Body Politic,* 85.

25. Rosanvallon, *La démocratie inachevée,* 53.

BRIEF CONTENTS

CONTENTS

Chapter One

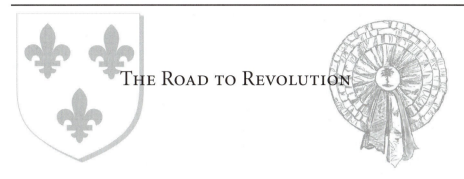

The Road to Revolution

Our Father, who art in Versailles. Abhorred be Thy name. Thy king-dom is shaken. Thy will is no longer done on earth or in heaven. Give us back this day our daily bread, which Thou hast taken from us. For-give Thy parlements who have upheld Thy interests, as Thou forgiveth those ministers who have sold them. Be not led into temptation by du Barry. But deliver us from that devil of a chancellor. Amen![1]

Louis XV reigned for fifty-nine years; ironically, just as the measles brought him to the throne by killing his father and older brother in 1712, so smallpox ended his life in 1774. France greeted Louis the once "Well-Beloved's" death with as much joy as his accession, because he had long lost the respect of his subjects, as the parody of the *Our Father* attests. His death placed his feckless grandson on the throne as Louis XVI, and made an Austrian princess, Marie Antoinette, France's queen. This unlucky pair would lose their thrones, and their heads, in a Revolution made inevitable by Louis XV's failure to reform successfully the French political system.

Louis XV had a deserved reputation as a lecher, a man easily misled by his seemingly boundless sexual appetite. The du Barry of the "prayer" is Jeanne Bécu, a Parisian prosti-tute whom Louis XV made his official mistress, giving her the title of countess of Barry. That a woman of such low social status could become a dominant figure in a Court at which one needed four generations of noble ancestry merely to be presented, gives us some idea of the extent of Louis's depravity. Eighteenth-century opinion held that du Barry owed her success to her ability to overcome the king's impotence. Sexual innuendo aside, the "prayer" also shows people directly tied the moral issue to the political one, to the "devil of a chancellor," seeking massive judicial and governmental reform.

The desacralization of the monarchy evident in the *Our Father* parody destabi-lized the French monarchy because the political order rested on the premise that the king, although unlimited (absolute) in his ability to make human law, was bound to God's law. The privileged of Ancien Régime France protected themselves and their property from the king precisely under "God's law," by means of contracts. Any weak-ening of the religious aura surrounding the monarchy, therefore, deeply threatened their position. The government had long preached the value of the king's unlimited authority to make law; when God's law checked such authority, elites could tolerate his claim. Spreading secularization among urban elites undermined one part of that

1

political consensus, Louis's blatant flouting of God's commandments, and the public rebukes he received for it from his own confessor starting on Easter 1739, completed the job. Elites began to look for a new way to protect their property and position, a search that led directly to the French Revolution.

Louis XV and Louis XVI ruled over a kingdom undergoing rapid transformation in basic demographic structures, in economic organization, and in social and cultural life. During Louis XV's lifetime, French adults began to live longer: life expectancies for those who reached twenty moved past sixty years of age. In the last third of the century, another dramatic demographic shift took place: more children survived. Infant mortality, which had been 50 percent in the period before 1750, dropped to 40 percent, anticipating the improvement in child survival in the nineteenth century. In the countryside, mortality of those aged one through nine dropped from about one in six to one in seven; in towns, the rate dropped from one in four to one in five. The greater life expectancy of adults and, to a much lesser extent, the decline in infant mortality, led to a sharp increase in the French population, which rose to more than 26 million. At the end of the century, the birth rate dropped slightly, perhaps in reaction to changing infant mortality, presaging the massive decrease in the birth rate in the nineteenth century.

The early eighteenth-century changes in the economy required new legal structures; however, the full force of the changes could not be fully effective because of the lingering legal and political impediments to economic liberty. Despite the modernization of many economic sectors, the old state structures remained in place; indeed, in many sectors the Crown amplified the structure of privilege. Virtually all commercial transactions theoretically involved a royal official, collecting a fee, or an individual, such as guild warden or a wine broker, who had paid a fee to the Crown in order to supervise a given activity and pocket the transaction fee. Although almost all economic activity should have come under such supervision, in fact, public annoyance at such interference encouraged an enormous black market sector, which, alas for historians, has left relatively few records.

Much of that activity took place inside the great agents of change: the towns and their suburbs. Paris stood far above any other French city, its population more than 600,000 by the time of the Revolution, so it deserves a description of its own. Rouen, Nantes, Bordeaux, Marseille, and Lyon, although only about a sixth (or less) the size of Paris, dominated their hinterlands and expanded rapidly after 1720. The middling towns, those of 20,000–50,000 population, followed widely different trajectories, while most smaller towns (10,000 or less) actually declined in population. The total urban population of France remained remarkably stable in the eighteenth century, but its distribution shifted markedly toward the larger cities.

∼ THE NEW URBANISM

Paris

> *Paris is the only city of the kingdom where sensations are at their most vivid, where the spirit and the heart acquire their maximum energy.*[2]

Parisian bookseller Nicolas Ruault, to his brother
(living in Evreux), August 1786

In the spring of 1757, the young Parisian Jacques-Louis Ménétra set out, like so many thousands of craftsmen before him, on his Tour de France. Ménétra traveled by way of Versailles to Orléans, thence through the Loire valley to other large towns such as Tours and Angers. After a brief stint with the Royal Navy at Saint-Malo, he ended up at Nantes. From Nantes, he visited the major southwestern towns: Poitiers, La Rochelle, and, of course, Bordeaux. Crossing France, he passed by way of Toulouse, through the great towns of Languedoc, like Montpellier, Narbonne, and Béziers, and up the Rhône valley, through Arles, Valence, and Lyon. He finished his great circle by way of Dijon and Auxerre, arriving back in Paris in 1763. He revisited this last leg of the route a year later, but then settled in Paris.

This intrepid wanderer left us a journal of his trip, one filled with countless details of everyday life. Ménétra borrows tales from others (taking on himself the role of hero); he exaggerates his own importance at every turn; he maltreats women and brags constantly about his successes as a lover. Despite his many flaws, Ménétra offers a penetrating look at popular attitudes toward many subjects: work, leisure, politics, and family life among them.

What did it look like, this France of 1757, as seen through the eyes of a young apprentice, later journeyman glazier? We can see elements of continuity. Ménétra often works for clergymen (churches, after all, had lots of glass) and for nobles. Again and again, he encounters aristocratic clients such as the abbess of Beaumont-lès-Tours, Henriette de Bourbon-Condé. As a journeyman, "he" has dealings with the major political figures of Bordeaux—intendant, First President of the Parlement, and governor of Guyenne—during a crisis involving recruitment of journeymen for the militia there in 1758.[3] The journeymen had a clear conception of the political rivalry among these men, using the First President against the intendant to achieve their goal. Later, back in Paris, we see him crossing paths with various Parlementaires and even, as a court tennis player, with the duke of Orléans and the prince of Condé. His work takes him to the palace at Versailles, where he sees the royal children.

Ménétra follows the normal life of a young artisan from Paris. As a young man, he takes his Tour de France, living fast and loose. Coming back from the Tour, he obtains work in Paris and soon settles down, getting married and starting his own shop. He raises two children and even, as a member of the fire brigade, becomes himself a member of the forces of order. As a guild master in a building trade, he lived through good times from the 1760s through the 1780s, because Paris expanded its habitat so rapidly in those years. Louis-Sébastien Mercier, writing in the 1780s, felt that a third of the city's buildings had been constructed since 1760. The duke of Orléans, who owned the largest forests near the city, became the richest man in France selling wood for this building boom.

Ménétra violates many of the rules of his own guild. He subcontracts work for others. He fights constantly with the guild wardens, accusing them of seeking to monopolize the trade of the city to their own benefit. At the fireworks for the marriage of the future Louis XVI and Marie Antoinette, his wife nearly becomes one of the scores trampled to death by the panicked crowd. In the chic café de la Régence, in what is now the Palais-Royal, he claims to have played checkers with a certain M. Rousseau: "We played I lost." The glazier informs us that "Both of us had the same clothes but not at all the same (breadth of knowledge) Between us (the difference) was like night and day."[4]

Ménétra's Paris changed dramatically, both in terms of the social distribution of the population and in terms of geographic size. The city of Louis XIV encompassed perhaps 1,000 hectares; that of Louis XVI included more than 3,400 hectares. As we can see from the city plan (see map, below), Paris engulfed such former suburbs (*faubourgs*) as Saint-Germain, Saint-Jacques, Saint-Honoré, and Saint-Martin. Places such as Montmartre that had been distinct villages in the seventeenth century became faubourgs in the eighteenth. Even so, Paris had a much tighter circumference than it does today. When the government erected the customs wall around the city in the 1780s, it established barrier posts at such sites as the current place Denfert-Rochereau, the place de la Nation, and the place Stalingrad. The sixteenth through twentieth *arrondissements* of today's Paris were then independent villages like Montmartre. Areas now in the heart of the city, such as the Invalides, only began to be integrated into Paris in the eighteenth century.

Starting from the Left Bank, we would find in late eighteenth-century Paris a poor workers' district near the place Maubert and the rue Saint-Jacques, extending out to the faubourg Saint-Marcel. At the center of the Left Bank lay the Latin Quarter, dominated by the Sorbonne and the students. Further west, the enclave of Saint-German-des-Prés, owned by the monks of that abbey, did not form a legal part of the city. Beyond this district, Paris expanded rapidly, particularly in the section near the Luxembourg Palace. Continuing along the river, the Invalides quarter and the Faubourg Saint-Germain had many new aristocratic homes.

Paris in 1767.

Rousseau at the Café de la Régence in 1771. Menétra may or may not have played checkers with Rousseau, but he could well have seen him at the Café de la Régence.

Source: Musée du Petit Palais.

Crossing the river to the Right Bank, the Marais, the center of elite society in the early seventeenth century, fell out of fashion: immigrant Jews from Alsace settled there. The most chic elements of Parisian society gathered in the Faubourg Saint-Honoré, near what is now the place de l'Opéra, and around the Champs-Elysées, where the government created the place Louis XV, known to us as the place de la Concorde. These sections of the city had relatively low population densities, as few as fifty or even twenty-five people per square hectare.

The Louvre and the Tuileries dominated the river bank down to the Pont Neuf, but just across from the palace one found a teeming popular quarter leading to les Halles. France's greatest market had thousands of merchants and shop owners, and tens of thousands of carters, porters, and day laborers, to say nothing of those working in the food trades: butchers, bakers, vegetable sellers, wine merchants, and countless others. People lived cheek by jowl in old parishes like Saint-Germain-l'Auxerrois or Saint-Jacques-de-la-Boucherie. The old center of the city became progressively more

The interior of the Café of Manouri. Most of the clients are men, some of whom also smoke.

SOURCE: Bibliothèque Nationale, Cabinet d'Estampes.

overcrowded with the poor: densities reached 1,300/ha^2 (square hectares) and never fell below 500/ha^2.

The east end of the city included the parish of Saint-Antoine and the Faubourg Saint-Antoine, quarter of artisans and immigrants. More than 60 percent of its metal, wood, and construction workers came from outside Paris, as did almost 80 percent of those in its food trades. Much of the economic activity in these suburbs escaped official supervision; Ménétra, although a sworn master of the glaziers' guild, illegally subcontracted work in the suburbs and collected his money under the table. The Bastille, looking down on the working populations of Faubourg Saint-Antoine, dominated the eastern end of the city. The profound social divisions within the city had important political consequences from the Revolution until the expulsion of many of the poor from Paris in the "urban renewal" after World War II.

Some elements of eighteenth-century Paris survive in the contemporary city. One gets a sense of the crowded, narrow streets in sections like the Marais or the rue Mouffetard. Many of the great aristocratic hôtels, such as the Musée Rodin (built for the financier Peyrenc in the 1720s) survive throughout the city; the monumental buildings dot its landscape. The eighteenth-century churches—Sainte-Geneviève (the Panthéon), Saint-Roch, the Madeleine, and Saint-Sulpice—can still be seen, in their Classical splendor. In a certain way, contemporary Paris, despite its many churches, substantially understates the remarkable number of ecclesiastical buildings the city once held: parish churches, convents, and abbeys. The interiors of many

had A, adaptation, but insufficient

of the parish churches bear witness to artistic embellishments of the eighteenth century, particularly in the ornate preaching pulpits, made usually of carved wood but, on occasion, as at Saint-Roch, of marble. Among the secular monuments, perhaps the two most enduring are the Hôtel de Ville, built to replace the town hall gutted by fire in 1772, and the place Louis XV/place de la Concorde.[5] The place de l'Hôtel de Ville, like the place de la Concorde, shows a greater emphasis given to open space, air, and light, in comparison with earlier conceptions of the city. One easily compares the place de la Concorde, with its vast open spaces and its broad array of avenues branching out in many directions, with the place des Vosges (built under Henry IV and Louis XIII), with its colonnaded sides and its tight enclosure, or even with the tightly enclosed place Vendôme, finished in 1697.

Eighteenth-century Parisians lived in a world in transition, one to which we would have difficulty adapting. Their city had limited, albeit much improved access to water; they lived in poorly heated and ventilated rooms, in houses known only to the initiated, on streets often without signs. In the late eighteenth century, the central and city governments fought to put numbers on the buildings and tried, with less success, to make all corner building owners put up a street sign so that people did not have to rely simply on the forest of shop, tavern, and merchant ensigns festooned on every building. The city government introduced a better police force, one with substations throughout the city and nearly three times as many men as under Louis XIV. The city fire company also took root; at first, people did not like this innovation, but they soon came to accept the obvious benefits of fire brigades. They and other Parisians demanded better lighting; in the 1760s, the city introduced the reflecting street lamp, greatly improving illumination.

Despite better lighting, improved sewage disposal, numbered houses, named streets, fire brigades, and a larger, more efficient police force, Paris remained a premodern city. Houses had better insulation—the poor less often hung cheap tapestries on their walls for warmth—but still could not provide amenities we would take for granted. Quite apart from the obvious lack of ready water, which had to be carried to upper floors by hand, most dwellings afforded little privacy: people performed bodily functions in hallway enclaves, in full view of passing neighbors. Families lived in single rooms, surrounding a fireplace, although after 1750 stoves slowly began to replace the hopelessly inefficient open hearth fireplaces. Many workers lived in holes-in-the-wall, using the public facilities around them as part of their "private" space. Thus artisans often ate in taverns or obtained meals from professional food preparers. The poorer elements of the population could not receive someone into their home, but rather met with others at the local tavern to share a meal or a drink. However much the police might call such taverns public space, and consequently demand the right to oversee them, neighborhood inhabitants viewed them as private space, as an extension of their homes. People lived in intimate connection, bound together by smell, sound, and sight. The German novelist Patrick Süskind has captured the essence of this world in a brilliant description of eighteenth-century Paris:

> there reigned in the cities a stench barely conceivable to us. . . . The streets
> stank of manure, the courtyards of urine, the stairwells stank of moldering

significance even Δ, adaptation, but state remained in decay

wood and rat droppings, the kitchens of spoiled cabbage and mutton fat; the unaired parlors stank of stale dust, the bedrooms of greasy sheets, damp featherbeds, and the pungently sweet aroma of chamber pots. The stench of sulfur rose from the chimneys, the stench of caustic lyes from the tanneries, and from the slaughterhouses came the stench of congealed blood. People stank of sweat and unwashed clothes; from their mouths came the stench of rotting teeth. . . . The rivers stank, the marketplaces stank, the churches stank.[6]

Our eighteenth-century Parisian rarely bathed, often bought prepared food or ate in a tavern (the latter more typical of men), and lived in a world of pungent aromas, with few modern creature comforts. Yet these people, above all the women, founded mass consumer society. The same consumer objects that suddenly appeared in households of rural notables in the middle of the century began to spread rapidly among the Parisian lower classes in the second half of the century. Women bought hand-held face mirrors and changed the style of their clothing. Previously, people had typically owned brown, black, and grey woollen clothing. In the days just before the Revolution, however, women bought blue, green, or yellow garments, often made of cotton. Women owned leather shoes, even multiple pairs! They wore silk or cotton stockings; some adopted cotton undergarments.

Men more slowly adopted these habits, but Ménétra's *Journal* bears ample witness to the changes. He has many of the old habits: he lives a violent life as a young man, constantly on the lookout for the police. Time and again, one of his friends dies in a fight, drowns, or is severely injured at work; he himself breaks a leg. He suffers from syphilis and takes mysterious powders, which he sells to others, for a cure. He drinks heavily, in taverns, where he goes to seek work and companionship. Yet he also participates in the emerging modern lifestyle. He eats meat all the time, sometimes orders "salad," drinks coffee, and, most notably of all, writes well enough to keep a journal. He provides an ideal example of the lower middle class of the towns, who provided the mass market so critical to the spread of the products of eighteenth-century manufacture and colonial trade.

Provincial Towns

> [Saacken] *said, "Now we'll burn Paris!"—"Do nothing of the sort; France will die of that alone!" Blücher replied, indicating the great ulcer gaping below them in fire and fume in the valley of the Seine.*[7]
>
> > Balzac, *Colonel Chabert,* reproducing the supposed
> > conversation of the Prussian generals in 1814

What about other French cities? One of the enduring elements of French culture is the contrast, often hostility, between the capital and provincial cities. Parisians have long looked down their noses at "backward provincials"; those living in provincial cities have long agreed with Blücher, viewing with disdain the "moral swamp" of Paris. Such surface hostilities aside, Paris has also provided a cultural model for

The new professions: a pastrymaker shows his wares in an eighteenth-century version of advertising.

SOURCE: © Ronald Sheridan/Ancient Art & Architecture Collection.

provincial elites. Fashions spread out from Paris to Nantes or Dijon or Marseille in the eighteenth century, just as in the twentieth. In the eighteenth century, the royal government encouraged such developments. Architects who found royal favor in Paris obtained important commissions in the provinces. One royal architect, Jacques Gabriel, father of Ange Gabriel, designer of the place de la Concorde, developed the baroque place Royale in Bordeaux, while another, Victor Louis, created the new royal theaters of Bordeaux and Nantes. The wealthy merchants of Bordeaux put up a new Chamber of Commerce building; they and their peers at Nantes built new houses in

Fishwives and launderesses. Women dominated certain professions, such as these two, or lace-making (and selling); they ran many shops in other trades.

SOURCE: © Giraudon/Art Resource, New York.

previously undeveloped quarters of their cities, such as the Ile Feydeau at Nantes. Where the Ile Feydeau section relies on streets only slightly wider than the traditional narrow ones, the later place Royale allows a half dozen broader thoroughfares to come together in an open, airy circle. These newer buildings, like the theaters, demonstrate the shift away from the Rococo style of the early eighteenth century, toward the neo-Classical style of its second half, but many of the mid-century developments remained Rococo.

Perhaps the most magnificent example of this airy, open square appeared in Nancy, the capital of Lorraine. The last duke of Lorraine, Stanislas Leszczynski, had constructed a central place; its focal point, as in similar new *places* at Nantes or Bordeaux, was a statue of Louis XV. The place Stanislas is one of the glories of European Rococo, bearing ample witness to the importance of eighteenth-century French provincial cities as cultural centers in their own right, yet it clearly demonstrates as well the dominance of Paris, in that a royal architect designed and executed it.

Today, one of the buildings of the place Stanislas houses a luxury hotel. In the eighteenth century, a similar establishment could be found on the place Royale of Nantes: the hotel Henri IV, a prototype of a new level of amenity for travelers. The Englishman Arthur Young, who traveled through France in the 1780s, cited the Henri IV as one of the finest hostelries in Europe. He contrasted it sharply with the ubiquitous traditional inns, somewhat rough-and-ready for the sophisticated traveler–tourist of the late eighteenth century, which he castigated as dirty, poorly managed, overpriced,

*The great stairway of the Opera House of Bordeaux, created by the
royal architect Louis Henry in the 1780s. Henry built a similar structure
at Nantes, one that also illustrates neo-Classical architecture reaching
the provinces.*

SOURCE: © Giraudon/Art Resource, New York.

and distinctly inferior to their English counterparts. Here again, we see one of the be-
ginnings of consumer culture: better-off people traveled in Italy and France for leisure
and education, taking what some already called the Grand Tour of Europe.

The growing provincial cities, like Rouen or Bordeaux, mirrored developments
in Paris. Bordeaux ripped out its old housing, but kept the narrow medieval streets;
Rouen's city center kept buildings and all, as the city's rabbit warren of narrow streets
today charmingly attests, and built around it. Caen created wider, airier spaces by

building up: 10 percent of its windows could be found on the third story of a building, as against the 0.3 percent of a nearby small town like Bayeux. At Nantes as in
Paris, the government tore down the houses on bridges, to improve traffic circulation. Many towns tore down their walls, evidence of internal security and of the
greater need for freedom of movement.

These provincial cities followed widely divergent paths in the eighteenth century.
Nantes and Bordeaux, doubling their populations, form something of an exception,
both in terms of their demographic growth and in terms of the rapid expansion of
their wealth. Other large cities, such as Caen or Lille, expanded due to the growth of
manufacturing, usually located in the suburbs. Towns that relied on domination of a
largely agricultural heartland, like Vannes or Châteaudun, or on their roles as administrative centers, like Rennes or Aix, tended to stagnate. Their economies remained
strongly traditional, with fewer dynamic elements of new trade or new manufacture.
France developed profound social, economic, and political rifts. One France expanded
in population, diversified and prospered in its economy, and evolved a new society. The
second France sent its children to the first, seemed to stick to its old ways, and, in many
ways, absorbed changes, such as increased popular piety, that had taken root in the first
France a century earlier. Yet many of these children came back to their villages, acting
as agents of cultural change in rural France. They brought with them new cultural objects and ideas, which penetrated even into mountain valleys. The contrast between the
"two Frances" should not obscure their fundamentally symbiotic relationship.

The great provincial cities provided a kind of halfway house for the transition to
the more modern society and economy. Ménétra's *Journal* offers extensive descriptions of many of the great towns and of an even larger number of small ones. He encounters many of the same socioeconomic upheavals common in Paris. At Nantes,
the journeymen are on strike against the masters. In the Loire Valley towns, the two
main groups of journeymen fight a pitched battle over hiring rights. In Bordeaux,
call-ups for the militia (during the Seven Years' War) lead to massive demonstrations
and to conflict between visiting journeymen and those from Bordeaux itself. In
Nîmes, Ménétra nearly marries a Protestant widow; nearby, in the Papal enclave of
the Venaissin, he finds the papal legate maltreating Jews. He recounts tales of mur-
derous innkeepers, of unsafe roads, yet also of widespread companionship and sociability. He finds himself welcome everywhere—his nickname on the Tour is the
Welcome Parisian—and spreads his tales of life in Paris. He and others like him
spread ideas and cultural norms into every corner of France. His journal provides
clear evidence that the great conflicts over control of labor that took place in Paris
and in other modernizing cities, took place as well in small provincial towns. The
pace of change may have varied, but not its ubiquity.

Urban tax rolls provide direct insight into the pace of change. The surviving
rolls for the Breton towns of Morlaix and Lannion (each holding between eight thousand and ten thousand people), which lay about twenty miles apart, show how
change created new identities and new professions. Morlaix had close ties to the international market, especially England and Ireland, as the center for export of linen
textiles from western Brittany. In the 1720s, its tax rolls offer listings for such professions as bookseller, café owner, coffee merchant, pastry maker, caterer (*traiteur*), and
lemonade seller. The rolls of Lannion, a town not directly connected to international

markets, do not indicate a single person following any of these trades in the 1720s. By the 1750s, however, Lannion, too, had cafés and pastry specialists and caterers.

KINGSHIP AND THE STATE

Louis XV: from the Bien-Aimé to the Old Roué

The character of our master is perhaps more difficult to depict than many have imagined; it is a hidden character, not only impenetrable in its secrecy, but even in the movements that take place in its soul.[8]

The duke of Luynes, speaking of Louis XV in 1743

The ruler of this rapidly changing France, Louis XV, had a tempestuous relationship with his subjects. The peace and prosperity of the 1720s and most of the 1730s gave way to the war and economic dislocation of the 1740s and 1750s. The entire country rejoiced when Louis and his wife, Maria Leszczynska, produced a son in 1729, and again in 1744, when he recovered from a dangerous illness. Yet Louis's reputation had started to decline in 1739, when he faced the extraordinary personal humiliation of being denied the sacraments. His confessor refused to give the king Easter communion because Louis's persistent infidelities demonstrated his lack of contrition. The king, refused communion, suffered the public humiliation of being unable to perform the ancient ritual of the king's touch.[9] His reputation in Paris suffered considerable damage from this lapse, although the evidence from the countryside suggests that the king remained popular there.

In the 1740s, Louis also assaulted the social sensibilities of his courtiers by choosing a commoner, Jeanne-Antoinette Poisson, as his "mistress in title," a position traditionally reserved for an aristocrat. Louis soon made her marquise of Pompadour. Mme de Pompadour came from a family associated with the General Tax Farm. She brought Farmers General socially into the highest echelons of Court life. Many in the old nobility resented it, and Louis had great difficulty getting someone officially to present her at Court.[10]

Popular opinion reviled Mme de Pompadour. Singers on the Pont Neuf denounced the "emptying of the king's treasury for buildings, for frivolous expenses; the State falls into decadence and the king gives order to nothing, nothing, nothing."[11] Unlike previous royal mistresses, Mme de Pompadour had an important say in government policy. She conducted business with ministers: the king once forced chancellor Lamoignon to discuss a decision with her and the surviving correspondence of many eighteenth-century ministers shows that they wrote directly to her about government affairs. She made and unmade royal ministers, such as the count of Maurepas, whom she forced out as minister of the Navy in 1749, or Machault d'Arnouville, whom she first raised to the highest positions and then discarded. Louis even admitted to Machault in the letter demanding his resignation that personality conflicts between Machault and Pompadour led him to dismiss a minister whom he felt to be supremely capable.

Most of the literature about Mme de Pompadour and later mistresses focuses on the scandalous and salacious, rather than on the important political role of the Court.

Given that courtiers often wrote or sponsored the street songs of Paris, the massive outpouring of abuse on Pompadour likely originated with unhappy courtiers and dismissed ministers.[12] Personal vendettas aside, Pompadour served as the representative of the Farmers General, who wanted control over the key royal oversight officials: the controller general, the minister of the Navy, and the Keeper of the Seals. Louis XV claimed that he fired (1745) Controller General Philibert Orry, a man of uncontested capacities, because Orry had "insulted" Mme de Pompadour. Orry's fall, however, surely stemmed more from the resentment of his former allies the Farmers General at his close supervision of their financial network than from an insult to their protector.

Pompadour's death hardly ended the connection between the royal mistress and the king's ministers. Louis XV's continued personal debauchery, and his choice of Mme du Barry as his final official mistress, exacerbated the government's problems. She allied with the ministers Terray and Maupeou to overthrow (1770) Pompadour's favorite, the duke of Choiseul. Well after his death, Louis XV's sexual escapades fascinated his former subjects. The *Anecdotes on Mme the countess of Barry* (1775) was one of the best-selling forbidden books of the last decades of the Ancient Régime. This salacious inside look at palace intrigue painted a picture of an old king devastated by his loss of virility. According to the anonymous author:

> Thanks to her apprenticeship with Mme Gourdon [a Parisian procuress], she [Mme du Barry] picked up tricks that would help arouse the feeble libido of the aging Louis XV, that would confound her competitors at court . . . In short, prostitution was the secret of her success. The duc de Noailles had said it all when the king expressed his amazement at the unprecedented pleasures he had experienced with his new mistress. "Sire," the duke replied, "this is because you have never been to a whorehouse."[13]

Talk of prostitution at the Court did much to sap the prestige of the monarchy. The reputation of Louis the malevolent and often pitiful roué tarnished the entire Court. Louis XV's personal conduct, combined with broader political, social, and cultural developments, delegitimized the government and desacralized the monarchy. After a brief interlude in the 1770s, the vitriol heaped upon Louis XV and Mme du Barry found a new target: the "Austrian"—Queen Marie Antoinette. Assaults on her moral turpitude provided a leitmotif of political discourse throughout the 1780s and into the early days of the Revolution.

The Fatal Wound: The Seven Years' War and the Death of the Old Regime

> *The country certainly suffered . . . from a deficiency in military direction, and in political and ministerial leadership . . . a deficiency all the more astonishing in that intellectual, manufacturing, and commercial cadres manifested an astonishing prowess.*[14]

> E. Le Roy Ladurie, describing France
> at the moment of the Seven Years' War

C H R O N O L O G Y	1754–1787

1754	Start of French and Indian War in North America
1756	Start of Seven Years' War in Europe
1757	French routed at Rossbach; French victories in North America
1759	British forces drive French from North America (Plains of Abraham); British Navy annihilates French at Quiberon Bay
1763	Peace of Paris; France loses Canada, Louisiana, and Sénégal
1772	First Partition of Poland
1778	French ally with the United States of America in War of American Revolution; Russian war with Ottoman Empire
1781	French Navy defeats British at Yorktown and in India
1783	Peace of Paris; United States becomes independent; French regain Senegal; Russia seizes the Crimea
1787	Prussians invade the Netherlands, suppress republican uprising; Russia attacks Ottoman Empire

Britain, France over India, U.S.

Intrigue at the Court of Louis XV destabilized his state, but the French defeat in the Seven Years' War struck the fatal blow to the political Ancien Régime. The Peace of Aix-la-Chapelle (1748), ending the War of the Austrian Succession, did little to restore relations between Austria and Prussia. In the New World, British and French colonists harbored deep-seated animosity, which burst into war again in 1753. A minor encounter in the wilds of Pennsylvania, in which a young Virginia colonel named George Washington surrendered the aptly named Fort Necessity to superior French forces, led a year later to a full-scale British invasion of the disputed region near today's Pittsburgh. General James Braddock marched two crack British regiments and a large contingent of Virginian militia into the wilderness. The small French force fled at first volley, but France's Indian allies took to the woods and slaughtered the cream of the British army.

Braddock's Defeat touched off the French and Indian War. In 1757, a combined French and Indian force drove south from Canada and captured the British forts on Lakes Ticonderoga and George, events immortalized in James Fenimore Cooper's *The Last of the Mohicans*. The tide turned decisively in 1758 and 1759, when Britain mounted three expeditions: one force turned Fort Duquesne into Fort Pitt; a second drove the French from the Hudson Valley; the third sailed up the Saint Lawrence River to Québec, capital of Canada. Trapped below the city, the English found a hidden trail up the cliffs, forcing the French to do battle on the Plains of Abraham, outside the city. On 13 September 1759, the famous opponents, Wolfe and Montcalm, met their deaths in the battle that made Canada an English colony.

The European fighting began in 1756, after the "diplomatic revolution." Since the late fifteenth century, the European system of alliances had revolved around the quarrel between the Habsburgs and the ruling family of France.[15] The Austrians played on the French desire to preserve the status quo in Europe, as the prince of Conti had successfully argued to Louis XV in a famous memorandum of 1747. Austria suggested that the two states had a common enemy, Prussia, because a third major land power, dominating central Germany, upset the balance of power. Frederick II, hearing of these negotiations, abandoned his French ally for an English one, in the Treaty of Westmister (January 1756). This new alliance system, France and Austria against Prussia and England, did not go over well in France, particularly among the army officers, who detested the Austrians.

The Seven Years' War produced a complete stalemate in Europe. One battle deserves special mention for its long-term impact on France: the catastrophic defeat of Rossbach (1757). Frederick the Great, outnumbered 54,000 to 21,000, routed a Franco-Imperial army, capturing 7,500 officers and men at a cost to his army of only 165 killed. French military commentators alternately blamed the troops, the large number of non-noble officers, and bad training. Non-military commentators blamed the noble officers, particularly the many who surrendered without a fight. The real culprit, the incompetent prince of Soubise, got a promotion.

The Peace of Paris (1763) restored the status quo in Europe, but it changed the map of much of the rest of the world. The decisive English victory in North America, and the Royal Navy's annihilation of its French rival at Quiberon Bay (1759), led to great French losses. The Treaty of Paris gave Canada and Florida to England, Louisiana to Spain (a French ally, in recompense for the loss of Florida), and stripped France of many other colonial enclaves, such as Sénégal, several Caribbean islands, and almost all its possessions in India. Economically, the return of peace demonstrated the economic benefits preserved by the skillful French negotiators. They managed to keep Saint-Domingue, Martinique, Guadeloupe, and the tiny islands of Miquelon and Saint-Pierre, off Canada, used by French mariners to work the Grand Banks, the world's richest fishing grounds.

France emerged from the war with virtually no navy, with a tattered army, with its finances ruined by debt, and with a fundamental conflict between the king and his most important judicial and political institution, the Parlement of Paris, over the nature and practice of government. The dismal failures of 1753–1764—in religious policy (1753–1757), in prosecution of the war (1758–1761), and in fiscal reform (1760–1764)—obliterated any chance that the status quo could continue and created a climate for fundamental, all-encompassing reform. In keeping with the evolving ministerial system of government, the state sought to enact such changes purely within the realm of administrative reform. Those outside the government, however, had begun to question the legitimacy of the state itself. During the initial phase of the dispute, in the 1760s, the opposition focused on strengthening traditional checks on the monarchy, above all the Parlements. By the 1780s, however, public opinion had come to reject both the ministerial system and the Parlements as means to reform the state.

How did this momentous change come to pass? What precisely did "institutional reform" mean in the France of the 1760s? Louis XV's state superficially resembled that of his predecessor, but the French government increasingly fell under the aegis of the royal ministers, rather than that of the king. People took to calling them

response = welfare.

the six kings: the king himself, plus the "kings" of Paris, finances, the army, the navy, and foreign affairs. This system, which contemporaries called "ministerial despotism," differed markedly from the monarchical government practiced between about 1660–1750. It lacked central direction, either provided by a Louis XIV or by a king working with a key minister, as during Cardinal Fleury's ascendancy in the 1730s. By the 1780s, the ministers of war or of the Navy would make substantial financial commitments without checking with the controller general to see if he had the money; individual ministers conducted what amounted to private foreign policies.

Louis XV screws up

Louis XV exacerbated the problem of ministerial infighting by a dramatic policy shift in the middle of the 1750s. Under Louis XIV and during the first half of the eighteenth century, the French state kept the key state positions in the hands of two distinct groups. The great nobility monopolized military commands and the important positions at Court, such as the first gentlemen of the king's bedchamber. Court positions did not carry any policymaking attributions, yet they gave their occupants daily access to the king. The king rotated the two positions of first gentleman every year, in recognition of their extraordinary importance to a noble family's ambitions.[16]

The leaders of the ministerial bureaucracy came from a different milieu, that of the highest families of the administrative and Parlementaire elite. Louis XV abruptly changed this division in the 1750s, inviting marshal Belle-Isle to be minister of war; he later appointed nobles to the Navy and foreign affairs ministries.[17] Under Louis XVI, the ministers of war and of the Navy remained titled sword nobles, while the old administrative and judicial elite kept the remaining ministerial positions. The two elites did not get along; indeed the marriage patterns of their leading members indicate profound social hostility.[18]

The entry of titled nobles into the Council of State had the unintended, and unpleasant, side effect of dragging Court intrigues ever more deeply into the already Byzantine struggles played out in the Council. The close connections of the ministers with lobbying interests exacerbated the problem. Here the split between the old noble families in charge of the ministries of war and the Navy, and the robe nobility families serving as controller general and chancellor (or Keeper of the Seals) abetted permanent ministerial infighting and governmental instability. With the exception of Jacques Necker, all of those running government finance from 1763–1787 came from the Parlement—l'Averdy, Terray, Joly de Fleury, d'Ormesson, and Calonne—or members of robe dynasties who had made a life in the high administration, like Turgot. In the 1760s, Controller General Terray and Chancellor Maupeou, both Parlementaires, fought the dukes of Choiseul and Praslin, ministers of war and of the Navy, just as in the 1780s Ségur and Castries, sword noble ministers of war, fought the career diplomat Vergennes (Foreign Minister) and the Parlementaire Miromesnil (Keeper of the Seals).[19]

These quarrels represented more than personal infighting. The most powerful groups in French society—the sword nobility, the Parlementaires, the financiers, and the bankers—all had, or sought, representatives within the Council of State and control of individual ministries. Like the key elements of modern American government, ministries represented both their own institutional needs and the desires of powerful interest groups. The controller general usually answered to the financiers, just as the minister of war represented the interests of the military complex.[20] The sword nobility favored an aggressive foreign policy because war was good business for them: more commissions, more chances for promotion, massive military spending. Little wonder that the duke of Choiseul plotted constantly for renewed war against England in the 1760s or that the duke of Castries pushed an active military solution to the Dutch crisis of 1786.

The state consisted of several interlocking elements, running down from the Council of State to the village tax collectors. The ministers and their staffs stood at the top, yet the central bureaucracy had scarcely four hundred full-time employees in 1750, and perhaps twice as many in the 1780s. They relied on a network of about forty provincial intendants, drawn from the masters of requests of the King's Household; the intendants had a local staff of about five hundred subdelegates, assisted by clerks. The army, the General Tax Farm, and the venal officers dwarfed these tiny nascent bureaucracies. The peacetime army had about 140,000 men, complete with a bureaucracy attached to the Ministry of War. The General Tax Farm employed platoons of inspectors, accountants, clerks, and "archers" (armed guards); it had so many long-term employees that it became the first French business to offer a retirement plan to its workers in the 1780s. The venal officers, who ranged from the proud presidents of the Parlements down to the humble collectors of taxes on tanned hides, numbered about 70,000; they provided the physical mass necessary for governance.[21] Historians who portray eighteenth-century French government as a struggle between these venal officers and the intendants ignore two fundamental realities:

1. Intendants all owned a venal office—master of requests.

2. Forty men could hardly administer a country of 26 million people.

The intendants increasingly interfered with every conceivable aspect of local life, and they did become the symbols of royal absolutism in the countryside, but their subdelegates, to cite only one example, invariably came from the ranks of the venal officers. Moreover, the old administrative system, built around the financial system of élections and the judicial one of bailiwicks and seneschalsies, still provided the government's first line of contact with most French people.

The royal courts, in particular, fleshed out the first line of government in the provinces. On a daily basis, the regular judicial pyramid (bailiwick/seneschalsy/provosty; presidials; Parlements) did more than any other institution to administer the kingdom. The many specialized courts, from the sovereign Chambers of Accounts, Courts of Aids (chief tax courts), and Currency Courts, down to ecclesiastical courts, Waters and Woods courts, courts of the constabulary, merchants' courts, and, of course, seigneurial courts, to which at least two-thirds of French people were still subject, handled the civil litigation that wove the fabric of everyday life. The Parlements, above all that of Paris, which had jurisdiction over about 40 percent of France, stood at the apex of this system.[22]

Royal officials had both judicial and executive functions; some of them, such as the Parlements, had *de facto* legislative ones. Our modern ideas of the separation of powers, although they date back to precisely this period (and in large measure to a specific eighteenth-century Parlementaire, the baron of Montesquieu), did not apply to eighteenth-century French government. The combination of executive, judicial, and *de facto* legislative power made judges the essential mediator between the government and civil society.

Nor should we ignore the largest number of government employees: the village tax collectors. The peasants themselves elected four to six collectors in each parish, about 160,000 men per year. These men served for a year, receiving a percentage of the money collected as their "salary." Yet even "permanent" royal officials usually had other interests and other jobs. Royal office provided relatively little direct financial return, but it offered the opportunity to share power and thus to obtain money in other ways. Tax officials could offer assessment breaks to their friends and relatives; guild wardens, acting on behalf of the state, could use their position to drive rivals out of business.[23] Royal judges could use their knowledge of upcoming property settlements to manipulate land markets.

The government failed so utterly during the Seven Years' War that reform of every aspect of state administration dominated the political agenda of the 1760s. The War demonstrated France's economic reliance on its empire, and so spurred reinvestment and reform in the Navy. The duke of Choiseul and his cousin, the duke of Praslin, overhauled everything, from ship construction to procurement, recruitment, and training. The humiliation at Rossbach spurred similar changes in the army: the troops received more training, better weapons, better sutlering, and improved permanent barracks. Regimental commanders lost control of recruitment and, to some degree, of responsibility for discipline, which began to be more systematic (and thus, in theory, more equitable). The government established a naval college, a training facility for civil engineers, the Royal Military Academy at Saint-Cyr, and the school of military equitation at Saumur. The corps of trained engineers helped greatly improve the road system of eighteenth-century France, cutting travel and postal times between Paris and other major cities: by 1765, couriers could ride from Paris to Lyon or Bordeaux in under a week.

These positive steps to reform the military included one fundamental mistake. The reforms eliminated many superfluous officers and created a relatively streamlined force, but, starting in the 1740s, the army's officer corps grew increasingly distant from the larger nation, due more stringent rules against commoners becoming officers.[24] The elite French Guards, 40 percent of whose officer corps of the early 1740s came from the families of financiers and judicial nobles, instituted (1745) rules requiring four and then five (1781) generations of nobility in the male line for new officers. The rule worked: only five of the five hundred men received as officers after 1745 got an exception.

The rules got tougher everywhere after the Seven Years' War. By the 1770s, the *rigidity* Royal Bodyguard demanded three hundred years of proven nobility for its officers. In 1781, the infamous Ségur Law mandated that all officers in the infantry, cavalry, and dragoons demonstrate four generations of male nobility in their families. The Ségur Law accurately reflected the intense quarrel between the administrative elite and the military one, although it also reflected the concerns of the reformers about the professionalization of the army. Nonetheless, the sharp split between the noble officers and their men had momentous consequences in June 1789.

The hue and cry for reform exacerbated Louis XV's post-1750 penchant for government by whim. His constant shuffling of ministers created permanent turmoil in the central administration. He changed controller general in 1754, 1756, 1757, 1759 (twice), 1763, 1768, and 1769. The often innovative reforms of a l'Averdy (1763–1768) or a Turgot (1774–1776) invariably failed due to a combination of resistance from entrenched interest groups, of Court intrigue, and of royal vacillation. The nonfinancial elements of the controller general's responsibilities offer an ideal example of the terrible effects of inconsistent policies. The government created a free market in grain in 1763, restored price controls in 1768, a free market in 1774, and finally went back to price controls for good in 1776.

Louis created instability in French foreign policy by conducting private diplomacy, known as the "Secret of the King." Louis first used his cousin, the prince of Conti, as a conduit for secret negotiations in Poland. When Conti fell into disgrace for plotting against the king, Louis took over this private network, without bothering to tell his own foreign minister about the parallel negotiations. When the chief clerk of the Ministry, who had handled both sets of correspondence, lost his ministry job in 1759, the "Secret of the King" lost its only connection to official channels. Two-track diplomacy hamstrung foreign policy.

The supercharged political climate of the 1750s, with its violent dispute about religious and jurisdictional matters, encouraged people to discuss reform, but the Seven Years' War brought such discussions to a halt. The dismal end to the war brought financial, political, and philosophical issues together again, and encouraged a flood of reformist pamphlets. In this climate of total reform, many legists even began to take up Montesquieu's ideas and to question the nature of sovereignty in France. Louis XV supported many of the ministerial reforms, but he explicitly rejected these ideas. In a dramatic shift in the French political landscape, his leading subjects, above all the Parlements refused to back down.

The Sovereignty Question and the End of Legitimacy

The sovereign power resides in my person only.

Louis XV, 1766

The quarrel over sovereignty at first remained hidden behind an ancient religious dispute: the dying embers of the feud between the Jansenists and the Jesuits. The Parlement of Paris, Gallican to the core, had long supported the Jansenists and objected to *Unigenitus* on the grounds of the public good: the king simply could not give away his rights over the French Church because he did not possess them.[25] They claimed to defend the right of the French kingship, an eternal entity and public office instituted to protect the common good, against the whims of a living individual, the actual person reigning as king. That person, although the living embodiment of the kingship, did not *own* anything related to the commonwealth, he merely had use and stewardship of it. The king could not act in as an individual to limit the powers and authority of his public office because he lacked the right to do so.[26]

The opponents of *Unigenitus* thus argued that an individual king, Louis XIV or Louis XV, could not accept a Papal bull that would limit the authority of the kingship. The royal government, supported by much of the Church hierarchy and, above all, by the Jesuits, continued to press for the interpretation that *Unigenitus* was a constitutional law of France. When the Parlements seized on the occasion of a civil lawsuit to confiscate the property of the Jesuits in France and then to expel them (1762), the king first sought to defend his old allies; two years later, he had to give in and sign the order for their expulsion. Without the Jesuits, Jansenism became irrelevant, so the debate turned to a purely secular issue that had lain at the root of the quarrel all along: who held the sovereignty?

By the 1760s, a state bureaucracy had essentially taken over the stewardship of the commonwealth from the king. The debate in the evolving public sphere thus sought to redefine the *res publica* (commonwealth) as the preserve of the nation; in time, that argument led to a rejection of both the king and the Parlements. Increasingly unsatisfied with a system in which the king alone made law, elites demanded that they have a hand in making the law. The most vocal proponents of such a view, precisely because they had an institutional venue, were the Parlements, notably that of Paris, and the lawyers who practiced before them.[27] These legal men focused on the authority to make law, which they situated in the nation, not the king. Steeped in two centuries of political theory that enshrined lawmaking as the defining mark of sovereignty, the Parlements now claimed, on behalf of the nation, to share that authority with the king.

The conflict became evident in a series of quarrels lasting from 1764–1771. The Brittany Affair, a dispute both jurisdictional and personal between the Parlement of Brittany, led by the king's attorney, Louis de La Chalotais, and the royal government, in the person of the duke d'Aiguillon, governor of Brittany, laid out the fundamental conflict. The intersecting lines of principle, personality, and politics created a chaotic situation.[28] Louis arrested La Chalotais and sought to break a strike by the Parlement by suspending the court and threatening to create a new one. The Parlements of Rouen and Paris leapt to the defense of their colleagues, insisting that the king had a responsibility to the "nation," represented by all of the Parlements, who together formed a "union of classes," a phrase they took from the sixteenth-century chancellor Michel de l'Hôpital.

The king and the Bretons eventually compromised, in large measure because Louis needed the cooperation of the Estates of Brittany to borrow money. Louis restored the Parlement and withdrew d'Aiguillon. The locus of conflict now shifted to Paris. The Parlement of Paris, taking up Montesquieu's argument in *The Spirit of the Laws* (1748), argued that the nation was the source of all sovereignty and that the Parlement itself, together with the king, represented the nation.[29] On March 3, 1766, Louis XV unexpectedly appeared at the Parlement, to hold a *lit de justice* and address the issue. The famous Seance of the Scourging left no doubts in anyone's mind about the king's position:

... the sovereign power resides in my person only ... my courts derive their existence and their authority from me alone ... to me alone belongs the legislative power ... the rights and interests of the nation, which some dare to regard as a separate body from the monarch, are necessarily united with my rights and interests, and repose only in my hands.

Four years later, the Parlement of Paris, trying the disgraced d'Aiguillon, explicitly stated that the nation held the sovereignty. The king responded quickly: he dismissed all charges against the duke and, in a final insult to the Parlement, even named him as Foreign Minister.

Louis XV sought to mollify the Parlement by bringing two of its key members into the government. First president of the Parlement of Paris, René de Maupeou, became chancellor, while a councilor, the Abbé Terray, became controller general. In 1770–1771, these two men masterminded another royal attempt at reform. Terray reduced payments on some forms of royal debt and rescheduled others, cut expenses, and streamlined parts of the financial administration; he carefully avoided tampering with the Paris annuities, the form of royal debt most owned by Parlementaires. Terray sought as well to reform the new land tax, the *vingtième,* which heretofore had relied on declarations of landowners as the basis of assessment.[30] He did not fully succeed. He and his cronies also practiced extensive corruption; shares in the General Tax Farm suddenly found their way into the hands of Mme du Barry, to members of Terray's family, to his notary, and to the king and two of his daughters.

Parlementaire opposition to some of Terray's financial edicts, coupled with existing conflicts between the king and the courts, led to a showdown in the winter of 1770–1771. The Parlement had accepted the debt rescheduling but balked at registering an edict that enunciated the absolutist principles of the Seance of the Scourging. The court declared a cessation of activities. Maupeou responded by suspending the Parlement of Paris and the Court of Aids. Soon, the suspension spread to other Parlements, which Maupeou abolished, setting up alternative courts in their place. This new court system functioned for three years, rendering justice in the king's name, and instituting much-needed reforms, such as the abolition of special fees (*épices*) paid to judges by all litigants. Maupeou's Revolution, as his contemporaries called it, alerts us to the differing opinions among French elites as to how to enact reform. As first president of the Parlement, Maupeou served its interest, but as the king's chancellor, this same man masterminded the abolition of the Parlements.

Louis XV's death derailed the Maupeou Revolution. The new king, Louis XV's grandson, Louis XVI, and his queen, Marie Antoinette, detested Maupeou, Terray, and their protector, Mme du Barry. Louis XVI quickly dismissed the two ministers, locked du Barry in a convent, and brought back the old Parlements, which provoked universal rejoicing. Parisian crowds stoned the carriages of the disgraced ministers and burned them in effigy, while the welcome-back ceremonies for the Parlements in cities such as Bordeaux lasted for days. Louis XVI recalled the 76-year-old count of Maurepas, disgraced by Pompadour in 1749, to be his chief minister, and began anew the game of musical chairs with the seats of his Council of State. The young

king turned to Anne-Robert-Jacques Turgot, former intendant of Limog
known Physiocrat, to be his new controller general.

Financial Woes

The government needs money; that says it all.[31]

Nicolas Ruault, January 1787

Turgot offers a particularly interesting example of a minister seeking reform, because of his close ties to the Physiocrats. Turgot and the Physiocrats represented a
step in the direction of modern government and modern economics, although they
remained also firmly rooted in the past. The Physiocrats denounced government interference in the economy, and sponsored free market ideas.[32] These ideas had some
currency in France in the 1760s: the government briefly created a free market in
grain and abolished the state monopoly West India Company in 1769. The free market in grain led to riots on behalf of fixed prices and against the so-called Famine
Pact. The latter belief, quite popular in the 1760s, held that Louis XV had made a
pact with the grain producers to help them increase prices; he and his corrupt
courtiers, of course, would get their share of the increased profits. Louis responded
by firing the minister who proposed the free market and by reinstituting controls.

Turgot restored the free market as part of a broad program of reform. Once
again, a minister set out on an ambitious search for progressive change; once again,
the powerful vested interests of the kingdom defeated him. Turgot's deregulation of
the grain trade, enacted on the eve of a widespread grain shortage, led to riots so severe they are known as the Flour War. He also attacked other forms of interference
with the free market, such as guilds. His attack on these privileges, in the Six Acts of
1776, led to his dismissal. Louis XVI henceforth followed his grandfather's dangerous example, constantly changing controllers general.

Turgot's failure alerts us to the remarkably charged atmosphere of the 1770s.
The dramatic economic growth of the eighteenth century had spun the French economy out of control. Old mechanisms of control, such as the guilds, could no longer
function in the same manner. The massive change in relations of production, market
conditions, and capitalization in some sectors of the economy far outstripped the
capacity of existing authorities to deal with the situation. Guild masters and journeymen fought tooth and nail for control over human labor; guild masters fought
each other for control of market segments; masters and merchant–manufacturers
fought for control of markets. The government did not follow a consistent economic
and tax policy. Reformers such as Turgot or Silhouette wanted to unleash free market forces, but because the government had sold massive amounts of its debt to
guilds—by means of offices and annuities—and other corporations, it could not afford to alienate them. The same forces had been at work in the Brittany Affair of the
1760s. Louis XV may have wanted to override the Estates of Brittany and humble its
Parlement, but he needed them to borrow money.

Borrowing.

The practice of borrowing money through corporations—provincial estates, the Church, town governments, guilds, royal officers—made the government dependent on those corporations. Most government reforms of the late eighteenth century, however, targeted the privileges of one or more of these corporations. Rousseau, in the *Social Contract,* provides us with a clear contemporary view of the danger of these corporations to the public good. He defines three wills—individual, corporate, and general—held by people in civil society. Modern commentators invariably focus on the conflict between the individual and general wills, but Rousseau singled out the corporate will as the most damaging to the social peace. He accurately reflected the opinion of his time that the great corporations stood in the way of any serious effort to reform state or society. Most reformers wanted to free individuals to choose their own actions. The abolition of the West India Company monopoly, the debates about the grain trade, the abolition of the guilds, the rise of the Physiocrats: all of these symptoms were evidence of the increased pressure to recognize individual rights. The government often supported such efforts, in theory, but found itself hamstrung in practice because of its financial dependence on the corporations.

Shortly after the fall of Turgot, political and diplomatic events combined to exacerbate the financial difficulties. France offered clandestine aid to the rebel British Colonies of North America in their fight for independence. Beginning in 1778, France joined the war. This time, with a reformed army and navy and an American ally, France won. The French Navy, in particular, acquitted itself admirably, both in American waters—where it played the determining role in the successful siege of Yorktown (1781)—and in the Indian Ocean. This military success came at a staggering financial price: the government sold more than 650 million *livres* of annuities to cover its costs, which ran to more than a billion *livres.* This debt, combined with the 1.5 billion *livres* borrowed during the Seven Years' War, left the government on the verge of bankruptcy. Moreover, the government's financial difficulties became matters of public discussion when Necker, head of finances after 1778 and disgraced in 1781, published what he claimed was an accurate picture of royal finances, the *Accounting to the King* (1781). The book was a runaway best-seller.

The government's finances, long a secret matter known only to the king and his ministers, had become the subject of open public debate. Necker's figures for pensions paid to the great nobility scandalized the public, and annoyed those courtiers who felt themselves underappreciated. Six years later, another controller general, Calonne, published his version of the budget (a more accurate one), showing receipts of about 475 million *livres,* but expenses of 600 million, half of it for interest. Despite the greater accuracy of Calonne's figures, public opinion tended to accept Necker's version of the story; Parisians made of this Swiss banker their prospective financial savior and, indeed, the savior of the nation.

French government finances required four immediate reforms: administrative stability; reduction of privileged exemptions (both full and partial); public control of public finance (i.e., an end to the General Tax Farm); and rational debt service policies. Very powerful forces opposed these reforms. The Farmers General and their financier allies wanted to keep control of state indirect taxation and to continue the ruinous debt service structure, from which they profited, and many of the powerful privileged, such as the nobility and the Church, wanted to keep their fiscal privileges. At the highest levels of government, the financiers demanded one set of policies, with full control to remain in the hands of the receivers general and the Farmers General. The bankers demanded different policies. Little wonder that reform proved so elusive.

The Death Rattle, 1781–1786

> *... the discontent of the wise and settled people, of the true people, of magistrates, even of nobles, that's what the Court must fear, inasmuch as this sedition is one of the spirit and is practically universal. It is not those who break windows, throw fruit at noses, who flog police informers, who are to be feared, but those who reason, who reflect.*[33]
>
>   Nicolas Ruault, August 1787

The government stumbled from reform to reform throughout the late 1770s and early 1780s. Ministers such as Necker and Calonne tried a wide range of administrative changes. Necker went the furthest, cutting down the number of disbursement treasurers in the military from twenty-seven to two and even abolishing the most powerful position in the royal direct tax system, the receivers general. His first disgrace, in 1781, led to the restoration of the receivers general and to the revival of the old financial mafia running the government's finances. The receivers general and the Farmers General retained an ever more iron-clad grip on the government's money: between 1781 and 1788, the share of money siphoned off by the tax farmers and the royal tax officials rose from 43 to 55 percent. The bankers, upset at the fall of Necker, were mollified by an increase in interest paid on life annuities, which rose to 10 percent in 1782.[34] The central government's expense for interest rose from 160 million *livres* a year in the late 1770s to more than 300 million *livres* by 1787. Available figures from town governments and provincial estates suggest that their interest expenses for forced government loans also nearly doubled in the final decade of the Ancien Régime.

The heart of the Ancien Régime's terminal political crisis was very simple. It could not raise enough taxes to pay interest on its loans. Moreover, by the late 1780s, the government had exhausted its credit. Potential creditors were very wary of lending more money, no matter what the rate of interest. When the king asked the clergy for a special grant of money in 1788, their official spokesman, the archbishop of Narbonne replied:

> You demand 80 millions from us. . . . Your Majesty knows that we will have to borrow it, that one cannot borrow without being assured of the public confidence, that the public confidence can only be acquired by a legal registration [of the edict], that the nation is accustomed to view as legal only a registration in the Parlement, that at this moment there is no Parlement, that the clergy cannot thus count on a registration, that there will therefore be no registration, and [therefore] the clergy cannot pay the 80 millions demanded.[35]

Moneyed elites wanted guarantees that they would actually get paid the interest on the annuities they bought. A key difference between the French monarchy of the seventeenth century and that of the late eighteenth century was that the moneyed elites would no longer tolerate a partial bankruptcy. Creditors, whether in France or Geneva or Amsterdam, no longer trusted the government; they wanted better assurances of repayment. In order to protect themselves, French elites demanded, purely and simply, control over taxation and government spending, as the cahiers for the Estates General of 1789 make quite clear. During the fiscal crisis of 1787, the Parlement of Paris declared again and again that it had no right to approve taxes and that previous approvals had merely been abuses: "it returned to the first usages of the monarchy and upheld once again the principle that it did not have the right to impose taxes on the people; that this right only belonged to an Estates General or to *the nation assembled by means of deputies*."[36] In that sense, something like the events of 1789 and their immediate outcome was inevitable. The French government simply had to change to a system in which the propertied elites would have direct say in tax and borrowing policy. Those elites had to put up the money and, without a say on taxation and lawmaking, they were no longer willing to do so.

The fiscal problems of the monarchy had an impact on every aspect of government policy, as the three great diplomatic problems of Louis XVI's reign demonstrated. In the 1770s, still able to borrow money, France could act decisively in foreign affairs, as in its intervention in the American War of Independence. In the 1780s, however, France became a passive observer of diplomatic events because its lack of money made it impossible to project military force. When Catherine the Great of Russia seized the Crimea in 1783, France could do nothing more than encourage Joseph II of Austria to refuse Catherine's deal for dividing up the Balkans. In 1787, the French had to stand idly by when the Prussian army invaded Holland (September), France's erstwhile ally, to restore the deposed House of Orange. France could only look on in dismay at the renewed Russian attack on the Ottoman Empire in that year.

France did take a more aggressive line outside of Europe. The success of the American Colonists gave France hope for new markets in the New World and the alliance with the Dutch (signed 1785) gave France the possibility of using the Dutch colony at the Cape of Good Hope as a springboard to an attack on British India. Throughout the 1780s, the French Council of State debated a variety of plans, some of them truly harebrained, for attacking the British in India and for annexing Egypt.[37]

The End of Royal Sovereignty, 1786–1787

> *We know that the sovereign alone has the right to make the law, but we also know that this law must be verified, recognized as good, useful, and conforming to the principles of the monarchy. And if the votes are not free in this verification, if the presence of the sovereign prevents this freedom of action, then one no longer finds there a sovereign, but a despot, a tyrant.*[38]

Nicolas Ruault, 26 May 1788

THE ODD COUPLE: LOUIS XVI AND MARIE-ANTOINETTE

Louis XVI and Marie Antoinette bear no little responsibility for the unraveling of affairs. Ruault called Louis a king "much beneath his century and his nation. No one can ignore his lack of an interior life, his absolute incapacity in the art of governing and in the control of his wife." In another letter, Ruault suggested that Louis's "unhappiness came from his overly weak and soft character. He is not fit to hold the reins of so great a state; he was born to be an Elector in Germany."[39] Louis faced the humiliation of his public avowal of impotence in the early 1770s; even when an operation enabled him to perform his husbandly duties, street theater (and others) continued to mock him.

Louis was not quick-witted and so cut a dismal figure in "smart" society; his younger brothers, the counts of Provence and Artois, were more socially adept. Ruault constantly reports plots to remove Louis and replace him either with his brother or with a regency in his son's name. Louis disliked Court ritual and detested hunting, an activity critical to the personal relationships of his ancestors and their Court nobility. He preferred to be by himself, hiding in his attic workshop, tinkering with his beloved collection of clocks and spying on the courtiers in the gardens. Maurepas found the new king lacking in royal dignity and rebuked him for his conduct at one royal ball:

> Foreign ambassadors who were present were scandalized; you entered without the captain of your guards and without having yourself announced; your chair was not even there, and you rushed to get in. We are not accustomed to seeing in public our sovereign count for so little.[40]

This rotund, slow-witted, vacillating man made a disastrous king at a time of crisis. Louis did not want for human qualities—he showed himself a man of great physical courage, he was a devoted family man, and he sincerely loved his subjects—but he lacked the ability to be king.

His wife's shortcomings exacerbated his own. Where he hesitated to act, she was impetuous. Where he took seriously the responsibilities of kingship, she was a frivolous, empty-headed, spoiled brat. Where he was a man of blameless personal morality, she led a life of constant scandal. Throughout the 1780s, French public opinion turned against the queen: Necker's publication of the massive pensions to her favorites, like the Polignac family, alienated less favored parts of high society (as well as ordinary taxpayers); the affair of the Diamond Necklace, in which a member of one of the highest French families, the Cardinal of Rohan, had to suffer a public trial for conspiracy to seduce and discredit the queen, dropped her standing even lower. The trial of Rohan demonstrates precisely how far the government had lost control: the Parlement of Paris acquitted him of the charges.

Nor should we underestimate the impact of such actions on the opinions of ordinary people. Shortly after the Rohan trial, the guild of the fishwives of Paris, who had had the immemorial privilege of sending a delegation to present their respects and a gift to the queen of France on her birthday, refused to visit Marie Antoinette, making known their moral disapproval of the queen's behavior. Crowds booed her when she appeared at the palace of Saint-Cloud on the outskirts of the city. The streets of Paris were filled with libels against the queen in the 1780s, often accusing her of infidelity with partners ranging from the king's brothers to her ladies-in-waiting. Her enemies (and his) invented many of these tales, but her personal behavior was far from beyond reproach and her penchant for profligate spending—preserved for posterity in *The Hamlet,* the mock village she had created for she and her friends to play at being milkmaids in the gardens of Versailles—provided a ready target for the monarchy's opponents. This unfortunate royal couple provided the final blows to the legitimacy of the state.

but weren't @ cause

the eighteenth century to the present day, historians and others have debated the question of whether or not Ancien Régime France could have reformed itself. Had the government reformed, so the argument goes, France could have averted its Revolution. This argument neglects one of the most obvious aspects of French history from the 1760s to the 1780s. The French government tried every sort of reform of which its leaders could conceive. They all failed because they did not address the basic issue facing the state: its loss of legitimacy. A state based on the shared fiction of the king's indivisible sovereignty, a state based on the concept of citizens without sovereignty, could not work.[41] Moreover, elites had begun to shift the focus away from the state and toward the nation. Nicolas Ruault stated the matter unequivocally in a letter to his brother in May 1788: "It is not the king who will charge himself to place limits to his authority. That supposes in him a wisdom, a philosophy, which he does not and cannot have."[42]

France needed sound public finances, which it could get only by obtaining the full confidence of the moneyed elites, who would grant it only if they received some measure of control over fiscal policy, as their counterparts in England possessed. Registration of fiscal edicts in the Parlements provided some measure of control, but the king's regular use of special powers to override Parlementaire objections (including periodic suspensions of the Parlement of Paris, such as the one cited by the archbishop of Narbonne in 1788), and the gradual loss of confidence in the Parlements themselves, made a new controlling body a necessity.

The fundamental conflict revolved around property: its definition and protection. The state, by its essence, could not solve this problem because it rested on three principles that could not survive the changing social, economic, and political reality of the eighteenth century:

1. Everyone was unequal.

2. The king held sovereignty, the ability to make law equally binding on all.

3. Protection of the rights of "citizens," especially their property rights, lay in the realm of contract rather than that of law.

The conflict between the first two of these principles is fairly obvious. Society accepted the principle that everyone was unequal and that unequal treatment of people (for example, by the law) was legitimate precisely because people were unequal, but the king demanded that everyone, of no matter what status, obey laws he promulgated. The conflict between these two views led to two distinct "parties." The ministerial advocates looked to the king's unlimited lawmaking authority as the means by which to reform society. The traditionalists, led by the Parlements, argued that "ministerial despotism" threatened the security of everyone's rights, especially their property. The Parlements' supporters felt that contracts supervised by the courts served as a brake on the authority of the king and his ministers. When the government tried to circumvent the old contracts, the Parlement became the defenders of the public interest. Yet as holders of important privileges, and as defenders primarily of the privileged orders, the Parlements could scarcely be relied upon to reform the abuses of the system. In sharp contrast to the 1760s, when an important segment of public opinion accepted the idea of Parlements as protectors of the commonwealth, in the 1780s, public opinion had come to reject both the ministerial system and the Parlements as means to reform the state.

In the eighteenth century, political discourse returned to the language of the sixteenth century, which stressed the preservation of the "public good" or commonwealth. The French political class had long recognized the distinction between the king's good and that of the public. From the 1760s through the 1780s it moved decisively to reject the government's proposition, defended for almost three hundred years, that the two were coterminous. They thus rejected the proposition's underlying premise, that the state, represented by the king, was the commonwealth. The leading French political thinkers of the eighteenth century harkened back to sixteenth-century ideas to demand a new form of government. Chancellor d'Aguesseau wrote of kingship:

> There has never been and never will be a power that does not come from bosom of God himself. It is He who, having formed men for society, wanted the members of which it is composed to submit to a superior power. . . . In consequence, it is He who is the true author of that power. . . It [the power] can be in the hands of a single person or of many, depending on the constitution of each State. . . . God has even found it good that the manner of this choice depend as well up to a certain point on the will, the genius or the inclination of each of the peoples who form these great societies that one calls a nation or a state.[43]

D'Aguesseau sounds here much like his sixteenth-century predecessors: power comes from God, but men themselves have a degree of choice in who wields it and how it is constituted. Anyone familiar with French legal history, as d'Aguesseau was, could not ignore the historical precedents. The Bourbons, like the Valois, owed their throne to French law, not to God.[44]

The royal ministers had developed a very different idea of government and the people. Charles Gravier, count of Vergennes, Minister of Foreign Affairs of Louis XVI, summarized these views in his response to the demands of the Estates of Brittany to name their own deputies to Court. The Estates cited their "natural rights" in this matter, but Vergennes argued Breton liberties were "simple privilege, founded on a specific concession [of the king]." The Estates argued that their liberties were "rights that the interest of your State did not permit them to forget," whereas Vergennes countered that "the State is the fatherland (*patrie*)."[45] As Vergennes's remark to the Bretons suggests, even in the 1780s, the royal administration continued to propound the view that the state itself could be the repository of the public good. D'Aguesseau's comments, made in the 1740s, show the same ambiguity about the distinction between the "state" and the "nation."

By the 1780s, French elites had clearly formulated an idea of the nation that lay outside, and above, the state. They no longer trusted *either* the state itself or the king to protect the public good. The public wanted a share in the guardianship of the public good, so that neither the programs of ministerial reform nor the ideas of the Parlementaires had any serious chance of success in the long run. Twenty years of discussion on this matter had produced a consensus that the nation was the source of all sovereignty and that its representative body had to share in the lawmaking power. The documents prepared for the Estates General in the spring of 1789 provide irrefutable evidence of massive, indeed nearly universal support for this idea. Unanimity about the sovereignty of the nation, however, did not produce a universal definition of the political nation itself. People could not agree on who constituted the nation, a problem that would bedevil the Revolutionaries, too.

The old, Aristotelian definition of the commonwealth as the collectivity of the citizens did not help much, because it left citizenship undefined. Jean-Jacques Rousseau's *Social Contract*, published in 1762, accepted the principle that all adult men constituted the nation, a definition not likely to find many takers in Parlementaire circles. Earlier, Voltaire had defined the English nation as "the most numerous, even most virtuous, and by consequence the most respectable part of men, composed of those who study the laws and science, of merchants, artisans, in a word, of all that which is not a tyrant."[46] The *cahiers* of 1789 once again make clear the popular preference: their authors had little doubt—all of the citizens called to participate in the drawing up the *cahiers,* together with their families, constituted the nation.

Many looked to England for a model of what to do, but whatever one's attitude toward the English Parliament, all agreed that an institution that gave propertied elites some say in the management of public finance had to exist. The heavy burden of taxation, and the massive abuses within the royal financial system, created a direct connection between the concern of elites about their private property and their concern about the public good. Powerful forces lobbied for change, for movement, and against stability and the old order. The monarchy, the very cornerstone of that old order, was not a likely implementor of the needed changes, however attractive some of the reforming initiatives of certain ministers may have seemed.

The Ancien Régime had fallen apart by the early 1760s, not only in an economic and social sense, but in a political and institutional one as well. The regime had lost its legitimacy. The key demands of elites make obvious the shortcomings of the existing system, and the underlying assumptions of the various parties. The king believed he had custody of the public good, so that only he and his advisors needed to know the workings of the government. The opposition, in contrast, believed the government should reveal its inner workings and make public all information relevant to the stewardship of the commonwealth.

The debate focused on royal financial affairs; it culminated in 1781, when Necker published his famous *Accounting to the King*. In the next six years, others published similar documents, so that informed public opinion for the first time had access to the inner workings of the government's finances. Once this information became public, everyone knew that the king and his ministers had not taken proper care of the *res publica*. The political nation resolved to take it back.

❧ CULTURAL AND SOCIAL CHANGE

In changing words, one changes ideas; and in changing ideas, one changes events.

Nicolas Ruault, June 1789

The French Revolution casts an enormous shadow over the second half of the eighteenth century. We know the Revolution took place, so the irresistible tendency is to look for its antecedents in the generation or two before it. In the nineteenth century, French scholars sought out intellectual antecedents in the Enlightenment. By the 1930s, historians had accepted the premise that the ideas of the Enlightenment played a critical role in the coming of the Revolution; some even argued that the changed perspective created by the Enlightenment led directly to the Revolution. Eighteenth-century observers, like the royal minister d'Argenson, argued that the radical changes in "public opinion" would lead to political change, even "revolution," although he would have given that term a less all-encompassing meaning than it took on after 1789.

In recent years, however, this old consensus has fallen apart. While some historians insist that the ideas of the Enlightenment led directly to the Jacobin Terror of 1793–1794, others insist on the uniqueness of the ideas of the Revolution. The latter point out the obvious disjuncture between the political discourse of, say, 1791 or 1792, and that of the early 1780s. Most would accept a clear split between the republicanism of late 1791 and 1792 and the ideas of the early 1780s, but others also insist on a disjuncture between 1789 and 1788. For them, the Revolution created its own political dynamic, one clearly distinct from the discourse of the Ancien Régime. These questions will concern us more in the next chapter, insofar as they relate to the Revolution itself, but they do force us to look carefully at social, intellectual, and cultural developments in the dying days of the Ancien Régime.

French political discourse underwent a fundamental transformation between the Seance of the Scourging (1766) and the calling of the Assembly of Notables in 1787. By 1787, French elites universally accepted the idea that the monarchy needed some sort of representative body to act as a check on the arbitrary behavior of the "six kings." Public opinion rejected the premise that the Parlements could serve this function. People supported the Parlements as the only existing line of defense against ministerial despotism, but also understood that the Parlements were part of the problem, not the solution. How typical Nicolas Ruault must have been in his reaction to the events of 1787, which led to the convocation of the Estates General: "Well, we are witnesses to a strange and rare event. An Estates General at the end of the eighteenth century!" Later, during the debates on how the Estates should meet, he would write: "The previous Estates Generals cannot serve as a model for this one. The spirit of former times is not that of ours: enlightenment has only spread for about a century; we have become a reasoning people."

Ruault reveals the critical factor of change between the 1760s and the 1780s: French elites had broken with tradition, had accepted the idea that reason should serve as the arbiter of the nation's political life. That willingness to accept change—to abandon tradition for tradition's sake—had its roots, as Ruault suggests, in the ideas of Descartes and the philosophers who followed him, but it also had roots in the broader changes in French culture, especially those that took place after 1750. The newly literate population—something like half of the men and a third of the women in northern France could sign their name to a marriage certificate—everywhere bought more books. Literacy brought more people into politics, at least as interested observers.

Women readers demanded more literary texts; production of novels rose markedly. Romantic novels, such as Rousseau's *Julie, or the New Heloise,* were the best sellers among nonreligious books. In the eighteenth century, far more people read Rousseau's fiction than ever read his political philosophy. Despite what we would view as his misogynist ideas, women formed the core of his readership. He and other Romantic authors offered women real benefits: prominent female characters, respect, security. Rousseau's bird-in-a-gilded-cage imagery, and his insistence on the emotionality (and hence nonrationality) of women grate our sensibilities; in a certain way, he denies the full humanity of women.

Looked at from the perspective of many eighteenth-century women, however, his ideas had a different resonance. In much of his writing, he places greater value on emotion than on reason; many of his readers shared that idea. Because women lived in a world of considerable physical insecurity, any man preaching respect for the physical safety of women would find a ready acceptance among women. Ménétra's *Journal,* with its constant tales of rape and sexual assault, makes chillingly clear women's justified concerns about physical security. Rousseau's ideas also blended well with the general cultural acceptance of the value of romantic love; by the late eighteenth century, people increasingly married for love. A literature that stressed that value, in France as in England, had a ready audience.[47]

Late eighteenth-century French literature ran the gamut from devout religious treatises to scandalous novels, like *Dangerous Liaisons* of Laclos, familiar to many today because of the recent films based upon it. People then as now bought mountains of ephemeral books. Most readers were far more familiar with adventure stories, supernatural tales, and romances than they were with Diderot's *Rameau's Nephew* or Rousseau's *Social Contract.* Some great literature had a broad audience: Rousseau's novels or his treatise on education, *Émile;* Voltaire's satires, notably *Candide;* Beaumarchais's plays, the *Marriage of Figaro* and the *Barber of Seville.*

The shift from Voltaire to Beaumarchais tells us much about the evolving nature of French society. *Candide,* published in 1759, assaults a wide array of targets. Voltaire mocks eighteenth-century warfare, implicitly indicts government spending priorities (the government in his fictional El Dorado focuses its resources on the public good, on the amelioration of the lives of its citizens), and preaches the simple life. Above all, however, he indicts the Catholic Church: its priests and friars are invariably villains, guilty of every conceivable sin.

Beaumarchais, writing twenty years later, focuses in another direction. He lampoons social mores, to be sure, but he offers a detailed indictment of the government, particularly of its financial system. The shift in primary target away from the Church and toward the government in these two works offers a fair indicator of the cultural change in the intervening generation. Beaumarchais also offers a much harsher critique of society itself.

From the 1760s to the 1770s, French writers published a wide range of materials, both in France and abroad. The authorities often winked at smuggling of banned texts, many of which made their way directly to Versailles in the government's own diplomatic pouches. People at Court simply had to know what was being said by a Rousseau or a Diderot in order not to appear ridiculous at the Parisian salons. The

Figaro: The Political Barber

In the *Marriage of Figaro,* in particular, Beaumarchais puts revolutionary social ideas in the mouth of the valet, Figaro.

> No, My Lord Count, you shan't have her! Because you are a great nobleman you think you are a great genius . . . Nobility, fortune, rank, position! How proud they make a man feel! What have *you* done to deserve such advantages? Put yourself to the trouble of being born—nothing more! For the rest—a very ordinary man! Whereas I, lost among the obscure crowd, have had to deploy more knowledge, more calculation and skill merely to survive than has sufficed to rule all the provinces of Spain for a century! And yet you would measure yourself against me! (*Act V, scene 1*)

The original version set the play in France, rather than in Spain, so it is little wonder that Louis XVI banned its performance in 1781. Little wonder, too, given the incessant guerrilla warfare at the Court, that his brother, the Count of Artois, tried to have it staged privately for himself and some friends and that, at first failing to do so, he and others finally got the king to approve (in 1784). Beaumarchais, in the interim, had diplomatically shifted the action to Spain. Artois's action confirms the relative powerlessness of the royal family in the face of cultural change: in order to maintain his image as someone at ease in the "beau monde," Artois had to sponsor a play that must have assaulted his sensibilities, given that he was a raving reactionary.

The Comédie Française put on the first public performance on 27 April 1784. Duchesses, footmen, soldiers—everyone lined up in the foyer of the theater and in the streets outside from early morning to get seats. Beaumarchais made some intemperate remarks about the problems of getting the play to the stage, leading to his arrest and five days in prison. When he was released, he received a hero's welcome at the evening's performance of the play, one attended, so the editors of a recent translation of the play inform us, by the king's ministers. One wonders what they thought of Figaro's lament: "How I would like to have hold of one of those Jacks in office—so indifferent to the evils that they cause."[48]

Beaumarchais's experience demonstrates the loss of governmental control over the cultural life of the country. Elsewhere in the speech cited above, Figaro spells out some of the cultural complaints of Parisian elites. Figaro would have those in office know that "stupidities that appear in print acquire importance only in so far as their circulation is restricted, that unless there is liberty to criticize, praise has no value." Later, released from prison (where he had moldered for offending some foreign potentate with his writings), Figaro decides to

> sharpen my quill again . . . [because] . . . there had been established in Madrid a system of free sale of commodities, which extended even to the products of the press, and that, provided I made no reference in my articles to the authorities or to religion, or to politics, or to morals, or to high officials, or to influential organizations, or to the Opera, or to any theatrical productions, or to anybody of any standing whatsoever, I could freely print anything I liked—subject to the approval of two or three censors!

government, perpetually befuddled by this dilemma, actually stepped up censorship in 1783, despite its obvious unpopularity among elites.[49] Elite political society had a dual attitude toward the government:

1. It held the government in the lowest possible esteem, often seeing the ministers as figures of ridicule.

   2. It wanted control of the state for itself, either by naming new ministers or by
   supporting a minister whose program met with a given group's approval.

Turgot was himself a *philosophe,* and contributed to the *Encyclopédie;* Necker's works
met with an overwhelmingly positive response from the Parisian elite. Members of
the highest nobility supported some of this dissent: the king's cousin, the duke of
Orléans, who owned a private enclave, the Palais Bourbon (now called the Palais
Royal) across from the Louvre, allowed the freest possible expression of ideas in his
self-policed reserve. Its cafés became hotbeds of political dissent.

   Yet the Enlightenment consisted of a mixture of the new and the old. Far too
often, we have tried to create false dichotomies, such as the one between the cult of
reason, supposedly enshrined in the Enlightenment, and the cult of emotion, represented by Romanticism. Literary criticism, in particular, has grown weary of this distinction. Scholars focusing on eighteenth-century French literature rightly emphasize
the symbiotic relationship between reason and emotion in both movements. Focusing on those Enlightenment ideas that we find most amenable conveniently ignores
the darker side of the *philosophes:* Voltaire, champion of religious tolerance, was also
an anti-Semite.

   Nowhere can we see the problem more clearly than in the visual arts. Eighteenth-
century French art, especially painting, often jars our sensibilities, yet some of the
artists have maintained or even enhanced their reputations. The great sculptors Étienne Falconnet (1716–1791), Jean-Baptiste Pigalle (1714–1785), Claude Michel (Clo-
dion, 1738–1814), and Jean-Antoine Houdon (1741–1828) have left enduring works
of art still appreciated. Falconnet's two most famous works could not be more different. In France, his 1742 *Sitting Cupid* provoked endless copies. The second piece, his
equestrian statue of *Peter the Great* (1782) in Saint Petersburg, Russia, offers a fitting
symbol of French cultural preeminence. Pigalle's fame rests above all on the magnificent funerary monument to marshal de Saxe in the Saint-Thomas church of Strasbourg, although posterity has judged less favorably the many busts he did for royal
commissions. Pigalle also headed the Royal Academy of Arts, so he frequently fought
with some of the more independent artists of the day. Houdon executed busts of many
of the leading figures of the end of the century, such as Thomas Jefferson (1789).

   Carle von Loo, the leading painter of the mid-century, has little reputation today.
His contemporaries François Boucher and Jean-Baptiste Chardin have endured better. Boucher's utopian peasants, in the *Autumn Pastoral* of 1749, remind us of the
rise of pastoralism, just as his *Triumph of Venus* (1740) and *Diana at Rest* (1742) illustrate the great vogue for nudes. Chardin, who received little respect in his own
day, is perhaps not surprisingly the most sympathetic of the mid-eighteenth-century
painters for our aesthetics. Chardin often painted understated domestic interiors,
reminiscent of those of seventeenth-century Dutch artists.

   Jean-Baptiste Greuze, who also painted in mid-century, has left an enduring
legacy of paintings not at all typical in their subjects, one best symbolized by *A Marriage,* which shows a rich peasant giving the dowry to his son-in-law. The painting
shows peasants living in a luxury few farmers could have imagined; it demonstrates
as well an important eighteenth-century dichotomy: the active men and the passive

women. Boucher offers a rare exception, in his famous portrait of Mme de Pompadour, which treats her with great respect as a *person*. (See Plate.) He shows her half reclining, fully dressed, in front of her bookcase, reading a book. Whatever else may be said against her, Pompadour was perhaps the greatest arts patron of her day, and an individual well versed in the culture of her time. In this, as in so many other things, she mirrored the tastes of the Farmers General, who also actively supported the arts. Most of Boucher's women, and indeed those of most painters, are treated as delicate, beautiful objects or, in some cases, as sentimental observers of male action. Later in the century, women became even more sentimentalized. Jean-Honoré Fragonard, perhaps best known for his four *Progress of Love* (1771–1773) paintings, done for Mme du Barry (who ultimately rejected them), remains the prototype of the painter of Romantic love.

The most famous painter of the late Ancien Régime, Jacques-Louis David, owes his greatest reputation to works done after 1789. Of his works executed under the Ancien Régime, the *Oath of the Horatii* (1785) and the portrait of the Polish noble Count Potocki, stand out as masterpieces. Potocki's portrait presages the later, more famous one of Napoleon crossing the Alps, while the *Horatii*, showing the sons of the Roman patriot Horace swearing an oath to defend the fatherland, offers a remarkable testimony to intellectual trends in the 1780s. David glamorizes the fatherland, and male loyalty to it above all, even to the king. The Romantic sensibilities of the two paintings are evident. David, like so many eighteenth-century painters, puts the women off to one side in the *Horatii*: they weep at the prospect of losing their loved ones. (See Plate 14.) Yet another David painting, *The Lictors Returning Brutus's Son,* shows the complexities of eighteenth-century attitudes toward such women: Brutus appears in the dark foreground, trying to remain Stoic in the face of his loss, while the womenfolk again weep. In this case, however, the illumination of the painting falls squarely on the women, who show that same sensibility so beloved by Rousseau, Richardson, Goethe, or so many other eighteenth-century authors.

Women played a vastly more important role in late eighteenth-century French art than they had in the past. Mme de Pompadour set a style others sought to follow. Women artists finally received some opportunities. Falconnet, mindful of his relatively weak skills as a portraitist, asked Marie-Anne Collot to sculpt the head of his Peter the Great. Diderot praised her skill, demonstrated as well in a bust of him. Two women painters, Adélaide Labille-Guiard and Elisabeth-Louise Vigée-Le Brun, had great success at Court in the 1780s, the latter painting official portraits of the queen (1783) and of the queen and her children (1787). (See Plate.) The Academy accepted both women as full members in 1783. Vigée-Le Brun's self-portrait with child bears testimony to her remarkable abilities, and to the singular esteem in which she has been held by the French artistic establishment: when I visited the Louvre in September 1999, it was the only painting by a woman born before 1800 hanging in the galleries.

Women also played a critical role in the Enlightenment, above all as patrons. They conducted the salons so essential to the development of Enlightenment culture. Women like Julie de l'Espinasse or Mme Geoffrin made of these salons the intellectual center of Paris, indeed one of the great centers of the Western world. One great writer after another read his work to a salon, and the sensibility created within their world, with its emphasis on equality and talent, did much to change political and cultural ideas. These women offered a place of conversation and intellectual inquiry to all of the *philosophes:* Voltaire, Diderot, Helvétius, Rousseau, indeed everyone of any consequence, passed through their doors.[50]

Many resented this newfound female power. Rousseau railed constantly against the salons and their learned women: doubtless he doubly resented his life-long dependence on female patrons. Lesser writers trained their poison pens on powerful political women, from Mme de Pompadour to Marie Antoinette. Pompadour and du Barry differed markedly from Marie Antoinette in that they were, by definition, committing adultery, and thus open to moral rebuke, but a more important distinction should be drawn between du Barry and Marie Antoinette, on one side, and Mme de Pompadour, on the other. Pompadour, unlike the other two, was a highly intelligent, well-educated individual; she intervened in politics as a politician, not as the mindless tool of Court intriguers. Yet even the other two could wield real power on their own. Du Barry commanded (and rejected) some of Fragonard's most famous work, and Marie Antoinette's decision to commission Vigée-Le Brun's official portrait of the royal family must be respected as a courageous, indeed stunning affirmation of women's abilities in a world more than a little reticent to do so.

The Enlightenment reached its peak of production, although not diffusion, between the late 1740s and the early 1760s. Few generations in one country have produced so much literature of so profound an historical significance. The central project of the period was the *Encyclopédie,* a self-described "systematic dictionary" that sought to provide broad definitions of terms both technical and philosophical. Its primary editor, Denis Diderot, wrote well-received novels, art and music criticism, and philosophical tracts. Diderot came from humble provincial origins, a member of the middle class of the small Burgundian town of Langres, educated there in its Jesuit *collège.* His collaborators included a wide range of the upper reaches of society, from nobles such as his co-editor Jean d'Alembert, financiers like Helvétius (one of the Farmers General), to learned doctors. Many of the leaders of this movement, like Diderot, received their education from the Jesuits: the *collège* Louis-le-Grand in Paris alone produced such figures as Voltaire and Helvétius. While in school there, they rubbed elbows with Turgot, both a *philosophe* and a royal minister, as well as the d'Argenson brothers (ministers under Louis XV and classmates of Voltaire) and Chrétien de Lamoignon, son of the chancellor, known to us by the name of one of his estates, Malesherbes.

Chancellor Lamoignon gave his son, Malesherbes, control of government censorship, and thus oversight of the book trade, from 1751–1763. The government's chief censor so much agreed with those he was supposed to regulate that he penned a defense of liberty of the press in 1758–1759, under the title *Memoir on the Book Trade.* Malesherbes had gone even farther in 1752: ordered to seize the second volume of the *Encyclopédie* just before it was to appear, Malesherbes wrote to Diderot to tell him that the book, as well as Diderot's papers, were about to be seized. When Diderot complained that he could not find someone to hide his papers on such short notice, Malesherbes volunteered his own house—an offer Diderot accepted. Thus the government censor's office searched Diderot's house for a manuscript hidden at

Mme Geoffrin's salon. Most of the guests are men, even though a woman runs the salon. Salon culture played a central role in political as well as cultural life, because in the salons the elite society to which the courtiers and ministers belonged passed judgments that could not be ignored.

Source: © Giraudon/Art Resource.

their chief's own house! Malesherbes believed the government could use its resources more wisely by producing literature to justify its action, rather than by wasting resources on suppression of the printed word.

If the official in charge of the book trade held such opinions, how likely was it that the government would be able to control free expression of ideas? Nor was Malesherbes an isolated case. In the county of Burgundy, the intendant, Bourgeois de Boynes, had an arrangement with a local bookseller, Charmet. The bookseller had bribed the appropriate customs officials at an entry point, and backed up his work by providing Bougeois de Boynes with copies of philosophic books theoretically banned from France. After a mix-up at the frontier, when the officials mistakenly seized some books, Charmet provided the intendant with two lavishly bound copies of Raynal's *Philosophical History;* in return, the intendant saw to it that the inspectors burned only those seized books likely to be difficult to sell.

How dramatically did mentalities change in these years? The list of titles tells the story: Montesquieu's *Spirit of the Laws;* Voltaire's *Candide,* his *Century of Louis XIV,* and *Philosophical Dictionary;* Rousseau's *Discourses, Émile, New Heloise,* and *Social Contract;* Quesnay's *Economic Maxims;* Diderot's *Rameau's Nephew;* Buffon's

Natural History; Helvétius's *On the Spirit;* the *Encyclopédie* (volume I appeared in 1751), to mention only a few of them. What country, what time could witness the publication of such texts without undergoing an intellectual revolution? Although historians debate the precise nature of that change, a close textual reading of works from the 1750s demonstrates that authors such as Montesquieu had an immediate impact. Foreign authors, particularly from Great Britain, men such as David Hume in philosophy and Samuel Richardson in literature, also destabilized received wisdom. Diderot and many other *philosophes* accepted English empiricism, yet subscribed wholeheartedly to Richardson's sentimentality. Richardson's *Clarissa* or his *Pamela,* widely praised by Diderot and other French readers, lay the groundwork for Rousseau and Romanticism.

The revolutionary nature of the change led to significant problems of contradiction within the writings of the *philosophes.* Rousseau's ideas on the state of nature appear utterly different in the *First* and *Second Discourses* (1749 and 1755) and *Émile* (1762), as against the *Social Contract* (1762). In the former, Rousseau lauds man in the state of nature and decries the corrupting influence of society, yet in the *Social Contract* he contrasts the superior nature of civil as against natural liberty. Civil liberty, unlike natural liberty, is based on moral choice: "with civil society comes moral liberty, which alone renders man master of himself; because the impulse of appetite alone is slavery, and obedience to a law one has given oneself is freedom." Such contradictions appear everywhere in the work and lives of the *philosophes.* Voltaire railed against despotism, yet believed in enlightened monarchy, typified by his friend Frederick the Great of Prussia (with whom he later fell out). Voltaire, sworn enemy of despotism and abused power, wrote pamphlets for the French government at the time of the Maupeou coup. Diderot detested and denounced the Académie Française, yet his co-editor of the *Encyclopédie,* d'Alembert, became its permanent secretary in 1772.

Diderot believed in a limited education for girls, but provided his own daughter (after some foot dragging) with what was, for a woman of the day, a first-class education, one far in excess of what his own writings suggested. His attitudes toward the people can perhaps sum up the general problem. Here he is writing about the unemployed:

> . . . these lazy men, young and vigorous, who find in our misused charity an easier and more considerable assistance that what they would procure by their labor, fill our streets, our temples, our large roads, our cities and towns, our countryside . . . This vermin could only exist in a State in which the value of men is unknown.[51]

Yet this same Diderot could write to Sophie Volland, on seeing the elaborate gardens of the royal château of Marly:

> . . . in my admiration which I couldn't refuse Le Nôtre [the great landscape architect of Louis XIV]. I called Henri IV and Louis XIV back to life. Louis showed this magnificent edifice to Henri, and Henri said to him: "My son, you're right; it's very beautiful. But I'd like to see the houses of my peasants

in the village of Gonesse." What would he have thought of finding all around these immense and magnificent palaces—of finding, I say, peasants without roofs, without bread, and on straw?[52]

Diderot, in the second passage, is very much the man of modern sensibilities; as Peter Gay suggests, we see in such thoughts the birth of the secular social conscience. In the first passage, however, we see a Diderot who cannot understand that an able-bodied man could be unemployed through no fault of his own. We see him echoing the sentiments of royal ordinances that such people were vermin: one royal adminis-trator of the 1690s, in a commentary on a poor relief edict, called them "garbage."

The distance between the Enlightenment and our own day appears most clearly in their attitudes toward women. Rousseau stands out for his blatant sexism, for his belief that women exist to "serve" men (as he says in *Émile*). Diderot explicitly re-jected the notion that men and women are equal, but did admit they should be treated more equally than they were. Others, like the marquis of Condorcet, a key figure of the late Enlightenment, or Helvétius, accepted female equality. Even so hard core a sexist as Rousseau is not so easy to decipher as we might think: he calls the perfect mate for Émile, Sophie (wisdom). Sophie has the natural wisdom of those uncorrupted by society; she has purity of sentiment, a quality far more prized in those days than in ours. We have taken the modern rationalist conceit from the fig-ures of the Enlightenment: the idea that reason provides the answer to all questions. They themselves did not accept that premise, however much they praised the use of reason to destroy the prejudices and ignorance built up over the centuries.

What did their contemporaries actually take from the *philosophes?* What can we say of the evolution of culture in late eighteenth-century France? One can distin-guish three levels of reading taste in the country. At the broadest level, people read cheap little books produced by the so-called Blue Library of Troyes (the books had blue covers). These publishers produced for a mass audience. Early in the eighteenth century, they produced above all for the lower classes of the towns; by the second half of the century, most of their production went to the countryside, to the newly literate peasantry. They bought religious books, lives of the saints more than any-thing else. They bought almanacs: compendia of proverbs, little stories, and advice much like the contemporaneous American best-seller, *Poor Richard's Almanac.* Buy-ers wanted songbooks, particularly, as the century wore on, of Christmas carols. They purchased primers with a strong religious element, much like those used in New England. Early in the century, they bought chivalric romances, loosely based on medieval epic poems, but later they shifted to fairy tales, which became available only after 1750. One searches in vain for any trace of the *philosophes*.

In provincial towns, people still bought religious literature, especially in areas like Lorraine or Brittany. In southern France, however, buyers sought secular literature. Elites bought "high" literature. In the 1770s and 1780s, the leading authors at the regu-lar booksellers included Voltaire (by far the best-seller), Helvétius, Rousseau, Simon Linguet, baron d'Holbach, Louis-Sebastien Mercier, and abbé Raynal. Side by side with these leading intellectuals, however, one finds the name of writers lost to histori-cal obscurity, like Pidansat de Mairobert, likely author of the scandalous *Anecdotes on*

Mme the countess du Barry. The best-selling forbidden titles ranged from serious works by Voltaire (*Questions on the Encyclopedia*) to pornography (some of it, like the *Maid of Orléans,* also by Voltaire). Legally published books included a range of specialized works on law or medicine, as well as the best-selling novels of the day, like Rousseau's *New Heloise.*

The middle- and upper-class readers of these philosophical works got together to discuss them at academies of arts and sciences, which sprang up in many large provincial cities. These academies recruited most heavily from among royal officers, especially if the town had a Parlement, as at Bordeaux. They also invited a small number of members of the clergy, usually from the cathedral chapters, military nobles, a substantial number of doctors and lawyers, and a smattering of others. One group remained dramatically absent: merchants. Merchants and others excluded from the academies later created their own reading societies, an interesting parallel to the increasing unwillingness of these same merchants to buy royal offices, as their compeers had done in the sixteenth or seventeenth centuries. Reading societies and academies existed side by side with other forms of sociability: provincial salons (more common early in the century) and Masonic lodges, which spread rapidly through France after 1750. All of these venues did much to create a climate of public discussion and to create among public officials and ordinary people alike a sense that public opinion (a phrase first used in its modern sense during these years) had come to be important and legitimate.

Parisian readers provide a much different view. Artisans and servants remained faithful, like their provincial counterparts, to religious works. The middle class, however, turned away from religion. By the 1780s, Parisian publishers scarcely printed religious works. Middle-class Parisian private libraries came to consist overwhelmingly of secular books.[53] Men bought historical works, certainly a reflection of the charged political climate of the times, while women bought novels. The authorities burned banned texts in the public squares, but such activities, as Malesherbes had warned in 1759, merely served to whet the public's appetite. Raynal's *Philosophical History,* which had exhausted its market by 1774, had a remarkable revival seven years later, when the authorities burned it publicly in front of the Parlement of Paris, touching off a renewed demand for the suddenly scandalous text.

Paris had a wide range of texts available to all. These texts ranged from those shouting scandalous stories in the streets and sellers of hastily printed handbills assailing government ministers, public policies or, often by the late 1780s, the queen, to those purveying their wares to the very Parlementaires and royal officials acting to have them banned. Parisians (and others) could also rely on externally published gazettes, the most famous of them the *Gazette of Leiden,* published in French, in the Netherlands, or on journals, such as the scandalous *Mémoires secrets,* issued by Bachaumont, or the more literary *Correspondance,* edited by the German Frederic Grimm. Grimm received letters from many leading figures in Paris, such as Diderot, offering them an outlet for their views. These ideas spread so widely that a Polish policeman confiscating the goods of a Jewish peddler in Galicia in 1788 found a copy of the *Gazette of Leiden* in his sack.

(handwritten annotations: "contradiction" "over ~~dictatory~~ within philosopher's beliefs (p. 38)")

Readers' tastes show us the cultural confusion of the 1770s and 1780s. They clamored for philosophical works, especially in the 1770s, and wanted as well to have more information about contemporary events. Little wonder that they would seek to combine the two, trying to provide some sort of philosophical underpinning for their pet program of reform. As in Eastern Europe under Soviet domination, writers sought often to combine political commentary with sex; in the case of eighteenth-century France, mildly pornographic writings, with obvious political overtones, came from the pens of many great *philosophes,* Voltaire and Diderot among them.

The social mores of the time, too, show its confusion. Fads came and went at a bewildering pace. Some members of high society decided to ape the English: serving afternoon tea (a custom that spread widely among the aristocracy), buying race-horses and betting heavily on them, dressing in English fashion. Gambling became a passion for many, ruining more than one family. The rich went to the Opera, to the Comédie Française, to the street entertainments, to the famous tavern (*guinguette*) of Ramponneau on the outskirts of the city. In Ménétra's *Journal*, again and again we see him rubbing elbows with slumming aristocrats, even playing court tennis with two princes of the blood.

The climate of the 1770s and 1780s seems that of cultural crisis. Robert Darnton's study of forbidden best-sellers reveals Mercier's *The Year 2440* to have been the runaway favorite of the 1780s. Mercier focuses on what this Utopian Paris of the future has eliminated: poverty, prostitution, the standing army, taxes, arbitrary arrest, and slavery. Children read so well that they use the *Encyclopédie* as a grammar school text. Everywhere, people denounce what they view as moral excesses: Mercier's Utopia has abolished coffee, tea, and tobacco as well as the blights noted above.

Pamphleteers issued slanderous libels about the sex lives of Louis XV and Mme du Barry; after Louis XV's death, the same authors soon turned their pens against Marie Antoinette. This seeming societal disgust with sexual promiscuity, however, must be balanced by the widespread acceptance of a culture of male marital infidelity, publicly proclaimed. Rich men flaunted their mistresses, particularly the actresses and singers whom they "sponsored." Courtiers engaged in endless rounds of sexual dalliance, games of love that often overlapped with high Court politics. Diderot could praise effusively the sentimental innocence and purity Richardson portrays in *Pamela*, yet simultaneously write pornography.

What did the Enlightenment leave to posterity? Did its ideas "cause" the French Revolution? Outside of France, we can point to the philosophies of the Scot David Hume and the German Immanuel Kant, to the economic changes of the Industrial Revolution, to the economic principles of Adam Smith, as some of the critical underpinnings of the modern world. To eighteenth-century France, Holland, and England (and its colonies), we owe the creation of modern political culture. The Enlightenment and the French Revolution, with considerable help from movements in other countries, created that political culture. The Enlightenment's emphasis on education, on reason, on equality have largely triumphed in the Western world, and became bedrock principles of modern politics due to the Atlantic Revolutions. Many observers at the time made a direct link between the American Revolution and the changing situation in France. Arthur Young wrote in October 1788: "Nantes is . . . enflammé in the cause of liberty . . . The American revolution has laid the foundations of another in France."[54]

The Enlightenment's curious amalgam of optimism—the belief that mankind can be improved—and pessimism—relying invariably on some higher authority to carry out the improvements—have proved a mixed blessing. Diderot and Voltaire corresponded with, and wrote on behalf of despots. They wanted these despots to be enlightened, to be philosopher kings or empresses, but they held out little hope for the people themselves, helping themselves. Even Rousseau, supposed apologist of democracy and (male) equality, provided the ideal society of his *Social Contract* with a Lawgiver, who would see what the mass of citizens could not.

Rousseau's works offer the ideal example of the confusing legacies left by the great Enlightenment thinkers. The Rousseau of the *Discourses* (1749 and 1755) emphasized the corrupting influence of society and touted the virtues of "natural" man and woman. These works, and his novel *The New Heloise,* building on the works of his English predecessors (like Richardson), established the foundations of Romanticism. The greatest German Romantic, Goethe, modeled his first novel, *The Sorrows of Young Werther,* directly on *The New Heloise.* Politically, early Romanticism tended to be conservative, yet Rousseau's primary political impact came on the Left, by means of his 1762 treatise, the *Social Contract.* From its stirring opening words— "Man is born free yet he is everywhere in chains"—to its denunciations of power based on force and of slavery, the *Social Contract* offered a devastating rebuke to the existing political and social system. His call for a society based on civil liberty derived from moral (rational) choice echoed loudly in the debates during the Revolution. Little wonder that the Revolutionaries enshrined Rousseau in their Panthéon of heroes or that those most openly claiming to be his heirs—the Jacobins—would have taken up his misogyny, denying women even the most minimal role in the political process.

The Enlightenment left us a split between a thoroughly de-Christianized elite culture, one perhaps best represented in its first generation by the deist Voltaire and in the second by the atheist d'Holbach, and a broader culture still steeped in Judao-Christian beliefs. In January 1788, Ruault summed up elite attitudes remarkably well in a letter to his brother about the Edict of Toleration (allowing Protestants to have some rights): "Never did a book of philosophy or of politics trouble the public order; even a religious book, a work of fanaticism, would only produce today the laughter of disapproval."[55] The leading intellectual circles of most Western countries have remained resolutely antireligious ever since, an attitude that spread eventually to many workers in the cities. At the same time, ordinary people, especially in the countryside, remained religious. The mutually exclusive vocabulary of the two sides has created a permanent and unbridgeable chasm, first made evident during the Revolution.

The story of Nicolas Gérard, a Parisian stonemason/hairdresser convicted of murder in 1783 illustrates just how profoundly ideas could penetrate from one social level to another. Accused of murdering his roommate, Nicolas Kerse, and then stealing Kerse's goods, Gérard proclaimed his innocence throughout the preliminary interrogations, the trial, and even the postconviction torture to which the Parlement subjected him. The bookseller Hardy, who kept a journal of Parisian events in those days, tells us about Gérard's last moments.

> He remained alive on the wheel for about one hour. It is said that this wretch had the audacity to speak with great insolence to his judges . . . Far from manifesting any sign of anguish or repentance at the Châtelet before execution, when the prison chaplain announced to him the arrival of the priest–confessor he said, "Voltaire and Rousseau died without a confessor, and I can do without one just as well as them."[56]

Notes

1. This parody of the Our Father appeared in a libel published in the early 1770s. It is reproduced in R. Darnton, *The Forbidden Best-Sellers of Pre-Revolutionary France* (New York: Norton, 1996), 166.

2. Nicolas Ruault, *Gazette d'un Parisien sous la Révolution. Lettres à son frère, 1783–1796*, ed. A. Vassal and C. Rimbaud (Paris: Librairie Académique, 1976), 73.

3. Ménétra describes himself as one of the leaders in these discussions. Although his description of the general phenomenon of negotiations among the journeymen, the intendant, the Parlement, and the governor rings true, one is less convinced that Ménétra himself played so large a role as he suggests. On his behalf, he says that the group of thirty leaders designated him as the thirty-first because "the council wanted a man who could write"; Ménétra's writing facility, to which the *Journal* itself bears witness, would have made him a useful member of the council.

4. J. Ménétra, *Journal of My Life*, ed. D. Roche, trans. A Goldhammer (New York: Columbia University Press, 1986), 182.

5. The Hôtel de Ville was gutted by fire again during the Paris Commune of 1871; today's structure is a reconstruction of the eighteenth-century one.

6. P. Süskind, *Perfume. The Story of a Murderer*, trans. J. Woods (New York: Washington Square Press, 1986), 3–4.

7. Cited in L. Chevalier, *Laboring Classes and Dangerous Classes in Paris During the First Half of the Nineteenth Century*, trans. F. Jellinek (Princeton: Princeton University Press, 1973), 375.

8. M. Antoine, *Louis XV* (Paris: Fayard, 1989), 405.

9. In this ritual, on Easter Monday, the king touched hundreds of people infected by scrofula. The royal touch supposedly healed those so infected. Louis's confessor refused him Easter communion again in 1740 and 1744.

10. Only those of ancient nobility, in theory going back to 1400, had the right to be presented officially to the king and queen. In reality, anyone whose nobility went back four generations was easily accepted at Court. Most contemporaries believed Pompadour to be the illegitimate daughter of one of the Farmers General, who convinced an underling to marry the pregnant mother.

11. Songs cited in R. Isherwood, *Farce and Fantasy. Popular Entertainment in Eighteenth-Century Paris* (New York: Oxford University Press, 1986), 14–15.

12. Mme de Pompadour's unpopularity stands as testimony to another phenomenon of late eighteenth-century French life, the changing role of women, to which we will return.

13. Story recounted in R. Darnton, *The Forbidden Best-Sellers of Pre-Revolutionary France* (New York: Norton, 1995), 142.

14. E. Le Roy Ladurie, *L'Ancien Régime. L'absolutisme bien tempéré (1715–1770)* (Paris: Hachette, 1991), 158.

15. This quarrel began as a fight between the House of Burgundy (a junior line of the French royal house) and that of France. When Mary of Burgundy married Maximilian of Habsburg in the late fifteenth century, the Habsburgs took up the cudgels in the dispute.

16. The great household positions also possessed considerable patronage power, such as naming the royal pages.

17. Belle-Isle, grandson of Louis XIV's disgraced superintendent of finances, Nicolas Fouquet, would not have qualified for a commission in some regiments; his father, grandfather, and great-grandfather had been nobles (by virtue of offices in the last two cases), but his great-great-grandfather was a draper from Angers.

18. Eighteenth-century intendants married the daughters of other intendants or of high-ranking judges or administrators; their eldest sons became administrators or judges, and they, too, married within the great clan. Military officers who served on the royal councils followed in the footsteps of military fathers (90 percent) and rarely married the daughters of magistrates (10 percent). Their sons married within the group. Mimicking their fathers and grandfathers, 72 percent of the sons pursued a military career and not a single one (among a sample of fifty-one) became a judge or civil administrator. See R. Andrews, *Law, magistracy, and crime in Old Regime Paris, 1735–1789* (Cambridge: Cambridge University Press, 1994), vol. I, Tables 4.1 and 4.3.

19. Some alliances across groups did take place; in the late 1760s, chancellor Maupeou allied with the duke d'Aiguillon. In the 1780s, minister Breteuil descended from high-ranking administrators who had intermarried with the sword nobility and taken on the latter's lifestyle.

20. If we might make a modern American parallel, the secretary of defense protects the interests of the military itself—demanding a certain weapon for purely military reasons—and those of the defense industry—pushing procurement policies that keep large-scale defense contractors in business or convincing the secretary of state that weapon sales abroad are a good foreign policy tool. The controller general had a trickier balancing act, as he often had to mediate the long-standing conflict between the financiers and the bankers.

21. We have long wondered about the exact number of such offices. I use here the figure provided in the most recent (and best) study of venal office holding: W. Doyle, *Venality: The Sale of Offices in Eighteenth-Century France* (Oxford: Clarendon Press, 1996), 60.

22. Provincial Parlements existed in Toulouse, Grenoble, Bordeaux, Dijon, Rouen, Aix, Rennes, Pau, Metz, Besançon, and Douai. Similar courts, often known as superior councils, existed in Colmar (Alsace), Bastia (Corsica, after its annexation in 1768), Arras (later transferred to Douai), Dombes, and Perpignan.

23. Ménétra complains constantly in his *Journal* of his guild wardens abusing their authority in this way.

24. The anticommoner bias had a long history, including edicts barring commoner officers from the infantry and cavalry in 1718 and 1727. The pressures of wars invariably led to the granting of exceptions, merely to keep the army staffed.

25. Gallicanism was the belief in a special status for the French Church. The Parlement supported both royal Gallicanism, the idea that the Crown had effective control of the French Church, and Parlementaire Gallicanism, which insisted on the court's judicial supremacy in legal matters related to the Church.

26. The most obvious manifestations of this principle were the king's inability to remove Crown officers, such as the chancellor, and his inability to sell any part of the royal demesne, of which he had the use but not the ownership.

27. Lawyers could print their court briefs without censorship; many politically minded barristers used this opportunity to urge government reform or to assail the legitimacy of the state. D. Bell's *Lawyers and Citizens* (Princeton: Princeton University Press, 1994), provides an outstanding presentation of this remarkable end run around censorship.

28. Matters of principle aside, La Chalotais was a client of Mme de Pompadour, whose death in 1764 cost him his protector; d'Aiguillon had ties to the rising mistress, du Barry.

29. Here the Parlement of Paris adopted a formula then current in England: the king *in* Parliament held sovereignty.

30. His reforms in this matter merely followed existing rules: as early as the 1750s, landowners had been required to furnish written proof justifying their assessments. The practice lapsed in many regions; Terray merely sought to revive it.

31. N. Ruault, *Gazette,* 78.

32. Adam Smith borrowed heavily from the Physiocrats. They differed from Smith, however, in their emphasis on agriculture, which they felt was the root of all prosperity.

33. Ruault, *Gazette,* 96–97.

34. The rate on annuities guaranteed on two lives, paid as long as either of the people remained alive, reached 9 percent. The government also offered special higher interest to those over sixty: 12 percent a year on life annuities. Necker's friends in the Genevan anks brilliantly manipulated this system. The purchaser did not have to specify his or her own life as the one in question. In 1784, the bankers of Geneva pooled 2 million *livres* to buy annuities guaranteed on the lives of thirty young girls; they then sold shares in the pool. When one of the little girls died young, the entire city attended her funeral.

35. Ruault cites this speech in a letter of 26 May 1788 (*Gazette*, 112).

36. Ruault, *Gazette*, 86, letter of 1 August 1787. Ruault had quoted the councilor Duval-d'Epresmesnil's speech to this effect in a letter of 8 July. Duval-d'Epresmesnil would later be arrested for his radical speeches.

37. The Egyptian plans usually revolved around the idea that Austria and Russia would divide up the Balkans, then ruled by the Ottoman Empire; France would get Egypt, which was a client state of the Ottomans. Joseph II actually proposed this idea to Louis XVI in 1782.

38. Ruault, *Gazette*, 111.

39. Ruault, *Gazette*, letters of 25 August and 19 April 1787.

40. Quoted in J.-F. Solnon, *La Cour de France* (Paris: Fayard, 1987), 433.

41. The phrase comes from Daniel Gordon's recent book, *Citizens without Sovereignty. Equality and Sociability in French Thought, 1670–1789* (Princeton: Princeton University Press, 1994). The implications of this problem, however, are perhaps closer to the heart of another new study: Patricia Wells, *Law and Citizenship in Early Modern France* (Baltimore: Johns Hopkins University Press, 1995), esp. ch. 5.

42. Ruault, *Gazette*, 109.

43. Cited in Antoine, *Louis XV*, 169–70. My translation.

44. French political theory had always held that the king received his power and legitimacy from the French nation, not from God. God sanctified the French choice through the anointing of the king at the coronation, but the source of legitimacy was the people and the law they made. Henry IV, founder of the Bourbon dynasty, offered irrefutable proof of this maxim: French law made him king, even though he was a Protestant.

45. Cited in M. Price, *Preserving the Monarchy. The comte de Vergennes, 1774–1787* (Cambridge: Cambridge University Press, 1995), 140.

46. From his *Philosophical Letters*, cited by J. Grieder, *Anglomania in France, 1740–1789* (Geneva, 1985), 4.

47. Not all eighteenth-century women lionized Rousseau. Mary Wollstonecraft made him her chief target in her *Vindication of the Rights of Woman* (1792).

48. Such is the translation in the Penguin edition, done by J. Wood: *The Barber of Seville and the Marriage of Figaro* (London: Penguin Books, 1964), 200. The French offers a translation problem here: Beaumarchais uses the phrase "ces puissants de quatre jours," literally, "those powerful ones of four days," perhaps colloquially rendered as "those four-day wonders." I would take this phrase as a reference to the incessant changing of royal ministers in the 1770s, when Beaumarchais wrote the play.

49. Ruault, in his letters, several times warns his brother that the postal service can no longer be relied upon for confidential correspondence.

50. France had some women writers: at any given time between the 1750s and the 1780s, about 3 percent of France's published writers were women. These numbers jumped dramatically in 1789.

51. Quotation from the article, "Hôpital," in the *Encyclopédie,* cited in R. Mortier, "Diderot et l'assistance publique, ou la source et les variations de l'article, 'Hôpital', de l'Encyclopédie," in *Le Cœur et la Raison* (Paris, 1990), 224.

52. Letter of 23 September 1763, cited in P. Gay, *The Enlightenment* (New York: Norton, 1969, 1977), vol. II, 39.

53. The poor most often bought their books from wandering peddlers, not from professional book shops.

54. A. Young, *Travels during the years 1787, 1788 and 1789* (London: W. Richardson, 1794), I, 105.

55. Ruault, *Gazette,* 102, letter of 25 January 1788.

56. Andrews, *Law, magistracy, and crime,* 577.

Chapter Two

The Death of the Ancien Régime, 1787–August 1789

I was enjoying myself and watching my days go by when the French Revolution came suddenly and revived all our spirits. And the word liberty so often repeated had an almost supernatural effect and invigorated us all.

Jacques Ménétra, Parisian glass maker

Charles Paquelin, a winegrower in the tiny Burgundian village of Chassagne, kept a *Notebook of Memories* during the days of the French Revolution. Paquelin's village, slightly south of Beaune, had some connections to the wider world, but it hardly placed him at the geographic center of events in 1789. What does this ordinary Frenchman tell us about his summer of 1789? Let us listen in:

> the 29th of July, at around 6 at night, terror is everywhere in the kingdom ... Everywhere in the region, they have started to ring the alarm ... all people are in consternation, women and children cry out every place, and try to save themselves by fleeing to the mountains ... they have sounded the bells to summon the assemblies in all the parishes to stand guard day and night ... because bands of brigands have formed, who murder, and who bring fire and blood everywhere; because they see no more law there ... How many men killed, how many brigands hanged; many nobles imprisoned; all the others have fled the kingdom in fear of the anger of the Nation. Many of the bishops in prison; everywhere they [the bishops] hide because they tried to bring famine; they are all grain merchants. Great numbers of châteaux have been burned and razed, great alarms and great repentance. It was during the wheat harvest. Before this great terror, we were greatly menaced by [the prospect of] civil war.[1]

Poor Paquelin. How confusing everything must have been to him and to millions of others. His own testimony shows us that he did not, in fact, write this particularly "memory" on the night of 29 July 1789, but somewhat later. Jean Bart, the leading French specialist on the Revolution in Burgundy, assures us that the village of Chassagne, Paquelin notwithstanding, remained calm in July 1789. Yet Paquelin offers us invaluable testimony about contemporary perceptions of what was taking place.

Paquelin highlights the existence of "terror . . . everywhere in the kingdom." He repeats the widespread rumor of armies of brigands spreading "fire and blood" and claims that village assemblies everywhere sounded the tocsin (alarm bell) to mount guard against these "brigands." He tells us of attacks on châteaux, and of the flight of many nobles. Finally, he suggests that ordinary people viewed bishops as little more than grain traders, partly responsible for the massive increase in bread prices in the spring and early summer of 1789. His memoirs ring true, so long as we use them with care. We now know, and indeed many contemporaries knew, that there were no brigands. Paquelin bears witness rather to the mass hysteria called the Great Fear of 1789: people in many parts of France *believed,* as he did, that such bands of brigands existed. Village assemblies did bring large bands of peasants into being; those bands, and not the brigands, often turned on the local châteaux. Modern research has demonstrated that the peasants rarely burned the châteaux, or killed any nobles. They focused on the seigneur's legal papers, which they burned in the hopes that by destroying the physical evidence of the old titles they could abolish the feudal rights of their owners. Paquelin's accusation against the bishops makes sense: bishops, abbeys, and cathedral chapters held almost all tithes in France, so bishops were "grain merchants." Bands of peasants that summer looted tithe granaries, often burning the emptied barns. What Paquelin does not tell us is that the regions subject to the Great Fear and those in which armed bands of peasants attacked the châteaux were not the same; indeed, we have no surviving evidence of the two events coexisting anywhere.

Paquelin's *Memoirs* bear witness to the astonishingly rapid collapse of the Ancien Régime. The rapidity of its disintegration, not simply in Paris, but *everywhere in France,* alerts us to its fundamentally rotten core. The political system of the Ancien Régime had ceased to serve the function of all states: the regulation of the shared interests of the members of the community. People demanded, and got, a New Regime in a few short months.

The speed of change should not startle us: we have seen a similar collapse in Eastern and Central Europe in 1989. Just as in France in 1789, the political system no longer served the needs of society. A system of seeming great strength thus collapses in a matter of months, with very little violence. People have debated the "inevitability" of the French Revolution since it happened; I am among those who believe it was inevitable. The specific events certainly could not be foretold, but the broader lines of Revolutionary events responded to all the discontinuities between social and economic, and political development in eighteenth-century France. The Ancien Régime tried reform and failed in the 1760s and 1770s. The Ancien Régime, feudal[2] to the core, based on privilege, could not survive. In its place, the French people placed the nation.

We must not, however, confuse the inevitability of political change with the serendipity of political events. The Revolution created its own political dynamic, rapidly moving in directions no one could have predicted. Once underway, its mo-

"so fast bic rotten core, but also bic created own momentum"

mentum dramatically altered the nature of political discourse. The startling shift in thinking of many of the deputies to the "Estates General" of early May 1789 and the same men as deputies to the "National Assembly" in late June 1789, for example, can only be understood as a response to the events themselves.

The evidence of change could not be more clear, because the political events of 1789 left an unparalleled record of popular political opinions: the *cahiers de doléances,* or lists of grievances, compiled by the inhabitants of every parish in the kingdom. They elected deputies who attended sub-regional assemblies in each of the more than one hundred fifty bailiwicks, where these deputies created a general *cahier* and chose the deputies to the Estates General. In towns, individual guilds wrote *cahiers;* in some guilds, in some cities, the journeymen and the masters wrote two separate *cahiers.* Rural women sometimes played a role in the process: in one sample of twenty-one Burgundian parishes, twelve had women participate in the electoral assembly. How could it have been otherwise in parishes such as Villeberny, in which the two largest taxpayers were the widows Bizot and Guedeney-Mongin? In many towns women's guilds, such as the fishwives or flower sellers of Paris, wrote *cahiers.* Convents, too, had the right to representation: the sisters met to appoint a male representative, often their overseeing priest, to their local assembly and to draw up a *cahier.* In Paris alone, fifty-seven convents sent representatives to the local assembly of the First Estate. Women seem not to have participated at the next level. None of those twelve Burgundian parishes sent a woman as a deputy to the regional assembly and the town-wide assemblies make no mention of them. Within each bailiwick, the clergy and the nobility compiled their own grievances. The vast majority of these documents have survived, providing perhaps the broadest sounding of public opinion in world history.

The Estates General of 1789 touched off a bewilderingly rapid chain of events that led directly to the overthrow of the monarchy (10 August 1792), to the executions of Louis XVI and Marie Antoinette, to a generation of international war, and to the many other remarkable changes we subsume under the name of the French Revolution. These events often must be followed day-by-day, particularly the momentous changes of May–October 1789, which fundamentally and permanently restructured not merely French but European politics. These political changes, themselves partly a response to social, economic, and cultural changes, in turn led to significant social and cultural shifts and, in the long run, to economic ones.

The historian seeking to reconstruct these events does so against a background of supercharged historiographical debate: few periods in human history so violently divide their interpreters. I have tried to synthesize the two most prominent schools, the Classicists and the Revisionists. With modification, I have followed the Classicists in three important ways:

1. I agree with most of them that the Revolution was inevitable because political systems must reflect the underlying economic and social structures of their societies, which the Ancien Régime no longer did by the 1760s.[3]

Classicry

2. I accept that the Revolution did create in France a unified, modern definition of property.

3. I believe that we can distinguish class differences among the different groups active during the Revolution and that, at certain moments, class differences led to varying political attitudes and action.

The Revisionists reject or would heavily modify these interpretations, particularly the second and third ones. In accepting point one, I am in no way rejecting the arguments of many Revisionists that changes in ideas led to fundamental changes in society.[4] The simplistic argument that noble ideas gave way to "bourgeois" ideas ignores the obvious amalgamation of different sets of values, and misrepresents the complexity of the ideologies of the nobility of Ancien Régime France. Rousseau, the man on whom the most radical Revolutionaries relied for their philosophy, has extremely strong ties to traditional ideas of the provincial French nobility.

The Revisionist argument that the Revolution merely extended pre-existing property relations to all of society and that modern private property existed under the Ancien Régime makes sense, if one makes two caveats. First, the Revolution eliminated other property forms, such as feudal property; second, the Revolution eliminated the private ownership of regulation of many sectors of the commercial economy by abolishing guilds and the venal offices, such as wine broker or inspector of hides, that had owned such rights of regulation. Relationships to property (and to ways of earning one's living) did affect how some people behaved during the Revolution—those involved in manufacturing tended to be far more radical from 1790–1792 than those from the world of law, as we shall see—but the Revisionists rightly renounce any theory that seeks to explain everyone's behavior in this way. In 1789, virtually all of the prominent actors had precisely the same relationship to property: they owned landed estates. Class differences do very little to explain attitudes or actions between April and July 1789, which far more often reflected the fissures of a society of orders. Again and again, we will find profound differences in attitude toward the Revolution expressed by those within the same profession.

As the previous narrative makes clear, I believe the social and economic transformation to the structures of a modern society had taken place well before the Revolution. The Revolution's main positive economic contribution was to bring laws into line with these changed realities.[5] In a direct sense, this change evolved from the modified legal and social structures. State confiscation and resale of property—above all, the property of the Catholic Church (about 10 percent of the land in France)—substantially modified land distribution and eliminated the largest single player in the country's most important market sector, the grain trade. The political process of the Revolution, with its emphasis on male democracy, had profound implications in social and cultural life. At the most basic level of human interaction, the Revolution's foundational principles—liberty, equality, fraternity—encouraged the abolition of traditional barriers of social hierarchy, as in the language of everyday speech. Gone were such honorifics as "monsieur" (my lord) and "madame" (my lady), replaced by "citizen" and "citizeness"; in the long run, the democratization encouraged by the Revolution extended "monsieur" and "madame" to all adult members of society.

This chapter focuses overwhelmingly on political events because I accept wholeheartedly the Revisionist argument that the Revolution was primarily a political event. That event needs to be studied in its political particulars and in the way in which an ever-evolving new world of ideas drove politics in directions all but unimaginable before the Revolution broke out. No document more clearly demonstrates this change than the letter Louis XVI left behind when he tried to run away in June 1791. Although he criticizes the excesses of the Revolutionaries, Louis does so entirely in the political vocabulary created by the Revolution; moreover, he accepts as irrefutable truths ideas he would have hotly contested just three years before. After the events of 1787–1791, even the king himself could no longer think in the same way or even in the same words. Let us turn now to the great events to find out why. In so doing, we must focus first on what happened in Paris, because of the primordial importance of events there; Chapter 13 will provide greater details on what happened in the provinces in 1789.

CHRONOLOGY	1787–5 May 1789
Spring 1787	Meeting of first Assembly of Notables
May 1787	Resignation of Calonne; Brienne replaces him
21 May 1787	Lafayette calls for an Estates General
June–July 1787	Court of Peers registers reform edicts— provincial assemblies; revised tax and fiscal system
July 1787	Louis XVI announces he will summon the Estates General by 1792
July 1787	Parlement of Paris exiled
November 1787	Parlement recalled
January 1788	Parlement registers tax reform edicts; limited toleration for Protestants
May 1788	King sends judicial reform edicts to Parlement
7 June 1788	Day of the Tiles in Grenoble
August 1788	King dismisses Brienne; announces Estates General for 1 May 1789; Necker returns to the government
September 1788	Parlement of Paris rules that Estates General will follow rules of 1614
Fall 1788	Second Assembly of Notables
Dec. 1788–Jan. 1789	King issues edicts on rules for the Estates General
March–April 1789	Electoral campaign for the Estates General; redaction of the *cahiers*
April 1789	Reveillon riots in Paris
5 May 1789	Estates General opens at Versailles

∿ The Estates General of 1789 and the *Cahiers de Doléances*

> *The King has read a great many of the* cahiers. *He must have seen with plea-sure that all of France loves him, is devoted to him, and competes with him to reform abuses. Among all those papers written by so many different hands, he will not find a single one that lacks the proper attitude and respect for the royal dignity.*[6]

Nicolas Ruault, 1 April

Failed reforms stretch back

The government of France staggered from policy to policy, from minister to minister throughout the 1780s. In the early part of the decade, the foreign minister, the count of Vergennes, dominated the government because of the close trust Louis XVI placed in him. After Vergennes's death (1787), Louis turned to successive chief financial of-ficials—Calonne, Brienne, Necker—for key advice. All of these men competed against the king's other ministers for control of state policy; no one individual had Louis XVI's complete confidence, so state policy lacked consistency. The wars of the American Revolution, which ended with the Peace of Paris (1783), brought the French state to the edge of bankruptcy. The new "American" debt, added to the exist-ing debts from the Seven Years' War, created a climate of chaos. By 1786, the royal government did not know where to turn for more money, because its traditional lenders, fearful of an imminent bankruptcy, became unwilling to purchase more government paper.

Desperately seeking an answer to this fiscal crisis, Louis XVI and his chief min-ister of 1787, Charles-Alexandre de Calonne, decided to turn to a device not used since the 1620s: the Assembly of Notables. An Assembly brought together a theoreti-cally handpicked body of the great men of the kingdom. Some people—Princes of the Blood, the great peers, certain archbishops and bishops, first presidents of the Parlements—virtually had to be summoned, so the government actually had far less say in who attended than one might think. These notables heard Calonne describe a government eager to make major reforms in both fiscal and judicial matters. The government wanted to get better control over expenditures and to expand its rev-enues. Calonne told the Assembly that the government took in about 475 million *livres* per year and spent nearly 600 million; he also informed them that France had borrowed over 1.25 billion *livres* in the previous ten years. His figures suggested that the government spent more than half its revenue on interest payments.

He wanted some administrative reforms as well, but there events outran his pro-posals. In the late winter and early spring of 1787, five major disbursement officials de-clared bankruptcy, among them a treasurer of the Navy whose losses amounted to 30 million *livres,* a treasurer of the army, and a receiver general of Rouen, a lynchpin of the syndicate collecting direct tax revenues. The French-language newspaper pub-lished in Holland, the *Gazette of Leiden* reported that royal financial paper declined in value every day; in such a climate, administrative reform became the order of the day. The Assembly of Notables, whose members had been strongly influenced by Necker's *Account Rendered to the King,* recommended a return to some of Necker's ideas, par-ticularly the consolidation of spending authority into fewer hands.

Calonne proposed two basic changes:

1. Greater control over expenses.

2. The elimination of many tax exemptions by creation of a single direct tax.

[handwritten: proposal:]

Calonne proposed a land tax, to be levied *in kind* (i.e., in raw produce), on all landowners. As one might expect of a group whose members made most of their income selling agricultural produce, the prospect of a new, massive seller on the market did not appeal to the Notables; they also raised quite legitimate concerns about the practicality of such a scheme. The Assembly balked at a blanket autho-rization to tax: they wanted the king to agree to a permanent representative body that would approve all taxes, in return for their acquiescence in the loss of tax ex-emptions. The king refused. Calonne, faced by an intransigent Assembly and crip-pled within the government by opposition from other ministers, had to resign. One of the chief spokesmen of the Assembly, Loménie de Brienne, archbishop of Toulouse, a disciple of Necker, took his place. He rapidly sought to put Necker's ideas into practice.

[handwritten margin note: debate = political over tax collection]

Brienne made a key concession: he accepted the Assembly's position that the king should collect the new land tax in cash, not in kind. The Assembly approved much of Brienne's program: new provincial assemblies, creation of a free market in grain, elimination of the public works *corvée,* and issuance of short-term loans. They agreed in principle with a land tax, but refused to vote for it on the (quite legitimate) legal grounds that they had no right to do so. The lawyers among them knew that no Assembly of Notables had ever approved the creation of a new tax: in the accepted legal view of the time, only an Estates General had such authority.[7] The marquis de Lafayette, one of the members of the Assembly, demanded that the king call the Es-tates for precisely that reason (21 May 1787).

Brienne and the other ministers quickly drew up the necessary edicts to enact these reforms and sent them to the Parlements for registration. The Parlement of Paris, sitting as the Court of Peers,[8] did register edicts reforming the fiscal adminis-tration, cutting expenditures, and, after some debate, even one extending limited civil rights to Protestants. The noble members of the Court of Peers, as well as the leaders of the Parlement, had sat at the Assembly of Notables, so it is little wonder that they took the same positions again. Like the Assembly, they ruled that only an Estates General could vote a new tax. In a self-serving gesture by the Parlementaires, the Court of Peers also opposed the government's plan to reform the judiciary.

Brienne and his chief ally, Keeper of the Seals Lamoignon, persisted. Giving in to the peers, the government announced (July 1787) it would call an Estates General "by 1792." The king sent more reforming edicts to the Parlement of Paris, which re-fused to register them; he then went to the Parlement, held a *lit de justice,* and forced them to register the acts. The Parlement renounced the forced registration, so Louis exiled them to Troyes. This familiar dance of opposition ended with the recall of Parlement and yet another *lit de justice* (19 November). Once again, Parlement op-posed the edicts; the king's cousin, the duke of Orléans, told Louis XVI, "it is illegal." The king replied, in classic absolutist style, "I want it, so it is legal."

[margin note: ⚠ fundamental belief A prior to revolution]

The day of such a system had passed: French elites would no longer accept the premise that the will of the prince was law. They now accepted the premise that the law stood above the king, and that the will of the nation, what the eighteenth-century philosophers Denis Diderot and Jean-Jacques Rousseau had called the general will, created the law. Moreover, those elites had turned not only against the king but against the Parlementaire opposition, seeing the Parlements as merely one institution more to be eliminated in the cleansing of the political system. In January 1788, Ruault would write, concerning the Parlement's condemnation of an almanach:

> pendantism, ignorance, prejudice, pretention have long dominated in these sorts of courts; natural reason cannot see the light of day in the Palace of Justice, among all those black robes which fill and darken it. If I were Parlement, one bright morning I would shake off all these ancient villanies and present myself as I ought to be in the midst of the capital of a lively, gay, spirited, and enlightened nation.[9]

Ruault here gives voice to the seismic shift in French politics between the 1760s and the 1780s; whereas in the 1760s elite public opinion had to choose between two parties—that of the ministers and that of the Parlements—by the 1780s, elites had emphatically rejected both of those options, in favor of a third one: the creation of a representative assembly to act as a check on "ministerial despotism." Gabriel-Honoré Riqueti, better known as the count of Mirabeau, who would become the dominant figure of the National Constituent Assembly, summed up the feelings of many in a letter to the royal minister Montmorin (April 1788): "I would never make war against the Parlements, except in the presence of the nation."[10] Once the nation had been assembled, Mirabeau and his allies intended to destroy not only the "absolute" monarchy, but the Parlements, which had been, under the Ancien Régime, the best source of protection from arbitrary governmental behavior.

The government convinced Parlement to go along with a land tax in January 1788. Calonne and Lamoignon introduced their judicial reform program in May. This all but eliminated the jurisdiction of the Parlements, setting up "Grand Bailiwick" courts to hear, without appeal, virtually all cases, creating a Plenary Court for political cases (government edicts, taxation), abolishing torture, and gutting the seigneurial courts. Public opinion favored many of the proposed reforms of local courts, but violently objected to the Plenary Court: Ruault called it "the shameful organ of the oppression of the people."

Brienne simultaneously gutted the existing financial system, going back to Necker's policies. He destroyed the power of the receivers general and other officials with authority to spend the government's money and reduced to five (from several hundred) the number of officials who could authorize spending. The personal credit of the receivers general and of the other powerful financial officers, such as the receiver of the clergy, the treasurers of the Estates of Brittany and Languedoc, and the Farmers General, had underwritten the government's finances for nearly a century.

=> Reforms of tax policy.   => Reduced courts power => resistance

Brienne's creation of a genuine Central Treasury, with complete authority over government spending, however much sense it made as an administrative measure, greatly upset the capital markets integrated into the old system and made it even more difficult to borrow money. His policies, like Necker's, responded to the desires of the bankers, especially foreign ones, in their ongoing conflict with the financiers, led by the Farmers General.

These reforms put the entire country in an uproar. Provinces like Brittany, in which the nobility had close ties to the Parlement, violently objected to the reduced power of the courts. Towns that had powerful local royal courts, like the presidial-seneschalsy of Vannes, protested. Some towns, those that stood to have Grand Bailiwicks, like Chalon-sur-Saône, just as strongly supported the change. In Brittany, the powerful commoners of Nantes and Rennes formed leagues against the nobles and Parlementaires; in Dauphiné, the population of Grenoble showered with roof tiles the royal troops sent to quell disturbances (7 June 1788). When the troops retired to their barracks, the city's population took control, holding the governor prisoner and forcing the Parlement to lead the resistance to the new edicts.

Brittany and Dauphiné provided diametrically opposed models to the rest of France. In Dauphiné, people from the three orders worked together to oppose "ministerial despotism." Popular resistance successfully faced down the troops and the legal elite then stepped in to provide an ordered structure for resistance. In Brittany, the crisis of 1788 sharply divided the nobility from the Third Estate. Their division grew progressively stronger and more violent; by November 1788, Breton barbers were even refusing to shave or give haircuts to any nobleman. In 1788 and early 1789, most of France reacted to events in a manner similar to Dauphiné, but, once the Revolution gathered momentum, the Breton pattern asserted itself. The fundamental division of May–July 1789 split people by order—nobility versus commoner—because the political system of the Ancien Régime relied on that division. In order to destroy the political system of the Ancien Régime, the Third Estate had no choice but to destroy its two greatest bulwarks: the nobility and the Church hierarchy, itself dominated by the great nobility.

The second Assembly of Notables, called in fall 1788, offered the king no more solace than had the first; indeed, if anything it proved more intransigent on every key demand. From Paris to Rennes, from Grenoble to the villages of Burgundy, traditional authorities crumbled in the face of massive demand for change. In August 1788, acting as a royal coroner, Louis XVI issued the long overdue death certificate of the Ancien Régime: he dismissed Brienne, reappointed Necker, and summoned the Estates General for 1 May 1789.

Some of those close to the king recognized the danger of letting the genie out of the bottle; the Princes of the Blood sent him a *Memoir* on 12 December 1788, cautioning him of the cataclysm to come:

> Sire, the state is in peril; your person is respected, for the virtues of the monarch assure him the homage of the nation; but, Sire, a revolution in the principles of government is being prepared; it is being induced by the fermentation

people further Louis XVI succumbs to pressure => Estates General, 1789 (May)

of minds. Institutions reputed to be sacred, and by means of which this monarchy has prospered for many centuries, are being transformed into problematical questions or even criticized as acts of injustice. . . . Who can say where the recklessness of opinions will stop? The rights of the throne have been questioned; the rights of the two orders of the state divide opinions; soon property rights will be attacked; inequalities of wealth will be presented as an object for reform; already it has been proposed that feudal rights be abolished as a system of oppression, a remnant of barbarism.[11]

Ruault's judgment of this unfortunate document echoed that of all of Paris. The initial sensation gave way to ridicule; he wrote on 8 January 1789 that the princes who had signed the *Memoir* no longer dared showed themselves in public because "the writer of this pitiful rhapsody of feudal rights and privileges has dishonored them in the eyes of the nation in having them sign it."[12]

 In Paris, as in the tiniest village, the call for the Estates General generated enormous anticipation. They had not met since 1614, so everyone wondered what they were. How would elections be held? Who could participate in them? How many deputies would come to Paris? What would be the rules governing actions of the Estates? The Parlement of Paris, which had garnered enormous popular support because of its opposition to higher taxes and because it had demanded the king call an Estates General to get new taxes, ruled in September 1788 that the Estates General would meet according to the rules followed in 1614.[13] This ruling made evident to all what leaders of elite public opinion had long recognized: in the new order of things, the Parlement, too, could have no place. Public reaction against the edict led the king, under Necker's influence, to make several key decisions about the rules for the calling of the Estates.

The government decreed that the three estates could meet either separately or together in the bailiwicks; the king further stipulated that each bailiwick would have an equal number of deputies. The king declared that the Third Estate would everywhere represent the countryside, as it had in 1614 in most of the kingdom, and that the Third would have as many deputies as the First and Second Estates combined. He left in abeyance the critical question of whether voting would be by head (individual deputy) or by order (one vote each for the clergy, nobility, and Third Estate). This second method would give each order veto power over all changes, because the immemorial custom of the Estates General was that all three orders had to agree to any binding action.

These rulings created the potential for enormous conflict. First of all, in the *pays d'Etats*, the provision allowing the three orders to sit together left open the possibility that the provincial estates would select the deputies for the Estates General, the practice they had followed in 1614. That situation led to violent conflict in some provinces, above all Brittany. Its dispute between the Second and Third Estates was so bitter that the nobility and the bishops refused to attend the Estates General. The Breton deputies to the Third Estate, once in Paris, created a political club that led the assault against noble privileges. The Breton Club soon attracted members from other provinces; in time, it took the name of the Paris convent in which it met starting in

decisions re : functioning of Estates General
=> conflict, cooperation btwn estates was impossible

October 1789: the Jacobins. In the other *pays d'Etats,* by way of contrast, the king intervened directly, ruling that deputies be elected in standard bailiwick assemblies.[14] The provincial estates of Languedoc, Provence, Burgundy, and Dauphiné theoretically lost their right to select the deputies, as their predecessors had done in 1614 (although Dauphiné, in fact, used the old method).

The Deputies

When the deputies arrived in Versailles, the three orders met separately. The First Estate (clergy) differed completely from its 1614 predecessor. Parish priests, perhaps 10 percent of the deputies in 1614, made up two-thirds of the original 295 deputies of the First Estate in 1789.[15] Conversely, bishops, invariably nobles, held only 14 percent of the seats in 1789, as against their 41 percent of 1614. The abbots, so powerful in 1614, obtained only ten seats in 1789. The deputies from the clergy stood out as well by education: over half had a university degree, usually in theology. They also tended to be a little older, a median just over fifty, as against the forty-five of the other two orders.

For the Second Estate, most bailiwicks allowed all nobles to participate in their electoral assemblies. They chose deputies who combined two defining elements of the traditional French nobility: pedigree and military service. Three-quarters of the noble deputies held a title, an extraordinary percentage in a country where fewer than five percent of the nobility could make such a boast. Seventy percent of them could trace their nobility back to 1500 or earlier; that, too, made them stand out in an overall nobility in which 70 percent of the families had been ennobled since 1600. Eighty percent of the noble deputies had served in the military, many of them in combat. The veterans included nineteen men who fought in the wars of the American Revolution, including the marquis de Lafayette. The nobles also stood apart from the other two orders in their lack of education and in the extreme concentration of men from Paris, with about half of them living in the capital. Another one hundred forty-three nobles sat either with the clergy (eighty-five) or the Third Estate (fifty-eight), the latter often recently ennobled men whose views differed from those of the aristocrats.

Allowing for widespread local variations, the Third Estate followed a simple basic pattern. In each parish, the taxpaying heads of households (aged twenty-five or over, resident for a year or more in the parish) met to draw up their grievances and to elect a few representatives to the bailiwick assembly.[16] In the larger towns, people often met by guild or by parish (or both), which sent deputies to the town assembly, which, in turn, sent people to the bailiwick meeting. In the chief town of the bailiwick, the deputies elected by the rural parishes and by the towns met together to elect deputies to go to Paris. They also combined the grievances of the individual parishes into a single, general *cahier.* In Paris itself, a violent dispute between the town government at the Hôtel de Ville and the bailiwick authorities at the Châtelet over who should supervise the elections led to a long delay. In the end, some 11,000 voters in the 60 districts of the city chose electors, who then met at the Hôtel de Ville to select the deputies to the Estates General. Because of the delays related to the procedural dispute, the deputies from Paris had still not been selected when the Estates General opened on 5 May 1789.[17] The deputies from the Third Estate resembled those of the clergy in one important respect: many of them had attended a university and the vast workers, but educated majority had completed secondary studies. Nearly 70 percent of these deputies had legal training.Royal judges or attorneys, usually from the bailiwick courts, held two hundred eighteeen of the six hundred five seats; self-described lawyers occupied another one hundred eighty-one places.

About one-sixth of the deputies to the Estates General lived in Paris; nearly half of them lived in a town of 8,000 or more people, and 75 percent lived in a town of 2,000 or more. Given that 80 percent of French people lived in the countryside, the heavy skewing toward urban elites created the potential for an urban–rural split in response to the actions of the deputies. The electoral procedures—above all those of the Third Estate—favored citizens from the leading town of each bailiwick. Chief judges of bailiwick courts sat as presidents of the electoral assemblies, and one-third of the assemblies chose their presiding officer as a deputy.[18]

Even allowing for this dramatic skewing toward urban interests, however, the deputies to the Estates General had much greater connection to the rural world than the men elected to the Legislative Assembly of 1791. Self-described "farmers" held 46 seats in 1789, but most of the deputies of the Second and Third Estates shared a common economic interest in agriculture because they got the largest share of their income from farm rents, even though they did not live in the countryside. They had only mixed success dealing with rural issues between 1789 and 1791, but their successors, who had even fewer rural ties, proved utterly inept, as we shall see.

The initial call for the Estates also went out to specific corporate groups. Within the Church, abbeys, convents, and cathedral chapters held internal assemblies to draw up *cahiers*. In towns, guilds met separately to draw up their grievances and to name deputies to the town assemblies. The king also wrote to the syndic of the Jews of Alsace to order individual communities of Jews in Alsace and Lorraine to hold meetings, elect representatives, and draw up *cahiers;* the Sephardic Jews of Paris wrote to Necker, protesting that they had not received a similar summons. The Jews of Metz hired the Polish Jew Zalkind Hourwitz to write a pamphlet on their behalf, in which he cited the rights of Jews to be treated the same as others: "The Jews are not foreigners, either by nature or by religion, but are so treated only because others regard them as such and cut them out of society. If they are given the right of Citizenship, then we will see they are French, like the other subjects of the kingdom."[19]

Some French colonies received summonses from the king, while others, such as Saint-Domingue, did not. The population of Saint-Domingue treated the snub as an accidental "oversight" and proceeded to hold elections anyway. The electoral process in Saint-Domingue touched off a multifaceted conflict, pitting white landowners against poor whites, all whites against those of mixed race and blacks (and some of the latter two groups against each other), and slaves against the free. In the end, the rich whites sent one delegation, while a coalition of mulattoes and some whites sent a competing one. This electoral dispute politicized the island and created among its entire population the expectation of important changes. When the political process did not give the people of Saint-Domingue the changes they demanded, they took matters into their own hands, much like the people of France.

The *Cahiers*

At the moment of a general regeneration in the State, all hearts open to flatter-ing hopes; we believe ourselves to live in days as happy for the subjects as they are glorious for the Monarchy, and all Europe already admires the head of a free nation, who shows himself to be the friend of healthy reason and of the truth.[20]

> Preamble to the *cahier* of the clergy of the parish of St-Paul in Paris.

The electoral assemblies also had to draw up general *cahiers,* to present to the king. What did people say? The nobility of the bailiwick of Bruyères, in the duchy of Lor-raine, summarized two key points in their first two articles:

> the deputy of the nobility of the bailiwick of Bruyères is to be specially charged to vote

1. For liberty of individuals, of citizens, and the suppression of secret letters, as well as the surety of their Estates.
2. To assure properties, such that no one can threaten them or make attempts against them by means of taxes which are not consented by the Estates General.

Everyone wanted protection of their liberty and of their property. In their fourth ar-ticle, the Bruyères nobility stated the key corollary of these demands: "no new law shall be binding unless it is sanctioned by the Nation." They wanted meetings of the Estates General every three years, at which deputies would vote all taxes. As Gouverneur Morris, an American envoy in Paris wrote in April 1789: "it appears from the Instructions given to the Representatives (called here *les Cahiers*) that cer-tain Points are universally demanded which when granted and secured will render France perfectly free as to the Principles of the Constitution."[21]

Clergy, nobles, Third Estate: everyone demanded that the "Estates General," their name for a representative body, have the authority to vote taxes, to supervise the ad-ministration of royal ministers, and, in many cases, to make (jointly with the king) or to approve new laws.[22] The *cahiers* invariably made these demands in a pragmatic, empirical fashion; few of them contained philosophical statements about the nature or locus of sovereignty. They demonstrated profound respect and affection for the king but also gave evidence of changes to come. The nobility of Crépy-en-Valois, for example, swore its allegiance to the nation and the king, in that order. The authors of the *cahiers* supported a constitutional monarchy in which a representative body would have to approve all laws and taxes and the king would be head of the executive branch of government. Morris unequivocally stated the key issue in February: "Your Nation is now in a most important Crisis, and the great Question, shall we hereafter

---

THE GENERAL *CAHIER* OF THE BAILIWICK OF D'AVAL

The most radical *cahiers* tended to come from the Third Estate, such as that of the bailiwick d'Aval in Franche-Comté. They began with the demand for a "National Constitution," with the exigent provisions:

1. That it be recognized that France is a free nation, that the kingdom is a monarchy governed by the king, following the laws, which cannot be destroyed nor changed without the consent of the nation, legally assembled.

2. That the monarchic power be maintained in all its plenitude and recognize the succession in the august ruling house, hereditary from male to male, by order of primogeniture, to the exclusion of women and their descendants.

3. That the nation cannot be represented except by an Estates General composed of deputies freely elected, of which half shall be chosen from the Third Estate and the others from the first and second orders.

4. That the Estates General shall meet every three years at the least, and votes will be counted there by head, in one and the same chamber.

6. That all laws will be consented to by the Estates General. All taxes, all loans will also be

consented to by the Estates General, who will determine the use of the money.

8. That all privileges or exemptions of any kind, whatever their cause, shall be abolished with respect to taxation levied for public expenses.

9. That individual liberty of all citizens and of their property, civil and political liberty shall be assured; and that *lettres de cachet* (arbitrary orders for arrest) be abolished.

These remarkable deputies went on to a long list of grievances. Under the heading of justice, they demanded abolition of venality of office. They demanded a completely new tax system: creation of a single tax, to be levied on land, with all landholders to be listed on one register; elimination of all interior tolls; creation of a single system of weights and measures; as well as abolition of the existing tax administration. They further insisted on the suppression of censorship and on the liberty of the press. The chapter "On the administration of Communes" had but one article: "Municipal officers in all the kingdom shall be elective, voted triennially, and non-venal."

---

have a Constitution or shall Will continue to be Law, employs every mind and agitates every heart in France."

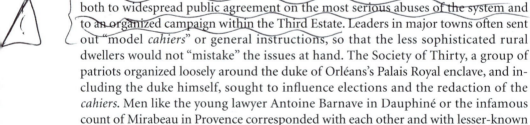

The similarity of so many of the general *cahiers* of the Third Estate bore witness both to widespread public agreement on the most serious abuses of the system and to an organized campaign within the Third Estate. Leaders in major towns often sent out "model *cahiers*" or general instructions, so that the less sophisticated rural dwellers would not "mistake" the issues at hand. The Society of Thirty, a group of patriots organized loosely around the duke of Orléans's Palais Royal enclave, and including the duke himself, sought to influence elections and the redaction of the *cahiers*. Men like the young lawyer Antoine Barnave in Dauphiné or the infamous count of Mirabeau in Provence corresponded with each other and with lesser-known patriots, such as the lawyer Jean Navier of Dijon. Navier sent a "Summary of Mandates" to the presidents of Burgundian village assemblies, in which he outlined the program of the patriot party in the Third Estate: voting by head; obligatory consent of the nation, by means of an Estates General, for taxes and laws; periodic and mandatory meetings of the Estates; and tax equality. The Third Estate everywhere, from the Paris suburbs to Burgundian villages, ordered its deputies to refuse to accept all humiliating social distinctions.

Navier, Barnave, Mirabeau, and their allies went beyond these demands, which had broad-based support; they had a more radical agenda. Navier's "Summary" demands support for provincial estates and local tribunals and insists that the primary function of the Estates General is to establish a constitution that would make individual liberty inviolable, respect property, and provide freedom of the press. He wanted the king and the military to take an oath to defend the constitution. Navier's "Summary" even addressed tactical issues. He suggested that if the clergy and nobles refused to vote by head, the deputies of the Third Estate should invite like-minded members of the other two orders to join them in telling the king that they were the Nation, and should then declare themselves the "National Assembly."

Navier's "Summary" makes obvious the political platform of one group within the Third Estate, including its intention to create a National Assembly if the other two orders would not go along with its political ideas. Ruault's letters of the spring of 1789 show that he, too, knew of such plans and reveal that he had great confidence in the Third's ability to carry them out: in February he wrote that "you can believe that the Third will defeat the nobility and the high clergy. If those groups grumble too much about it, we will find a way to get around their votes, which will lead to an even greater revolution."[23] The main leadership of the forthcoming National Assembly—Mirabeau, Brissot, Barnave, Condorcet, and the others—had already begun agitating for a constitutional monarchy in the mid 1780s. When the king announced the calling of an Estates General, these people realized that their opportunity had come; they seized it.

Their radical program faced opposition even within the Third Estate: Navier failed to gain election at Dijon. Yet the opposition failed to see the internal logic of the patriot demands. Most people wanted a representative body to vote laws and taxes; their *cahiers* used the only name they knew for such a body, an "Estates General." That term did *not* mean they wanted *the* Estates General, that is, the actual historical body that had sat most recently in 1614. The most politically sophisticated elements, men such as Navier or Ruault in the Third Estate or the men meeting in the assemblies of the nobility in Paris, understood fully that what they wanted was a "National Assembly": a body elected by the citizens, that is, the men of property. Those who wanted such a "National Assembly" made clear their opposition to the current form of government, but felt that Necker and, to some extent, Louis XVI, supported them.

The patriot party voiced demands widely shared with others, but used a vocabulary most people, even in the Third Estate, were unwilling yet to accept. Two elements helped them convince people to adopt the new vocabulary, and the new thinking it represented. First, the pamphlet literature inundating France during the electoral campaign of 1789 educated people in the new politics. This campaign also greatly heightened tensions between nobles and commoners, making the nobility (the *aristos*) and the bishops into the great enemy of needed reforms. Second, the political developments of May and June 1789 drove those clinging to the old vocabulary and to timid measures of reform into the mentality and reality of revolution.

In the villages, the coalition of legal men who provided virtually all of the presiding officers of electoral assemblies assured the success of the urban middle class program. These "presidents" often did not live in the village; some presided over multiple assemblies. Through these men, the patriot party of Barnave, Mirabeau, Navier, and others out-organized their opponents and elected a solid majority of deputies who were sympathetic to their ideas. The same political process occurred within the nobility. The conservatives, titularly led by the king's brothers, and actually directed by the *parlementaire* Jean-Jacques Duval d'Eprémesnil and the count d'Antraigues, got out their vote. The electoral success of the liberals in the Third Estate and of the conservatives in the Second Estate reduced the prospects of compromise.

The nobility suffered from a critical internal problem in the great political struggle of May–July 1789. Many of its members, such as those who had met in the Paris district assemblies, agreed with the Third Estate that France needed a constitution. They further agreed with the deputies from the Third about almost all of the key elements of that constitution. The conservative nobles, who dominated the elections in the outlying bailiwicks, could not agree on this fundamental point: they hoped to share power with the king, but rejected some of the principles their liberal noble colleagues (and the members of the Third) felt should provide the fundamental underpinnings of that constitution. When the critical moment came, in late June 1789, the liberal nobility sided with the Third Estate.

Parish *cahiers* did not stop with the clauses from the model *cahiers*. Numerically, the peasants dominated these assemblies. They often elected ploughmen to represent them at the bailiwick meetings, and used their village *cahiers* to set out the key demands of rural society. The peasants demanded the elimination of the existing tax system and the creation of a new one based on a fairer system of assessment. The *cahiers* of the clergy tended to fudge a little on how much they would pay, but the nobles and Third Estate almost universally demanded a new system based on a land tax. A majority of the noble *cahiers* even agreed to give up their tax exemptions. One *cahier* after another denounced the salt tax, interior tolls, the absurd proliferation of weights and measures, excessive government spending, venality of office—in short, virtually everything the Ancien Régime stood for. They demanded a permanent "Estates General," which would supervise government ministers, oversee taxation and spending, vote taxes and laws, and "represent" the nation.[24]

Local *cahiers* often mentioned specific grievances or demanded old-fashioned protectionism—like the butchers of Rochefort, who wanted to forbid outside *charcutiers* from bringing cooked meat into the city—but they could also tie broad philosophical principles to local government. We are not surprised to hear the lawyers of Rochefort refer to "this class of citizens [the Third Estate] . . . so long vilified, so often oppressed, which will retake in the national assemblies its rights and the degree of influence that the barbarism of previous centuries has taken from it, that Gothic prejudices still dispute but which reason and equity render unto it." The city's surgeons presaged the attitudes the National Assembly would take when they demanded the abolition of monasteries and convents, which were of "no utility to either religion or the government," and were perpetuated only by "laziness or the caprice of parents." The ordinary inhabitants of the parish of Notre Dame, outside the city walls, gave local voice to the democratic urges so evident at the national

J.-L. David, Napoleon Crossing the Alps (1800). Here we have the cult of the romantic hero in full bloom; Napoleon sits astride not only his horse, but an entire historical era.

Elizabeth Vigee-Le Brun, Marie Antoinette and her children, (1787). Vigee-Le Brun's prominence as a painter is amply demonstrated by this extremely important commission, a remarkable coup for a female artist in the 18th century.

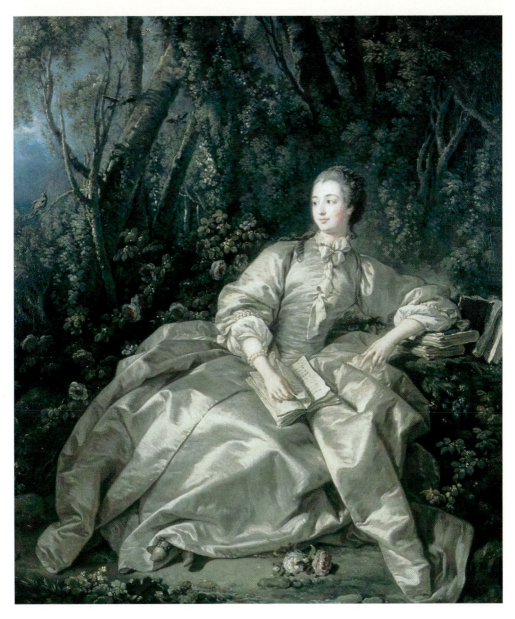

Francois Boucher, Mme de Pompadour. Boucher painted several portraits of this important royal mistress, who was arguably the most important patron of the arts in her day. As in most of these paintings, she holds a book, this time reading in her garden.

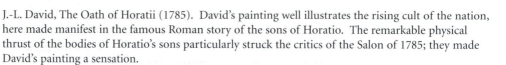

J.-L. David, The Oath of Horatii (1785). David's painting well illustrates the rising cult of the nation, here made manifest in the famous Roman story of the sons of Horatio. The remarkable physical thrust of the bodies of Horatio's sons particularly struck the critics of the Salon of 1785; they made David's painting a sensation.

level: they demanded the right to elect the local syndic and his assistant, who were to serve two-year terms.[25]

In Paris, the district assemblies of April 1789 immediately put this idea into practice. Their actions demonstrate conclusively that the political nation, particularly the Third Estate, had already determined that they would henceforth have representative, partly democratic government. These people viewed the Estates General as the means to enact such a "revolution." The preamble of the *cahier* of the provosty of Paris, which met in late April, began: "A revolution is being prepared. The most powerful nation in Europe is about to give itself a political Constitution."[26]

The royal convocation letters in Paris had named presidents and secretaries for each district assembly. The voters immediately removed their officers and elected presiding officers, either the old ones, if they were willing to serve because they had been elected, or, if they refused, new ones. Jean-Sylvain Bailly, soon to be mayor of Paris and the first presiding officer of the National Assembly, wrote in his memoirs of his feelings on the glorious twenty-first April, when he attended his local assembly:

> When I found myself in the midst of my district assembly, I felt that I breathed new air; it was the phenomenon of being something in the political order and by the single quality of being a citizen, or rather of being a bourgeois of Paris, because we were still bourgeois and not citizens . . . That assembly, an infinitely small part of the Nation, nonetheless felt both the strength and the rights of all.[27]

The Revolutionary Content of the *Cahiers*[28]

[Before voting any taxes, its deputies] *"must have solemnly declared, recognized, and clearly stated the following rules: 1) That all the French are born free and equal, and that all power must come from the Nation."*

Cahier of the Third Estate of the parish of Filles Saint-Thomas, Paris

We must be absolutely clear on the revolutionary nature of these demands. Many historians, misled by the traditional vocabulary, have suggested that the *cahiers* did not have a "revolutionary" character: not so. If we examine the specific recommendations, and get beyond the rhetorical devices, we can see that the Ancien Régime had virtually no support in France in 1789, save among some a few hidebound aristocrats (both lay and ecclesiastic) and some elements of the poorer provincial nobility. The Estates General—that is, the real institution that had met in 1588 or 1614—had virtually none of the characteristics the men of 1789 attributed to their "Estates General." The *cahiers* demanded a revolution: a complete demolition of the Ancien Régime, root and branch, and the establishment of a constitutional monarchy. They demanded, as Morris rightly said, the substitution of law for will, of liberty and equality for arbitrariness and privilege. Like the Third Estate of d'Aval, they insisted that law derived from "the consent of the nation, legally assembled"; that demand—repeated again and again in the *cahiers,* especially those of the Third Estate but also, let us not forget, in many of those of the nobility and clergy, completely rejected the legitimacy of the Ancien Régime. Moreover, no compromise between this principle and the principle of royal absolutism was possible.

Many *cahiers* demanded local assemblies, also voted by citizens. The idea that people had the right to representation, and that their representatives should control the state, was ubiquitous, as the action of the Parisian districts—electing their presiding officers—made abundantly clear. Oddly enough, the royal government had done much to resuscitate such views, when it created regional assemblies of estates in 1788. Many of the deputies to these local assemblies sought, and obtained, election to the Estates General.

Among the bailiwick *cahiers* of the Third Estate, and even in many noble *cahiers,* such as that of Paris, the principle of a constitution stands out: everyone insisted that the first duty of the new assembly was to write a constitution. The *cahiers* demonstrate the total collapse of the old system. Few spoke up on its behalf. The language shows respect for the king, often referred to as the father of his people, and for monarchic authority, but the specific clauses invariably assault every principle of royal power. The king would keep only executive authority, losing his hold over both the legislative process and the judiciary. The *cahiers* assert the principle of the sovereignty of the nation, even if they do not use the word. For their authors, there could be no doubt: the nation, not the king, made the law. Here the distinction between the more radical *cahiers* of a city such as Paris, and those of outlying areas, became clear. The Parisian *cahiers,* those of the nobles, as well as the ones of the Third Estate, usually specified that the Estates General would make the law, which the king would then sanction.[29] Given that monarchical political theory rested on the principle that the king made the law, their assertions about the role of the Estates in that process are the essence of the revolutionary message. They believed in liberty, for persons and property.

The *cahiers* provide a remarkable road map of what would happen in 1789; the results of May through October 1789 corresponded very closely to what the *cahiers* had demanded. The relative unanimity among the general *cahiers,* that is, in the sentiments of the political elite, led quickly to a set of constitutional principles based directly on those sentiments. The National Constituent Assembly, as it would call itself, made the *nation* the source of sovereignty (lawmaking); gave the Assembly full control over taxation, borrowing, and state administration; established legal equality of individuals, freedom of the press, protection of individual liberty, inviolability of most forms of property, and a judiciary independent of the king's will; and abolished the greatest of the old abuses, such as venality of offices and all forms of privilege. They also agreed on some limitations: many of the *cahiers,* like that of d'Aval, with its insistence on the Salic Law's exclusion of women, demonstrated strong opposition to rights for women. The Assembly took longer to enact legislation over more contentious issues, such as freedom of religion or a "free" market.

"Enlightened" opinion among members of the Third Estate, clergy, and nobility agreed on the fundamental principles. They violently disagreed over other issues, including Church property, compensation for feudal rights, the existence of noble status, and control of the future Assembly. Their two key demands—liberty of people and protection of property—made them look to the king as the executive branch of government, a virtually unanimous clause in the *cahiers*. The *cahiers* of a few radical urban districts, however, revealed a level of hostility and a degree of intolerance for the Ancien Régime that foreboded violent conflicts to come.

The Voiceless

We the inhabitants of the countryside have no deputies in the assembly of the province.

Complaint of the peasantry of Époisses, in Burgundy

During the reading of the cahier, *the least among us were satisfied because we did not reject their complaints.*

Third Estate of parish of Saint-Germain l'Auxerrois in Paris

One little researched aspect of this process deserves mention: the conflict between the opinions expressed in the general *cahiers* and those expressed in the parish assemblies. Everywhere, lawyers or notaries from nearby towns presided over the village assemblies. Within the villages, economic interest usually divided the notables—lawyers or merchants or ploughmen—and the poorer peasants. As noted above, the notables often got the village assembly to enact a "model" *cahier*, adding a few articles about local concerns, or intimidated the poor into silence. Villages in which the seigneurial judges ran the meeting (and the royal letters stipulated that the "local judge" should do so) had particularly divisive meetings. Burgundy, which still had widespread serfdom, was especially fertile ground for "wild" assemblies: those who met after the official assembly and created their own *cahier* (known as the *cahier sauvage,* the "wild" or perhaps "free" *cahier*), the voice of the poor. The *cahiers sauvages* tended to address local issues, such as grievances of tenant farmers against their landlords or of peasants against the local seigneur. In some towns, the poor, usually excluded from the assemblies, likewise protested that their complaints had not been addressed. The self-serving addition of the good citizens of Saint-Germain l'Auxerrois notwithstanding, the Parisian poor in particular felt excluded; self-appointed spokespeople for this group published "*cahiers* of the poor," small pamphlets that set out the grievances of day laborers, porters, water-carriers, and the countless other poor workers of Paris.

At the next level, the bailiwick assembly, the rich ploughmen often provided half or more of the deputies, and many of the wealthy urbanites owned rural estates, so that concerns of rural property holders received a full hearing. The overwhelmingly urban deputies elected by these assemblies took away from the bailiwick meetings a package of important reforms for rural life, yet many deputies often lacked the expertise to understand how such reforms would have to be enacted. They shared with the peasants an abiding interest in destroying the existing taxes and in creating

urban vs. rural—different desires

THE PARISIAN RADICALS: BLUEPRINT FOR REVOLUTION

Reading the *cahiers* of the district assemblies of the Third Estate of Paris reveals the astonishing degree to which the urban radicals had a specific agenda, which they successfully forced upon a country little in sympathy with it. The forty-five voters of the district of Theatins, in the quarter of Saint-Germain-des-Prés, put together a remarkable document, which, in addition to the standard demands, made some far more radical ones. In article 25, they demanded that priests be allowed to marry, "because marriage is in no way incompatible with their functions, nor is it forbidden to them by divine law"; in article 26, they demanded that divorce become legal, "as an indissoluble contract is contrary to the inconstant nature of man"; in article 29, they insisted on religious toleration, because "tolerance is one of the most essential virtues in civil society." Article 30 demanded the abolition of religious orders,

> as contrary to the social will and the good of the fatherland, of which they diminish the population. By this means both simple and gentle, the regular orders of both sexes will be gradually extinguished in France, and their goods, thus acquired by the Nation, will serve for the payment of the public debt and for a multitude of objects of public utility. This article is one of the most important of this *Cahier*.

Just as the citizens of Filles Saint-Thomas predicted the confiscation of Church property and its use for paying off the state debt, so, too, they predicted that the state should divide all ecclesiastical revenues and make sure all parish priests get a salary of 1,200 *livres* (the precise amount the Assembly would later designate). They even asked the Assembly to finish off the Louvre according to the old plans of the architect Perrault: they wanted the expanded palace to include a library, an art museum, a cabinet of natural history, and a gallery of maps—all to be open to the public every day!

One of their articles (37) asked the Assembly to abolish all "bastilles," a demand echoed in several other Parisian district *cahiers* (and discussed at the general electoral assembly) and one that convincingly suggests that the storming of the Bastille on 14 July was far from an "accidental" incident. The inhabitants of the parish of Saint-Joseph, in the quarter of Les Halles, gave the most eloquent presentation of this demand:

> Article 6: That the Bastille crumble and rot; that this same ground, watered with the tears of victims of arbitrary power, shall henceforth be watered only by tears of relief and thanks; that the locale, condemned by the continued existence of this living sepulcher, shall henceforth be ennobled by a national monument, in honor of our good King, which will recount to posterity the memory of his virtues and his love for the French, of whom he is the father; that the demolished remains of this vast tomb serve as the foundations of a temple to Liberty in honor of the Estates General; and, like the brave Americans, who transformed into defensive weapons the statue of their oppressor, we will transform this abode of tyranny and the tears shed within it into a place of liberty and concord; in a word, let us be French, that is, free, and the support of the Throne and the Fatherland.[30]

a land tax that would be paid by all proprietors, no matter what their status. They also well understood the need to abolish many seigneurial privileges, such as the universally decried hunting monopolies and dovecotes.[31] The village and bailiwick *cahiers* often objected to other seigneurial rights—dues, milling monopolies, courts—but demands for specific changes varied sharply from place to place.

ignoring peasant demands in Estates General. *in practice.*

The deputies to the Estates General knew perfectly well that the peasants had expressed their grievances and knew, from reading village *cahiers* or even *cahiers sauvages,* what those grievances were. At the parish and bailiwick meetings, the deputies had heard the peasants voice these complaints. The deputies knew that they themselves had played a critical role in preventing peasant complaints from being sufficiently heard at the national level. All over France it was the same: the farmers who made up the largest segment of the population had few deputies among those sitting in Paris, and those few came from among the wealthiest ploughmen.

Ignoring rural opinion would have profound implications. Historians usually make the modern assumption that the "privileged orders" (clergy and nobles) could only represent themselves, so they take for granted Louis XVI's decision to allow the Third Estate to represent the countryside. These historians forget that the medieval Estates General and most of the provincial estates of France had a different system: the landlords (i.e., the clergy and nobility) represented the countryside.[32] The Estates General of 1560, 1576, 1588, and 1614 used a mixed system: in the areas without provincial estates, the Third Estate represented the countryside; in the *pays d'États,* the nobility and clergy usually did so.

The traditional system made more sense in certain ways. The clergy and nobles often had more common interests with the peasants on tax issues than did the deputies from towns. Urban merchants invariably supported higher direct taxes, levied essentially on landed property; landlords preferred indirect taxes, like duties on wine, because urban dwellers drank more often in taverns than rural ones. Provincial estates, such as those of Brittany and Burgundy, also had many resident rural nobles sitting in their assemblies. The Estates General would have scarcely fifty such men. This rural nobility shared cultural values, above all religious ones, with the peasantry: both groups remained much more closely tied to the Catholic Church than did the urban elites who dominated the Estates General.

On the one hand, by ruling that the "Third Estate" included the rural dwellers, Louis XVI enfranchised the rural mass of the population: about 70 percent of rural men could attend the parish assemblies of 1789. The rural dwellers could count on the Third Estate to support its demands against the nobility. On the other hand, the peasantry's attitudes toward a new tax system and toward the Catholic Church more closely mirrored those of the nobility and clergy, so the Third Estates's actions in those areas were not likely to get much support in the countryside. By ruling in favor of the Third Estate, Louis had recognized a fundamental transformation of French social life: the powerful landowning nobility of late eighteenth-century France no longer lived in the countryside, as its predecessor of 1614 had done. Many of the small-town notaries, lawyers, and judges who sat in the Estates General shared economic interests with the nobles and the peasants because they owned rural estates, but the roots of the rural–urban split that would devastate the Revolution in 1790 and after lay in the creation of an Estates General in which those who actually lived in the countryside had so little voice. When the Legislative Assembly came to power in 1791, the near total absence of rural men exacerbated this initial problem and helped pave the way for counter-revolution.

=> *counter – revolution*

❧ THE BIRTH OF MODERN FRANCE: 27 APRIL–11 AUGUST 1789

Once the spirit of subordination is lost, the love of independence will start to grow in all hearts.[33]

The Parlement of Paris, remonstration against the Six Acts of 1776

C H R O N O L O G Y	27 April 1789–11 August 1789
27–28 April	Reveillon Riots in Paris
5 May	Opening of Estates General
7 May	Nobility votes to verify credentials on its own
26 May	Negotiations between Third Estate and nobility break off
4 June	Death of the Dauphin
10 June	Third Estate begins process of constituting itself as the full assembly
13 June	Parish priests begin joining with the assembled Third Estate
17 June	Declaration of the "National Assembly"
19 June	Clergy votes to join the Third in the new Assembly
20 June	Tennis Court Oath
23 June	Royal seance; Assembly refuses king's order to disband
24 June	Clergy disbands, joins the Assembly
25 June	Forty-six nobles join the Assembly
27 June	King orders all deputies to join the National Assembly
11 July	King dismisses Necker
12 July	Royal German regiment attacks crowd in the Tuileries Garden; electors of Paris form the Commune, new city government; customs barriers around Paris destroyed
13 July	Parisian crowds begin to search for grain and arms
14 July	Crowds seize arms at the Invalides, storm the Bastille, murder the Mayor of Paris and the two chief officers at the Bastille
15 July	King appears to the Assembly; vows to work for reform
16 July	Necker reinstated

CHRONOLOGY	(continued)
17 July	King appears at the Hotel de Ville of Paris, accepts the revolutionary cockade; nobles begin fleeing the country
22 July	Murders of Foullon and Bertigny
July–August	Great Fear in the countryside; reorganization of municipal governments
4–5 August	Assembly abolishes "feudalism" and privileges
5–11 August	Assembly debates precise abolition of privileges, issues decree of 11 August "entirely destroying the feudal regime"

The events of the spring of 1789 drove the process ever more in the direction desired by the Society of Thirty and the urban deputies of the Third Estate. The harvest of 1788 had been poor in most of northern France and grain prices rose steadily, peaking in July 1789, just before the new harvest came in. The high price of grain and the climate of political instability led to riots in many cities, such as the Reveillon riots in Paris (April 1789). The government feared precisely such disturbances: Morris and Lafayette discussed potential revolts in Paris as early as 17 April and Morris noted in his diary that the king moved 10,000 troops into the Paris region in anticipation of trouble.[34]

The worst rioting took place shortly after the electoral assemblies held in Paris's districts between 21 and 23 April. The disturbances about bread prices began in earnest on 24 April but worsened sharply on 27 April. At the assembly of the Sainte-Marguerite district, the paper manufacturer Reveillon had publicly stated that the price of bread should be reduced to a level affordable for workers making 15 shillings a day; the saltpeter manufacturer Henriot had said the same in another assembly. Their remarks reached the streets as support for wage reduction, leading crowds of artisans to loot Henriot's house and to destroy utterly Reveillon's house and manufactory (27–28 April). Troops called in to quell the disturbances killed between twenty-five and two hundred people and wounded scores more.[35] Reveillon sought and obtained protective custody in the Bastille, making him one of its last inmates.

Coming on the eve of the opening of the Estates, this riot did not bode well for the political stability of the capital. Contemporaries found these riots particularly suspicious because Reveillon had an outstanding reputation among the workers of Paris; he had spent large sums on relief for his own workers in the winter slowdown of 1788–89 and paid his workers far more than 15 shillings a day. The surviving evidence, such as police arrest records, indicates that none of Reveillon's own workers participated in the riots.[36] Some of those participating in the riots included artisans whose small workshops were threatened by Reveillon's products; these men may have been particularly upset that Reveillon represented the faubourg Saint-Antoine at the city's electoral assembly (which took place the very day of the riot).

Given that one *cahier* after another from the Third Estate had specifically mentioned that their deputies should not suffer any "humiliating distinction" with respect to the other two orders, the physical events of early May greatly strengthened the hand of the hard liners among the Third Estate. One group of deputies of the Third made their displeasure more evident by meeting on the evening of 5 May to destroy immediately the pretense that the group meeting in Versailles was an Estates General. They decided henceforth they would call themselves the "Commons," a term taken from the English; the French word, "communes," had, since the twelfth century, had a frankly revolutionary connotation. The next morning, the Third returned to the great hall, to find that the other two orders had been given separate quarters; the sheer size of the Third dictated that it would meet in the Hall of Menus Plaisirs.

The Estates had a profound political question to answer right at the start: would the Estates vote by order, with one vote each for each order, or by head, with one vote for each deputy? Given that the deputies from the Third Estate outnumbered those of the other two, control of the Estates hinged in the balance.[37] Those who knew the traditional procedures of the Estates General worried that one order could prevent action by its veto: the Estates General had always operated under the principle of consensus—the orders had all to agree for a motion to pass.[38] Given the dominance of the military aristocracy in the Second Estate, they seemed (and were) a formidable barrier to change. Those in the laity who demanded serious reform of the Church and of religious policy worried that the First Estate would use its veto to prevent the creation of religious toleration and to avoid reform within the Church, as had happened in 1560.

At the opening session, the royal spokesmen had proposed to the Estates that some questions might best be settled debating in common and others debating by order. The king would leave the question up to the Estates themselves. This proposal fueled the flames. Throughout the electoral season, pamphlets appeared setting forth the position of the two sides. Pamphlets supporting the position of the Third Estate dominated the field, particularly the incendiary *What is the Third Estate?* of the Abbé Sieyès. In response to his own question, he answered that by all rights the Third Estate was "everything" but that it unjustly had been made to be "nothing." What does it demand to be? "Something." Sieyès argued that the Third Estate *was* the nation, because it represented 95 percent of the people. In May 1789, more and more deputies to the Third Estate came to agree with him. When the nobility voted overwhelmingly (7 May) to verify credentials of nobles on its own and then declared itself duly constituted four days later, the Third Estate hardened its position. The clergy, too, verified independently, but made no declaration. Talks among the three orders dragged on from 7 to 26 May and broke off.

The king tried to get them back together on 29 May, but, as was so often the case, he vacillated. When his oldest son died, on 4 June, his paternal grief overwhelmed any interest in other matters. The Third Estate finally took matters into their own hands on 10 June, passing a motion by Sieyès that it alone was the "national assembly" and inviting the other two orders to join it. Here we do well to remember the "Summary" instructions written by the Dijon lawyer, Navier, which had proposed (in March) precisely this course of action. Given that Navier was in close

5 May 1789

The complications of setting up so unprecedented an occasion led to some delays, so the Estates General did not open until 5 May, at Versailles. The ceremonies themselves introduce us to the critical role of symbolism in the Revolution, and make clear the various currents of opinion. Morris tells us that at the great public procession of 4 May, the crowds shouted "Vive le Roi!" at every opportunity, but that the queen "meets not a single acclamation." His sources at Court told him that the queen and king were greatly offended by the ceremony: the king objected to the duke of Orléans marching with the deputies, rather than as a Prince of the Blood, and to the cold reception granted the queen. When Marie-Antoinette complained to a courtier about "these unworthy French" ("ces indignes Français"), the king's aunt, Madame Adelaide, reportedly replied, you should "say these indignant French, Madame" ("dites indignés, Madame").

At the opening ceremony on 5 May, the clergy and nobility appeared in elegant finery, the Third Estate, by order of the royal master of ceremonies, in simpler black costumes; moreover, in the great Hall of Menus Plaisirs of Versailles, where the opening session took place, a balustrade separated the deputies of the Third Estate from their social superiors. The master of ceremonies, the marquis de Brézé, who tried to regulate the meeting of the Estates using the same criteria he applied at Court, outraged many members of the Third Estate because of the elaborate and, to them, humiliating protocol of the great procession of 4 May 1789. He began the opening ceremony on 5 May by making the Third Estate enter through a side door, rather than the main

one used by the king and the other two orders. Morris, an eyewitness to the session, commented at length on the elaborate finery of the nobility, in their waistcoats and waist-length "lappets" made of "Cloth of Gold," and contrasted it to the simple black cloth of the Third.

One deputy from the Third, Louis-Marie La Revellière-Lépeaux, "ostentatiously wore brightly colored clothes," while another "old Man who refused to dress in the Costume prescribed for the Tiers and who appears in his Farmer's Habit, receives a long and laud Plaudit." In another break with ceremony, many deputies of the Third, led by Jean-Sylvain Bailly, soon to be mayor of Paris, ostentatiously redonned their hats, despite Brézé's ruling that only the deputies of the first two orders could replace their hats once the king had done so. Morris tells us that "when he [the king] puts it [his hat] on again his Nobles imitate the Example. Some of the Tiers do the same, but by Degrees they one after the other take them off again. The King then takes off his Hat." He we can see a ceremonial confusion on everyone's part: the deputies from the Third know full well they are violating precedent by keeping on their hats, and so slowly acquiesce to old habit. The king, in his turn, perhaps somewhat embarrassed by this situation, responds by removing his hat, which then forced all deputies to do the same. One gets a sense of the general inclination toward reconciliation with the monarchy in another key element of Morris's description: "The Queen rises, and to my great Satisfaction she hears for the first Time in several Months the Sound of *Vive la Reine!* She makes a low Curtesy and this produces a louder Acclamation, and that a lower Curtesy."

contact with those—such as Mirabeau, Barras, Barnave, and the group associated with the Society of Thirty—who led the movement toward a National Assembly from May to June 1789, there is little doubt the premeditated plan of some of the leaders of the Third Estate had been broadly disseminated before the Estates General met. These men planned to accomplish precisely what they did between May and August 1789.

Timothy Tackett suggests that four key factors transformed the middle group favoring compromise into men ready to act unilaterally: "the growing group consciousness of the deputies, the didactic effects of Assembly oratory [especially by the Bretons], the impact of the crowds, and the attitudes and behavior of the Nobility."[39] Moreover, the specific policies recommended by many *cahiers,* even those phrased in the traditional language of the Ancien Régime, in fact supported just such a course of action. The *cahiers* of the Third Estate almost everywhere had insisted on the vote by head. In Paris, the people grew increasingly restive at the unwillingness of the nobility and clergy to turn the Estates General into the first National Assembly. The bookseller Hardy, who kept a diary of events, wrote on 4 June:

> One sees not only with sadness but with much uneasiness that there still exists in the capital as in many other parts of the kingdom, a seed of discord, a germ, a yeast of insurrection, whose flame, hidden and shrouded beneath misleading cinders, can at any moment cause the most considerable fire.[40]

Creating the National Constituent Assembly, 10 June–13 July 1789

If this revolution is fulfilled, it's true, the kings of France will no longer be legislators; they will no longer dispose of that monstrous double power to make the laws and to execute them. But is that losing or is it returning to the principles of reason, equity, and justice that must govern all the world?

Nicolas Ruault, to his brother, 8 July

The clergy and nobles failed to respond, so the Third began its work. On 13 June, three priests joined them, followed by sixteen more in the ensuing days. On 17 June 1789, the group took its most momentous step: on another motion by Sieyès, it adopted the title, "National Assembly" (soon changed to "National Constituent Assembly," to emphasize its primary function of creating a constitution) and further declared all current taxes to be illegal. It covered the government's legal tracks by offering a temporary continuation of existing taxes, but stipulated that the permission would lapse should the National Assembly be dismissed.[41] The letters sent home by individual deputies suggest that all of them feared for the future of their Assembly, and that many of them feared for the security of their persons, indeed for their very lives.

On 19 June, the First Estate voted to join the National Assembly. The next day, when the deputies to the Assembly found their meeting room locked, they adjourned to a nearby tennis court, where they took an oath not to break up until they had established a constitution. The Tennis Court Oath (20 June), immortalized in Jacques David's famous painting,[42] raised the stakes in the political poker game among the royal government, the nobility, and the Third Estate.

Three days later, at a royal sitting of the Estates General, the king sought to mollify all elements, although the nobility expected his statement to support their position: Morris tells us his noble friend the marquis de Boursac "anticipates a World of Triumph to the Noblesse in the Séance of to Morrow. He will I think be mistaken." The king entered to wild enthusiasm from the first two orders, who shouted, as was traditional, "Vive le roi!"; the Third Estate received him in silence. He accepted the principle that the Estates General alone could vote new taxes and loans, promised to abolish the most severe abuses of human rights, such as serfdom and *lettres de cachet*, and agreed to set up provincial estates throughout the kingdom.

Many historians have argued that these promises satisfied the demands of the *cahiers* written just two or three months before, but that they failed because they did not deal with the political events of May and June. In fact, the king did *not* satisfy the most critical demand of the *cahiers*: that the first duty of the Estates General was to draw up a constitution, and thus, that the Estates General, as the representative of the nation, did so on behalf of the principle that the *nation,* not the king, held the sovereignty. The *cahiers* had insisted that the "Estates General" vote both taxes and *laws*; the king had not acceded to this critical second demand. Here we can recall

J.-L. David, The Tennis Court Oath *(1791). David suggests that all three orders participated, whereas only those nobles sitting for one of the other two orders took part. His deliberate falsification gives us some indication of the role of artistic propaganda in creating legitimacy for the new regime.*

SOURCE: The Granger Collection, New York.

Morris's letter of February 1789, which isolated the great question: "shall we have a Constitution or shall Will continue to be Law?" Louis XVI's speech of 23 June left him firmly on the side of Will and so cannot be seen as acceding in any way to the central political demand formulated during the electoral campaign. The deputies of the Third Estate acted in May and June 1789 exactly as their *cahiers* had overwhelmingly instructed them to do: they sought to transform the Estates General into a National Constituent Assembly that would write a constitution, thus establishing the principles that the nation made the law and voted the taxes and that personal liberty and property were inviolable.

The king refused to accept the actions taken by the Third Estate in the previous week, ordered the three estates to continue to meet separately, and gave the privileged *de facto* veto power over any change in their status. He concluded by telling the deputies to disband and suggested openly that:

> If you were to abandon me in this worthy undertaking, then I should continue on my own to act in the interests of my subjects. I command you to disperse immediately and to return tomorrow morning to the rooms set aside for your orders so that you may resume your discussions.

The deputies who had created the National Assembly, bravely ignoring the large number of royal troops surrounding the building, refused. Bailly, who had chaired the meeting taking the Tennis Court Oath, replied to the royal master of ceremonies, "the nation assembled does not have to take orders." Mirabeau was even more direct: "Go tell your master that we are here by the will of the People and that we will not leave unless driven out by bayonets." François Furet has recently reminded us of Victor Hugo's reaction to Mirabeau's words—*"Your master!"* The king had been declared a foreigner.[43] Mirabeau had taken the final step in the long journey away from a kingdom in which the king could claim to be the personification of the public good, of the nation, and into a state in which the nation, the manifestation of the public good of its citizens, stood apart from and above the king.

The king, for reasons much debated by historians, decided to allow them to stay. Some suggest that he was distracted by the news that Necker had resigned—news passed to him as he left the room (the king dissuaded Necker later that day). Others claim that the king did not dare to resort to force, because of the tumultuous state of nearby Paris. Still others argue that the liberal nobles, led by the marquis de Lafayette, implored the king, who in this version had ordered his bodyguard to dismiss the deputies by force, to act with restraint. Whatever the truth of the matter, Louis did not disperse them. Morris's diary entry for the 23 June is highly instructive. After noting that the aristocrats were "delighted with the King" he makes a more sober assessment: "In the Course of the Conversation they tell me some Anecdotes which convince me that the King and Queen are both confoundedly frightened and I am thence led to conjecture that the Court will still recede."

Events proved Morris right. The people in Paris and Versailles took his interpretation. Everyone, from the man or woman in the street, to the troops, to the deputies to the National Assembly, believed that the Assembly had won a signal victory. In

Paris, large crowds cheered patriot orators and the French Guards refused to act against "fellow citizens" (several Guards ended up in prison for their action). The bookseller Hardy would soon be writing of "an insubordination that spreads progressively, like gangrene." Spectators had been attending the sessions of the Third Estates since late May and they continued to urge on the deputies. Other troops soon followed the example of the French Guards; in early July, minor mutinies broke out among the troops stationed in or near Versailles.

On 24 June, the clergy disbanded as an order and merged with the National Assembly. A day later, forty-six nobles, led by Lafayette and the duke of Orléans, the king's cousin, did the same. The National Assembly received them with wild applause that lasted fifteen minutes. On 27 June, the king invited those deputies from the clergy and nobility who still held out, to join the Assembly. Ruault wrote that "the victory of the Third Estate over the two privileged orders is complete. There are no longer orders in the state." People danced in the streets of Paris. Morris wrote to John Jay: "The King after siding with them [the nobles] was frightened into an Abandonment of them. He acts from Terror only."

As part of a spirit of compromise toward the nobility, the president of the Assembly, Bailly, declared a recess, so the two hundred-odd holdouts could enter with dignity. The Assembly moved quickly to get down to business, establishing thirty working committees, thus creating groups of manageable size; moreover, in a gesture of solidarity, the deputies elected individuals from the two privileged orders to head each work bureau. The most important of these committees was the Constitutional Committee, which, as its name suggests, received the charge of proposing the new constitution. In the main assembly, the deputies arranged themselves in a semi-circle around the president of the Assembly, an office rotated on a regular basis. The more radical deputies began to gather in the seats on the left; the conservatives responded by sitting together on the right: Left and Right, to describe liberals (or radicals, in some cases) and conservatives, have ever since been part of the world's political lexicon.

The king and his supporters bided their time. Public order seemed to be breaking down everywhere. On 30 June, 4,000 people stormed the prison in which the mutinous French Guards were held, releasing them. The king, using the excuse that public order appeared threatened by such disturbances, began to move troops into the vicinity of Versailles: in less than a week, the government moved more than 15,000 soldiers into the environs of Paris, seemingly ready to make a show of force. On 8 July, Mirabeau publicly proclaimed in the Assembly that the king had already brought 35,000 troops to the Paris region and planned to bring 20,000 more, both figures substantial exaggerations, but accurate reflections of public opinion. Many of those around Louis—notably his wife and his brother, the Count of Artois—encouraged him to use these troops to teach the "rabble" a lesson.

Although the king's actual plan remains a matter of debate, contemporaries unanimously agreed with Hardy, who worried about the many troops and artillery flooding into the area around Paris, especially the encampments on the Champs de Mars and the plain of Grenelle, "as if one proposes to undertake the siege of Paris." The Assembly sent the king a delegation on 9 July, asking him to remove the troops and to rely on the loyalty of the nation. The deputy Camusat, from Troyes, wrote that day:

all of the places near Versailles and the capital are filled with soldiers; all of the passages, all means of communication are guarded. Convoys of artillery are arriving from all parts; ten to twelve regiments are expected in eight days, and altogether these different troops will form a body of 50,000 men. . . . Everyone is convinced that the approach of the troops covers some violent design.

Camusat and others did not have long to wait. On 11 July, the king dismissed Necker and created a new ministry. Informed the next morning, Camusat wrote (at 9 A.M.) to his constituents: "It is clear today that they invested Paris and Versailles with cannons and soldiers in order to contain the populace at the moment when they would find out about the disgrace of the only man who still had credit."[44] The Parisians and the deputies particularly feared the foreign regiments that the king had introduced into the area. Their fears proved well founded on 12 July, when the German cavalry set upon a crowd in the Tuileries gardens and its commander sabered to death an old man who dared to offer verbal resistance. All observers agreed that French troops would side with the people: Ruault's letter of 9 July speaks of entire regiments going over to the side of the people in the suburbs of Paris.

Taking the Bastille

On the morning of the 14th, that forever memorable day.

Nicolas Ruault, in his diary

The 14th of July, that day forever memorable.

Bookseller Hardy, in his diary

Yesterday's journée will be forever memorable.

Commune of Paris, 15 July

Parisians organized themselves at four key centers. At the Hôtel de Ville, the roughly four hundred electors of the city of Paris (those who had chosen the deputies to the Estates General) met to deal with two equally disturbing phenomena: the royal offensive against the National Assembly and the decline of civil authority. They took two decisive actions that mirrored those taking place elsewhere. First, they decided to create an urban militia, soon to be called the National Guard, and second, they made themselves into a permanent governing body for the city. They called themselves at first the "permanent community" but ten days later, they became the Commune. Many of the electoral assemblies of the sixty districts of Paris also set up permanent meetings, starting on 12 or 13 July. Some did so on their own initiative, but most at the direct order of the electoral assembly (11 P.M. on 12 July). On the morning of 13 July, the electoral assembly ordered each district assembly to arm two hundred men; later that day, they amended the order to six hundred men per district (48,000 men), to be raised in three days.

Two other centers of action emerged. The cafés of the Palais-Royal hosted large politicized gatherings, doubtless attracted by the protection of the duke of Orléans. He and his fellow members of the so-called Society of Thirty, a group of roughly that size who met regularly in the late 1780s to discuss reform, seem to have had some hand in certain of the demonstrations of July. The final group was the people themselves. In some cases, we can speak of groups of artisans, politicized by the activities at the Hôtel de Ville and at the district assemblies; in a few cases, more dubious elements sought to take advantage of the impending anarchy, but these formed an extreme minority, except in the looting of 12 July.

The long-standing tradition of the French Revolution in July 1789 is that "mobs" formed in the city and sought vengeance on the symbols of royal absolutism. A careful reading of the chronology of events, however, definitively suggests that such was not the case. The crowds who acted on 13 July and 14 July were far from mobs; they were well-organized, usually quite disciplined, and very specific in their goals. Plenty of evidence survives of disorder in the city—of arbitrary arrests, of harassment of the wealthy by the poor, of looting and pillaging by gangs of thieves—but the larger crowds, especially the citizen militia, did not act in this way. In fact, the action of the brigands did as much as anything else to call into being the citizen militia that would carry out the great deeds of 14 July. Even Hardy, whose fear of disorder was such that he refused to leave his house, had to comment on the "good order" of the bourgeois militia that formed on 13 July.

Although we have no surviving written documentation, in terms of direct orders, there can be little doubt that the combined efforts of the district assemblies and the permanent committee (at the Hôtel de Ville) gave considerable direction to the popular movements. The population of Paris did not act blindly or stupidly, nor indeed did they use excessive violence.

The Parisian people took matters into their own hands on 13 and 14 July, seeking to do five things:

1. Maintain order in the city.

2. Find grain to help drive down the price of bread.

3. Obtain arms and ammunition for the new militia.

4. Force the king to restore Necker to power.

5. Carry out some of the demands of the *cahier* of Paris's Third Estate.

The first act in the drama, the looting of forty of the fifty-four gates of the entry duty (*octroi*) barrier (12 July), seems to have been the work of self-interested parties, above all smugglers, wine shop owners, and thieves.[45] Yet the general *cahier* of the Third Estate of Paris had specifically demanded this course of action, as had that of the nobility.

The spectre of such violence encouraged the solid citizens who sat in electoral assemblies to act immediately to restore order. They did so, by calling into being impromptu companies of armed citizens, who then coordinated two efforts already underway: the search for grain and that for arms and ammunition. The effort to find grain did not bear much fruit: the price of bread reached an eighty-year high on 14 July. In this case as in so many others during the Revolution, the high price of bread played a critical role in inciting rebellion or popular action.

The crowds, primarily made up of artisans and shopkeepers, sought next to get their hands on military stores, such as weapons and ammunition. They looted the armorers' shops on 12 July; ominously, the French Guards sent to stop the looting instead fraternized with the crowd. On 13 July, the crowd seized gunpowder from a barge in the Seine and received more succor from royal troops: the two regiments quartered at Saint-Denis sent written word of their commitment to the popular cause. The chief royal official of Paris (the merchants' provost), Jacques de Flesselles, sought to distract these forces by sending them to supposed stores of military goods that proved to be empty. Angry artisans did not forget his "treachery."

On the morning of 14 July, about 8,000 people broke into the military hospital, the Invalides, removing cannons as well as small arms and ammunition. Another large crowd set out for the great royal fortress whose guns overlooked the faubourg Saint-Antoine: the Bastille. Thousands milled around the Bastille, demanding its surrender. A combination of bungling by the garrison and the determination of the radical elements of the crowd led them into the interior courtyard, where the five score defenders, panicked at so vast a throng, opened fire, killing between twenty-five and two hundred, depending on whose estimate one believes.[46] The French Guards joined the crowd and trained five of the Invalides's cannons on the main gate of the Bastille: it surrendered.

Generations of historians have castigated the attackers for what happened next: they murdered seven of the one hundred defenders. Given that those same defenders had just killed or wounded some one hundred fifty to two hundred of their fellows, what seems remarkable is less the murder of the seven than the sparing of the re-maining ninety-three. The crowd took out its main fury on the man they held re-sponsible for the deaths of their comrades, the commander of the fortress, de Launay. In a highly traditional gesture, they beheaded him (and his chief lieutenant) and pa-raded the heads on pikes through the streets. The German officer de Flue, who wit-nessed close at hand the murder of de Launay, received rough treatment at the hands of the crowd, but "I was astonished that they spared me." They spared his men, too; the Swiss soon enrolled in another regiment.

Another detachment, incensed at what it viewed as the perfidy of Jacques de Flesselles, sought revenge outside the Hôtel de Ville. Many defended de Flesselles as an innocent victim of misinformation, but one discontented artisan put a bullet through the provost's head and the crowd soon afforded de Flesselles the same treat-ment it had given de Launay. Although some rowdy elements suggested that other heads should join them—one rallying cry reportedly was "all bishops to the lantern post," in fact the city did not witness massive violence. One deputy wrote home on 16 July that "much more was accomplished through fear than through the desire for the good."[47] The English ambassador, the duke of Dorset, wrote that "the regular and resolute conduct of the population surpasses all that can be imagined."

The Storming of the Bastille, *14 July 1789. The artist has embellished the scene, but rightly emphasizes the key role of the cannon taken from the Invalides in the garrison's decision to surrender the Bastille.*

SOURCE: Reproduced from the Collections of the Library of Congress.

Hardy, who deplored the revolutionary crowds, made a stunned exception for the takers of the Bastille. In a classic summary of the events, he wrote:

> One cannot hold back one's astonishment when one reflects on the outcome of events to which we have been witness since the beginning of the week. One can only recall with horror and with trembling the infernal project that existed to introduce into the capital on the 14th or 15th, 30,000 men, seconded by brigands, to run down its citizens and then to clap into irons all those whom the sword had spared. One regards as something absolutely supernatural the taking of the Bastille *in less than three hours,* and as another sort of miracle the calling together and establishment of a bourgeois militia in less than 24 hours.[48]

The crowd in Paris could act with sudden violence: eight days later, they murdered a royal minister, Foullon, and his son, Bertigny, the intendant for Paris. Foullon, who had been the hardliners' choice to replace Necker, had been hiding in the country near Paris. When he tried to run further away, local peasants arrested him, placed him in a cart, his mouth stuffed with straw—a reference to his supposed remark that the starving people could eat grass if they had no grain. Brought back to Paris by a detachment from the new National Guard, the crowd at the Hôtel de Ville pummeled him to death and placed his head on a pike, its mouth again stuffed with straw. Another detachment arrested Bertigny, who suffered the same fate as his father-in-law. These events horrified the solid citizens: letters written home by the deputies themselves suggest that they recoiled far more from this act of violence than from the actions of 13 and 14 July. Morris exclaimed "Gracious God, what a People!" after viewing Foullon's severed head.

This incident aside, however, the great revolutionary days of the summer of 1789 passed with remarkably little violence. George Washington, writing to Morris in early October 1789, correctly stressed the absence of bloodshed in his view that the Revolution was not yet over: "I fear, though it [France] has gone triumphantly through the first paroxysm, it is not the last it has to encounter before matters are finally settled. In a word, the revolution is of too great a magnitude to be effected in so short a space, and with the loss of so little blood."

The Death of "Feudalism," 15 July–11 August 1789

The National Assembly destroys entirely the feudal regime.

Opening words of the National Assembly's decree of 11 August 1789

Louis XVI consulted his ministers and his army commanders; marshal Broglie, head of the army around Paris, assured the king that he could not rely on his troops, especially his French ones. Quite apart from the reliability of the troops, the king also had to consider his ability to borrow money. Capital markets were extremely sensitive to his actions; the government's credit was already feeble by mid-July. A massive military intervention in Paris would have destroyed what little credit France had left. Louis had only to read the *cahiers* to know that. The citizens of the Sorbonne district of Paris had written what was on the minds of all: "it shall be established and recognized as a fundamental maxim, which alone can assure the tranquility and property of citizens, that only the Estates General shall have the right to consent to loans and taxes."[49]

The king took three momentous decisions. First, accompanied by his brothers and a mere handful of soldiers, the king appeared at the Assembly on the morning of 15 July and vowed, in a speech written by the bishop of Autun, Talleyrand (a key leader of the Assembly itself), to work with them to restore the nation. The deputies erupted with joy: several fainted and one "died for joy" from a stroke.[50] Second, on 16 July, Louis recalled Necker, who had fled to Switzerland. Third, the king and the deputies headed to Paris to calm things down. On 17 July, bravely setting forth with a tiny escort, he set out for the Hôtel de Ville, where Bailly gave him "the keys to your good town of Paris, the same ones presented to Henry IV. He reconquered his people;

Bertigny de Sauvigny being led to execution; the head on the pike in front of him is that of his father-in-law, Foullon. This incident shocked contemporaries more than any other in the summer of 1789.

SOURCE: AKG London.

today, the people have reconquered their king." After Bailly's laudatory address, Louis responded, "I will always love my people," and accepted the Revolutionary cockade, an amalgamation of the white of the Bourbons surrounded by the blue and red of the city of Paris.[51] "Then, and not till then, [Louis] received the general shouts of Vive le Roi!" [Morris] from the initially suspicious crowd. All observers recalled how those in the streets shouted this refrain over and over, joined soon by those who had remained indoors; even the sick came to their windows to add their happy voices. Rétif de la Bretonne would later compare the king's presence to "the beneficial sun, seeming to dissipate the thick clouds that covered our horizon," and claim that "the king's arrival gave salve to my wounds."[52]

Once the people of Paris had stormed the Bastille, the Revolution took off in entirely new directions. The symbolic impact of this event is difficult to overestimate. The people had taken, by force, the most universally known (and detested) symbol of "despotism." Reaction throughout France was immediate. Cities, towns, and villages wrote to the Commune of Paris expressing their approval. Châteauroux wrote of "its joy at the happy revolution," while Le Havre spoke of the "Revolution that assures for ever the national liberty." Angers went even further: "A people grown

Louis XVI comes to Paris, 17 July to accept the cheers of the citizens and the keys to the city. On this fateful day, Louis accepted the tricolor flag, created by combining the traditional white of the Bourbons with the colors of Paris, blue and red.

Source: Culver Pictures.

old in slavery, bent down under the yoke of tyrants, has risen up at a stroke, broken its chains, and, on the ruins of despotism, founded the edifice of liberty." The people of Caen, on hearing the news, immediately stormed the enormous medieval castle of the dukes of Normandy, which still overlooks their city. Many of the nobles, among them the king's youngest brother, the Count of Artois, and the clique around Marie-Antoinette, fled the country.

The new order began everywhere. The Commune of Paris took over the maintenance of order in the city, through the means of the National Guard. Immediately, in towns all over France, other urban elites did the same. Urban assemblies like that of Paris sprang into being. Revolutionary committees seized power in sixteen of France's thirty largest towns and shared power in ten others. In the countryside, the Great Fear, the groundless reports of "brigands," led people to organize themselves; entire village communities came together to create a new order. This transition took place with remarkable speed: almost everywhere, a new order was in place by August or September. After some confusing moments in the fall of 1789, the municipal elections of January 1790 established the legal foundation both for new municipal governments and for the principle of elective government.

At the national level, the Assembly went to work on its officially declared new purpose: the creation of a constitution. They had several models before them, most recently that of the new United States of America (1787). Leaders in the Assembly recognized the first key stumbling block: privileges. The Great Fear and the attacks on the châteaux, all luridly described in the popular press of Paris, created an atmosphere of naked fear among urban elites. Ruault's journal of 25 July noted that the Assembly discussed attacks on châteaux: "the country people have pillaged, devastated, sometimes even burned a large number of châteaux belonging to nobles, designated 'aristocrats,' and have taken, dispersed, and thrown into the fire titles of nobility." In a letter to his brother on 8 August, he made a telling historical comparison:

> We live today in a state of constant alarm created by the large number of evil subjects, by a turbulent, restless population, which wants to burn down half the city so that it can loot the remaining half. *Liberty* is today the catchword to carry out good on one side and evil on the other. With this single word, one can torch a city, burn châteaux, houses, ravage all the countryside; that's what peasants in various cantons of France are doing today, in hatred of their seigneurs. Liberty can lead to so many evils! This fury resembles that abominable madness, the Jacquerie, which covered all of France in mourning after the battle of Poitiers.[53]

He blamed the events on the hatred of the peasants for their seigneurs.

In such an atmosphere, one faction of the Assembly decided it could move decisively against the old order. The Breton Club, made up of the radical deputies of the Third Estate from Brittany, plotted to introduce a measure abolishing feudalism on the evening of 4 August, when one of their number, Le Chapelier, would be chairing the meeting. They convinced the duke d'Aiguillon to introduce a motion calling for abolition of serfdom, seigneurial dues, and labor services, in return for compensation. The viscount of Noailles followed him and soon the flood began. In a frenzy of self-sacrifice on the altar of the nation, the deputies denounced or renounced all matter of privileges: hunting, wood gathering, private courts, urban and guild rights, provincial liberties, royal pensions, the tithe, venal offices. As Mirabeau (who actually missed the session), had said in the spring, "privileges are essential as a defense against despotism, but an abomination used against the nation."

Waking up on the morning of 5 August, like a drunkard hung over from a binge, the deputies wondered what they had wrought. Many deputies had spoken cautiously on the night of 4 August, stating that they had to refer back to their constituents to make binding declarations. The deputies from Nantes wrote back to their constituents asking for such authority; in a special assembly held on 14 September, the inhabitants of the city voted to approve the deputies' action and to accord them full powers "in order to cooperate for the well-being of the state." Even the Breton nobility, who were boycotting the Assembly, accepted the actions of 4 and 5 August. In both Nantes and Quimper, local meetings of nobles affirmed the decisions taken by the Assembly. These cautious steps remind us of how weakly many deputies grasped the essence of the changes. The National Assembly had already ruled (2 July) that, as deputies to the National Assembly, its members could not hide behind the traditional obligation of members of an Estates General to refer back to their constituents before taking any action not authorized in their mandates.[54]

The Assembly took a week to sort through the main actions of the night of 4–5 August. They passed a definitive decree on 11 August; Furet rightly calls this decree the death certificate of the Ancien Régime. They abolished various "feudal" [their word] privileges: dovecoats, seigneurial courts, *cens*, hunting monopolies. They also abolished other privileges of the Ancien Régime, such as the tithe of the Church (abolished without compensation) and venal offices (abolished with compensation). They eliminated forever all "pecuniary privileges" of individuals or groups (such as towns, provinces or the Church). Clause 11 made all "citizens without distinction of birth" admissible to all public and ecclesiastical offices and abolished derogation of nobility.

The (male) members of French society agreed that the nation, composed of legally free and equal (male) citizens, would be the new form of political association. As François Furet has written, the decrees of early August

> are among the founding texts of modern France. They destroyed, from top to bottom, aristocratic society and its structure of dependancies and privileges. They substituted for it the modern autonomous individual, free in all that the law does not forbid.[55]

These actions confirmed Morris's judgment of early July, of the "Sovereignty of this Country as being effactually lodged in the Hands of the Assemblée Nationale." Now the Assembly had to use its sovereign authority to create a new constitutional system.

Notes

1. I rely here on the citation of Paquelin available in J. Bart, *La Révolution française en Bourgogne* (Dijon: La Française d'Édition et d'Imprimerie, 1996), 127. My translation.

2. I use feudal in the sense that contemporaries used it: a legal system based on privilege, on private ownership of public authority (seigneurial courts), and on property rights rooted in extra-economic factors. The vast majority of French people in 1789 lived under the judicial authority of a private individual, paid small feudal dues in recognition of such jurisdiction, had to abide by monopolies, such as mills and wine presses, and did not have unrestricted use of their landed property. Eighteenth-century Frenchmen invented the term *féodalité* to describe this system. Some half million people, mostly living in the Burgundies, were still serfs. They lived with great restrictions on their rights to move, to marry, and to inherit property.

3. The date I accept for the disjuncture, the 1760s, well precedes that accepted by most historians from the Classical school, who focus on the 1780s and on change immediately before the Revolution.

4. The philosophical underpinning of the argument here thus accepts only partially the Marxist tenet that social being determines consciousness; I would agree

that such is often the case, for large numbers of people, whose material conditions of life leave them few options. I believe, however, that consciousness, particularly that of individuals, can change for more purely intellectual reasons; furthermore, such change is most likely precisely at moments of extraordinary historical transformation, such as the French Revolution.

5. Its main immediate effect was the devastation of the French economy, on which see Chapter 15.

6. N. Ruault, *Gazette d'un Parisien sous la Révolution. Lettres à son frère.* (Paris: Librairie Académique Perrin, 1976), 129, letter of 1 April 1789.

7. We now know that the Estates General of the fourteenth century did not, in fact, make binding votes about taxation. We also know that the famous vote of a permanent direct tax (*taille*) in 1439 did not take place. In the 1780s, however, all observers believed the Estates General had made binding votes of taxation (those of 1560 actually did do so) and that the royal *taille* dated from the "great meeting" of 1439.

8. The Court of Peers consisted of the regular Parlement, along with the Princes of the Blood and the thirty-five peers of France.

9. Ruault, *Gazette,* letter of 19 January 1788, 102.

10. Cited in F. Furet and M. Ozouf, *Dictionnaire Critique de la Révolution Française* (Paris: Flammarion, 1988), 301.

11. "Memoir of the Princes," in *The French Revolution,* ed. P. Beik (New York: Walker, 1970), 11. Beik attributes the actual memoir to Antoine Auget, an associate of the king's youngest brother, the count of Artois. In addition to Artois, the memoir was signed by his cousins the prince of Condé, the duke of Bourbon, the duke d'Enghien, and the prince of Conti. The third royal brother, the count of Provence, refused to sign it.

12. Ruault, *Gazette,* 121.

13. In fact, the Parlement did allow for some exceptions. In 1614, members of the Parlements had to sit with the Third Estate; in 1789, they would sit with the Second.

14. This ruling applied to all *pays d'États;* it came in response to the turmoil in Brittany, where the two sides had already fought to the finish before the king issued his ruling. In 1614, most of these titular parish priests (curés) did not actually administer their parishes; the actual number of resident parish priests was therefore tiny.

16. As noted above, some parish assemblies allowed women heads of households to participate. Little evidence survives of individual women, living alone, being involved; the heads of households in question were invariably wealthy widows.

17. Many district assemblies in Paris—both of the Third Estate and of the nobility—also protested that the two groups met separately; many nobles insisted that they, too, were citizens of Paris and should meet with the other citizens in a single assembly.

18. This detailed look at the deputies relies on the outstanding recent book of T. Tackett, *Becoming a Revolutionary. The Deputies of the French National Assembly and the Emergence of a Revolutionary Culture (1789–1790)* (Princeton: Princeton University Press, 1996).

19. Ch.-L. Chassin, *Les Élections et les Cahiers de Paris en 1789* (Paris: Jouast et Sigaux, 1888), 4 vols., III, 327.

20. Chassin, *Les Élections*, I, 50-51.

21. Gouverneur Morris to George Washington, 29 April 1789, in *A Diary of the French Revolution*, ed. B. Cary Davenport (Boston: Houghton Mifflin, 1939), two vols., I, 60. Morris was one of the key framers of the American Constitution. All future references to Morris's letters or his diary come from this collection, which is organized chronologically.

22. The *cahiers* of both the nobility and the Third Estate of the Paris districts all contain precisely the same demands in this respect: lawmaking authority rests with the nation, in its Estates General; the state shall respect the freedom of the individual and the inviolability of property; the Estates General shall create laws to guarantee freedom of the press and various other rights; the Estates General alone shall have the right to vote taxes or approve loans. They disagreed on some other issues, notably the vote by head or by order.

23. Ruault, *Gazette*, letter of 24 February 1789, 126. Ruault's bookstore abutted the Palais Royal, chief meeting place of the Society of Thirty. His knowledge of these plans adds further credence to the role of the Society in disseminating this strategy.

24. I say "Estates General" because the traditional Estates General had no right to vote laws. Estates General meeting during a royal minority did have the authority to supervise royal ministers and government spending; those meeting under an adult king, as in 1576, had the right to offer advice about such matters, but no binding authority.

25. Jacques Duguet *et alia, La Révolution Français 1789–1799 à Rochefort* (Projets Editions: Poitiers, 1989). The citation from the lawyers appears on p. 17, that from the surgeons on p. 18, and that from the inhabitants of the parish of Notre Dame on p. 24.

26. Chassin, *Les Élections*, IV (1889), 427.

27. Cited in Chassin, *Les Élections*, I, 307.

28. Some time after I had written this section, a remarkable book by John Markoff and Gilbert Shapiro, *Revolutionary Demands: A Content Analysis of the Cahiers de Doléances of 1789* (Stanford: Stanford University Press, 1998), appeared. Their analysis, as the title suggests, strongly supports the interpretation set forth here.

29. Outlying areas sometimes reversed this wording, making the Estates General approve laws made by the king. A small number of *cahiers,* such as that of the clergy of Paris, insisted that the king alone made the law and upheld the traditional interpretation of the king as absolute but limited. They wrote: "That the French

government is a purely monarchical one; that the sovereign and legislative power resides exclusively in the person of the king. But, in the exercise of his authority, the monarch is bound by fundamental and constitutional laws."

30. Chassin, *Les Élections,* I, 449. Remarkably enough, three days after Parisians had stormed the Bastille, when Louis XVI came to Paris to show his support for the new order, the city government of Paris voted to erect a statue in his honor—on the site of the Bastille.

31. Nobles had the right to keep birds—doves, pigeons—and to prevent anyone from killing them. Peasants everywhere complained that the birds ate the seeds sown in the fields. The *cahier* of the provosty of Paris not only attacked hunting and dovecoats but insisted that all people currently awaiting trial on charges of violating such privileges be released. *Cahiers* often praised the role of seigneurial courts in resolving local disputes between peasants; they insisted on maintenance of similar local courts. They strongly denounced, however, seigneurial courts that resolved disputes between seigneurs and peasants.

32. The Estates General changed format in 1484 in some regions, allowing the Third Estate—formerly just the "communes" (i.e., self-governing towns)—to represent the countryside. These Estates also deliberated in common.

33. Cited in Chassin, *Les Élections,* II, 510. The Six Acts abolished guilds, in the name of the "right to work," possessed by all men. As noted in the previous chapter, opposition to the Six Acts led to their rescission and to Turgot's dismissal.

34. In a letter of the same day, he cited 15,000–20,000 men as the total number of troops recently introduced into and around Paris.

35. Contemporary estimates vary wildly; the likely figure is closer to twenty-five than to two hundred.

36. Nicolas Rétif de la Bretonne, then living in Paris, in his *Les nuits révolutionnaires* (Editions de Paris: Paris, 1989), 28–29, specifically accuses reactionary aristocrats of freeing prisoners from Parisian prisons and encouraging these hoodlums to carry out the riots. Rétif de la Bretonne tends to embellish his stories—the specific accusation lacks proof—but his general point, that forces seeking to destabilize Paris on the eve of the Estates General fomented the disorders, rings true. Morris and other observers had similar suspicions.

37. Deputies straggled into Paris every day, so that on any given day the precise numbers of deputies differed. The best estimates are offered by Tackett, who tells us that by mid-July the Third Estate had six hundred four deputies, the clergy two hundred ninety-five, and the nobility only two hundred seventy-eight (the Breton delegation of nobles refused to participate in the assembly).

38. Modern historians, unaware of the rules of the Estates General, invariably suggest that everyone feared that the two privileged orders would outvote the Third. Not so. During the debates of the nobility of Paris about voting by head or order, some speakers specifically mentioned the desire to avoid one order blocking the will of the other two. When the deputies of the nobility of Paris returned to them in late June, explaining why they had joined the National Assembly (and agreed to vote by head), they cited the Assembly's fears of single-order veto. Logic would also dictate that the First Estate, dominated by parish priests (whose social origins placed them in the Third), would far more often have combined with the Third than the Second: the events of late June bear out that assessment.

39. Tackett, *Becoming a Revolutionary,* 138.

40. Excerpts of Hardy's diary are reproduced in Chassin, *Les Élections,* III.

41. All of these steps, it should be emphasized, had been recommended by many of the *cahiers,* such as those—both of the Third and of the nobility—of the electoral districts of Paris.

42. David somewhat disingenuously shows the nobles participating; no deputy to the Second Estate was present, although nobles sitting as members of the Third Estate, such as Mirabeau, did take part.

43. Furet and Ozouf, *Dictionnaire,* 301.

44. The tale of Camusat comes from L. Hunt, *Revolution and Urban Politics in Provincial France, Troyes and Reims, 1786–1790* (Stanford: Stanford University Press, 1978), 70–71. Morris's diary entries give credence to a plot to arrest key deputies, dismiss the Assembly, and starve Paris into submission; Ruault, in early July, worried about imminent violence.

45. They did not, however, destroy the gate whose duties ended up in the pockets of the duke of Orléans, one of the leaders of the revolutionary forces, which suggests that even they did not act blindly in their destruction.

46. The German lieutenant de Flue, serving with a small detachment of Swiss at the Bastille, dismissed the common figure of one hundred-sixty killed as too high, because the garrison had fired for so short a time. (Chassin, *Les Élections,* III, 535, n. 2).

47. The deputy Jean-François Gaultier de Biauzat, a lawyer from Clermont-Ferrand, cited in Tackett, *Becoming a Revolutionary,* 166. In note 74 on that page, Tackett suggests other deputies expressed similar sentiments in letters to their families.

48. Chassin, *Les Élections,* III, 575.

49. Chaussin, *Les Élections,* I, 422. Foreign ambassadors gave the same assessment to their governments; Louis had to go along with the Assembly because he lacked the money to do otherwise. Without their help, he could obtain no further funds.

50. Morris, 164.

51. This tricolor of blue-white-red became the symbol of the new France and, in time, the national flag. Dozens of countries, all over the world, have followed France's choice of a tricolored flag. In recent times, we can point to the new Russia flag, with its horizontal stripes of white, blue, and red, and to those of the newly independent states created by the collapse of the Soviet Union and of Yugoslavia.

52. Rétif de la Bretonne, *Nuits,* 45; Ruault, *Gazette,* 438–440; Morris.

53. Ruault, *Gazette*, 447 and 162 (letter). He makes reference to the greatest French peasant rebellion, which took place in 1358, in the aftermath of the English capture of King John at the humiliating defeat of the battle of Poitiers (1356).

54. The cardinal of la Rochefoucauld had made a declaration to the Assembly on 2 July that he could not agree to the deputies meeting together, rather than by order, because his mandate did not authorize such a change, and because the constitutional laws of the monarchy protected his order's right to meet separately. Mirabeau vehemently (and successfully) protested that representatives of the nation could not act in such a manner. Had the Assembly not so ruled, many of the deputies of the nobility and clergy—whose *cahiers* had specified that voting be by order—could have legally claimed the need to refer back to their constituents before agreeing to vote by head. The noble deputies of Paris, who lived close enough to do so easily, actually did take this step.

55. Furet and Ozouf, *Dictionnaire*, 131.

Chapter Three

THE DEATH OF THE MONARCHY

The tumultuous populace of large cities are ever to be dreaded. Their indiscriminate violence prostrates for the time all public authority, and its consequences are sometimes extensive and terrible.[1]

George Washington, to the Marquis de Lafayette, 28 July 1791

The National Constituent Assembly's actions of early August 1789 revealed both the continuity of March through August 1789 and the ruptures to come. The Assembly moved rapidly to enact the program of legislation laid out in the *cahiers*. Virtually everyone agreed the Assembly should make laws, vote taxes and loans, hold ministers accountable, abolish useless and harmful privileges, and create a more responsive and effective government. The Assembly acted to fulfill these goals in July and early August 1789. In so doing, however, it ran up against three fundamental problems that would eventually destroy everything it had built:

1. The extent of the king's power as head of the executive branch of government and in lawmaking.

2. The delicate balance between liberty and property.

3. The role of the Catholic Church.

The decrees of 4–11 August created two precedents whose logical elaboration would prove very damaging. By simply abolishing the tithes, the Assembly eliminated a form of property that had existed for over a thousand years. Did the failure to respect property rights in this form have consequences for other forms of property? Contemporary property owners everywhere expressed such fears and demanded that the state take action to protect their property. Furthermore, by abolishing privileges, did the Assembly make inevitable the abolition not only of nobility but of corporate bodies? (As it turned out, yes.) The plot paranoia that provided a leitmotif to most of the Revolution often stemmed from the fear of mysterious "factions": at first that meant the "aristocrats," but later it came to encompass just about any group of people the writer or speaker wanted to attack.

The popular press—people like Jean-Paul Marat or Camille Desmoulins or Jacques Hébert in the *Père Duchesne*—regularly made ridiculous assertions about one plot or another. In June 1789, Arthur Young expressed "amazement at the ministry permitting such hotbeds of sedition or revolt"; after the fall of the Bastille, these journals became progressively more seditious.[2] The constant drumbeat of attacks against the aristocracy and the queen, in particular, hardened popular opinion against them. Rumors spread everywhere; in Bordeaux, the lawyer Pierre Bernadau reported in October:

> Here, they said that the nobles are assembled to massacre the Third Estate; there, that the count of Artois, with Spanish troops, was at the gates of the city; later, that Bordeaux was entirely mined or that the monks were arming themselves, etc. . . . etc.[3]

Young's journal suggests French people associated Marie Antoinette with a high explosive counterrevolution. In July, at Colmar, people told Young that the queen intended to blow up the National Assembly and massacre the population of Paris; a month later, Auvergnat villagers suspected Young as her agent, sent to blow up their local mine.[4]

People in the provinces swung back and forth. The king's visit to Paris on 17 July sparked many hopes: Bernadau, usually a hostile observer of the Revolution, wrote in his diary on 4 August that "as soon as we learned that calm returned to the capital, our electors wrote a letter of thanks to the Estates General." After a description of Bordeaux's celebrations on that day, with the "brilliant" fireworks, Bernadau warily mused, "Are we now free of danger, so that we can rejoice?" Bernadau's deep breath lasted little more than a week. When he heard of the events of 4–5 August in Paris, and of local reaction to them, he sang a different tune: "We feel every day how much the premature deliberations of the National Assembly expose us to the evils of anarchy."

The 5 October march to Versailles, and the forcible removal of the royal family and National Assembly to Paris, further heightened tensions. Many provincials, such as the nobility of Toulouse, sent off vigorous protests that the king had been made a prisoner and, alone among the French people, did not benefit from the freedom of movement decreed by the Assembly itself in August 1789. The confiscation of Church property in November 1789 added to the unsettled situation, although many worried more about how to get their hands on the land than about the fate of the Church.

The chaos of the summer and early fall of 1789 gave way to a remarkable degree of stability by the start of 1790. Young left Paris on 28 June and spent September to December in Italy. When he returned to France in late December 1789, he found the situation much calmer: no longer did he face arbitrary arrest at every little town. The relatively peaceful municipal elections that began the new year buoyed everyone's hopes. Lafayette wrote hopefully to Washington that "we have come thus far in the Revolution without breaking the ship either on the shoals of aristocracy, or that of factions, and amidst the every reviving efforts of the mourners and the ambitious we are stirring towards a tolerable conclusion."[5] Others took a less sanguine view of events, worried about the lack of an effective executive authority. Once the king and Assembly had been forced to move to Paris (5 October 1789), the king lost any real independence; he became, in effect, a prisoner in his own capital. Yet this prisoner remained the chief executive officer of government, with the authority to name government ministers. He also retained the strong loyalty of the officer corps of the army.

Abolishing tithes and many feudal dues, and the widespread popular perception that people did not have to pay the old taxes anymore, led to economic and political chaos in many regions. The local political climate calmed greatly after the elections of January and February 1790, but the economic problems lingered on. Moreover, the Church, having lost its revenues, could no longer care for the poor. The government, unable to collect taxes, could hardly take its place. Many wealthy families lost their income. Some of them depended on feudal dues for their main support, but far more lost heavily when peasants, no longer forced to go to the lord's mill or wine press, took their business elsewhere. Other peasants simply stopped paying their rent and their taxes. The traditional courts and part of the old tax system still existed in early 1790, but they had lost much of their authority. The inability of the government ministers to provide effective executive leadership hamstrung state action at the national level. When mutinies broke out in the army and the navy, the central government had great difficulty organizing a repression sufficient to restore order without alienating public opinion.

Lafayette would write more tellingly to Washington in March 1790, fleshing out his loose description of the potential shoals the ship of state had to avoid. He worried that the people "mistake licentiousness for freedom" and that "hatred to the ancient system," rather than clear thinking about a new one, dominated the Assembly's agenda. He further noted the continued presence of "two parties, the Aristocratic that is panting for a counter revolution, and the factious which aims at the division of the Empire, and destruction of all authority and perhaps of the lifes of the reigning branch, both of which parties are fomenting troubles."[6]

The apparent success of the Revolution in 1790 did not prove lasting. The events of 1789 and 1790 provided the critical foundation of all that was to come. The precipitant actions of the summer of 1789, which focused on destruction without first considering that something needed to be in place to provide the structures of political society, did much to create the dangerous momentum that led to civil war and the Terror. The inability of leaders in Paris to create an effective national government in 1790 guaranteed that the unstable elements remaining from the compromises of 1789 would overwhelm France. The Assembly could not be both executive and legislative branches, and it would not, perhaps could not, let the king and his officials freely perform executive functions.

George Washington accurately predicted to Gouverneur Morris (13 October 1789) that the discontent of the aristocrats and nobles, the mortification of the royal family (this even before he knew of the October Days), and the "licentiousness of the People" were sources of certain trouble to come. The fundamental splits between the nobility and clergy, and the supporters of the new regime deepened constantly in 1790 and 1791. The Assembly took a progressively harder and harder line against the two former privileged orders: confiscating the property of the Church, abolishing monastic orders, abolishing nobility itself. Little wonder that the local administrations of 1790, which usually contained a broad cross-section of society, including nobles and clergymen, gave way to much more narrowly recruited bodies in 1791. Nobles and clergymen all but disappeared. When the Constituent Assembly gave way to the Legislative Assembly, in September 1791, the same process repeated itself at the national level.

The failure of compromise in 1790 ensured that the carefully constructed Constitution of 1791 had no chance of success. Moreover, the Constitution's chief executive officer, Louis XVI, had already abandoned it before it took effect. The king and his immediate family fled Paris on 20–21 June 1791, forever destroying any chance of compromise among the aristocracy, the Crown, and the people. Some of the left-wing leaders, such as Marat, had been demanding the end to the monarchy long before Louis's flight, which Marat had long predicted. Once Louis had borne out such predictions, the momentum toward a new form of government could not be stopped. In hindsight, we see the republic, established in September 1792, as the sole alternative to the constitutional monarchy set up in 1791, but contemporaries took a different view. Many political leaders sought to create a Regency, usually on behalf of Louis's young son.[7]

The republican position had the overwhelming advantage of internal coherence; many of those who might have been strong supporters of a regency for Louis XVI's son refused to countenance the deposing of the king. The crowd in Paris rallied strongly to the republican side; in August 1792, they stormed the Tuileries Palace and put an end to more than 1,200 years of monarchy in France. The Republic they created lasted only seven years but the change in political culture and social myths survives to our own day.[8]

❧ THE DEFEAT OF THE KING AND THE OCTOBER DAYS

What a beautiful day, Sire, that Parisians are going possess your Majesty and his family in their city![9]

Mayor Bailly of Paris, to Louis XVI, 6 October 1789

CHRONOLOGY	26 August 1789–21 June 1791
4–11 August 1789	Abolition of Ancien Régime
26 August 1789	Declaration of the Rights of Man and of the Citizen
11 September 1789	Debate on king's veto power; he receives suspensive veto only
5–6 October 1789	Parisian women, followed by the National Guard, march to Versailles; forcibly bring royal family to Paris (Tuileries Palace)
2 November 1789	Confiscation of Church property
3 November 1789	King signs August Decrees

CHRONOLOGY	(continued)
14 December 1789	Reorganization of municipal and local governments
Jan.–Feb. 1790	Municipal elections
17 April 1790	*Assignats* become legal tender
June 1790	*Bagarre de Nîmes*
12 July 1790	Civil Constitution of the Clergy
14 July 1790	Feast of the Federation
31 August 1790	Repression of mutineers at Nancy
February 1791	Second *Camp de Jalès*; municipal elections
2 March 1791	Guilds suppressed
March–April 1791	Pope condemns the Civil Constitution of the Clergy; district elections
2 April 1791	Mirabeau dies
14 June 1791	Le Chapelier Law
20–21 June 1791	Royal family flees Paris; family arrested at Varennes

The Declaration of the Rights of Man and of the Citizen, 26 August 1789

Man is born free, and he is everywhere in chains.

J.-J. Rousseau, *The Social Contract*

The National Constituent Assembly had to determine the foundational principles of the constitution it would write and to enact legislation that would both eliminate the abuses of the old system and put into practice the principles of the new one. The abolition of privileges decreed between 5 August and 11 August paved the way for serious debates about the rule of law. Many deputies demanded a statement of principles to serve as a guideline for their deliberations; the *cahier* of the Third Estate of Paris, like several others, had explicitly demanded "that there be made an explicit declaration of the rights that appertain to all men, and that it declare their liberty, their property, and their security." Lafayette drew up just such a statement and showed it to his friend, Thomas Jefferson, then the American ambassador to France and living in Paris.[10] Various other "patriot" leaders, such as Sieyès, drew up similar documents. The Assembly debated the details and produced one of humankind's most important documents, "The Declaration of the Rights of Man and of the Citizen," passed on 26 August.

They borrowed heavily from Jefferson's *Declaration of Independence* and from George Mason's *Virginia Declaration of Rights.* They began:

> The representatives of the French people, constituted as a National Assembly, and considering that ignorance, neglect or contempt of the rights of man are the sole cause of public misfortunes and governmental corruption, have resolved to set forth in a solemn declaration the natural, inalienable, and sacred rights of man: so that by being constantly present to all the members of the social body this declaration may always remind them of their rights and duties.

The *Declaration* contained remarkably careful language. The Assembly met under the auspices of the "Supreme Being," not of "God," because, to a French person in 1789, the word "God" meant the God of the Catholic Church. The phrase "Supreme Being" not only brought forth memories of the deist principles of Voltaire, it allowed the *Declaration* to be ecumenical in its outreach to members of all religions, even those, such as Judaism, illegal in most of France prior to the Revolution. Once again, as with the abolition of feudalism, principle outran practice for a while: the Jews of eastern France did not get full civil rights until 1791.

Motions of principle were all well and good, but the Assembly had to take specific action. In the wake of the abolition of certain property rights, they quickly moved to protect what we think of as modern property rights. They denounced all "feudal" obligations related to personal status, such as serfdom, as an assault on the basic human right of liberty; the Assembly abolished them without compensation. The deputies ruled, however, that feudal rights based on land were redeemable property: peasants subject to such dues had to pay their owners compensation, later fixed at 25 times the annual payment for the dues in question. Most peasants, hearing that the Assembly had abolished feudal dues, simply stopped paying: "(T)he declarations, conditions and compensations are talked of; but an unruly, ungovernable multitude seize the benefit of the abolition, and laugh at the obligations or recompense."[11] Peasants immediately destroyed dovecoats, weathervanes, and seigneurial bancs in churches, and ostentatiously hunted and fished in forbidden forests and streams. Because seigneurial courts still existed in 1789, seigneurs immediately took their peasants to court to insist on full payment of dues and respect for property. This conflict got out of hand in regions such as Brittany and Guyenne, where large peasant bands burned châteaux and, in some cases, murdered their seigneurs. The large-scale passive resistance of the peasantry paid off in the long run; in 1793, the central legislative body (the Convention, elected in 1792) abolished all seigneurial dues without compensation.

The Assembly also decreed reimbursement for venal offices, hardly surprising in that about 30 percent of its members owned one. The state had no money to pay for these offices; in fact, it had almost no money to pay for anything. Many people refused to pay the old taxes. If we can believe Bernadau, matters got so bad at Bordeaux that the receiver of the old *vingtièmes* on income quartered troops in the

The Declaration of the Rights of Man
and of the Citizen, 26 August 1789

The *Declaration* begins with a paraphrase from Rousseau's *Social Contract*: "Men are born and remain free and equal in rights," but rapidly abandons Rousseau for the more careful doctrines of John Locke. Clause two shows us the key distinction: "The purpose of all political association is the preservation of the natural and imprescriptible rights of man. These rights are liberty, property, security, and resistance to oppression." Here the Assembly sided with Locke and the Americans, and those who had written the *cahiers*, against Rousseau, who did *not* believe property was a natural right. The deputies stressed the inviolability of property, a matter of great concern to the men of property who dominated assemblies at all levels.

The rest of the *Declaration* brings forth classic principles of modern democratic government: the sovereignty of the people ("nation"), freedom of conscience, freedom of the press, rights to a fair trial, equality before the law, equal obligation to pay taxes, the right to consent to taxes, separation of powers, governmental accountability to "society." The last clause (17) came back to property: "Property being an inviolable and sacred right, no one may be deprived of it except when public ne-

cessity, certified by law, obviously requires it, and on condition of a just compensation in advance." The deputies added this clause, in part, to cover their tracks for the actions taken on 4 and 5 August, when the Assembly had decreed the elimination of so many different forms of property. It needed to reaffirm the principle of property as a natural right and tie that principle directly to confiscations.

The Assembly also made sure, as many contemporaries put it, to protect liberty from license. Clause ten, for example, allowed free expression of opinions, even religious ones, "provided their manifestation does not trouble public order as established by law." Freedom of the press had a similar limitation, because one could print freely only if one accepted "responsibility for any abuse of this liberty in the cases set by the law." In creating these loopholes for future action, the Assembly assured that whoever held the right to make the laws in question would define natural rights. One of their critical mistakes in the coming months would be that they often did so in quite specific terms. They did not learn from the salutory experience of the Americans, that vagueness ("We, the People") has its uses.[12]

houses of the judges of the Parlement of Bordeaux, in order to make them pay their assessments.[13] Desperate for a way to pay off the staggering national debt, the Assembly quickly focused on Church property as the answer.

The clergy were the biggest losers in the new order. The Assembly had abolished the tithes in August 1789, leaving the parish clergy with no means of support. This action alienated many curés who had, up to that point, supported the Revolution, but the Assembly did later vote them a state-paid salary.[14] In November 1789, the Assembly confiscated all the property of the Catholic Church, on behalf of the nation. (See the following text.) The Assembly issued bonds, called *assignats*, secured on the proceeds of the sale of the seized Church property; officers initially obtained reimbursement for their confiscated offices by means of such bonds. This robbing of

Peter's Church to pay for Paul's offices brought together the two greatest conflicts engendered in the fall of 1789: treatment of the Catholic Church and settling of the government's debts.

Provincial Reaction, July–September 1789

> . . . *something was to be done by great folks for such poor ones, but she did not know who nor how, but God send us better, because the* tailles *and dues crush us.*[15]

Unidentified peasant woman, speaking to Arthur Young, 12 July 1789

The greatest events of the summer of 1789 took place in Paris, yet the country did not remain inert. Provincial reaction weighed constantly on the minds of the deputies and the king. The dramatic events of mid-July helped fuel a massive outpouring of disorder in provincial France: local authorities reported more than a 1,000 separate incidents of violence in that month alone. This violence led to a climate of terror, one best symbolized by the Great Fear of late July and early August, which spread through several regions of the kingdom. The decrees of 5–11 August gave the Assembly's response to the disquiet in the provinces.

The storming of the Bastille, and the concomitant creation of the Commune of Paris led to the creation of local Communes in many French towns. Some cities, such as Dijon, changed their governments on their own. Pro-Revolution forces seized power on 15 July, before word of the taking of the Bastille could have reached them. At Caen, on 21 July, the city's population, imitating the action at the Bastille, stormed the great Château of the dukes of Normandy that dominates the city, seizing the arsenal held there; at Strasbourg, the day after they heard the news from Paris, the artisans stormed and looted the Hôtel de Ville. At Orléans, however, the news of the fall of the Bastille prompted no violence, only a special election of 20 men, authorized to be the new government (21 July).

Most towns created new governments; others, like Reims or Montargis, co-opted new men into the old group. At Troyes, a new committee seized power but could not keep control. On 9 September, the old mayor, Claude Huez, and the new committee convened a special hearing on grain supplies. Dissatisfied with the results, a crowd, mainly unemployed textile workers, seized Huez as he stepped down from the platform. When he fled into an adjoining room, they battered down the door and literally tore the old man to pieces. Women and children dragged his corpse through the streets, dumping it in front of the town hall. The crowd then pillaged Huez's house and those of three other leading citizens. In short order, the old royal officials, backed by troops, returned to effective power at Troyes.

Everywhere, the fear of chaos galvanized propertied elites. They sensed that the political order had lost its legitimacy and could no longer be relied upon to protect them or their property. Cities and villages reorganized their local governments in large measure to defend themselves against possible rebellions by the lower classes. The villages affected by the Great Fear invariably met under the auspices of their leading citizens, who took a leadership role in mobilizing them against the dreaded "outsiders."

Both the Great Fear and the actions of the National Assembly in early August had some relationship to real unrest in the countryside. Peasants in Lower Normandy burned twenty-five châteaux in the two weeks prior to 5 August. The 5 August abolition of feudalism led to more violent local action in many regions. Bernadau wrote from Bordeaux that:

> The people, interpreting in its own way the edicts of its representatives, takes the excess of licence for the exercise of liberty. There is not a single country proprietor who dares to count on tomorrow. The peasants permit themselves everything, first against the nobility and the clergy, then against all those whose coat is cut differently from theirs. From every corner of the province, we receive details of the most disastrous scenes: châteaux burned, prisons opened, houses pillaged, citizens insulted, comestibles sold at prices fixed by the buyers.[16]

In July, Arthur Young reported château burnings in the Franche-Comté, lootings in Burgundy; in August and September, he cited widespread resistance to paying dues, rents, and taxes, and witnessed orgies of hunting in Provence.

In Paris and in the provinces, propertied elites, above all members of the legal profession, acted to create a new governing system in the summer and fall of 1789. In town after town, royal officials lost power to a coalition of lawyers, clergy, nobles, merchants, and even, in manufacturing towns like Troyes, richer artisans. The National Assembly's decree of 14 December 1789, creating new local and municipal administrations, provided the framework for the final steps: the municipal, district, and departmental elections of January–February 1790. These fairly democratic[17] elections demonstrated the broad-based support for the Revolution among many groups. Limoges was typical, its voters selecting five lawyers, three nobles, four merchants, a priest, two shopkeepers, and a doctor. Even Troyes elected a new municipal government that included a noble, members of the clergy, former royal officials, lawyers, merchants, and artisans. The largest towns, such as Lille or Paris, had a much greater presence of people from the world of commerce and manufacturing than did smaller ones in 1790; in this matter, they presaged important changes in local governments in 1791 and 1792.

Rural areas, as Young's journal suggests, reacted strongly to the events of the summer of 1789. The peasant *cahiers* of 1789 had demanded abolition of the salt tax and the *taille*; they wanted the Church to use the tithes to pay the local priest and to keep up the poor; many denounced seigneurial obligations. The Assembly abolished feudal dues and tithes and, after the riots and tax strikes of 1790, eliminated the *taille* and the salt tax. Yet they insisted on compensation for many of those dues and often relied on the registers of the *taille* and *vingtième* to determine local assessments for the new land tax. To most peasants, it was just a different name for the hated *taille*. The countless specific local peasant grievances got short shrift from the urban leaders of the Revolution. When the Assembly sided with the landlords in a dispute over whether to call one Breton land tenure arrangement "feudal," the entire region around Vannes revolted. Troops shot more than a score of the rioters; local voters responded by boycotting the

Just Desserts: Arthur Young's Summer of 1789

Arthur Young, the English agronomist, traveled through France and Italy in 1789. He spent June in Paris, recording his precious observations about the great events, but left the city on 28 June. In July and August, he wandered throughout France, and offers us a remarkable view of the variety of local reactions.

Young first heads east, toward Strasbourg. At Château-Thierry on 4 July, he cannot find a single newspaper; in fact, he is shocked to find not a single coffee house! He writes in his journal: "not a newspaper to be seen by a traveller, even in a moment when all ought to be anxiety. What stupidity, poverty, want of circulation! This people hardly deserves to be free." Five days later, Young learns from an army officer that troops were converging on Paris, a rumor confirmed when he reached Metz (14 July). The next day, at the large city of Nancy, Young finds the locals unwilling to act on their own. They cautiously tell him: "We are a provincial town, we must wait to see what is done in Paris."[18]

Reaching Strasbourg on 20 July, Young hears of the storming of the Bastille and witnesses the riot at the Hôtel de Ville. At Colmar, a letter from a local deputy to the Assembly convinces everyone that the queen intends to blow up the Assembly and massacre the Parisians (one wonders if it was the same deputy whose inaccurate letter on the August Decrees touched off riots in the Alsatian countryside). Young comments: "Thus it is in revolutions, one rascal writes, and an hundred thousand fools believe."

Moving southward toward the Franche-Comté, Young is repeatedly stopped by local militias or National Guard; everywhere, they tell him to wear the cockade of blue-white-red. After one such incident, he admits, "I do not like travelling in such an unquiet and fermenting moment; one is not secure for an hour beforehand." Arriving in Besançon, he reports that

> many châteaus have been burnt, others plundered, the seigneurs hunted down like wild beasts, their wives and daughters ravished, their papers and titles burnt, and all their property destroyed: and these abominations not inflicted on marked persons, who were odious for their former conduct or principles, but an indiscriminating blind rage for the love of plunder. Robbers, galley-slaves, and villains of all denominations, have collected and instigated the peasants to commit all sorts of outrages.[19]

Young here repeats the standard accusations that led to the Great Fear; in fact, we have little evidence of armed bands of evil-doers, nor did many seigneurs lose their lives, nor their wives suffer sexual assault.

Finally, in Besançon, Young again finds newspapers, albeit rather old ones. The countryside around the city, in contrast, remains in nearly complete ignorance of events: "for what the country knows to the contrary, their deputies are in the Bastille, instead of the

elections of 1791, whose local turnout averaged only 5 percent. Little wonder that this region proved to be a hotbed of counter-revolution from 1792–1793. In the southwest, between December 1789 and March 1790, peasant bands from the traditionally radical regions once roamed by the Croquants attacked over 100 châteaux, seeking an end to seigneurial dues. Nor did the rural community care too much about the social origins of landlords they attacked: their assaults targeted nobles (35), clergy (18), and commoners (29) alike.[21]

The peasants had also demanded access to land; the confiscation of Church property gave the government the means of appeasing some of this land hunger by selling high-quality meadows, woods, and arable fields. In some regions, like the

---

(CONTINUED)

Bastille being razed." Young finds it inconceivable that the nobles do not organize to protect themselves and criticizes the "universal ignorance" of the provinces. At Dijon, on 30 July, he again complains of lack of newspapers and seems astonished that he is the first person to bring news of the riot at Strasbourg. Once again, reports spread everywhere about rural looting (although few murders or burned châteaux). At last Young is able to see if the rumors about brigands—which he had repeated himself—are true: his informant at Dijon, the chemist Morveau, assures him they are not. Young quickly accepts Morveau's proof and conclusions.

At Moulins (7 August), we hear more complaints about the lack of newspapers, but Clermont proves better. There, on 12 August, citizens hear of the great events of 5 August:

> The great news has just arrived from Paris, of the utter abolition of tythes, feudal rights, game, warrens, pidgeons, &c. have been received with the greatest joy by the mass of the people . . . but I have had much conversation with two or three very sensible persons, who complain bitterly of the gross injustice and cruelty of any such declarations of what will be done, but is not effected and regulated at the moment of declaring.

Wandering through the Midi, Young meets up with the same situation he had seen in the east. Everywhere, people lack information: Le Puy, like Moulins, has no newspapers. The lack of information encourages wild rumors and suspicion of all strangers: Young faces arbitrary arrest in a village near Clermont (13 August) and again on both 19 and 20 August, in the countryside of the Vivarais. When he reaches Marseilles (5 September), however, Young finds a quite different situation: "Marseilles is absolutely exempt from the reproaches I have so often cast on others for want of newspapers."

Young's comments, which strongly reinforce other evidence we have about events in provincial France in that summer of 1789, remind us of the stunning changes that overwhelmed society. Provincials often had to act on insufficient information. Individuals, such as the over-zealous Alsatian deputy, could have an enormous impact on local opinion simply because of the scarcity of competing sources of information. Rural people especially relied on rumor; they heard the vague outlines of what had happened (as on 5 August) and reacted to it. Given the agonizingly slow transmission of news from Paris out to many rural areas, and even to some towns, it could not be otherwise. As Young wrote at Besançon on 29 July:

> Thus it may be said, perhaps with truth, that the fall of the King, court, lords, nobles, army, church, and parliaments, proceeds from a want of intelligence being quickly circulated, consequently from the very effects of that thraldom in which they held the people: it is therefore a retribution rather than a punishment."[20]

Cambrésis in the far north, peasants bought an average of 60 percent of the initial properties put up for sale.[22] Yet confiscated rural property in most of France ended up in the hands of the urban middle classes because the state sold most of the land in large blocks. In the regions close to large cities, like Bordeaux or Paris, urbanites often bought 90 percent of the nationalized lands.

The Revolution offered many apparent benefits to peasants, but peasants in many regions of France felt they had been robbed of the full benefits of the new order. They reacted with direct action against landlords, whether it was the peasants of the duke of Liancourt, east of Paris, who simply divided up his wastelands and brought them under their ploughs, or those of the southwest burning châteaux.

These conflicts died down in the fall of 1789—Young spoke of seeing a peasant hanged in Provence for attacking a château—but the evil feelings that underlay them did not go away. Aside from the rich ploughmen, who everywhere bought up confiscated Church property, and those relatively few happy villages in which the peasantry itself, in broad numbers, bought up these lands, most French peasants suffered from unfulfilled expectations by 1790. When the Revolution turned against the Church, the clergy of many regions found ready antigovernment allies among the disillusioned peasantry.

The October Days: The March to Versailles (5–6 October 1789)

The high price of bread was the pretext: the design formed by some since the motion by Saint-Huruge—to have the king and the National Assembly in Paris—was the true motive. It's true that such is the only means to avoid a shortage and to reanimate the commerce of Paris.[23]

Rétif de la Bretonne, speaking of the October Days

The Assembly focused its main efforts on creating a constitution. Should France have a single legislative body or should it, like England and the United States, have a bicameral legislature? Mindful of the potential for the nobility to prevent reform, the Assembly voted (10 September 1789) for a unicameral legislature. After much debate, they also defined the powers of the state executive, that is, the king. He could veto legislation for the duration of a sitting of the new National Assembly but, if a second elected Assembly passed the same law, it took effect over his veto. The king would have no veto over constitutional or financial bills. This debate over the royal veto took place against a restive political climate in Paris. Bread prices rose again, and the king had called in troops once more. Moreover, Louis had not yet signed the decrees of 11 August. Finally, on 5 October, the market women of Paris, incensed by reports that army officers at Versailles had defiled cockades bearing the national colors, and probably egged on by the agents of the duke of Orléans, took matters into their own hands.

Thousands of them marched to Versailles demanding bread and the removal of the king and of the National Assembly to Paris.[24] Lafayette and the National Guard of Paris, some 20,000 strong, soon followed. On the morning of 6 October, the usual misunderstandings led panicky royal guards to fire on the crowd, killing a few; the crowd, in turn, massacred a few of the guards and put their heads on pikes. Some elements of the crowd moved threateningly toward Marie Antoinette's apartments; she fled in her nightgown to the king's room. The royal family had little choice but to join the crowd, now swelled to 60,000, in a procession back to Paris. Led by pikes bearing the severed heads of Louis's guards, the procession slowly wended its way from the great palace of Versailles to the dingy halls of the vacant Tuileries. Henceforth, the royal family lived as prisoners in the Tuileries Palace, right next to one of the most turbulent neighborhoods of Paris. The Assembly, too, moved to the capital. The Paris crowd could now intimidate the government; it was not reticent to do so.

The October Days highlight the critical role of the people in the success of the Revolution. As Morris confided to his diary, "They all suppose, as was supposed in

The March to Versailles, 5 October 1789. Women led this critical popular movement, which brought the royal family and the National Assembly to Paris.

SOURCE: © Giraudon/Art Resource.

the American Revolution, that there are certain Leaders who occasion every Thing; whereas in both Instances it is the great Mass of the People." The March to Versailles completed the triumph of the Parisian radicals. Every step taken from June 1789 (the creation of a National Assembly), through July (storming the Bastille), August (a declaration of rights and abolition of "feudalism"), and October (bringing the king and the Assembly back to Paris) directly responded to articles from the *cahiers* drawn up by the Third Estate of Paris in April 1789. These initial steps, however, left aside the critical question of the new constitution. As Young had written on 20 July, they had two alternatives: a practical constitution (ideally one modeled on that of England!) or "to frame something absolutely speculative. In the former case, they will prove a blessing to their country; in the latter [case], they will probably involve it [France] in inextricable confusions and civil wars, perhaps not in the present period, but certainly at some future one."[25] Young's chauvinism for the English constitution notwithstanding, his larger point rang true, as events would bear out.

As for the man contemporaries viewed as the chief instigator of these events, the duke of Orléans, he quickly lost all credit with the public, as well as with the authorities. The Swiss banker Huber reported that Lafayette had a short conversation with the duke:

> Monseigneur, I am afraid that there will soon be on the scaffold the head of a person bearing your name.[26]

Orléans took the hint: he fled to England, where he remained until July 1790.

∼ THE NEW REGIME TAKES SHAPE

> [M. Bellefontaine] *is to be the interpreter of our attachment, of our entire de-*
> *votion to the Fatherland and to the King, of our sentiments of fidelity to the*
> *new Constitution, of our firm resolution to struggle with all our might, with*
> *all our means, to maintain the laws and the prosperity of the Kingdom, and,*
> *finally, to take, for us and in our name, the oath of the Federation.*[27]

The naval workers of Rochefort, naming their representative to the Festival
of the Federation, 1790

The Assembly acted with dispatch and effectiveness on most matters. The deputies
created effective local and regional administrations, particularly in the judicial branch.
They produced a Constitution, sound in most respects. Despite its many successes,
the Assembly ultimately failed because of its inability to deal with four key matters.
First, it hopelessly bungled the creation of a place for the Catholic Church in the new
France. Second, it could not solve the interrelated issues of state debt and taxation.
Third, despite the prominent leadership roles played by many nobles (Lafayette,
Mirabeau, the Lameths), the Assembly could find no place for the nobility in the new
France. Fourth, the deputies failed to create a sound executive branch of government.

The Assembly had encouraged French people to think in new terms by quickly
(December 1789) replacing the provinces with a system of smaller jurisdictions,
called departments (at first, eighty-three, a number since increased). Within the departments, the Assembly created districts, themselves divided into cantons. The new
departments generally took the name of geographic features, such as the name of a
river (Cher) or of mountains (Maritime Alps). The elections of February and March
1790 created new councils at each of these levels of government. Rural landowners
obtained many of the new positions, along with the legal men more often found on
town councils; departmental councils rarely included the merchants, manufacturers,
and artisans found on municipal councils. Individual groups did not monolithically
support or oppose the Revolution. At Toulouse, where barristers obtained election as
mayor, as councilors at the three local levels of government, and as attorneys general
of the district and department, two-thirds of their fellows opposed the New Regime
and some became leaders of the Counter-Revolution. In Paris, barristers provided
one-quarter of the members of the Commune, but most of their brothers refused to
practice law in the new courts.

Municipalities used direct election by all "active" citizens; departmental and district councils used a method of indirect election, in which active citizens chose "electors," who then chose the councils.[28] The restrictive clauses—a minimum
twelve-month residence in the locale and a contribution of three days' wages in
taxes—eliminated few rural men, but disenfranchised almost all of the urban poor.
Something like 70 percent of adult men could vote in the first tier elections and even
the rules about electors, those sitting in the second tier assemblies, left perhaps a
million men eligible.[29] The rules eliminated all women, some of whom, it will be remembered, had voted in 1789. The Assembly's remarkably broad suffrage, far
broader than the existing systems in either Great Britain or the United States, di-

rectly tied the majority of male adults to the political system and gave them a firm and immediate connection to representative government. Just as the broad principles of the *Declaration* suggested, the general will—the male adults—would make and administer the law, either itself or through its representatives, who would merely give voice to the general will.[30]

Here and there, the elections led to problems. The small Burgundian town of Vitteaux provided the extreme case: when Jean Filsjean, lord of Saint-Colombe, a seventy-five-year-old noble, showed up at the electoral assembly, local peasants, outraged at the participation of someone widely believed involved in grain speculation in the 1775 Flour War, took him outside and lynched him. They told the police that he had been a "milord who betrayed the Nation." Elsewhere in Burgundy, where the continued existence of serfdom had poisoned relations between peasants and seigneurs, nobles faced physical attacks.

The two new councils had considerable local power. The district councils had the authority to sell the confiscated Church lands and to apportion taxes among the communes. Municipal governments took over many important functions, such as the maintenance of local order and poor relief. The Assembly, in response to the extensive complaints about the old judicial system, abolished seigneurial courts (1790) and created an entirely new system, based, like the municipalities, on elections. Each canton would have a justice of the peace, elected by the active citizens, for minor cases; each district would have a bureau of peace and reconciliation and a district court of five elected judges, chosen by district or departmental electors.

Civil cases could go to the tribunals only after they passed through the hands of the bureau of peace and the parties had obtained a certificate saying that reconciliation had failed. These new institutions, like the electoral regime itself, reinforced the idea of the nation as a cooperative venture, in which citizens jointly sought the common good, through justice and equity: "the strength and vigor of municipal life constituted one of the most striking characteristics of Revolutionary France."[31] This new local judicial system seems to have worked quickly and cheaply, even in Paris, a notorious hotbed of litigation!

At the national level, the Assembly created an Appeals Court that could rule only on procedural or factual error, and, in time, a High Court of the Nation, for cases involving government misconduct. The delays in creating the High Court proved to be an appalling precedent, because they encouraged the Assembly itself to get involved in such matters, preventing the creation of an immediate, effective judicial process for those accused of crimes against the nation. In the prevailing paranoia of 1789–1794, when opposition to state policy often carried a charge of treason ("*lèse nation*"), political interference in what should have been judicial matters inevitably led to violence.

The Assembly created a judiciary that answered to the people and the Assembly, not to the king. Once again, these actions directly responded to unequivocal demands of the Paris *cahiers*: "The judicial power must be exercised in France, in the name of the King, by tribunals composed of members absolutely independent of all acts of executive power."[32] Alas, that the *cahiers* did not say "independent of the constituted sovereign power," an oversight that soon had tragic consequences.

The provisions about central administration and general constitutional doctrines similarly attacked royal power and previous practice. The Assembly borrowed from the Ancien Régime the rule that the king had to consult with his six ministers (war, Navy, finance, interior, justice, and foreign affairs) and could send the Assembly no proposal that did not have the requisite minister's signature. They radically changed that rule's meaning, however, because the new constitution made ministers directly responsible to the Assembly, not the king, for their conduct. The Assembly circumscribed the king's suspensive veto, barring him from using it on financial bills or constitutional law. They forbade him from declaring war or peace without their consent.

As for the Assembly itself, once it finished writing the Constitution, it would give way to a new body, the Legislative Assembly, which would have seven hundred forty-five deputies. The two-year Legislative Assembly would be chosen by electors selected by the active citizens. The members of the Constituent Assembly, in one of their many unselfish acts, decreed that no one among their number could sit in the upcoming Legislative Assembly. This measure, no matter how nobly conceived, had the unfortunate effect of eliminating from the national legislature the only people in the kingdom with any legislative experience. Many of the deputies of the incoming Legislative Assembly had experience in district and departmental councils, but that did not compensate for their lack of national political experience.

The Constituent Assembly moved cautiously forward but it progressively became more and more radical in its rejection of the Ancien Régime. Having rejected the fundamental basis of that system, privilege, the Assembly began systematically to dismantle every privilege associated with the old system. The Assembly abolished manufacturing monopolies and the monopoly trading companies, and created a free market in grain. True to the grievances their constituents had drawn up, the deputies wanted specific reforms: a fairer tax system, better protection for property rights, a more just legal system, representative government. These pragmatic reform proposals led inexorably to a discussion of philosophical principles that had not appeared in many of the *cahiers*. The more the Assembly debated one change, and the relationship of that change to a given principle, the more it realized it had to make other changes.

The new system, based on law and on the nation, required a new vocabulary: the language of the Ancien Régime clearly could not be used to describe the New Regime. The Assembly, as the *Declaration of the Rights of Man and of the Citizen* makes clear, turned to the one alternate vocabulary then available, that of the Enlightenment. The recent events in the United States of America offered a particularly useful practical application of such a vocabulary. Many leading French intellectuals made that explicit connection. When Young visited Marseille in September 1789, Abbé Raynal told him that "the American revolution had brought the French one in its train." Raynal presciently mused that the constitution being proposed was too "democratical" and would lead to a "species of republic, ridiculous for such a kingdom as France."[33]

The Constitution of 1791 and the laws passed by the National Constituent Assembly created a new France; most of their reforms became permanent. They abolished privilege and put legal equality in its place. They established civil rights for Protestants and Jews (delayed),[34] eliminated the old usages and institutions, instituted uniform weights and measures (the metric system), unified tariffs, and legislated a wide variety of civil rights: freedom of expression, of religion, of assembly, all, of course, somewhat limited by law. They freed the serfs, although not the slaves, abolished internal tolls, tithes, the seigneurial system, the old taxes and privileged tax exemptions, and the temporal holdings of the Catholic Church. They created a new system of courts, relying on elected judges, justices of the peace, and juries. They helped initiate a national citizen militia and popularly elected regional, local, and municipal governments. They legalized divorce, made marriage a civil contract, and extended many civil rights to women, although they did not give women political rights. Before we are too quick to criticize the National Assembly and its Constitution, we must recognize their remarkable achievements.

The Revolution and the Church: Phase One, 1789–1791

> *It must be shouted even from the temples: philosophy has resuscitated nature; philosophy has recreated the human spirit and restored heart to society. Humanity died by servitude; it is reborn by thought.*[35]
>
> Abbé Fauchet, funeral oration for those killed in taking the Bastille, 5 August 1789.

Each move forward alienated a different constituency. The confiscation of the property of the Catholic Church (November 1789) naturally upset the clergy, who still possessed enormous influence in many regions, especially rural ones. Their chief spokesman, the Abbé Maury, alerted his fellow deputies to the wider issue raised by the confiscation:

> our possessions serve to guarantee yours. Today it is we who are under attack; but do not deceive yourselves, if we are stripped bare, your turn will come soon. . . . It [the people] will exercise over you all those rights which you exercise over us; it will say that it is the Nation, and that one cannot prescribe against it.[36]

Whatever else may be said about the Church's use of its property, it did provide the material basis for most poor relief in the Ancien Régime. The state's confiscation of Church property implied a nationalization of relief efforts. During the course of the eighteenth century, many royal officials, acting as private individuals, directed local hospitals; the state now took control of them. The roughly fourteen hundred hospitals responding to the initial state inquiry informed the commissioners that their collective income had declined from 21 million *livres* in 1788 to 14 million in 1790. This decline bespoke the disastrous consequences for the poor of the loss of the Church's property and boded ill for their future. Government control of poor relief meant rapid devolution of authority in this matter to local governments, such as municipal authorities. This highly localized organization of relief naturally meant that its quality varied sharply from one town to the next.

The Assembly also abolished religious orders (January 1790), making exceptions only for teaching and charity work. Contemporaries were familiar with stories of "useless" monks and with the age-old tales of lascivious friars and nuns. The utilitarian values of the late eighteenth century had little use for contemplatives, many of whom were, in fact, younger children of wealthy families who had forbidden them to marry so that family property would stay intact. Ordinary people, those a little less affected by the stereotypes of Enlightenment literature, knew the other side of the religious orders: they provided virtually all of the nurses and teachers of eighteenth-century France. People may have detested the wealthy abbots, but they had a much more positive view of the Christian Brothers, who ran schools for poor boys, or of the "grey sisters" who staffed most French hospitals. The Assembly, by abolishing the religious orders, grievously wounded the systems of poor relief and education.[37]

The combined actions against the Church alert us to the greatest gap between the deputies and the rural majority of the French population: the anticlericalism of the deputies. Like Abbé Fauchet, they looked to "philosophy," meaning the great thinkers of the Enlightenment, for answers to moral and political questions. In June 1789, the newly created National Assembly consciously voted not to hang a crucifix in its meeting chamber. Six weeks later, when a priest demanded that mass be celebrated each morning at the Assembly, the deputies burst into laughter. Like the people of Paris, the deputies particularly disliked the monks and the bishops, whose luxurious lifestyle contrasted so sharply with their pious protestations on behalf of the poor. The *cahier* of the Theatins section of Paris had summarized general urban feelings about the religious orders:

> In the future, religious professions must be extinguished and suppressed, as contrary to the social will and to the good of the fatherland, whose population they diminish. . . . (T)heir goods, acquired by the Nation, will serve for the payment of the public debt and for a multitude of objects of general utility.[38]

One of Paris's great cultural successes of the fall of 1789, the play *Charles IX* by Marie-Joseph de Chénier, illustrated the widespread anticlericalism of the capital. In this retelling of the Saint Bartholomew's Day Massacre of 1572, the cardinal of Lorraine urges Charles IX to slaughter the Protestants and blesses the swords of those who will carry out the deed. Chénier costumed the actors in the style of Charles's time and even used the bell of the church of Saint-Germain l'Auxerrois that, legend had it, had rung to signal the start of the massacre, as a prop. Morris commented that "this Piece, if it runs thro the Provinces as it probably will, must give a fatal Blow to the Catholic Religion."

Few deputies of the Third Estate were active Catholics; even many of the nobles, a group generally better disposed toward Catholicism, were not churchgoers. The deputies took a pragmatic attitude toward the religion of the masses: "Like nineteen-twentieths of the Assembly, I believe that religion is useful and that we must therefore allow public worship," wrote one deputy. Another suggested that "religion is the first foundation of the social order."[39] This condescension toward rustic believers had bloody consequences, as we shall see.

The Church had had a mixed reaction to the first stirrings of Revolution. The parish priests largely supported the agenda of the Third Estate in June 1789. They could even see their way to the abolition or modification of tithes; after all, they rarely received the money. The violent split between the church hierarchy and the parish priests in 1789, and between the secular and regular clergy, played into the hands of those who wanted to destroy the power of the Church. On the famous night of 4 August, after a bishop had suggested the abolition of seigneurial rights related to wood gathering, a noble proposed the abolition of tithes. That sort of internal division within the privileged orders carried over into the clergy itself. Abbé Sieyès, after all, had written the most influential and incendiary pamphlet on behalf of the Third Estate in 1789. The bishop of Autun, Charles Talleyrand-Périgord, proposed in October 1789 the confiscation of church property, touching off a violent conflict within the Church.

Mindful of the doubtful loyalty of many ecclesiastics, and possessed itself of a deep anticlericalism, the Assembly sought to ensure the clergy's loyalty by means of a special "Civil Constitution of the Clergy," which spelled out the clergy's rights in the new France. Priests and bishops would become servants of the state, chosen by the departmental or district electors and receiving a state salary. For many parish priests, the 1,200-*livres* salary would have been an improvement over their old income. The Assembly abolished the old bishoprics; each bishop now ruled over a department. The Assembly asked the Pope to approve (literally, to "baptize") these changes in the summer of 1790. He hesitated, both because he detested the principles of the Revolution as blasphemous and because he worried that the Revolutionary government was about to annex his personal enclave within France: Avignon and the Comtat Venaissin.

Four months of futile negotiations led the Assembly to act on its own, demanding that all French ecclesiastics take an oath of loyalty to the Civil Constitution of the Clergy. The bishops almost universally refused: only seven took it. The parish clergy split evenly, primarily along regional lines: priests in the Paris basin and the southeast took the oath, those in the north, the east, and much of the west did not. In some rural areas, the laity demanded that their priest refuse, as a symbol of their unhappiness with the course of the Revolution. Many urban priests, such as those of Dijon, also refused.

The situation worsened in late 1790 and early 1791. The inhabitants of Avignon forcibly annexed Avignon and the Comtat to France. The Pope, further incensed by this action, issued two bulls denouncing the Civil Constitution (spring 1791). The Constituent Assembly, in its last official act (September 1791), ratified Avignon's incorporation into France. Henceforth, the Catholic Church would be an unshakeable enemy of the Revolution. That hostility extended to republicanism everywhere, throughout the nineteenth century. The Catholic Church also associated the Revolution with recognition of the rights of Protestants. In some regions, such as Nîmes, where several hundred Catholics died at the hands of the Protestant National Guard in the *bagarre* (brawl) of April 1790, outright violence could not be controlled.[40] In the summer, 20,000 armed Catholic National Guardsmen responded to the Protestant threat by meeting together at the Camp de Jalès in the Ardeche. When a similar meeting took place in February 1791, thousands of National Guardsmen from an area extending from Marseilles to Lyon converged, only to find the Catholics dispersed. The

National Guard arrested and murdered the Catholic leader, dumping his corpse in the Rhône.[41]

The alienation of many parish clergy greatly exacerbated the rural–urban split. Rural priests were natural leaders of their communities: literate, broadly respected, sharing deep bonds of sympathy with their parishioners. In Breton areas soon to be in open rebellion against the government, the priests refused the oath because of pressure from their congregations. These "refractories" then came full circle, providing a leadership group for those in rural areas who felt betrayed by the Revolution. Other village notables, too, felt increasingly alienated from a Revolution driven more and more by urban concerns. The failure to make a clean abolition of feudal rights provided another serious rural grievance against the Constituent Assembly.

The alienation of the Church from the Revolution was part of a larger process; it did not, in itself, lead to counter-revolution, but helped provide a major piece of its substructure. The great anti-Revolution movements of 1792–1793 often took place in regions in which the local clergy had refused to take the Oath for the Civil Constitution; however, rather than look to those events for causality, we would better understand them as stages in a continuing process. The enormous mental gap in perceptions of the Church between the deputies of the Constituent Assembly and the rural majority illustrates the larger cultural chasm separating the two groups.

Fiscal Madness

> *The deranged state of the finances has obliged them to make a present use of part of the 800 millions, which were intended to pay off so much of the Dette constituée. It having been proved to them that the probable expenses for the three last months of the year will amount to above 230 millions, and that the receipt will be less than 94 millions.*[42]
>
> Earl Gower, English Ambassador to France, October 1790

Virtually all historians agree that the financial crisis of 1786–1789 precipitated the French Revolution, but few have seriously examined the fiscal system of the Revolutionary government. Two centuries of hindsight have focused on broad philosophical issues, yet the documents of 1789 through 1791 show that the Revolutionaries themselves spent much of their time debating the methods of financing the state, paying off France's enormous state debt, and avoiding bankruptcy. No systematic examination of the portfolios of the deputies to the Constituent Assembly tells us how many of them owned shares in the state debt, but the presence of so many royal officials among the deputies guarantees that a majority of them did so. One member of the Assembly's finance committee estimated the total state debt, including venal offices, to be 4.7 billion *livres*.

Where could the government come up with enough money to pay off these debts and finance the everyday workings of the state? Taxation did not offer an attractive alternative, because the *cahiers* of 1789 had almost universally demanded the abolition of all existing taxes. Although the Assembly voted a temporary continuance of these taxes in 1789, people simply refused to pay. In February 1790, a crowd at Béziers lynched five salt tax collectors. Perhaps responding to the Béziers incident, the Assembly abolished the hated salt tax a month later. In the next eighteen months, it abolished the direct taxes, internal tolls and customs, entry duties, and sales taxes. State revenue plummeted. Necker tried to float a loan (fall 1789); it failed, as did his ludicrous scheme of convincing people to give 25 percent of their income as a "patriotic contribution." His stock with the public fell so far that his dismissal in September 1790 "produced no effect either on the public mind or public funds" (Morris).

The *cahiers* had supported a land tax, levied on all owners; the Assembly enacted one of 400 million *livres* (1791), of which it collected at most 240 million *livres*, spread over parts of two years.[43] Revenues from taxation declined from 180 million *livres* in fiscal year 1790–1791 to 106 million *livres* in fiscal year 1791–1792. Given that the government spent between 600 and 700 million *livres* a year, it had only two choices: increase taxes or generate money from other resources.[44] Moreover, these figures ignore the substantial expenditure that took place at the local level. Writing in September 1790, Jefferson's secretary, William Short, rightly castigated the government for its unwillingness to take the harsh necessary measures: "you will readily believe that a government like this will not adopt the harsh business of forcing taxes so long as they can make use of that gentle means of striking paper to satisfy their demands."[45]

The Assembly quickly proved Short right, by changing the nature of the *assignats*. The Assembly first moved cautiously, retiring some governmental debt by decreeing that the confiscated Church lands would be sold to pay it. They issued *assignats*, large-denomination paper bonds guaranteed by the sale of the confiscated Church property: these bonds bore interest and could be used to buy up the seized land, called the *biens nationaux* (national property). The Assembly then began to use the *assignats* to pay state debts, such as reimbursement of venal offices, a matter of great interest to the many deputies who owned one.

The Assembly's next step eventually proved to be the fatal one. Realizing that the drastically reduced tax revenues could not pay for ongoing state expenses, they made *assignats* into a form of paper currency (September–November 1790). Yet this policy initially had more positive than negative consequences. The initial modest issue bore some relationship to the value of lands backing them, so the *assignats* maintained almost 90 percent of their face value until July 1791.[46] They provided an important respite to the government, putting into circulation about 1.2 billion *livres* by early 1791. The *assignats* provided the only financial solace the state or its creditors got; moreover, as one local official put it, even "the enemies of the Revolution themselves have an interest in this operation [land sales], because it is the only means by which they will be paid the liens they might have on the State." Local commissioners sold millions of *livres* worth of property, and some creditors and officers did get some money back, but both groups lost enormous amounts of capital in the Revolution.

The confused tax situation fitted in closely with major changes in the distribution of rural output. The abolition of the tithe, which removed a charge of about 8 percent on gross production, ended up profiting the landlords; they merely raised rents by a proportional amount. The extinction of seigneurial dues created much more uneven savings, but, once again, landlords kept the savings. Peasants reaped some savings because their direct taxes dropped so sharply in 1791: per capita direct taxation appears to have declined by 55 percent between 1789 and 1791 and to have bottomed out at 9 percent of the 1789 level in 1794.[47] Massive regional disparities in land tax rates continued, because the New Regime often used the tax distribution charts of the old one. Tax policy bore out the fears expressed about insufficient consideration for rural interests: landed interests paid almost all the taxes levied from 1791 to 1794, except for the forced loan of 1793.

The unwillingness of the deputies to vote sufficient taxation and the means to collect it led to three terrible consequences:

1. A loss of public credit, because the state debt could not be repaid.

2. Inadequate funds for departmental administration.

3. A decrease in commercial activity, in part related to the inflation caused by the *assignats*.

The one area in which one can say the Assembly acted with utter irresponsibility is state finance.

⟿ The King and the Assembly: The Flight to Varennes

I do not know if this [the abolition of nobility] *accords well with the spirit of the Monarchy and if, without thinking about it, we are rapidly heading toward a Republic.*

Nicolas Ruault, to his brother, 22 June 1790

The Revolution maintained enormous reservoirs of support throughout France. People wanted representative government, at local, regional, and national levels. They urgently waited to see what the new constitution would say. In the spring of 1790, in response to the revolutionary events of 1789, peasants all over France organized local festivals, often around the ancient may pole. They festooned the poles with the tri-colored ribbons (cockades) of the Revolution and constructed bonfires of the symbols of seigneurial authority: church pews, weathervanes, and coats of arms. They forced seigneurs to host banquets and to fraternize with them. Soon these *ad hoc* celebrations became more ritualized and codified; they took on the name of federations. The federation celebrations led the Paris authorities to the idea of a great Festival of the Federation, to take place on 14 July 1790, at the Champs de Mars in Paris.

These mixed signals alert us to the extremely tenuous situation of 1790. The economy languished: Young wrote in January 1790 that only the colonial sector remained healthy. Production in one sector after another had fallen off dramatically, a situation that particularly affected the urban workers. The bountiful harvest of 1789 had helped, because bread prices remained low throughout the fall of 1789 and spring of 1790, but massive unemployment left tens of thousands of people on the public dole. Young claimed that over 20,000 Lyonnais, most of them silk weavers, lived off of charity by December 1789. Manufacturing towns like Troyes or Reims, which had already lapsed into recession before the Revolution began, housed thousands of starving workers. The government Committee on Begging's 1791 survey got reports from local officials in 51 of the 83 departments that nearly two million of their 16 million inhabitants (12.5 percent) were beggars. Even allowing for the inclusion of seasonal laborers in this figure, it still suggests a staggering poverty problem.

The titular ruler of this tinderbox of a country, Louis XVI, and his wife, Marie Antoinette, felt increasingly uncomfortable with the course of the Revolution. Louis signed the edicts grudgingly. He did not like the despoiling of Church property or the Civil Constitution. He or the queen personally detested many of the Revolutionary leaders, such as Lafayette. He and his advisors tried to maintain some semblance of control over the process by means of bribery, but the most important leader corrupted by royal money, Mirabeau, died in April 1791. Louis's relatives, above all his brother Artois and his cousins in the Condé family, agitated abroad for the Revolution's defeat. The king and queen corresponded with foreign rulers, first with Marie's brother Joseph, ruler of Austria and the Holy Roman Empire, and then with his successor, her nephew Leopold. The latter proved more sympathetic. He and the king of Prussia, Frederick William II, grew increasingly restive at events in France.

The relationship between the royal government and the Constituent Assembly seemed to be progressing relatively smoothly in early 1790. The king, after several weeks of planning a theatrical gesture, appeared unannounced at the Assembly on 4 February to reassure the deputies that he supported their work. He pledged to support the constitution and to raise his son according to its principles. He concluded, "Let us all, from this day forward, following my example, be moved by one opinion, one interest, one purpose—attachment to the new constitution and ardent desire for the peace, happiness and prosperity of France."[48]

The king's speech prompted the deputies to swear an oath to "be faithful to the nation, the law and the king." Provincial authorities postponed scheduled balloting so that citizens might hear the king's speech read aloud: in Rouen, the assembly voted to illuminate the town that evening and to have the local clergy chant a *Te Deum*, the traditional religious ceremony celebrating great royal victories. The outburst of joy notwithstanding, Morris noted that "I can conceive of no other Effect there [in the provinces] than to encrease Animosity. The Noblesse will consider it as the Effect of Thraldom in which he is held, and the Populace as a Declaration of War against their Superiors."

Louis waxed and waned in his attitude toward events. All observers agreed to his genuine concern for his people and his abhorrence of violence. He believed in some of the reforms of 1789—he often reiterated his willingness to accept consent to taxation—but other aspects of the Assembly's work deeply troubled him. Its anticlericalism, best symbolized by the Civil Constitution of the Clergy, particularly upset the king. His visit on 4 February 1790 and his actions that spring, however, gave hope to many. The great national Festival of the Federation, celebrated at the Champs de Mars (near the present Eiffel Tower) to commemorate the first anniversary of the taking of the Bastille and to signal the birth of the renewed France (official statements focused on the latter), gave

*The king and his family walking in the Tuileries garden, without an
escort. Louis and his family sought to establish a greater rapport with
their subjects by such contact, and by propaganda such as this image.
The royal family wears the much simpler modes of dress made popular by the Revolution.*

SOURCE: Bibliothèque Nationale, Estampes, c. Hachette.

the king the public opportunity to take an oath of loyalty to the nation and to the
constitution.

"Federalists," mainly members of the new National Guard, came from all over
France to Paris to join Lafayette and the king in taking such an oath. Some observers
felt the king displayed little enthusiasm for the events, but others, such as Earl Gower,
thought that "the ceremony of the fourteenth was conducted with astonishing regu-
larity." The nobility was conspicuous by its absence. All of Paris, save the nobles, had
helped construct the giant works for the Festival. One group proposed to arrive at
the ceremony "behind a hearse decorated with toads, vipers, and rats, intended 'to
represent the ruin of the clergy and aristocracy.' "[49] However much the Festival of
the Federation, celebrated throughout France on 14 July 1790, emphasized unity, its

The Festival of the Federation 14 July 1790. This massive festival in Paris mirrored those taking place elsewhere in provincial cities, as the entire nation celebrated the anniversary of the fall of the Bastille.

SOURCE: Bibliothèque Nationale, Estampes, coll. De Vinck n. 3761.

underlying message suggested a unity that did not include the aristocracy. Louis, whatever else he may have been, was also one of them.

The happy couple of 14 July 1790 did not last long. Already more radical political groups had begun to organize. The Breton Club, officially renamed (January 1790) the Society of the Friends of the Constitution, but universally known as the Jacobin Club, soon had more than four hundred chapters throughout France. Middle-of-the-road Parisians, like Ruault, feared that the radical club had more real power over events than did the Assembly itself.[50] The Cordeliers Club, led by Parisian radicals such as Jean-Paul Marat and Georges Danton, rallied Lafayette's opponents on the Left, while the monarchical party tried to create a coalition on the Right. Lafayette had reached "the zenith of his influence," as Jefferson's secretary, William Short, put it, "but he made no use of it . . . the time will come when he will repent having not seized that opportunity of giving such a complexion to the revolution as every good citizen ought to desire." Lafayette had many fine qualities, but, as Morris wrote of him in September 1789: "This Man is very much below the Business he has undertaken and if the Sea runs high he will be unable to hold the Helm." In the hurricane swells of 1790–1792, Lafayette, as much as any other individual, helped capsize the ship of state.

The coalition of 1789 suffered from considerable strains in 1790, but it remained strong in many areas. During 1790, many nobles—the Lameth brothers, Mirabeau, Lafayette—continued to play leading roles in national politics, or on departmental councils. The 1791 elections returned very few nobles, indicative of the collapse of the broader coalition of 1790. The Legislative Assembly, also elected in the summer of 1791, contained few nobles or clergymen, a stark contrast to the Constituent Assembly, where they made up about 40 percent of the membership. The Constituent Assembly, in part because of the important presence of nobles and clergymen, had a coalition of monarchists—those who wanted to preserve some power in Louis's hands. The Legislative Assembly had far fewer defenders of the king.

The royal speech of 4 February and the Festival of the Federation provided a somewhat misleading veneer of success. The Constituent Assembly alienated both of the privileged orders by measures such as the Civil Constitution and the legal abolition of nobility (June 1790). In August 1790, provincial events intervened in a critical way: the unpaid troops stationed at Nancy rebelled against their officers. The commander of the nearby garrison at Metz, the marquis de Bouillé, marched on Nancy and stormed the city, leaving 300 dead. After the surrender, Bouillé either hanged or broke on the wheel 33 captured soldiers. The Parisian workers and many middle-class politicians denounced his action, but Lafayette, Bouillé's cousin, defended his relative.[51] The general quickly lost popularity in Paris.

The revolt at Nancy formed part of the nearly universal loss of discipline in the armed forces. Earl Gower reported regularly to his superiors about the inability of the French Navy to find crews to man its ships. The naval base at Brest seems to have been in a state of semi-insurrection for most of 1790 and 1791: "attendance at Constitutional Clubs has occasioned a general disposition among the soldiers to cashier their officers; and, among the many new experiments now making in this country that of an army in which the soldiers are to have the command seems not to be the most promising."[52]

Some of the most important leaders of the Constituent Assembly, men like Antoine Barnave of Dauphiné or Isaac René Le Chapelier of Brittany, sought to create a consensus around the status quo. Barnave and his supporters believed the Revolution had achieved its goals: equality before the law, control of the political process by men of property, elimination of the abuses and "irrationalities" of the Ancien Régime, and a constitution. Most French people from 1790–1791 supported their view, but, as is so often the case in politics, organized groups of dissidents undermined a loosely guarded consensus. The radically revised political order of 1789–1791 created enor-

MIRABEAU

Gabriel Honoré Riqueti, count of Mirabeau, more than any other individual, provided centrist leadership in the National Constituent Assembly. Mirabeau came from a family of old nobility in Provence, but he had been disowned by his family and his order long before the Revolution. He lived the life of a complete wastrel, squandering his wife's fortune (which led to a prison term on the Ile de Ré), running off to Holland with Sophie de Mounier, young wife of an aged president of the *Cour des comptes* of Dôle. The long arm of French justice tracked him down and dragged him back to the prison at Vincennes, where he spent three years (1777–1780). As Furet has remarked, "The count of Mirabeau had taken from the Old Regime an incomparable experience. His future colleagues in the Constituent Assembly were men of law, judges, lawyers. He was a defendant, a prisoner, a litigant."[53]

In the 1780s, Mirabeau became a prominent writer, often working for important politicians, but penning pornography, too. He became friends in Paris with many of the subsequent leaders of the patriot party, such as Brissot; in 1788, he helped found the Society of Friends of Blacks, the French abolitionist organization. Unable to become a deputy of the nobility, he enrolled as a merchant in Marseilles, which elected him to the delegation of the Third Estate. His thundering voice—what Michelet called the "great voice of Paris"—and his imposing presence—Michelet speaks of Mirabeau's huge head, hideous and astound-

ing in its countenance—made him one of the dominant figures of the Assembly.

No man better represented the contrast between deplorable private morality and support for upright public action. At night Mirabeau would carouse and gamble; by day, he argued for the abolition of slavery and the rights of man. He stood forthright against the excesses of royal absolutism—the *lettre de cachet*, which had imprisoned him more than once, was no simple theoretical abuse to Mirabeau—yet he accepted large bribes from the royal Court. The King bought off 200,000 *livres* of his debts, paid him 6,000 *livres* a month (plus 300 more for his copyist!), and promised a further million *livres* at the end of the Assembly. Yet Mirabeau insisted that such payments did not sway him; rather, he felt he led the Court in the direction he wanted to go.

Mirabeau's death, on 2 April 1791, robbed the Assembly of his leadership at a critical moment, and left the king with much less influence in that body. Earl Gower lamented his death because "the Jacobins will no longer be curbed by Mirabeau." All France mourned the loss of the great orator; the Assembly immediately voted to inter his remains at the special shrine for France's heroes, the Panthéon. Gower claimed 28,000 people followed the hearse and that three-fourths of Paris turned out for the procession. After the arrest of Louis XVI , when investigators discovered that Mirabeau had been receiving money from the Court, his remains were ignominiously removed.

---

mous opportunities for organized groups to step into the void and consolidate local, regional or national power. In Paris, Lafayette and several key collaborators cleverly maneuvered to create a hierarchy of professional officers and a core of paid soldiers in a National Guard that would be loyal to its commander, Lafayette. This effort failed: Lafayette once told Morris that the Guard would follow him into battle but that he could not get its members to stand guard duty when it rained.

On the Right, the king and his supporters longed to push the clock backward, to restore some of his power. On the Left, deputies such as Maximilien Robespierre and Jérôme Pétion organized to eliminate all vestiges of monarchical authority. Indeed, by the late spring of 1791 more and more deputies become convinced, like the radical Jacobins whom Young had called enragés in January 1790, that France needed to become a republic.

The king played a critical role in this uncertainty, because he played a double game with everyone. To his most trusted friends, he admitted that he opposed many of the measures in the proposed Constitution, such as the oath for the clergy. By the spring of 1791, he was ready to take critical symbolic actions, such as receiving communion on Palm Sunday from a refractory priest. When the royal family attempted to move from the Tuileries Palace to the château of Saint-Cloud on Paris's outskirts on Easter, the National Guard of Paris surrounded the Tuileries and refused to let the carriages pass. Antiroyal demonstrations in the capital increased; the left-wing press vilified the king, Lafayette, and other "traitors." The king plotted to escape from his *de facto* imprisonment in the capital.

The Revolutionary Press and Radicalization

> *A single instant will suffice to lead to it* [civil war], *if you are sufficiently imbe-cilic not to prevent the flight of the royal family. . . . bring the king and the dauphin within your walls, guard them well, lock up the Austrian, her brother-in-law and the rest of the family.*[54]

> L'Ami du Peuple, 17 December 1790

The revolutionary press played a critical role in the politicization of the people throughout this period. In Paris, the relaxation of censorship in the aftermath of the passage of the *Declaration* accelerated the growth of periodicals: one hundred forty (twenty-seven of them daily newspapers) sprang into being in 1789 alone, and roughly a quarter of these survived for a year or more. In the provinces, the dreary advertising circulars, often called *Affiches* (literally, notices), transformed themselves into real newspapers. First, in May and June, they began to report news from Paris; next, they started to publish major speeches, then political commentaries and summaries of key events in Paris and throughout France. The semi-respectable Parisian press, readily available at cafés throughout the city, ran the gamut from the left-wing *Ami du Peuple* (*Friend of the People*) edited by Jean-Paul Marat to the *Ami du Roi* (*Friend of the King*) of Royou. The less socially acceptable papers included the workers's favorite, *Père Duchesne*, published by the radical Jacques Hébert. The thousands of writers, editors, and illustrators of Paris also published countless pamphlets and broadsheets. These tended to be more radical in their politics (either to Left or Right) and, often, to rely on lewd scandal-mongering. Marie-Antoinette ("The Austrian") provided a particularly popular target for the left-wing publicists, who accused her of a wide range of sexual misdeeds and of political treachery.

The proliferation of published materials led to rapid growth in the printing industry, which boasted over two hundred shops by the late 1790s. The small scale of these printers encouraged radical political thinking, because they had little capital invested in physical plant. The largest printers, like Charles-Joseph Panckoucke (who

Lafayette touches the "res publica" of Marie-Antoinette. This pornographic wood-cut (1790) is typical of the attacks against the queen. This particular image sullies Lafayette, too, and deliberately ignores the fact that he and the queen detested each other.

SOURCE: Bibliothèque Nationale.

had twenty-seven presses in his shop), not surprisingly published less incendiary material; his chief newspaper, the *Moniteur*, served as the paper of record for the successive legislative bodies. The leading papers often had circulations of only 3,000 a day, but the total circulation in Paris ran into two or three hundred thousand. Individual issues of certain papers, such as *Père Duchesne*, could, on occasion, sell 60,000–80,000 copies. The audience far exceeded these numbers, because cafés and reading societies subscribed and many subscribers read articles aloud in the cafés and cabarets throughout France.

The limited figures available on subscribers unsurprisingly suggest that right-wing papers had heavily noble and clerical subscriber lists, while left-wing papers went to lawyers, business people, and artisans. A Jacobin paper such as the *Journal de la Montagne* went heavily (in the provinces) to lawyers and business people; the more radical *Ami du Peuple* was read by business people, government officials, and artisans, who subscribed twice as often to it as to the *Journal*. Professionals, largely lawyers, made up 30 percent of the *Journal*'s subscribers, but only 8 percent of those of the *Ami du Peuple.*

Here we see another split, this one within the Left. In the early stages of the Revolution, up through 1791, the lawyers dominated the Left; starting in 1792, the readers of the *Ami du Peuple,* those involved in commerce and production, began to take over, especially in Paris and other towns. Although lawyers maintained a strong presence on departmental and district councils through 1792 and 1793, they progressively lost ground on town councils, such as those of Caen or Limoges. They had led sectional assemblies in Paris in 1790 and 1791, but rapidly gave way to small- and medium-scale manufacturers in 1792 and after. The revolutionary commissioners of 1793 in the section of Faubourg-Montmartre, for example, included not one lawyer among the fifteen men; in the section of Gravilliers, in 1792 and 1793, only one of the twenty-six commissioners was a lawyer. Haberdashers, tailors, sawyers, paper manufacturers, and others involved in production led the section.

The Flight to Varennes, 20 June 1791

> *Stop or I'll fire into the coach.*
>
> The postmaster of Ste-Ménéhould
>
> *In that case, stop.*[55]
>
> Louis XVI

What did these men read in the *Ami du Peuple* and similar publications? Marat tirelessly attacked the king, seeing an aristocratic plot behind every difficulty. Throughout the winter of 1790–1791 and into the spring of 1791, he predicted the king would attempt to flee Paris. On June 20, 1791, in one of the decisive events of the Revolution, Louis proved him right. Louis had well disguised his intentions, even issuing a formal declaration to other European monarchs about his support for the Revolution. He conveniently left behind a manifesto explaining his motives, stressing that the *cahiers* of 1789 had given the deputies a clear mandate: "the making of the laws should be done in concert with the King." He stated, accurately, that "in violation of this clause, the Assembly placed the King entirely outside the constitution."[56] In a long and rambling text, Louis essentially demanded back some of his authority. He accepted the voting of taxes and shared responsibility for the promulgation of laws, but he presented himself as the people's "father, your best friend," who would save them from the factionalism to which the Assembly was prone. Even he used the language of the Revolution to attack it:

> What pleasure will he not take in forgetting all his personal injuries, and in seeing himself again in your midst, when a constitution, which he will have accepted freely, will cause our holy religion to be respected, the government to be established on a firm foundation and to be useful by its actions, the property and position of every person to be disturbed no longer, and laws no longer to be violated with impunity, and, finally, liberty to be established on firm and immovable foundations.

Louis and his family did not get away. Although they slipped neatly through the lines around the palace, a series of little delays made the journey slower than expected. The military escort arranged for the king grew tired of waiting and retired. Finally, the local postmaster of the town of Sainte-Ménéhould recognized the coach and its

The return of the king from Varennes. Surrounded by the National Guard, Louis and his family return to a sullen Paris.

Source: © Gianni Dagli Orti/Corbis.

occupants. He raced ahead to the tiny town of Varennes, where he called out the National Guard, soon joined by the entire population. The Assembly sent deputies and troops to bring them back; four days later, the procession entered a sullen Paris, whose crowds refused to remove their hats as the king passed and who shouted, "Long live the law" and "Long live the nation." On the morning after the flight, thousands of Parisians had entered the unlocked Tuileries, wandering its hall. Ruault, an eyewitness, states that they took only one item: the king's portrait. They tore it to shreds.

Louis claimed that he intended only to go to Montmédy, near the border, to be under the protection of that same marquis de Bouillé who had massacred the mutineers of Nancy. His opponents believed he intended to flee abroad and to organize a monarchist crusade against France. Certainly Marie-Antoinette conducted secret negotiations with her relatives in Austria to do the latter, and the king's brother, the Count of Provence, who did make good on his escape, declared that Louis had intended precisely such a course of action. The king, a traitor to the Nation: what would the Assembly do?

The vast majority of French people in July 1791 believed in a constitutional monarchy. The Assembly created a document that met with widespread approval, but the king's flight greatly exacerbated the split between the moderate mass of citizens and a strident, urban minority of radicals. In most quarters, public respect for

THE LONGEST NIGHT: THE FLIGHT TO VARENNES, 20–21 JUNE 1791

Louise-Elisabeth de Croÿ-Havré, duchess of Tourzel, was the governess of the royal children during the French Revolution. She miraculously survived the Terror (Gower initially thought her dead in the September Massacres of 1792) and left memoirs of her times of troubles with the royal children. She witnessed firsthand all of the great events, from the March to Versailles through the trials of the king and queen. Let us listen in to some of her reminiscences of the Flight to Varennes, on which she accompanied the royal family.

> I was on pins and needles, even though I showed no anxiety, when Madame said to me, "There is M. de La Fayette." I hid Mgr the Dauphin under my skirts, and reassured them both that they could be quite at ease. I was certainly not so . . . Messieurs Bailly and La Fayette had come to attend the king going to bed, and disputed with him; in order not to give them any suspicions, that prince pretended to be in no hurry to go to bed. The king thus had to undress and go to bed; he then had to redo his toilette and put on a wig, to disguise himself. . . . When

he had climbed into the carriage, he held her [the Queen] in his arms, kissed her, and repeated, "How happy I am to see you have arrived!" . . .

> We had to put up with several little incidents which prove only too well that the slightest causes influence great events. M. de Fersen, worried that the bodyguards had taken a route other than that indicated to them, was forced to re-cross the barrier to rejoin them, and preferred to take a longer route to avoid inconveniences, which made us lose another half-hour, which, added to the three-quarters of an hour delay in the king's bedchamber, put us an hour and a half behind schedule. . . . To make matters worse, the horses of the king's carriage fell twice between Nintré and Châlons; all of the harnesses broke, and we lost more than an hour repairing this disaster.

> [The group changed from the broken-down small carriage to a large one at the barrier of Clichy.] We traveled in a great, commodious berlin carriage, but one that had nothing extraordinary about it . . . I was supposed to be the mistress, under the name of the baroness of Korff; the King passed for my valet, the Queen for my lady's maid, and Madame Elisabeth [the king's aunt] for the nursemaid. . . .

the Assembly increased after the king's flight, because they reacted so effectively and so expeditiously to the situation. They suspended the king, required all ministers to report directly to them, and sent a delegation to lead the royal family back to Paris. The urban radicals, such as the Cordeliers Club in Paris, reacted very differently. They denounced the king. The Cordeliers, leading a delegation of 30,000 Parisians, presented the Assembly with a petition demanding a republic or, at least, a plebiscite on the king's position. The Assembly demurred, deciding instead to rule that Louis could be reinstated as king if he agreed to accept the constitution. Departmental councils wrote praising the Assembly's action; in September 1791, they similarly lauded the king's acceptance (13 September) of the constitution. Louis, ever the vacillator, had taken ten days to do so. In Paris, the Left took his ten-day delay as the sign for renewed action.

Events throughout the summer had cast Louis in an ever dimmer light. When the Cordeliers organized a demonstration in favor of a "new organization of the executive power" at the Champs de Mars (17 July), Lafayette's 10,000 National Guardsmen fired on the 50,000 demonstrators, killing fifty, wounding scores, and arresting more than

(CONTINUED)

"At last I am out of that city of Paris," said this good prince, "where I have had to drink so much bitterness. Be assured that once I have my butt in the saddle, I will be very different than you have seen me until now." He read to all of us the memoir he had left in Paris to be brought to the Assembly; and he rejoiced in advance of the happiness of which he hoped to give France a taste, of the return of his brothers and his faithful servants, and of the possibility of reestablishing religion and of repairing the evils [done by the Assembly]. . . . Looking at his watch, which marked 8 o'clock, he said, "La Fayette is currently quite personally embarrassed."

. . . Arriving at Pont-de-Sommervel, how great was our sadness and our anxiety when the couriers reported to us that they could find no trace of the troop [awaiting us] nor anyone who could give us any indication about them . . . But our happiness was at an end. The Heavens, which wished to try our August and unhappy sovereigns to the end, allowed the duke of Choiseul to completely lose his head. The enterprise was well beyond his capacities. His heart was pure, and he would have died to save his King, but he did not have that calm courage and tranquility that allows one cold-bloodedly to judge events and the means to remedy unforeseen circumstances. [The duchess goes on to explain how Choiseul, worried that the King was more than two hours late, decided that the enterprise had been called off and sent home all the troops that were to escort the King on his voyage. The carriage soon reached Ste-Ménéhould.]

M. d'Andouins, captain in Choiseul's regiment, came up to the carriage and whispered to me, "the measures have been badly taken; I will move away so as not to arouse suspicion." These few words pierced our hearts; but there was nothing to do but keep on our route . . .

Evil would have it that the infamous Drouet, son of the Ste-Menehould postmaster, ardent patriot, stood at that moment at the door and, having had the curiosity to look in the carriage, thought that he had recognized the King and positively assured himself of it by comparing the face of that prince with [the portrait on] an *assignat* that he had in his pocket. [Drouet rode ahead to Varennes, where he alerted the local patriots, who stopped the carriage.][57]

two hundred fifty people. Public opinion in Paris turned definitely against Lafayette and moved sharply leftward. A little more than a month later, an event outside of France sharply accentuated that trend: the Emperor Leopold (Marie-Antoinette's nephew) and King Frederick William II of Prussia issued the Declaration of Pillnitz, which called on all European powers to restore Louis XVI to his full rights as King of France. The Revolutionaries now could be certain of the hostility of Austria, Prussia, and the Pope. Powerless to do anything against the first two, they legalized the seizure of the French possessions of the latter, Avignon and the Comtat.

THE LEGISLATIVE ASSEMBLY AND THE FALL OF THE MONARCHY

What patriot, what aristocrat could ever write that he who so villainously turned his back on us on June 21st has suddenly become our friend on September 14th?

Nicolas Ruault, to his brother, 20 October 1791

The Constitution of 1791 created a new France, much of which had already taken root before the vote approving the constitution itself (summer 1791). Many of their greatest reforms became permanent: legal equality; the guarantee of such civil rights as freedom of expression, of religion, and of assembly; the abolition of feudalism and legal privilege; the creation of popularly elected regional, local, and municipal governments; the metric system of weights and measures. Some innovations, such as legalized divorce and greater civil rights for women, survived for only a few years. Indeed, many of the civil rights existed more in theory than in practice under later authoritarian rulers, such as Napoleon. In an immediate sense, however, French people strongly supported every major element of the new constitution, save one. The Flight to Varennes had created one intractable constitutional question: how could a king who so violently opposed the new order be trusted with its implementation?

In the last year of its existence, the Constituent Assembly had played an elaborate game with the king. He spent a lot of money to get support from key leaders in the Assembly, above all Mirabeau, and he also dangled control over prospective appointments to ministries in front of key deputies. From July 1790 to April 1791, the king effectively played off Lafayette against Mirabeau, using their great influence over the Assembly to try to preserve some of his own power and to counteract the authority of the radical Jacobins. Already in January 1791, Earl Gower had noted the increasing hostility of the various parties within the Assembly.

> The violence of party is at present so great in the National Assembly that no terms of abuse are omitted by the speakers on either side, and the style of language which used to be confined to the markets, and therefore called *le langage des halles*, is now very frequently adopted in that place.[58]

The rhetorical violence progressively stepped up, especially after the king's flight.

The death of Mirabeau (4/2) meant that the king had to switch to the brothers Alexandre and Charles de Lameth, Adrien Duport, and Antoine Barnave, a quartet whom their contemporaries called "the triumvirate." They belonged to the Jacobin Club, but followed policies to ensure the consolidation of the Revolution's gains. They had strong antimonarchist credentials from the debates of 1789–1790, because they had led the fight to limit the king to a suspensive veto and had also lobbied for a single chamber legislature, to prevent aristocratic influence. By 1791, however, they sought an alliance with some aristocrats and the king, because they wanted to avoid further destabilizing democratization. Barnave summed their view in mid-July: "any new step forward would be a culpable act . . . a further step in the direction of equality would mean the destruction of property."

Inside the Jacobin Club, other elements reacted vigorously against these compromises. The question of rights for people of mixed race in French colonies led to a violent debate in May 1791, in which Barnave and his group supported the whites, while the new Left, led by Robespierre, agitated for the rights of mulattoes.[59] The faction led by Barnave seceded (16 July) from the Jacobins and formed a new political club, named after the convent in which it met, the Feuillants. Lafayette, too, threw his support to this new group.

By September 1791, civil disturbances had broken out in many areas. Catholics and Protestants fought bloody battles in the Midi; anti-noble and anti-urban riots broke out in Quercy and the Auvergne; peasant bands formed in Brittany and the west; parts of Alsace seemed ready to seek the protection of the Emperor. The implementation of the Civil Constitution of the Clergy provided a flash point for this agitation. Supporters of the new order sought to intimidate parish priests into signing the oath of loyalty to the new constitution; they physically drove out priests who refused to sign. The active hostility against non-juring priests soon led to a counterattack against juring ones. Peasants in many regions drove off priests who had taken the oath. Although many non-juring regions, such as the Vannetais, had pre-existing grievances against the Assembly, the implementation of the oath for priests provided an effective rallying point for discontent of all kinds.

The takeover of municipal governments by the commercial and manufacturing interests led to conflicts between those governments and departmental ones, still dominated by lawyers and landowners. Moreover, the commercial and manufacturing group had profound splits within its own ranks. In June, the National Assembly had passed the Le Chapelier Law banning workers' and producers' organizations, which outraged guild members and journeymen, who lost their associations, the *compagnonnages*. Guild members tended to maintain informal bonds in place of the formal ones, and the *compagnonnages* survived, illegally, into the nineteenth century, but the Le Chapelier Law increased the militancy of the *sans-culottes* artisans in every town in France, above all in Paris.

The greater militancy of the Paris *sans-culottes* provided the increasingly mercantile leadership of the sectional assemblies with a large, militant, readily mobilized force. The more moderate legal men, often allied with the Feuillants, had steadily lost ground to the merchants and manufacturers in elected assemblies: in 1791, legal men dropped to a mere 13.6 percent of the electors, less than half the percentage of 1790. In section after section, the average age of those chosen as electors declined from year to year, as did the percentage of those who had been chosen previously, which dropped from just under half in 1791 to less than 20 percent in 1792.

The new national representative body, the Legislative Assembly, also differed markedly from its predecessor. The active citizens had met in June 1791, that is before the king's flight, and chosen electors. The electors met between 29 August and 5 September to choose the new Assembly. Virtually all of the new deputies held positions in local administration. Eighty percent of the deputies from one sample of 17 departments served as local officials, most often on departmental councils.[60] As in the local elections of Paris, the national elections of 1791 highlighted the rise of a new generation to political power. Whereas the average age of the deputies chosen in 1789 was about forty-five, half of the deputies elected in 1791 were under thirty. In the Legislative Assembly, as in local assemblies, men with substantially less stake in the Ancien Régime, those committed to the principles of a new order that rejected everything about the old one, became far more prominent.

The old leaders of the National Assembly continued to hold sway behind the scenes because none of these new deputies had national experience. The Feuillants divided into two groups, one led by the Lameths, Duport, and Barnave, and the other by Lafayette. Together, these groups had the allegiance of three hundred forty-five deputies. The more radical Jacobins, led by Maximilien Robespierre, Jacques-Pierre Brissot de Warville, and Pierre Vergniaud, could claim one hundred thirty-five. Control of the Legislative Assembly thus rested with the uncommitted group of about three hundred deputies.

Many observers in September 1791 believed that the Legislative Assembly would be unable to control the situation because the new state lacked the means for effective action. Unable to collect the new taxes, the Legislative Assembly issued more and more *assignats*, which declined to 63 percent of face value by January 1792. Discipline in the army remained poor; many of its officers, upset at the treatment of the king after his flight, did little to disguise their hostility to the new regime. Between September and December 1791, more than two thousand army officers emigrated from France, bringing the total who left between July 1789 and December 1791 to over 6,000. These desertions left entire units without trained officers.

No money, no army: what was the Legislative Assembly to do? One faction wanted to increase the power of the king. After all, the chaotic situation of the fall of 1791 required strong executive action, and the king was, for good or for ill, the executive branch. This faction gave out feelers to the Court and to the aristocracy. In the climate of the time, any hint of cooperation with the aristocracy created political problems. The second faction believed the king could not be trusted. The most radical among them, such as the leaders of the Cordeliers Club—Danton, Marat, Desmoulins—demanded the deposition of the king and the creation of a republic. The Legislative Assembly sought a middle course, taking a hard line on some issues important to the radicals—thus passing laws demanding that the Counts of Provence and Artois return to France and setting a deadline for all emigrés to return or face confiscation of property and rights—but insinuating Feuillant-backed candidates into the ministries. The king vetoed the two decrees and similarly vetoed a law requiring priests to take an oath to the Constitution of 1791 in place of one to the Civil Constitution of the Clergy. In the midst of this standoff between the king and the Feuillant leadership, the Lameth brothers and Barnave left Paris in disgust, effectively decapitating the Feuillant club. Gower wrote ominously on 2 December 1791:

> An universal expectation of an approaching crisis prevails. Every body acknowledges that France cannot long continue in it's [*sic*] present state; but what the *dénouement* of this tragi-comedy will be remains to be known.

The Revolt on Saint-Domingue

... this day [31 March 1792] *15,000 slaves rose up ... we have abandoned our properties, which are in the power of our slaves, who no longer work; it's the mulattoes who have pushed them to it.*[61]

M. Clausson to Guittard de Floriban, 23 April 1792

The Feuillant leadership had alienated the Left and the popular classes in Paris by the Le Chapelier Law, by the Champs-de-Mars massacre, and by a brief effort to suppress the political clubs and the radical press (August 1791). The king's veto of the three decrees in the fall of 1791 showed that they did not have support on the Right, either. Events outside France made the situation even more precarious. The critical French colony of Saint-Domingue, wracked for two years by disputes among its white and mulatto elites, erupted in revolt. The whites sent a delegation to the Estates General, using an electoral process that excluded the many free blacks and the mulattoes, who owned one-third of the plantation property, a quarter of the slaves and of the land. Mirabeau strongly objected to seating the white delegation:

> We will demand of them . . . whether they intend to rank their Negroes in the class of men or that of beasts of burden. If the colonies desire that their Negroes be considered men, let them free them, let them permit them to vote, let them allow their Negroes to hold office. In the opposite case, we will ask them to notice that in apportioning the number of deputies to the population of France we have not counted the quantity of our horses and our mules; in the same way, the claim of the colonists [for 20 seats, based on Saint-Domingue's total population] . . . is ridiculous.[62]

Mirabeau's forces won a partial victory: the whites got only six seats.

As for the mulattoes, they, too, sent deputies to France. The Society of Friends of Blacks, an abolitionist group in France that included such important figures as Condorcet and Brissot, led a campaign to seat the mulatto deputies alongside the white ones. Mirabeau and the Abbé Grégoire tried to get them seated in the Assembly, demanding to know how the whites could deny representation to blacks and mulattoes who had met the qualifications for being active citizens. The Assembly tabled the measure.

In response, one of the mulatto leaders, Vincent Ogé, returned to Saint-Domingue and led a revolt. He, his brother, and Jean-Baptiste Chavannes, who had fought in the American Revolution, briefly seized control of the town of Grande-Rivière. The white authorities moved swiftly against them, executed the leaders and displayed their severed heads at major towns (February 1791). Six months later, the slaves took revenge for the murdered men. A revolt in the northern part of the colony burned fourteen hundred sugar and coffee plantations to the ground and wiped out their white population. The revolt spread quickly to the other parts of the colony, laying waste to town and plantation alike. The French government never regained control, although in 1794 one of its commissioners, Léger Sonthonax, legally validated what the slaves's own actions had accomplished: emancipation.[63]

The loss of Saint-Domingue, the riots on Tobago, Martinique, and Guadaloupe—"in truth, it is difficult to say in what part of the French dominions there are not commotions"—crippled the French economy.[64] France had imported something like 180 million pounds of sugar a year in the late 1780s, an amount worth about 75 million *livres*. France re-exported most of this sugar to other parts of Europe (above all Holland and Hamburg). Total trade with the West Indies may have involved as much as 500 million *livres* per year, and the re-export of sugar to the rest of Europe a massive sum as well. The slave, sugar, and coffee trades provided the foundation of prosperity of great ports like Bordeaux (sugar), Nantes (slaves), La

Rochelle, and, to some degree, Marseilles (sugar). Orléans, Bordeaux, La Rochelle, and Marseilles had many refineries. Orléans alone had twenty-seven, which gave employment to six hundred fifty workers. All told, the refineries there poured 1.3 million *livres* into the local economy, either in wages (about 300,000) or in purchasing goods. With the loss of Saint-Domingue's sugar in the fall of 1791, the economic situation in Orléans and Nantes quickly turned desperate. When refiners, shippers, and merchants went bankrupt in these cities or in Bordeaux or Marseilles, they took many other suppliers and backers with them. Thus perished the one sector of the nonagricultural economy that survived intact the cataclysms of 1789.

Agitation on the islands continued from 1791 onward. The white planters of Saint-Domingue, outraged at the Constituent Assembly's mild efforts on behalf of free blacks, stalked out of the Assembly and threatened to declare themselves independent. The initial success of the black rebellion in northern Saint-Domingue led to violent repression, but the seed of rebellion soon spread. French troops and sailors often refused to sail to the West Indies, in part because of the horrifying levels of mortality (due to disease) they suffered there. The mulattoes fought for their political rights, in the name of those principles that motivated the French deputies of 1789. Slaves fought for their freedom, too—fought to make Rousseau's dictum, "man is born free," a living reality. The political climate of 1791 did not bode well for blacks in the West Indies, in part because several leaders of the Assembly owned plantations. The inability to achieve a workable solution in the islands added another element of instability to French politics.

Diplomatic Developments

I find that it is risking a lot: we shall see everything that comes of it.

Guittard de Floriban, reacting to the declaration
of war against Austria, 20 April 1792

Diplomatic developments outside France also affected the course of the Revolution. In eastern Europe, the great powers—Russia, Austria, and Prussia—sought to take advantage of France's weakness. They greedily devoured Poland, partitioned in 1792 and 1795. The Poles initially had the temerity to protest. Their nobility, a far larger group than in the West, constituting perhaps 10 percent of the population, tried to create a new basis for their Commonwealth. In 1791, they promulgated the liberal Constitution of the Third of May, based on the principles of the Declaration of the Rights of Man and of the Citizen, albeit with a different definition of citizenship, which they extended only to nobles and to some town dwellers. When Russia invaded Poland to put a stop to such shenanigans, the other powers, preoccupied with the situation in France, did nothing.

France's example disturbed Western Europe as well. Morris wrote to George Washington in January 1790 that "never perhaps were the Affairs of Europe in a Situation which admits so little of forming any solid Opinion; and this from the spreading of what is called the french disease: Revolt. Hungary, Part of Germany, Italy and

Savoy with France and Flanders are already in different stages of that Disease. Poland is constitutionally afflicted with it." Great Britain looked with trepidation on the sight, worried especially that France would take control of the southern Netherlands. Beginning in 1793, those fears came true. Holland, too, which had had its own abortive revolution in 1787, became less and less stable.

The areas immediately around France faced particular difficulties. The small German states, above all the ecclesiastical electorates of Trier and Mainz, had the special problem of the French émigré communities, whose counterrevolutionary activities had become a major bone of contention by fall 1791. The Legislative Assembly demanded that Louis XVI put pressure on these small states to expel the émigrés, in order to stop their support for counterrevolutionary activity in Alsace and southern France. The Legislative Assembly had to intervene to prevent patriots in Provence from marching on Arles, a center of counterrevolution. This intervention proved to be a temporary respite; in March 1792, a motley volunteer army of 7,000 men laid siege to Arles and captured the city. Parallel peasant rebellions, often focused on anti-noble activity, broke out throughout the region. Peasants in the Midi persecuted refractory priests, grain dealers, and others. Peasants in Brittany and the Vendée, in contrast, turned against juring priests. The first of many Breton rural rebellions began in the winter of 1792.

Louis XVI, under heavy pressure from the Legislative Assembly, sent letters to the Elector–Archbishop of Triers, demanding he expel the emigrés. On 6 January 1792, the Elector legally did so, but his half-hearted action did not mollify the war party in France. Increasingly, Brissot and the leaders of the Assembly demanded war against the German states. Emperor Leopold II massed troops on his side of the border (February 1792). Counterrevolutionary forces everywhere—outside of France, in Brittany and the West, in the Midi—redoubled their efforts. People from all sides wanted war. The patriots believed war would get rid of all the "conspiracies" and would enable them to get firm control of society. The king believed France would lose the war and he would get back his power; the emigrés felt a foreign invasion would restore them to power. Only a few political leaders, Maximilien Robespierre chief among them, spoke out against the war.

In April 1792, the Legislative Assembly declared war on Leopold II. Louis dismissed his Feuillant ministers and brought in members of the Jacobin Club, allies of Brissot. The disorganized French armies immediately suffered defeats; one army lynched its general after a loss. The Austrians waited for the Prussian army to appear. Frederick William II of Prussia declared war only on 21 May. Emigrés soon marched behind the Austrians and Prussians, sure they would control France. The Allied armies, however, dallied near the frontiers. French generals conducted secret negotiations with their Allied counterparts. The king and queen secretly wrote to the Allies, encouraging them to overthrow the Revolution. The Legislative Assembly responded by issuing a new decree exiling non-juring priests and by another to raise 20,000 fresh National Guardsmen to replace the royal guards; the king vetoed both decrees (11 June 1792). Everywhere in France, the situation spun out of control. The value of the *assignats* began to tumble. and unrest spread even more widely in the provinces.

In mid-June, Louis again dismissed his ministers, touching off a march to the Tuileries by the workers of the Saint-Antoine suburb. Seven thousand of them paraded in front of the king, who sat wearing a red cap, symbol of the revolutionary workers. Louis listened to two hours of insults and threats, but never wavered; he even drank a toast to the health of the Nation. The disappointed *sans-culottes* finally went home. Eight days later, Lafayette appeared at the Assembly, seeking a decree against the rioters of 20 June. The Assembly refused. The king and queen distanced themselves from the general, who returned to the front.

Federation Day approached, and with it thousands of provincial National Guardsmen began to appear in Paris for the festivities. Unsure what to do in the crisis, the Legislative Assembly created a new legal device, the official declaration that "the fatherland is in danger," enabling it to institute permanent sessions of all governing bodies and to enlist National Guardsmen into the regular army. These Guardsmen tended to come from the most radical of the cities, such as Brest or Marseilles. The volunteers from the latter arrived in Paris in late July, singing "The Song of the Army of the Rhine." Parisians, much taken by its blood-curdling cries for patriotism, its announcement that "the hour of glory has arrived," and its stirring cadences, rechristened it, "The Marseillaise."

The End of the Monarchy, 10 August 1792

Like the ewe that watches the fight between the dogs and the wolves, I rooted for the former.[65]

Rétif de la Bretonne, watching the
storming of the Tuileries, 10 August 1792

The Parisian sectional assemblies, like other government bodies, began to meet on a permanent basis, starting on 25 July. On 20 July, the section of Théâtre-Français on the Left Bank became the first to admit passive citizens to its meetings. Soon, another half dozen radical sections had done the same. The commander of the Allied army marching on Paris, the duke of Brunswick, declared that he would exact "exemplary and forever memorable vengeance" on Paris, if the king were to be harmed.[66] One section after another in Paris now called for the king's removal and the declaration of a republic. In early August, some of the key leaders of the Legislative Assembly spoke up on his behalf; the sections responded by denouncing the Assembly as well. Newspapers openly called for an assault on the Tuileries palace, where the royal family lived.

On 10 August, the assault took place. Thousands of Parisian *sans-culottes*, aided by National Guardsmen from Paris and from the provinces, stormed the palace. Mme de Tourzel claims that Pétion replaced the National Guards on duty at the last minute, with companies on whom he could completely rely. The royal family sought asylum early in the morning at the Legislative Assembly. Some one hundred eighty Guardsmen died in the assault, as did six hundred of the nine hundred Swiss Guards defending the king—many of the latter slaughtered after the king had ordered them to lay down their arms. Vergniaud took the podium to announce the death of the monarchy:

THE MARSEILLAISE

Allons, enfants de la patrie,	Rise up children of the fatherland,
Le jour de gloire est arrivé	The day of glory has arrived!
Contre nous de la tyrannie	Against us the bloody standard
L'étendard sanglant est levé!	Of tyranny has been raised!
Entendez vous dans les campagnes	Do you hear in the countryside
Mugir ces féroces soldats?	Those ferocious soldiers cry out?
Ils viennent jusque dans nos bras	They come right into our midst
Égorger nos fils, nos compagnes	To cut the throats of our sons, our wives.
Aux armes, citoyens,	To arms, citizens,
Formez vos bataillons!	Form your battalions!
Marchons! Marchons!	March! March!
Qu'un sang impur	Let an impure blood
Abreuve nos sillons!	Water our furrows!

English translation adapted from: E. Kennedy, *A Cultural History of the French Revolution* (New Haven: Yale University Press, 1989), 277–278.

> The dangers to the fatherland, which are at their worst, come about because of the defiance inspired by the conduct of the head of the executive power in a war undertaken against liberty and our national independence. Addresses from all parts of the empire demand the revocation of the authority granted to Louis XVI; and the Assembly, not wishing to augment its own power by any usurpation of power, proposes that you decree the establishment of a national Convention whose modalities of convocation it will propose; the organization of a new ministry, with the existing ministers provisionally conserving their power until its nomination.[67]

The Legislative Assembly suspended the king, fired his new ministers, and restored the earlier ministry, adding to it the radical leader Georges Danton, the chief architect of the assault of 10 August. So ended the Capetian monarchy founded in 987.

No longer a monarchy, yet still not a republic; a lame duck Legislative Assembly in power; enemy armies poised on the eastern border; peasant rebels in arms in the west: what was France to do? The Legislative Assembly took decisive action. With the king now out of the way, they quickly put into effect the decrees against refractory priests, giving them two weeks to leave the country. The Assembly next accepted Vergniaud's proposal to convoke a convention to draw up a new constitution. Despite the chaos, France held the first round of elections on 27 August, even with the expansion of the electorate by "universal" manhood suffrage, only about 20 percent of the voters turned out for the primary assemblies. The second stage of the process, the electoral assemblies to choose the deputies, took place in early September.

In Paris, workers, on the authority granted by their sectional assemblies, started arresting priests, locking many of them in local convents converted into prisons. The

Prussians invaded France, capturing Longwy and driving toward the capital. The British government informed its French counterpart that it hoped "nothing would happen to the King or his Family because that would escite the Indignation of all Europe." The American ambassador, Morris, took the British note to mean that they "will make War immediately if the Treatment of the King be such to call for or justify Measures of Extremity."

Panic stricken, the government, at Danton's direction, introduced "domiciliary visits," which produced three thousand new detainees in Paris's prisons. Radical papers called for death to traitors and claimed evidence of conspiracies everywhere. When news arrived on 2 September that the Prussians had passed Verdun, the last fortress between them and Paris, the *sans-culottes* took matters into their own hands, executing more than eleven hundred people. They started with about two hundred non-juring priests, moved on to some prominent nobles and the remaining Swiss Guards, and finally to common criminals. The September Massacres had echoes outside of Paris: one crowd butchered the duke of La Rochefoucauld, being taken to Paris for trial, in front of his wife and mother. Crowds at Reims, on the Prussian line of march, massacred non-juring priests. The death of people like La Rochefoucauld, a liberal noble who had distinguished himself in his calls for the abolition of seigneurialism and in his opposition to slavery, signaled the radical triumph. His old friend Lafayette escaped only because he was not in Paris. Sure he was to be arrested and executed, the marquis crossed the lines and was captured by the Prussians.

On 20 and 21 September, two events drew these matters to a close. On 20 September, at Valmy, the French army, led by General Dumouriez, defeated the Prussians, who immediately withdrew back to the Rhine. The next day, in Paris, the new Convention met. Ambassador Morris ironically wrote in his diary: "Nothing new this Day except the Convention has met and declar'd they will have no King in France." George Washington, although farther away, had a better sense of the meaning of the events set in motion on 10 August. He wrote to Morris on 20 October: "We can only repeat the sincere wish that much happiness may arise to the French nation, and to mankind in general, out of the severe evils which are inseparable from so important a revolution." Yet the Revolution, and the evils, had only just begun.

Notes

1. George Washington, *Writings*, ed. John Rhodehamel (New York: Literary Classics of the United States, 1997), 780–781.

2. A. Young, *Travels during the years 1787, 1788 and 1789* (London: W. Richardson, 1794), I, 117–118.

3. M. Lhéritier, ed., *Les débuts de la Révolution à Bordeaux d'aprés les Tablettes manuscrites de Pierre Bernadau* (Paris: Société d'histoire de la Révolution Française, 1919), 101.

4. Young, *Travels,* I, 174–175.

5. *The Letters of Lafayette to Washington, 1777–1799,* ed. L. Gottschalk (Philadelphia: American Philosophical Society, 1976), 346, letter of 12 January 1790. Lafayette wrote these letters in English.

6. *Letters of Lafayette to Washington,* 347, letter of 17 March 1790.

7. In 1789, many had clamored for the duke of Orléans to take Louis XVI's place, but the duke had lost favor by October 1789, as we shall see.

8. Cultural matters are treated in Chapter 15.

9. J. Chalon, ed., *Mémoires de Madame la duchesse de Tourzel, gouvernante des enfants de France de 1789 à 1795* (Paris: Mercure de France, 1969), 33.

10. Interested readers can follow their work in detail in G. Chinard, ed., *The Letters of Lafayette and Jefferson* (Baltimore and Paris: The Johns Hopkins University Press and Les Belles Lettres, 1929), esp. 136–142. Jefferson's official title was minister-in-residence.

11. Young, *Travels,* I, 189.

12. The United States Constitution does not define "people." In twelve of the thirteen original states, it meant "adult white male property owners," but the document did not say that. The U.S. Constitution and its amendments do not say who can vote, but who cannot be denied that right.

13. Bernadau, *La Révolution à Bordeaux,* 100.

14. By 1789, most of parish priests got only a portion of the tithe from its owner, often a bishop or cathedral chapter, but that portion was their main source of income.

15. Young, *Travels,* I, 148.

16. Ibid., 81 and 85.

17. At this stage in French political life, levels of "democracy" refer only to males. All elections banned women as voters and were thus fundamentally undemocratic.

18. Such caution made sense in a conversation with an outsider, to whom they would have been unlikely to reveal any plans they had made.

19. Young, *Travels,* I, 160. Young here uses stereotypical imagery drawn from the memories of the Jacquerie. We have virtually no evidence of peasants raping noble women and very few seigneurs lost their lives. The peasants did burn the papers and, on occasion, the château.

20. Citations are from relevant dates in Young, *Travels,* I, which is organized chronologically.

21. P. Jones, *The Peasantry in the French Revolution* (Cambridge: Cambridge University Press, 1988), 80, table 3. I have combined the totals for nobles (27) and their agents (8).

22. The Church owned 40 percent of the land in the bishopric of Cambrai, as against a nationwide average of about 10 percent.

23. N. Retif de la Bretonne, *Les Nuits Révolutionnaires, 1789–1793*, ed. M. Dorigny (Paris: Les Éditions de Paris, 1989), 55. This work is a selection of texts from Retif's much longer *Les Nuits de Paris.*

24. Some observers, like Rétif de la Bretonne, suggest that prostitutes and criminals (including men disguised as women) played a significant role in the march, but historians generally agree that such people formed a tiny minority of the marchers. Much evidence exists—including police testimony by many of the marchers—to buttress his remarks that the market women (les Dames de la Halle) forced every woman they encountered to join the march.

25. Young, *Travels*, I, 154.

26. P. Burley, *Witness to the Revolution. American and British Commentators in France, 1788–1794* (London: Weidenfeld & Nicolson, 1989), 84.

27. *La Révolution Française à Rochefort*, 94–95.

28. This system directly parallels the American Electoral College and the original indirect election of U.S. Senators.

29. Survey histories of the Revolution, with the notable exceptions of Sutherland and Palmer, typically suggest that the three-days wages restriction eliminated 45 percent of the male population from the voting rolls, and claim that only 50,000 men were eligible to be electors. My research on local tax rolls shows that in 1789, 75 percent of rural taxpayers contributed three days' wages or more. Yet Lille, a town of about 66,000, had only 5,464 eligible voters. Studies of other towns show a similarly limited pool of active citizens. The elections of 1790–1791 actually followed closely the rules of 1789. Malcolm Crook, the leading expert on Revolutionary elections, suggests that more people voted in 1789 than in later elections. He also notes that roughly 50,000 participated in electoral assemblies each year, a figure that led to the second error.

30. Here again, the Assembly departed radically from the ideas of Rousseau, who specifically denounced the use of representatives.

31. A. Soboul, *The French Revolution* (New York, 1974; original French edition 1962), 194–195. Criminal cases proceeded through a separate system, one that had local police courts, district ones, and a departmental Criminal Court. The reforms also created juries, chosen by lot from among a list taken from among the active citizens, although not including them all.

32. Ch.–L. Chassin, *Les Élections et les Cahiers de Paris en 1789* (Paris: Jouast et Sigaux, 1888), 4 vols., III, 333 ff.

33. Young, *Travels*, I, 192–193.

34. Protestants got civil rights in 1789, the Jews of Alsace only in 1791. One manifestation of the extension of civil rights to Jews came with the sale of church property. The Sephardic Jews of Bordeaux made extensive use of their new civil status to buy up such lands.

35. Ruault, letter to his brother, 8 August 1789, 162–163.

36. Cited in F. Aftalion, *The French Revolution, an Economic Interpretation*, trans. M. Thom (Cambridge: Cambridge University Press, 1990), 63.

37. Although the Assembly did not abolish teaching and charitable orders, it did prohibit them from recruiting new members, essentially dooming them to slow extinction.

38. Chassin, *Les Élections*, ii, 436.

39. Tackett, *Becoming a Revolutionary*, 71.

40. The *cahiers* of 1789 pointed to future problems over the issue of Protestants. Even relatively liberal *cahiers* from local clergy demanded that Catholicism remain the state church and adopted an intolerant position toward non-Catholics.

41. Sutherland, *Revolution and Counter-Revolution*, 110–113. Sutherland integrates the extensive counter-revolution back into its rightful place in the revolutionary narrative.

42. *The Despatches of Earl Gower*, ed. O. Browning (Cambridge: Cambridge University Press, 1885), 37.

43. The Assembly soon added a tax on moveable property and a commercial licensing fee, the *patente*. Although these taxes eventually (post-1797) became the sound foundation of a new system of state revenue, in the short run, they failed miserably.

44. Earl Gower, the English Ambassador, reported the February 1791 estimate for the current year's spending to be 658 million *livres*. (*Despatches*, 59.)

45. Many areas of France had no land registers, so assessments of the land tax ended up depending on Ancien Régime assessments for the *taille* and the *vingtième*. Taxpayers naturally viewed the "new" land tax as simply the *taille* under a different name.

46. Their value declined sharply after July 1791 (see following text).

47. Once the state established itself on a firmer footing—certainly by 1797, direct tax rates returned to their old levels; in fact, in most parts of France, they seem to have increased by about 20 percent.

48. Cited in M. Fitzsimmons, *The remaking of France. The National Assembly and the Constitution of 1791* (Cambridge: Cambridge University Press, 1994), 94.

49. M. Ozouf, *Festivals and the French Revolution*, trans. A. Sheridan (Cambridge, MA: Harvard University Press, 1988), 47.

50. Arthur Young, who was inducted as a member in January 1790, claimed that the many leaders of the Jacobins were already republicans at that time.

51. Lafayette had, in fact, sent Bouillé a letter urging a harsh repression.

52. Gower, *Despatches*, 94.

53. Furet and Ozouf, *Dictionnaire Critique*, 299.

54. Jean-Paul Marat, *Œuvres Politiques 1789–1793. T. III: Septembre 1790—Décembre 1790*, ed. J. De Cock and C. Goëtz (Brussels: Pole Nord, 1989), 1954.

55. Rétif de la Bretonne, *Nuits*, 74. He surely takes this story from Parisian newspapers.

56. The text of Louis's manifesto can be found in Beik, *French Revolution*, 158–167.

57. Madame de Tourzel, *Mémoires*, 192–200, selections. My translation.

58. Gower, *Despatches*, 53 (28 January 1791).

59. The final compromise gave rights only to mixed-race people born of two free parents.

60. Only three people identified themselves as farmers; in 1789, the provosty of Paris alone had two of them. Two Constitutional bishops (Ariège and Calvados) also can be found in the sample. The only department among the seventeen that sent a priest was the Vendée, which sent two (of nine deputies). Departments of Ain, Aisne, Allier, Basse Alpes, Haute Alpes, Ardeche, Ardennes, Ariège, Aube, Aude, Aveyron, Bouches-du-Rhône, Calvados, Cantal, Charente, Morbihan, and Vendée.

61. Guittard de Floriban, *Journal*, 162.

62. Cited in A. Cooper, *Slavery and the French Revolutionists (1788–1805)*, trans. F. Keller (Lewiston, NY: Edwin Mellen Press, 1988), 58. Letter from Mirabeau to his constituents in Provence. The classic book on the Haitian Revolution remains C.L.R. James, *The Black Jacobins: Toussaint Louverture and the San Domingo Revolution* (London: Allison & Busby, 1936, 1980). C. Fick, *The Making of Haiti: The Saint Domingue Revolution from Below* (Knoxville: The University of Tennessee Press, 1990), contains a precise narrative of events.

63. In Paris, the legislative body serving in February 1794, the Convention, ratified the actions of those who freed the slaves, abolishing both slavery and the slave trade. By then, however, France was at war with Spain and Great Britain, and those two powers had control over much of the island. The sections of the island that those powers did not control, the blacks themselves did.

64. Gower, *Despatches*, 10 (2 July 1790). Gower kept the British government closely informed about events in the West Indies, which were of the greatest interest to them.

65. Rétif de la Bretonne, 92. He rooted for those fighting for the king.

66. Historians often speculate on the impact of the Brunswick Declaration on the Paris crowd, yet Guittard de Floriban only makes mention of it on 3 August, when the government ministers officially announced it to the Legislative Assembly.

67. Mme de Tourzel, *Mémoires*, 369.

Chapter Four

TERROR AND TRIUMPH, 1792–1794

During this time terror hovered over France and particularly in Paris where everyone lived not only in the greatest penury but also in horror of every kind in (the midst of) murders Everything was in the greatest disorder The French breathed blood They were like cannibals and were real man-eaters Neighbor cold-bloodedly denounced neighbor Blood ties were forgotten I witnessed those days of horror.

> Jacques Ménétra—artisan, *sans-culottes*,
> national guardsman, section militant, Jacobin—
> recounting the Times of Terror, (1792–1793)

Some years after the fact, Ménétra recoils in horror from the deeds in which he himself had played a significant part. His memoirs seek to minimize his own role, yet he served two months as a member of his section's revolutionary committee, or committee of surveillance, which kept an eye out for enemies of the Revolution, accusing and arresting those suspected of insufficient revolutionary ardor. He notes with relief that he lost election to the Paris Commune in that year. His successful opponent and all other members of that body were executed in the aftermath of the fall of Maximilien Robespierre and the Jacobins on 9 Thermidor of the Revolutionary Year II (28 July 1794).[1]

Ménétra and his neighbors, like many Parisian artisans, formed the revolutionary mass of the *sans-culottes*: they stormed the Tuileries on 10 August 1792, participated in the *journées* of 31 May to 2 June 1793 that brought the Jacobins to power, and joined the march against the Convention in April 1795 (the Germinal rising). His section, Bonconseil, intervened to save some local patriots from the September Massacres of 1792, denounced moderates in the fall of 1793, supported the prosecution of the radicals in 1794, and adopted a wait-and-see attitude on 9–10 Thermidor.

Ménétra mentions acquaintances and friends guillotined in those dark days, like his drinking buddy, Barbet Mathieu, a journeyman hosier, and, as the glazier tells us, a man "from Lyons that was a capital sin."[2] These poor unfortunates formed part of the group of about 2,700 people executed in Paris during the Terror (September

1793 to July 1794). Nearly 60 percent of the victims fell in the final three months, during the mindless internecine warfare within the Left or as part of the mass executions of Ancien Régime elites. Tens of thousands more perished in the provinces, above all in cities themselves the center of counterrevolution, such as Lyon, or located near rural insurgencies, like Nantes. Thousands of rebels-in-arms died in the provinces, but the Terror executed many innocents, like Mathieu, denounced for uttering an incautious word at a tavern one night.

Every surviving account of those terrible years stresses the insecurity, disillusionment, and naked fear charactistic of the time. The Terror intimidated citizens everywhere, even in those regions in which few fell as official victims. The region around Paris had not a single official execution, yet these villages, too, suffered. Richard Cobb, in his study of Paris's relationship with its surrounding area between 1792 and 1802, offers one of the most vivid descriptions of the Terror:

> [In Paris] the nights of the Terror, we may suppose, were still and silent ones, unrelieved by the reassuring clatter of the carriages of the gamblers, as they returned from the tables, . . . But the *rural* night was even more silent and potentially more horrific and there was little to allay the panic fears of an isolated peasant family as its adult members tossed, listening to the shrieks of the owls and awaiting the crows of the cocks that would spell the end of the dark tunnel of nocturnal terror.[3]

Throughout the nineteenth century, the fearful remembrance of the Jacobin dictatorship of the Year II served as a rallying cry against democratic change everywhere in Europe. In time, the Left adopted Robespierre and the Jacobins as the precursors of modern revolutionary action; the Right made them into totalitarians. In the late 1980s, a leading French historian touched off a firestorm when he referred to the suppression of the Vendée rebellion by the Jacobins as a "genocide." How did things come to such a pass? What happened in France in the fall of 1792 and spring of 1793 to create the atmosphere conducive to government by Terror? For the answers, let us return to the immediate aftermath of Louis XVI's fall.

∿ THE BIRTH OF THE REPUBLIC, AUGUST–NOVEMBER 1792

Nothing is more cruel than fear.

Jules Michelet

C H R O N O L O G Y	August 1792–August 1793
10 August 1792	Storming of the Tuileries; end of the monarchy
August	Decrees establishing new government; mandatory house searches
2–6 September	September Massacres
20 September	Battle of Valmy: French defeat the Prussians

C H R O N O L O G Y	(continued)
21 September	First meeting of the Convention; declaration of the Republic
6 November	Battle of Jémappes: Dumouriez defeats the Austrians
December 1792	Trial of Louis XVI begins
21 January 1793	Execution of Louis XVI
1 February	Declaration of war against Great Britain and Holland
10–11 March	Massacre at Machecoul, start of Vendée uprising
31 May–2 June	June Days: riots in Paris, collapse of the Girondin government
June	Vendéans capture Saumur and Angers; are repulsed at Nantes; Jacobins gradually take over the government
24 June	Convention approves the Constitution of the Year II
13 July	Assassination of Marat by Charlotte Corday
27 July	Robespierre joins the Committee of Public Safety
23 August	*Levée en masse* (mass conscription)
27 August	British capture Toulon

Jules Michelet, the great nineteenth-century historian, tells a story relayed to him by one of the participants in the attack of 10 August against the Tuileries. The old man recalled a conversation he held with a "rich baker of the Marais" while under fire in the Tuileries courtyard: "Still, it's a great sin thus to kill Christians; but, in the end, that's so many the fewer to open the door to the Austrians." Such sentiments ran high in Paris throughout August and September, because people believed Prussian-led Allied force would soon lay siege to Paris. These fears did not abate until firm news of the withdrawal of the Allied army reached Paris on 2 October.

The sequence of events in late August did little to allay the fears of Parisians. After the *journée* of 10 August, an Insurrectionary Commune, consisting of six men each from the forty-eight sections, replaced the old Commune. This group came overwhelmingly from the world of large-scale artisans, small-scale manufacturers, and merchants. Elections within the forty-eight sections continued throughout August, as one section then another replaced individual deputies. On 24 August, the government required all citizens in Paris to take an oath of civic loyalty, which, for the first time, omitted reference to the king.

The sections and Commune urged decisive action on the Legislative Assembly. That body named an Executive Council to act in place of the king, and took a series of radical steps to reestablish order. They voted to hold elections for a new constitutional Convention, based on "universal"[4] manhood suffrage (although still using a two-tiered system of indirect election), to deport all refractory priests who refused to take a new oath of allegiance, to eliminate even the teaching and hospital religious orders, to ban the wearing of priestly garb in public, to empower municipal governments to arrest "suspects" thought to be enemies of the nation, and to mandate the keeping of civil registers (births, deaths, marriages) by communal authorities, not by the Church. The government actually managed to hold elections amid the chaos of late August and early September. This new legislative body, the Convention, took power on 21 September. Its first official act declared France a republic.

In response to the law of suspects, authorities rounded up refractory priests and other suspected counterrevolutionaries; in Paris alone, they detained nearly a thousand. The Assembly took two other key decisions in late August. First, they created an Extraordinary Criminal Tribunal, to hear cases against traitors. Second, they mandated, and the Commune immediately carried out, a house-to-house search in Paris for arms held by counterrevolutionaries. Two of the most radical sections, Luxembourg and Poissonière, voted, in the words of the latter, "considering the imminent dangers to the Fatherland and the infernal maneuvers of priests, [the section] decides that all priests and suspect persons, held in the prisons of Paris, Orléans and elsewhere, shall be put to death."

The September Massacres, in which Parisians broke into the city's prisons and murdered over one thousand people, followed naturally from the fall of the monarchy. The collapse of the only governmental system France had known for over a millennium destabilized every aspect of society. Developments everywhere boded ill for the new government: General Lafayette surrendered to the Prussians; Longwy surrendered virtually without resistance, allowing the Prussians to surround Verdun, the last fortress on the road to Paris. A massive uprising began in the Vendée. The minister Roland suggested that the government flee Paris.

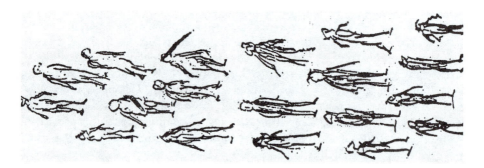

The September Massacres, *1792. The Parisian Guittard de Floriban bears witness to the face of terror, in this sample drawing in his diary.*

Source: C. Guittard de Floriban, *Journal de Célestin Guittard de Floriban, Bourgeois de Paris sous la Révolution,* ed. R. Aubert. (Paris: Éditions France-Empire, 1974).

The Commune of Paris, meeting on the morning of 2 September, voted to sound the tocsin (alarm bell) and to call out the National Guard. Danton, then serving as minister of justice, strongly allied to the Commune, went to the Legislative Assembly to demand measures against traitors. He defended the Commune's sounding of the tocsin, in his most famous speech:

> The tocsin that is being sounded is not an alarm signal; it is the order to charge on the enemies of the Fatherland. To defeat them, messieurs, *il nous faut de l'audace, encore de l'audace, toujours de l'audace* [we will need audacity, still more audacity, always audacity], and France will be saved.

The Assembly dithered in its response, adjourning from 2 P.M. to 6 P.M., that is, precisely when the massacres started. The proposed legislation had demanded the death penalty against those who "refused to serve in person or to give up his arms"; in fact, a second motion went further, demanding the death penalty for all who "directly or indirectly refuse to execute or who in any manner whatsoever interfere with the orders given by and measures taken by the executive power." The Commune voted to arrest Roland, but Danton, whose opposition had prevented the government from leaving, personally tore up the arrest warrant.

The events of July to September 1792 exacerbated a split within the Paris Jacobin Club that had begun in the late spring of 1792. Even in early August, a group around the deposed interior minister Charles-Nicolas Roland and the deputy Jean-Pierre Brissot had sought to compromise with Louis XVI. Historians often call this group the Girondins, because several of its leaders, like Pierre Vergniaud, came from the department of the Gironde (Bordeaux); their contemporaries usually called them the "Rolandins" or the "Brissotins." Roland's wing of the group naturally wanted to increase the powers of the ministers. In the provinces, the Girondins allied strongly with the conservative departmental councils, heavily dominated by large landowners and legal men. These councils remained bastions of constitutional monarchists even after the king's fall.

The Jacobin faction known as the Mountain, led by Maximilien Robespierre, demanded more power for the Convention. Although many leading Jacobins, like Robespierre himself, were men of law, they drew their strongest support from people like Ménétra, the commercial and mercantile interests, and thus had obvious ties to the district and municipal councils, now dominated by those interests.[5] The department of Haute-Vienne offers a good example: 85 percent of the municipal councilors of Limoges were Jacobins, whereas only 42 percent of the departmental councilors belonged to the Club. Outside of the cities, Jacobin clubs spread mainly to rural communes in areas like the Rhône valley that felt threatened by the noble counterrevolution, because people identified the Jacobins with "patriotism," that is, with a policy of vigorous repression of counterrevolutionaries.[6]

In Paris, the Montagnards made common cause with the group focused around the Cordeliers Club, led by Danton, and with the spokesmen of the *sans-culottes*, like the street orators Jacques Roux and Jean Varlet, and the journalists Marat and Jacques-René Hébert, editor of the incendiary *Père Duchesne*. The new Paris Commune, and

THE SEPTEMBER MASSACRES

The inhabitants of the area around the Abbaye prison started the Massacres on 2 September by killing twenty-four priests about to be transferred there; soon, the crowd burst into the Abbaye and massacred its prisoners. The massacres moved from prison to prison for five days: the Carmelite convent, the Maison de Force, the Conciergerie, the Salpêtrière, which housed mainly prostitutes, and, finally, Bicêtre, home to the infirm poor, to the syphilitics, and to unwed mothers and their children. The Massacres of 3–6 September often involved hastily convened popular tribunals, which voted life or death for the poor unfortunates in their grasp. In the end, between eleven hundred and fourteen hundred people died, nearly 75 percent of them simple criminals, with no obvious political misdemeanors.

Célestin Guittard, whose diary contains a sketch of bodies lying about to mark the start of the September Massacres (2–6 September 1792), offers the interpretation promulgated by Marat's *Ami du Peuple*, and accepted by many Parisians:

> Today in the prisons they killed all prisoners condemned to death and refractory priests. . . . Necessity required carrying out such executions. Part of Paris was leaving tomorrow and soon after to join the armies: Paris was going to be denuded of armed men, so all of these unfortunates would have been able to slit our throats during the absence of all the citizens. How sad it is to be obliged to come to such extremities, but they say it is better to kill the devil than to have him kill us. . . . Never since the start of the Revolution had Paris found itself in such a crisis as we found ourselves today. The Fatherland finds itself in danger and the enemies are, so to speak, at our door. It is thus the outcome of the battles

that will probably be joined this month, that will decide our fate. Thus they massacred today all afternoon everywhere in Paris.[7]

The September Massacres provide one of the three dominant, lingering, popular images of the Revolution: the storming of the Bastille, the September Massacres, and the Terror. Each carried, and still carries, a specific mneumonic value. The storming of the Bastille is a symbol of the unity of all good citizens in the face of despotism, but carries the overtones of the potential for unchecked violence on the part of the lower classes. The September Massacres stand for the mindless political violence of the lower classes: the French coined the word *septembriseur* to describe those who participated in the massacres, and it soon became an all-purpose invective used against all radicals. The Terror came to represent what happens when the lower classes actually get a share of government.[8] All three share the element of violence and of popular participation. They provided nightmares to the middle class of Europe throughout the nineteenth and into the twentieth century, making them profoundly suspicious of the political participation of the mass of the male population. Those living in Paris hesitated somewhat in their initial reaction, but then the official response became one of approbation for a deed that, if perhaps a little over-enthusiastic, was necessary to save the "Fatherland in danger." Out in the provinces, local elites took a much dimmer view of developments; the September Massacres confirmed all their worst fears about the Parisian masses.

the sections, were their strongholds. As in the provincial cities, so, too, in Paris, the commercial–manufacturing elite now had complete political control. In the aftermath of 10 August, they forced two major reforms of the National Guard: first, its elite formations, bastion of the relatively wealthy (the only ones who could afford the fancy uniforms), had to disband; second, the Parisian Guard broke into forty-eight battalions, one for each section. The merchants, manufacturers, and master artisans thus took from the legal men control of the three levers of power in Paris: the Commune, the sectional assemblies, and the National Guard, whose new commander, the brewer Antoine Santerre, aptly represented the changeover. The Paris elections of August 1792 ratified the changes, and they returned a radical group of men to the Commune and to Paris's seats in the Convention. Almost everywhere in France, with the exception of the departmental councils and the national legislature, the political leadership shifted from the lawyers of 1791 to the mercantile and business elites of 1792.

The two "parties," the Montagnard Jacobins and the Girondins, did not have clear-cut programs in mind, indeed many historians question whether the latter existed at all, other than as a loose coalition. From the perspective of provincial France, the Executive Council ministers had impeccable "patriot" credentials because they had been cashiered by Louis XVI in June and forcibly restored in August. The Parisian radicals mistrusted the ministers, except for their man, Georges Danton, minister of justice. The central factions used every means at their disposal to empower their provincial allies. The Girondin-dominated Executive Council sent its orders to the departmental councils, whereas the Convention relied on the district and municipal councils run by provincial Jacobins.[9] In December 1793, the Montagnard-dominated Convention abolished the departmental councils; when the Girondin group returned to power, in the fall of 1794, they restored the departmental councils and abolished the district ones.

The election (August–September 1792) of the new representative body, the Convention, took place against this rapidly changing political background. The Paris Jacobins sent pamphlets to their associated provincial clubs, urging members to support two hundred fifty deputies from the Legislative Assembly who had "remained faithful to the cause of liberty": one hundred ninety-four of them obtained election. The Feuillant faction, whose policy of constitutional monarchy had been rendered obsolete by the events of 10 August, failed to elect a single deputy. Most of the *conventionnels*, as they were called, belonged to the "Jacobin" clubs, yet aside from exceptions such as the departments of the Loiret or the Orne, where the Girondins manipulated the vote, most provincial electoral assemblies showed little understanding of the Parisian split. In Paris, factional newspapers campaigned openly for their men: the electors supported the Mountain, picking such radicals as Robespierre (the highest vote-getter), Danton, the painter Jacques David, and, in the end, even the paranoid journalist, Marat.[10]

In Paris as in most of the provinces, the elections of 1792, even though conducted under the principle of universal manhood suffrage, suffered from low turnouts. In the Côte d'Or, where 70 percent of those eligible turned out in 1790, only a quarter did so in 1792, exacerbating a trend that started in 1791. The newly enfranchised urban workers generally failed to vote: Paris, political hotbed though it was, had a turnout below 10 percent. In this respect, the election of August to September 1792 followed the standard pattern. Indirect elections for choosing electoral colleges everywhere had substantially lower turnouts than municipal ones, in which the voters actually made the final choice. In Paris, several sections sought to overcome what they viewed as an antidemocratic measure by insisting, in writing, that the electoral assembly refer back to them for approval of the deputies selected. The electoral assembly refused.

The emerging factional split in Paris had close ties to the second and third major political problems of 1792:

> Citizens with little political sophistication easily believed the most absurd possible accusations, but

> France *did* face a staggering array of internal counterrevolutionaries and external opponents.

This general lack of political sophistication extended from the upper classes to the artisans or peasants, as the journals of Guittard, Ménétra, or Young make clear. The lack of an ability to process political information in a sophisticated way had much to do with a political culture formed under a monarchy that revealed as little as possible of why it did what it did. That said, the relatively slow movement of information in the eighteenth century encouraged rumor mongering and paranoia everywhere: in Great Britain or the new United States of America, just as much as in France. Surely the astounding events of the late eighteenth century, which created a climate of nearly unimaginable instability, also encouraged people to look everywhere for deep, dark plots.

French artisans and shopkeepers harbored social and political grievances against the former ruling groups. Ménétra's journal entries for 1789–1790 indicate his hostility to the "nobles with their old parchments and their ancient gallant knights from whom they claim to trace their ancestry when most of them are descended from servants lackeys [and] coachmen" and the clergy, which sought to preserve men in "their ancient Gothic prejudices" and which wanted "to rule by their dogmas and fabulous mysteries." Parisian artisans saw treachery everywhere; they immediately suspected any noble or clergyman of wanting to return to the Ancien Régime, yet, like Ménétra, they would make exceptions for "good" nobles or priests whom they personally knew, and whose conduct since 1789 had not given rise to suspicions.

The lack of experience in open, *public* practical politics, a legacy of the Ancien Régime's limited political culture, combined with the theoretical framework within which the Revolutionaries operated served to create a lethal combination.[11] Robespierre and his supporters relied heavily on the works of Jean-Jacques Rousseau. Men like Barnave, Brissot or Boissy d'Anglas looked to John Locke or to Montesquieu. The former enshrined their ideas in the Constitution of 1793, the latter in the Constitutions of 1791 and 1795. The political actors of France in the 1790s shared their chief failing with their American contemporaries: they could not understand the purpose of political parties. The French carried it to the extreme that there were no declared candidates for election as deputy. Many local elections relied on voice votes. Guittard reports that the approval of the Constitution of 1793 by his section took place by voice roll call vote: "everyone said yes." In cases where they did not, the humiliated minority oftentimes stalked out of such meetings, which then reported a unanimous vote.

The French saw in every coalition or political group a "faction" or a manifestation of what Rousseau called the "corporate will," which he had described, in *The Social Contract* (1762), as the greatest danger to honest government. The unwillingness to accept the legitimacy of group action, particularly action against the group in power, led to an inability to compromise. The Left, in particular, suffered from this malady. Gouverneur Morris correctly foresaw the coming split in September 1792, writing to Jefferson that:

> You will see by the Gazettes that there is the same Enmity between the present Chiefs which prevailed heretofore against those whom they considered as their common Enemies, and if either of the present parties [Jacobins and Girondins] should get the better, they would probably again be divided, for Party, like Matter, is divisible ad infinitum, because things which depend on human opinion can never be tried by any common Standard.

In this way, the situation in France strongly resembled that in the United States of the 1790s: profound suspicion of party/faction yet a need to create parties; a fear of conspiracies yet the existence of real plots; recognition of the need to compromise, as in the U.S. Constitution of 1787 and the French one of 1791, but an inability to accept the legitimacy of opposition.[12]

Politics easily became intensely personal, as Young had written even in January 1790, and major policy disputes overlapped with personal vendettas. In France, this process started to get out of hand in September 1792 and led to riots in the spring of 1793.[13] Both the United States and France also had great difficulty reestablishing legitimacy in the countryside; Shay's Rebellion (1787) and the Whiskey Rebellion (1794) stand as American counterparts to the Chouans and Vendeans of France. One important constant stood out in both countries: the large landowners supported greater powers for regional authorities, states or departments, while the urban merchants, and some lawyers, wanted a stronger central government, often allied with municipalities.

The Mountain and Girondins had divided sharply in the summer of 1792 about the overthrow of the monarchy. They briefly closed ranks on the issue on 10 August but the trial of the king brought out their underlying differences once again. The Girondins, whether a united faction or not, stood for certain policies more in tune with the needs of provincial France. They wanted to try Louis XVI for treason, of which he was certainly guilty, but did not want to execute him. Knowing of the peasants' broad sympathy for the king, many of them wanted his sentence put to a plebiscite. They wanted a separation of Church and state, but did not push for radical action against priests who supported the Revolution. They supported a more federal approach to government, with more power devolved on the departmental councils, so their provincial supporters soon became known as Federalists. The Montagnards wanted to execute Louis, to destroy all vestiges of the Church's power, and to impose the will of the central government on the provinces. Although the first two goals rested on principles as well as practical considerations, the last one, greater authority for the central government, had more to do with the evolving chaos of French society than with any antipathy to local government.

The split between the Montagnards and the Girondins in the late summer of 1792 stemmed, above all, from a dispute about the nature of the new state. The Montagnards, supported firmly by the Parisian populace, rightly believed France needed strong central leadership. Given that civil war had broken out in the west and south, that foreign armies stood perched on France's northern frontier and inside her eastern borders, and that millions of people lived on the edge of starvation, their argument made a lot of sense. The Girondins stood for a federalist France, with more diffuse power and greater local autonomy. Their policy reflected the reality of 1790 and 1791, when some prospect for federalism seemed possible. By the spring of 1793, the foreign war and the massive civil disorder made federalism an essentially untenable option. Little wonder that the conflict between the Girondins and the Montagnards ended in favor of the latter in June 1793.

The Girondins also suffered from an inherent contradiction of their position in the Convention. They supported more authority for the Executive Council, because they dominated it, but that policy weakened their position in the Convention, whose deputies felt it should wield power. That the Montagnards and Girondins acted out of expediency on this issue seems beyond question. At the war ministry, each successive minister systematically purged the bureaucracy of officials from the opposing faction. The first war minister of the post-monarchy era, the Girondin Servan, set the tone for all his successors when he immediately dumped twelve of his thirteen senior officials, setting off howls of protest in Paris. When the Jacobin Pache took over in October 1792, he quickly stacked the ministry with men holding close ties to the Paris sections. No one in Paris protested the accumulation of power in this minister's hands! By the fall of 1792, ministers such as Roland, Clavière, and Servan controlled bureaucracies of between one thousand and two thousand officials, which gave them considerable patronage. In November, Roland used his jurisdiction over elections to issue circulars to local officials; his efforts helped insure the victory of many of his allies to departmental councils.

The precise relationship between the Executive Council and the Convention hamstrung effective governance. Morris summed up the two key problems facing the new government in a letter to Jefferson (23 October 1792):

> whether they can establish an Authority which does not exist, as a Substitute (and always a dangerous Substitute) for that Respect which cannot be restored after so much has been done to destroy it; whether in crying down and even ridiculing Religion they will be able on the tottering and uncertain Base of Metaphisic Philosophy to establish a solid Edifice of Morals; these are the Questions which Time must solve.

The First French Republic, which lasted only seven years, had no such temporal luxury. It failed categorically in its efforts to recreate an executive branch of government to replace the discredited monarchy and in its efforts to root out Catholicism as the moral foundation of ordinary people's lives.

The Death of the King

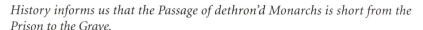

History informs us that the Passage of dethron'd Monarchs is short from the Prison to the Grave.

Gouverneur Morris to George Washington, 23 October 1792

The Convention faced a dismal situation. They needed to absorb the authority of the Executive Council and the old Legislative Assembly and, within Paris, to reach a working agreement with the Commune and its allies, the sections, which now met every day. In the provinces, things could hardly have been worse. Peasants in Brittany and the Vendée rebelled against conscription; fighting between republicans and monarchists seemed endemic in the southeast, as peasants in Provence burned one noble château after another in the fall. At Auxerre, a crowd had torn out the heart of a National Guardsman who refused an oath to the new order; at Dijon and Beaune, the municipalities carried out house-to-house searches and arrests; in the countryside, rumors of brigands spread like wildfire. Food shortages appeared in many areas. Serious bread riots broke out in November, starting in the traditionally rich grain lands of the Beauce (near Chartres) and spreading throughout central France.

The defeat of the Prussians at Valmy (20 September)—little more than an artillery duel, but decisive all the same—led to a rapid improvement in the military situation. By the late fall, Revolutionary armies swept to victory in the Low Countries, in Savoy, and in the Rhineland. Drunk with success, the Revolutionaries turned now to their greatest immediate challenge: what to do about "Louis Capet." The political split intensified in the fall of 1792. The Girondin leaders remained members of the Jacobin Club in Paris until October 1792 when, led by Robespierre, the Club expelled Brissot. The other Girondins soon came under attack: the Paris Jacobins expelled Roland on 26 November, and issued circulars attacking Condorcet, Pétion, and other "Brissotins." This approach did not play well in the provinces. Among provincial Jacobin clubs whose attitude we can determine by their written proceedings from the fall of 1792, supporters of Brissot and the Girondins outnumbered those of the Mountain two to one. Clubs in major cities such as Bordeaux, Montpellier, Angers, and Marseille broke off relations with the Paris mother club.

As 1793 began, public opinion, even in the Jacobin clubs, stood firmly in the Girondin camp. When Pétion resigned as mayor of Paris to be a deputy in the Convention, the electors originally chose him again. When he steadfastly refused, the electors turned to the former royal Controller General Lefebvre d'Ormesson, who also refused. Finally, on 30 November, Parisians chose a Girondin mayor, who defeated the Montagnard candidate nearly 2 to 1, but they chose a Jacobin state's attorney, Anaxagoras Chaumette.

The provincial cities, and their Jacobin clubs, largely rejected *sans-culottes* extremism: most of them subscribed to moderate Leftist papers such as Jean-Louis Carra's *Annales patriotiques* rather than to Marat's radical *Ami du Peuple*. The clubs, and other convivial societies (some overtly political, others not) contributed to the enormous demand for Parisian newspapers. Postal inspectors reported that 80,000 of them left Paris for the provinces every day in 1793. This single figure demonstrates the fundamental change that had transpired between 1789, when Young consistently complained about the lack of availability of Parisian newspapers in provincial cities, and 1792, when news poured out of Paris to quench provincial thirsts. That fundamental transformation, to a society with an active, public political process, proved to be the Revolution's most enduring legacy. Henceforth, French citizens, even under authoritarian rulers like Napoleon I, believed that they had a right to know about transpiring political policies and events. The massive information flow of 1792 enabled provincial clubs to make up their own minds about the Parisian events. Virtually without exception, local Jacobins denounced the September Massacres, and reserved their harshest words for Marat. They used the generic term *maratisme* to stigmatize Parisian radicalism.

The international situation, although it improved, still gave cause for concern. Prussia turned away from the French fighting toward Poland, seeking to profit from the upcoming partition of that country, overrun by Russian troops in August. The Austrian army in the southern Netherlands suffered a catastrophic defeat at Jémappes (6 November) at the hands of Dumouriez's army, but the Convention rightly worried about the general's loyalty. After losing the battle of Neerwinden, he went over to the Allies (April 1793). On the Savoy front, much the same thing happened: the victorious general Montesquiou deserted to the enemy (October 1792). The Convention annexed Savoy and Nice (November 1792), and the Rhineland and Belgium (early 1793). The annexation of Belgium, together with the execution of Louis XVI (January 1793), drove the English into the coalition. War against England and Holland became official on 1 February.

Five problems dominated French political life in the fall of 1792 and winter of 1792 to 1793: the government's inability to raise money, the trial of the king, subsistence, conscription, and war. These problems naturally fed on each other. The war required more troops, leading to expanded conscription, and more government spending; falling tax revenues forced the government to issue more *assignats* to pay these higher bills; the greater volume of *assignats* led to inflation, which drove up food prices.[14] Fighting between cities seeking to requisition grain and the surrounding countryside spread from one end of France to another. Peasant hostility to conscription exacerbated hostility between town and country. By late 1792 departments such as Morbihan, on the south coast of Brittany, or the Vendée, had virtually ceased to belong to France. No one voted; no one joined the army or navy; no one paid taxes. The department of Gers, in the Pyrenees, contained not a single tax register. The Convention slowly began to collect arrears for 1791 at the end of 1792, but even in Paris many citizens did not pay their 1792 taxes until the fall of 1793.[15]

Unfortunately for the people, and the government, the harvest of 1792 continued the pattern of spotty production of the major cereals. In the west, local officials claimed farmers harvested only half the usual wheat crops, although they did bring in a normal rye harvest. Shaky harvests combined with the inflationary issuance of new *assignats* (3.5 billion *livres* between April 1792 and September 1793) to double grain prices in 1792. They rose another 60 percent in the first half of 1793. Prices of basic goods such as soap, sugar, and coffee doubled for those who did not have access to hard currency. Although catastrophic for ordinary consumers, *assignats* provided an ingenious remedy for the government's need to buy agriculture produce to feed and move its armies. The large- and medium-scale farmers sold produce for *assignats*, which they used to buy up nationalized land. The government could thus use the nationalized land quite efficiently to pay for its chief operating expense: the army.

That thought hardly comforted urban consumers. In December 1792, the Convention, after a heated debate, decided to create a free trade in grain, abolishing all price controls and hindrances to circulation (except export). Hungry artisans and peasants had different ideas. They forced local authorities to ignore the Convention and impose price controls in almost every town. The Paris Commune spent 500,000 *francs* a day to subsidize the price of grain in the city's markets, yet the city's artisans grew ever more restless. In February 1793, the market women of Paris presented a petition to the Convention demanding price controls; the laundresses demanded the death penalty for soap hoarders. Parisiennes responded to the denial of their petition by breaking into stores and selling sugar, soap, and other goods for "fair" prices. By 26 February, this "popular price setting," had given way in many cases to simple looting. The National Guard had to restore order. Among male politicians, only Jacques Roux, leader of the radical *enragés*, supported the women.

The Trial of the King

> *People, I die innocent.*
>
> Louis XVI, at the scaffold, 21 January 1793

War, grain and sugar riots, breakdowns in local authority—against such a backdrop the Convention had to decide what to do with Louis XVI. After some months of indecision about whether to try Louis, and, if so, how, the Convention decided to try him itself. On 11 December 1792 the king made his way from the Temple prison to the Convention amid sullen, silent crowds. On the floor of the Convention, he insisted on his innocence and demanded the right to legal counsel. The deputies, most of whom were lawyers, agreed to his demand, appointing the famed Enlightenment figure Malesherbes. The deputies had little doubt of Louis's guilt, because an armored box discovered in the Tuileries contained his correspondence with foreign rulers about overthrowing the Revolution. What should they do with him? Should he be condemned to death? Should the people of France vote on his execution?

The Convention's voting took place in an eerie atmosphere. Starting on 13 January, all house lights had to remain on through the night; on 14 January, all public spectacles closed for the day and the government doubled the guards on prisons. On 15 January 1793 the deputies voted 693 to 0 for a verdict of guilty. In the following days, they divided sharply on the question of an appeal to the people: 424 to 283, with the Girondins going down to defeat.[16] Many local clubs that had supported Brissot and Roland in their quarrel with the Paris Jacobins, now turned against the Girondins. Marseille shifted allegiance to the Mountain, bringing the rest of Provence with it.

Indeed, the idea so outraged the Marseille Jacobins that they sent out a circular (1 February) demanding the recall of all deputies who had voted for the appeal to the people.

The deputies divided again on the death penalty: three hundred sixty-one voted for death, seventy-two for death with a delay for clemency, and two hundred eighty-eight against. The next day, another vote tallied three hundred eighty for death and three hundred ten for clemency. Some of the latter, Thomas Paine among them, had no special concern for Louis; they simply opposed the death penalty itself, on principle. Others believed, rightly, that executing Louis would lead to war with England.

All Paris lived uneasily during these January days. On 20 January, the day before the scheduled execution, the Convention, led by the Girondins, voted to seek prosecution of those responsible for the September Massacres. That evening, a monarchist assassinated the Jacobin deputy Le Pelletier de Saint-Fargeau. The Convention doubled the guard at the Temple, fearing that the broadsides plastered through the city proclaiming, "Save the King" "Burn the Guillotine" "Murder the Deputies" might actually lead to an insurrection. The next day, some 80,000 National Guardsmen lined the route from the Temple to the Place de la Concorde. Some witnesses suggest that Louis marched through silent streets, massive crowds struck dumb by a spectacle that would have been unimaginable just months earlier. Louis-Sébastien Mercier, in contrast, denied such reports:

> No alteration could be seen on people's faces, and they lie who printed that stupor reigned in the city. . . . The day of the execution did not make any impression: the shows opened as usual; the cabarets ringing the bloody square emptied their pitchers as usual; cake and paté sellers hawked their wares in sight of the decapitated corpse.

On the square itself, 20,000 men, among them Conquerors of the Bastille, surrounded the guillotine. Louis needed help from his confessor to mount the steep steps; at the top, he spoke to the crowd: "People, I die innocent. I pardon the authors of my death. I pray God that my blood will not fall upon France." Murmurs spread through the crowd, but the drums drowned out the rest of his words. Seconds later, the son of the executioner, Sanson, held up the king's severed head, to cries of "Vive la République!" "Vive la nation!" and "Vive la liberté!" Mercier reports that schoolchildren at the *collège* of the Quatre-Nations tossed their caps in the air at the news. On the scaffold itself, one of the executioners started selling little packets of the king's hair and the crowd surged forward to carry away bloodstained bits of clothing.

∽ THE JACOBIN REPUBLIC, 1793–1794

> *The monarchy, jealous of its authority, swam in the blood of thirty generations; and you would hesitate to show yourselves severe against a handful of the guilty?*[17]
>
> Louis-Antoine de Saint-Just, March 1794

The execution of the king allowed the Convention to focus on its other three problems—local disorder, subsistence, and the war—and to begin serious work on its original purpose: the creation of a new constitution. No specific group had control of the Convention at this time. The Girondins, above all the philosopher Condorcet, completely dominated the Constitutional Committee. They produced a draft of 402 articles by mid-February 1793.[18] Yet the real battle of early 1793 did not take place over constitutional principles. The desperate daily situation required immediate answers based on practical reality, not philosophic niceties. In the gritty political warfare of January through July 1793, the Jacobins took the measure of their Girondin foes.

Given the lack of a directed executive branch of government, the individual ministers often acted as independent executive agents. The Convention sought to rein them in by means of committees. In October 1792, they created a Committee on General Security, which had responsibility for public security, specifically for identifying and arresting enemies of the Republic. Its thirty members came from all political stripes, although it had a strong initial Montagnard contingent. The Girondins reduced the Committee to fifteen and stacked it with their men on 9 January, but the disorder created by the assassination of Saint-Fargeau (20 January) and the death of the king (21 January) led the Convention, on 21 January, to turn again to the hardline Jacobins. Two days later, the radicals forced Roland to resign as minister of the interior, but failed to elect their candidate to replace him. Nor did the Jacobins have much initial success gaining the ministry of justice, vacated on 22 January, or that of war. Two changes of minister of war between January and March led to the appointment of the apparently neutral nonentity Bouchotte. His chief clerk, however, was the Jacobin F.-N. Vincent, who purged the ministry of all Girondins and packed it with Jacobins.

The Convention had created a new committee (1 January 1793) to act as a liaison between the legislature and the Executive Council of Ministers. This arrangement left vague the lines of executive authority. The Convention clarified the matter on 6 April by giving the committee authority over the entire executive branch, except the Ministry of Finances. They gave this new body its cruelly ironic name: the Committee of Public Safety. Six weeks later the Girondins, having shipped more than eighty Jacobin deputies off to the provinces as the Convention's "deputies on mission," used their majority to create yet another commission, the Committee of General Security, which they gave power over the ministries of the interior and of foreign affairs, and the brand new Committee of Public Safety.

The frenzied political infighting took place against a backdrop of instability, counterrevolutionary plots, and mounting hunger. In addition to the various quasi-executive commissions, the Convention created (10 March) a Revolutionary Tribunal to hear cases involving state security and established (21 March) revolutionary committees of surveillance in all communes and large city sections. In Paris, the creation of these committees gave the quasipermanent sectional assemblies, who already possessed an armed force, a powerful new weapon to intimidate their opponents. The mounting price of bread added fuel to the revolutionary flames. The Convention, responding to pressure from the Parisian crowds, mandated a special tax on the rich, to be used to subsidize bread prices, and made *assignats* the sole legal currency. These measures had little immediate effect: on 17 April, Guittard wrote that Paris had had no bread for five days and that armed National Guards stood watch at every bakery in the city. The urban poor everywhere struggled just to eat. A revolutionary explosion could not be far off.

In the countryside, the Convention's February conscription decree for 300,000 men created another explosion.[19] Unlike the "voluntary" military drafts of 1791 and 1792, this one was to resort to force if necessary. Most communes chose their soldiers by the traditional, and universally detested Ancien Régime method: drawing lots. Following in the aftermath of the bungled abolition of feudalism and of the supremely unpopular assault on the clergy, the attempted imposition of a military draft was certain to produce violent opposition. Peasants all over the west shouted "down with the lottery" and took up arms. The revolt in Brittany, the Chouannerie, settled down quickly to a low-level guerrilla warfare, due to prompt and substantial military intervention, but just south of the Loire, in the Vendée, the rebels got the upper hand. In a few weeks, armed bands of 10,000 men roamed the countryside, starting a civil war that would end with tens of thousands of deaths. The government responded to the news of the insurrection by passing a law (19 March) allowing the summary trial and execution of rebels captured in arms. Its initial attempts at suppressing the Vendeans failed miserably; peasant guerrillas bamboozled the government troops, trapped hopelessly in the forbidding hedges of the *bocage* country. By May, the guerrillas had driven out the troops and gone on the offensive.

The Girondins, who had control of the Executive Council of Ministers, naturally received the blame for this disaster, as well as for the other miseries of the spring of 1793. The army's defeats in Belgium, and the treason of the Girondin's favorite general, Dumouriez, further undermined their position. The political debates in the Convention now turned increasingly personal. Robespierre demanded the arrest and trial of Brissot; other radicals demanded the removal of certain deputies as agents of Counterrevolution. Everyone likely agreed with Guittard, who wrote on 13 March: "One cannot be tranquil for a moment!" On 28 March, sections conducted house-to-house searches for arms held by "emigrés, nobles, non-juring priests, servants of nobles, and other suspect persons."

The Montagnards organized their chief allies, the Paris sections, for dramatic action. On 18 April, they circulated a petition in the sections to be sent to all departments, urging the Convention to expel and arrest twenty-two Girondin deputies. The Girondins responded by arresting and trying Marat. When the Convention acquitted him (23 April), he led a triumphal procession through the streets of Paris. A week later, besieged by foreign armies in the north and east and by peasant rebels in the west, the Convention declared the "Fatherland in danger" and ordered all male citizens between the ages of eighteen and fifty to take up arms for the purpose of marching against the western rebels.

Events spun out of control everywhere, especially in Paris. The Girondins tried to use the Committee of General Security to bring the Paris Commune to heel; the Jacobins relied on the Commune and the sections to intimidate the Girondins. The dénouement started in early May. On 1 May, a crowd of 8,000 to 10,000 marched on the Convention, demanding price controls on grain and bread. A delegation of women from Versailles also occupied the Convention itself, refusing to leave without a promise of price controls. The Convention caved in the following day and promulgated the decree on 3 May.

Women and Politics: The June Days

The police reports suggest that women, especially market women, led the opposition to the Girondins. On 13 May, one police agent wrote: "the women perservere in the project of demanding the recall of the twenty-two deputies . . . ; they even have the hope that they will be seconded by the men." Another agent wrote: "evil influences, under the mark of patriotism, have excited these revolutionary heroines to riot and to take up arms so as to dissolve the Convention and cause rivers of blood to flow in Paris." The leading radical women organized a new political club, the Club of Republican Revolutionary Citizenesses on 14 May, perhaps led by Claire Lacombe and Pauline Léon. A Girondin deputy warned the Convention on 25 May of an impending massacre of the Rightist deputies: "the pretext will be a manufactured outbreak of disorder in the Convention; the women will set things going; indeed a regiment of them has already been formed for this iniquitous work." [22]

These events would have enormous long-term implications for the political participation of women in the French Revolution. The Jacobins distrusted women in politics in part because of the important role played by Marie-Jeanne Philippon, wife of the minister Roland. The Convention sought to arrest both she and her husband during the June Days. She actually went to the Convention itself on the night of 31 May to try to convince them of the innocence of her husband. She would be released and re-arrested, finally going the scaffold on 8 November 1793. Her husband committed suicide two days later.

The Jacobins feared, too, the role of the radical women led by Lacombe and Léon. Their alliance with the male radicals, like Hébert, made them potential enemies. Surely the Jacobins also feared the galvanizing role women had played in some of the great Revolutionary days, such as the march to Versailles or the June Days. When they obtained full power, the Jacobins denied women political rights, closed their clubs, and executed or imprisoned their political leaders. The central role of women in the June Days, the very event that brought the Jacobins to power, thus instigated the Jacobins' destruction of women's rights.

On 28 May, a crowd of about three hundred women, in all likelihood organized by the Club of Republican Revolutionary Citizenesses (CRRC), marched on the Convention, demanding the right to bear arms to protect themselves, saying "they wanted to stand guard, like the men."[20] The leaders of the forthcoming insurrection organized in the sections on 29 May, created a central committee for their activities, and then invited the Commune to join them (30 May). The next day, at 4 A.M., the Commune sounded the tocsin. Because Friday 31 May 1793 was a heavy work day, artisans took slowly to the streets.[21] Poor Guittard suspected great things: he spent the day shivering in fright, "wanting to vomit, finding myself all day weak in the legs and with trembling hands." He expressed great relief at the end of the day that nothing had happened, yet recorded 31 May in his diary along with 14 July 1789, 20 June 1791, 10 August 1792, and 21 January 1793 as "four or five truly remarkable days." Saturday, 1 June saw relatively little action until late in the evening, when the workers left their shops and took up arms. Sunday, 2 June, they turned those arms on the Convention. A massive gathering of National Guardsmen and *sans-culottes,* certainly over 75,000 armed men, surrounding the Tuileries Palace and forced the Convention to arrest twenty-nine of its own members, as well as two Girondin ministers. The Mountain had now broken the Girondins, but it took the

TWELVE WHO RULED[23]

The Convention created the twelve-member Committee of Public Safety in April 1793 to provide a liaison with the executive branch ministries; the Committee soon became the *de facto* executive branch of the government. Unlike the ministers, who could not be deputies in the Convention, the Committee of Public Safety consisted of deputies drawn from the Convention, renewed by vote of the assembly every six weeks. Danton and his allies dominated the initial membership, although two of the later Twelve who ruled during the Terror had seats from the beginning: Bernard Barère and Robert Lindet, both lawyers. The Committee added three more of the famous Twelve on the eve of the June Days: Georges Couthon, another lawyer; Louis-Antoine de Saint-Just, a young (twenty-six) former wastrel whom his own mother once imprisoned by *lettre de cachet;* and Marie-Jean Hérault de Séchelles, a member of an ancient noble family and the king's attorney of the Parlement of Paris in the late 1780s. Hérault de Séchelles provided the key leadership for the group during the difficult days of early June 1793, but Couthon, who was confined to a wheelchair because of meningitis, gave several impassioned speeches that deeply affected his colleagues. Hérault de Séchelles maintained close ties with Danton even after the latter's fall from grace. In March and April 1794, he allied with Danton and the Indulgents to try to put a stop to the Terror.

He joined Danton and Desmoulins on the scaffold.

The renewal of the Committee on 10 July led to the removal of Danton and some of his allies. The Convention added two more of the Twelve, André Jeanbon Saint-André, a former Protestant minister; and Pierre-Louis Prieur (called Prieur of the Marne), a lawyer. Seventeen days later, the Convention took the dramatic step of naming the preeminent figure of the Jacobins, Maximilien Robespierre, to the Committee. Soon, the final four members joined: Jean-Nicolas Billaud-Varenne, a lawyer from La Rochelle and failed playwright; Jean-Marie Collot d'Herbois, an actor (and minor playwright) with close ties to Parisian radicals; and two military engineers, Lazare Carnot and Claude-Antoine Prieur-Duverny (called Prieur of the Côte d'Or).[24] Carnot had known Robespierre at Arras, where both belonged to a local literary society: Robespierre had even acted as the lawyer for Carnot's servant in an inheritance lawsuit.

These twelve men well represented the Convention. They came from all over France: three from the Southwest; two each from Burgundy, Picardy, and Paris. Like most of their fellow deputies, eleven of the twelve had had advanced education, eight of them in law. They belonged to the literary public sphere of the late Ancien Régime: eight of them had published a book, pamphlet or play by 1790,

Montagnards until early July to consolidate their position and actually take power themselves.

The Jacobins took over in an atmosphere of utter chaos. In the west, the Vendean rebels swept all before them. They captured town after town in their region. Thouars, Fontenay, and finally, on 9 June, the substantial Loire river city of Saumur fell, defended by none other than the Parisian militia recruited in March, under Santerre. In the south, matters looked just as bad. Factional fighting broke out in Marseille in March, leading local Jacobins to impose new taxes on the rich and enact stern police measures. The local merchants and their workers rose up against the Jacobins, driving the deputies on mission from the city and deposing the Jacobin municipal council. Just up the river, at Lyon, a Jacobin municipality suffered for its failure to control bread prices, a third higher than those of Paris. Once again, discontented workers

(CONTINUED)

and most of them had subscribed to literary societies in their hometown. Like their fellow deputies, they were remarkably young for men asked to take over their country. Nine of them were under forty when they took power. Of the remaining three, Collot d'Herbois was forty-three, Jeanbon Saint-André, forty-four, and Lindet, forty-six.

The Twelve did not have real factions but two clear blocs could be distinguished: the radicals, with strong ties to the *sans-culottes* and the Paris sections—Robespierre, Saint-Just, Couthon, Collot d'Herbois, Billaud-Varenne, and, perhaps, the fickle Barère—and what might be called the functionary wing, Lindet, Carnot, and Prieur of the Côte d'Or. This trio specialized in organization, above all of the military; the public opprobrium that followed 9 Thermidor largely excluded them. Carnot especially kept his reputation. Alone among the Twelve, he remained on the Committee into the fall of 1794 and he became one of the original five Directors of the government created in 1795. The radicals fared less well. Their split in July 1794 led to the execution on 28 July 1794 of Robespierre, Couthon, and Saint-Just. Two of their three chief accusers, Billaud-Varenne and Collot d'Herbois, were later (1795) sentenced to exile in French Guiana, "the dry guillotine," for their part in the Terror. The third member of those who toppled Robespierre, the ever

slippery Barère, managed to obtain an acquittal at the 1795 trial.

The streets of Paris bear permanent witness to the historical memory of these figures: only Lindet and Carnot have given their names to streets in the capital.[25] One of the great avenues that flows into the Arc de Triomphe bears Carnot's name, as does a major boulevard. Robespierre's name briefly (1946–1950) graced a small street and the square on which the Jacobin Club formerly met, evidence of the Communist influence in the Paris of 1946. That influence quickly waned. In 1950, the city fathers renamed the square the place du Marché Saint-Honoré and even changed the name of the tiny street, to the rue de la place du Marché Saint-Honoré, perhaps seeking to efface the memory of so controversial a figure. In the great provincial cities, too, major avenues bear Carnot's name and blandly describe him as "the organizer of the victory." His role in the Terror, in which he fully participated (i.e., voting in favor of the execution of Danton and Desmoulins), is conveniently forgotten. As for Robespierre, only Leftist cities, such as Brest, where the main street bears his name, dare to evoke the memory of the soul of the Jacobins.[26] Thus do the avenues and boulevards of every French town become the places of memory for each contemporary political group's version of a mythical French past.

armed themselves and overthrew the municipality. Events in Marseille, Paris, and Lyon had this in common: the party perceived to be in power was attacked by the armed workers of the city, desperate for bread and work. Guittard wrote in his journal that "[the bread shortage] began on July 10th and lasted until September 10th . . . You had to be at the baker's door by 4 A.M. There were those who lined up at midnight." In Paris, workers aimed their hostility at the Girondins who opposed price controls; in Lyon and Marseille, it meant revolt *against* the Jacobins. Word of the Lyon revolt reached Paris in early June, exacerbating tensions there and leading to cries for stern measures against counterrevolutionaries.

Bordeaux, whose deputies headed the Girondins, reacted violently against the actions of 2 June. It declared itself in insurrection against the Convention, sent delegates urging other cities to do the same, and raised troops to march on Paris. Lyon and Marseille joined forces to take Avignon and declared their region in rebellion. Montpellier joined in on 11 June and Toulon, the great Mediterranean naval base, a few days later. In the west, the Breton departments responded with joy and sent troops toward Caen, which had also revolted against the Convention.[27] The Federalist revolt received support in many regions of France, but by no means in a majority of them. The three key centers of Federalist resistance were the west, in an area running from Caen to Upper Brittany; the area around Bordeaux; and the Rhône valley. To that, we must add the Vendée, whose insurrection had nothing to do with Federalism: the Vendeans wanted the return of "their priests and their king." The Federalists wanted neither.

The Montagnards acted quickly on several fronts. They focused immediate attention on the need to draw up a constitution. Rejecting many of the principles brought forward by Condorcet and his committee, the Jacobins hurriedly pushed through a constitution based on a unicameral legislature, directly elected by all male citizens. Their declaration of rights included rights to public assistance, to education, and to resistance of oppression. The Constitution of 1793 also abolished all feudal rights, without compensation, and divided the nationalized property (of the Church and émigrés) into smaller lots, for sale to poor and middling farmers. Amazingly enough, something like 2 million men voted in the constitutional plebiscite of July 1793. Almost all of them voted in favor, but the voting assemblies often held vigorous debates and many of them forwarded proposed amendments to Paris.[28] Turnouts could vary from under 20 percent (17 departments) to over 40 percent (six). Although the Convention ruled that, in the given emergency, it could not enact the Constitution, the plebiscite provided the Convention with desperately needed legitimacy at one of France's most difficult moments.

The Convention turned first to deal with the Federalist rebellion. A small army sent to Caen (August) immediately broke the Federalists there; the rebels of Bordeaux capitulated by October. In both cities, the deputies on mission from the Convention carried out few reprisals. The situation in the southeast, however, was another matter. The anti-Jacobins of Marseille and Lyon had executed local supporters of the Convention, including the deputy on mission in Lyon, Chalier, who quickly became a Revolutionary martyr (all the more so after the publication of his prison memoirs). The Vendeans occupied Angers, a city of 20,000, but the failure of their two-day assault on Nantes led them to return to their *bocages*. The government desperately needed this victory, because Nantes was the only one of France's three greatest ports in its hands.

The war situation deteriorated steadily from March to August. The Austrians captured Condé and Valenciennes; the Savoyards attacked Nice; the Spaniards crossed the Pyrenees, an area which already had a low-level peasant insurgency against the Convention; the Allies recaptured Mainz; and the British sent troops to capture France's West Indian possessions, above all Saint-Domingue. As if defeat in war, treason in the southeast, and rebellion in the west were not enough, on 13 July one of the supporters of the Caen Federalists, Charlotte Corday, assassinated Marat while he was taking a bath. The Convention became more militant in its policies: it removed Danton, now become the symbol of insufficient rigor, from the Committee of Public Safety and replaced him two weeks later with Robespierre, the embodiment of revolutionary vigilance. He led the Convention to its most dramatic move on 11 August: one day after the celebrating the approval of the new Constitution. On Robespierre's motion, the Convention suspended its implementation during the "emergency."

In August 1793, facing continued military threats and runaway inflation, the Convention voted (23 August) the "levée en masse," mass conscription of men aged eighteen to twenty-five, coupled with mobilization of women for work, of nondraft animals for army usage, and of old men to march to public squares, there to proclaim the virtues of patriotism. In early September, in response to the massive *sans-culottes* demonstrations about bread prices and wages, the Convention created "Revolutionary Armies": armed patriots who would seek out traitors and hoarders. They also approved a 40-shilling payment to citizens attending twice weekly meetings of their sections, decided to salary the presidents of revolutionary committees, and agreed to make "terror the order of the day," launching what we know as the Reign of Terror.

THE REIGN OF TERROR

I am without indulgence for the enemies of my country; I know only justice.

Louis-Antoine de Saint-Just, Speech of 8 Ventôse II (26 February 1794)

CHRONOLOGY	September 1793–July 1794
September 1793	Terror made into official government policy; wage and price controls introduced (Law of the General Maximum)
September/October	Curtailment of women's political rights; closing of Club of Republican Revolutionary Citizenesses; arrest of women's leaders
9 October	Convention's forces recapture Lyon
16 October	Execution of Marie-Antoinette
16 October	Jourdan defeats Austrians at Wattignies
17 October	Defeat of Vendéans at Cholet
31 October	Execution of most of the Girondin leaders; others commit suicide
29 November	Execution of Barnave
12 December	Defeat of Vendéans at Le Mans
19 December	Recapture of Toulon; reprisals begin
13–24 March 1794	Hébertists arrested (13 and 14 March) and executed (24 March)

CHRONOLOGY	(continued)
28 March	Condorcet commits suicide
30 March–6 April	Danton, Desmoulins, and "Indulgents" arrested (30 March); tried, and executed (6 April)
April–July	Height of the Paris Terror
8 June	Festival of the Supreme Being
26 June	Jourdan wins battle of Fleurus
27–29 July	Fall and execution of Robespierre, Saint-Just, Couthon, and their allies (9 Thermidor)

Saint-Just's words have the same frightening, implacable coldness today that they bore two hundred years ago. The Jacobins knew only "justice," untempered by mercy; yet they, like political actors from time immemorial, had first to define it. They first focused on the purity of the congregation, weeding out the heretics from their own ranks, purifying the Revolutionary "priesthood." The Leftist newspapers of 1793 and early 1794 mainly attacked each other, casting out the wildest, most hideous accusations. They accused their opponents of hoarding grain amidst a famine; they plotted to restore "Capet's son" (the child of Louis XVI) to the throne; they plotted to marry their leader to Capet's daughter; they plotted to restore the monarchy, with Philip of Orléans as king; they plotted with aristocratic exiles, with peasants rebels, with the British, with the Austrians and Prussians to overthrow the Republic; they plotted to unleash anarchy, by destroying private property and allowing man's basest desires to have unchecked license. Well might Nicolas Ruault lament on 11 June 1793 that "one of the greatest plagues that the Revolution has produced is the frightening license of the newspapers; they pervert public opinion."

From a distance of two hundred years, these accusations seem so ridiculous that we cannot even imagine that people believed them. Yet they did believe some of them and they often acted in direct response to these perceived threats. The accusations focused on people's real and legitimate fears. These included the restoration of the monarchy; the return of the aristocracy; the danger of foreign invasion; the threat of civil war in the Vendée or in the southeast; the shortage of bread; and massive unemployment. These terrible realities had nothing to do with imagination; they were the stuff of everyday life in France in the summer of 1793. People wanted the government to do something to solve these problems. Even Ruault, hardly sympathetic to the Jacobins, would write to his brother on 8 July 1793: "We hope that . . . personal interest will save the Republic and produce the general good, that we will never speak again of Girondins, as if they had never existed."[29] A few weeks later, he would congratulate his brother on the collapse of the Federalists at Evreux and the restoration of "order and obedience to the law."

The Terror can best be understood as three distinct movements:

1. The special case of Paris, tied directly to national politics.

2. The fight against the counterrevolution.

3. An intimidating climate of fear almost everywhere else.

Local officials, invariably directed by a deputy on mission from Paris, did occasionally execute someone. They guillotined non-juring priests, those who aided non-jurors, the odd speculator, some nobles, and a smattering of ordinary people. The authorities used a broader campaign of arrests (70,000+), backed up by the threat of execution, much more than execution. They used intimidation to restore a functioning government: to obtain bread for the starving people of the cities; to collect state revenue; to organize the army; to restore civil order in areas not in rebellion.

Historical memory largely ignores this third Terror; throughout the nineteenth and twentieth centuries, the Terror has meant the grotesque carnival of blood in Paris and, to a lesser degree, the brutal excesses at Lyon, Nantes, and a few other places. The Convention created the legal underpinning of Paris's Terror on 17 September 1793, when it put teeth into the mandate of the Revolutionary Armies by passing a Law of Suspects, allowing the revolutionary committees to arrest Federalists, former nobles, monarchists, and other "enemies of liberty." Twelve days later, the Convention instituted mandatory wage and price controls (the Law of the General Maximum), although it implemented the latter much more quickly than the former. The Convention also struck out at those it viewed as politically suspect. It began a trial of Brissot and the Girondin leaders, arrested the radical Jacques Roux, and closed down the Club of Revolutionary Republican Citizenesses, who had been so instrumental in the May demonstrations and who had been allied with Roux throughout the summer. It simultaneously acted to satisfy the people's need for bread. Guittard tells us on 10 September:

> at last there is bread today in all of the bakers' shops and they have thus dissipated the people who still wanted to gather there. What for, because everyone has as much bread as he wants today. I hope we are finally delivered from this crisis. . . .

The Convention tried and executed the Girondin leaders—Brissot, Vergniaud, and nineteen others went to the guillotine on 31 October. "They were convicted," Guittard writes, "of having plunged themselves into a conspiracy directed against the unity and indivisibility of the Republic, against liberty and the security of the French people." Throughout October and November, the revolutionary tribunals and the Convention sent other notables to the guillotine, among them earlier leaders of the Revolution now fallen from favor, like Barnave, Bailly, Philip of Orléans, and Mme Roland. Many of those who escaped the blade, like Roland or the former mayor of Paris, Pétion, committed suicide. The Convention arrested sixty-five of its own deputies, who had signed a secret denunciation of the events of 2 June, but it did not try them. It tried, convicted, and executed Marie Antoinette (16 October), and several generals suspected of treason.

Generations of historians have recoiled from the "mindless" Terror of 1793–1794, yet the events followed an extremely logical (if deeply perverted) pattern. The Paris Terror began with the fall 1793 assault on the Jacobins's most dangerous political rivals. The country still overwhelmingly wanted something like a constitutional monarchy and the reformed Catholic Church of 1790. The Jacobins thus murdered or drove to suicide all those associated with the compromise solution of 1789–1791—Bailly, Barnave, Philip of Orléans, and many others—and the moderate Girondins, such as Brissot, Roland, and Pétion. Having literally decapitated their most dangerous opponents outside their own movement, Robespierre and his allies moved to consolidate their supremacy on the Left: they naturally murdered all potential rivals, from Danton to Jacques Roux and Hébert.

The Terror, in Paris and in part of the southeast, thus served a partisan political purpose: that of eliminating political threats to Robespierre. The second Terror, the one that killed the most people, formed part of the response to counterrevolution and civil war. Terror by intimidation focused on the subsistence crisis and the creation of a functioning government. The old government structure had completely broken down. Lacking any obvious basis for legitimacy, given the widespread claims by the Convention's opponents that it was illegitimate, the government sought to use brute force and intimidation to establish short-term legitimacy. By January 1794, all three Terrors had succeeded. The Left had destroyed the leadership of the Center and Right; the government had gained the upper hand against counterrevolutionaries; and the state had frightened most French people into obeying their government. These successes, apparent by early 1794, led Danton and others to suggest that the Terror end. Robespierre and his allies disagreed. Desperate to justify continued government by Terror, they made the devastating blunder of turning against their allies on the Left. Once they had killed them (April), they resorted to the old political ploy of persecuting a scapegoated minority. In the France of 1794, the choice of scapegoat was easy: the nobles and the clergy.

The phrase "Reign of Terror" recalls for us the image of the Revolution consuming its own children in Paris. The three phases of the Parisian Terror targeted very distinct groups:

1. The fall 1793 executions of the early leaders of the Revolution and the Girondins, fewer than two hundred people.

2. The internal massacre within the Left, culminating with the death of Danton in early April.

3. A last paroxysm of viciousness, targeted on the scapegoated privileged orders.

Nearly two-thirds of the eleven hundred fifty-eight nobles officially executed during the Terror died between April and July 1794; roughly a third of the clergy executed died in June and July 1794.

While the Convention executed Marie Antoinette, the people of Paris and other major cities stepped up their campaign of organized vandalism against all symbols of the Ancien Régime. They decapitated the royal statues on the portal of Notre

The Last Night of the Girondins

I must tell you of the last night of the Girondins. I have it from Anarcharsis Clootz, who came to see me the night before last. When they were condemned to die at about 11 P.M., they all, minus Valazé, who had stabbed himself in front of the tribunal, met together in a single room to have supper. They had served a very good meal of all that could be obtained at that hour in the Palace quarter: roasts, pastries, delicate wines, liqueurs. They elected a president, it was *la Source* [whom Ruault does not identify], who proposed that

they die right there. 'I feel myself sufficiently courageous, he told them, to kill you all, and myself last, and thus prevent that we should die publicly on the scaffold.' The band of the condemned received this proposition in different ways; they began to eat and drink. In the midst of the meal, they lengthily debated the question of the existence of God and the immortality of the soul. Seventeen of the twenty-one recognized both the one and the other and refused to die at the hand of the president.[30]

Dame and dug up the coffins of France's kings and queens (even good king Dagobert, buried in the seventh century!) at Saint-Denis. Ruault wrote to his brother: "All these monuments to human grandeur and vanity have been destroyed, burned in quicklime last October, at the same time that they tortured the last queen of France and publicly immolated the twenty-one Girondins. Such sad times these are, when the living and the dead are both persecuted for . . . their opinions."[31]

The government's military situation improved in early September 1793, when a French army routed the Austrians at Wattignies, driving them across the frontier. In the south, the newly created Revolutionary Army from Paris joined regular troops and captured Lyon in early October. The Convention demanded vengeance for Lyon's treachery, but the deputy on mission in charge of the repression, Georges Couthon, settled for a few exemplary punishments and for the destruction of the houses of the richest merchants. His replacement, Joseph Fouché, had some seventeen hundred prisoners lined up over hastily dug graves and mowed down with cannon and musket fire. The troops who took Lyon then headed south, to Toulon, where rebels fleeing Marseille had joined local Federalists to invite British intervention. When the French army retook Toulon, in December, seven thousand rebels left with the British. The army shot eight hundred people the next day and guillotined two hundred more in the ensuing month. The Convention mandated that these two cities take new names, Mountain-Port and Ville Affranchie (Freed Town), to efface the shame attached to those of Toulon and Lyon. One minor element of the siege of Toulon is worthy of note. A Corsican artillery captain named Napoleon Bonaparte earned a promotion to brigadier general by directing the bombardment that drove the British fleet from the harbor. Paris celebrated the news of these victories with a mammoth parade in their honor.

The massacres in regions of counterrevolution provide yet another historical example of the brutality of civil war. The cycle of repression–reprisal of the Vendée or the Rhône is, sadly, as old as time. The Terror of Paris, with its blatantly political and social side (the latter in late spring 1794), sprang from the fall of the monarchy

Destroying royal images in Paris: here the crowd demolishes the statue of Louis XIV in the Place des Victories. Today's statue is a later copy of the original.

Source: © Corbis.

and the execution of the king. Killing Louis XVI established the precedent for the elimination of political rivals. The atmosphere in which he was tried, the charges against him—with their emphasis on foreign plots[32]—all led up to the increasingly vituperative, personal, bloody politics of 1793–1794. The Convention took the critical step in June 1793 of arresting its own deputies and charging them with treason. Their execution in October 1793 started the Convention down the slippery slope sure to lead to failure. The foolish executions of the leading deputies of the Left in March and April 1794, carried out *by* deputies from the Left, led to the Left's inevitable collapse in the summer of 1794. Before we get to that episode, however, let us consider the other two elements of the Terror.

The violent Terror took place primarily in four cities: Toulon, Lyon, Nantes, and Paris. Just as the authorities shot hundreds in Lyon or Toulon, so they drowned eighteen hundred at Nantes. The deputy on mission, J.-B. Carrier, and the local authorities began the procedure by tying ninety non-juring priests to a barge, which was then taken to the middle of the Loire and sunk. Local authorities repeated this procedure six times, not only for priests but for Vendéan rebels—men, women, and children—and even common criminals. Carrier got a hero's welcome when he returned to the Paris Jacobin Club.[33] Nantes had the dubious distinction of executing the most people during the Terror: almost thirty-five hundred in its department as a whole.

The *noyades* (drownings) were just part of the repression of the Vendée rebellion. In October, the army defeated the main rebel force at Cholet. The rebels then marched to Normandy, hoping to link up with the British at Granville. Cut off by the army, they turned back toward the Loire, suffering the loss of ten thousand people in fighting near Le Mans and of another three thousand at Savenay. In the Vendée itself, the "blues" (the royal army) brought fire and sword to every hamlet. In the words of their commanding general, Turreau, they were to "employ every means to discover the rebels, everyone will be bayoneted; the villages, farms, woods, wastelands, scrub and generally all which can be burned, will be put to the torch." The local population dropped by as much as one-third. People abandoned entire towns, like La Roche-sur-Yonne, which Turreau burned to the ground. Tens of thousands of people died in the repression, touching off more warfare. The Republic did not gain full control of the Vendée for another two years, when General Hoche captured and executed the main rebel leaders.

Terror and counterrevolution went hand-in-hand. The three departments most affected by the Vendée rebellion accounted for 43 percent of the total executions during the Terror, and the four most compromised in the southeast for another 18 percent. The majority of "unofficial" executions, certainly more numerous than the official ones, also came in these two areas. Although the climate created by the Reign of Terror hung like a pallor over all France, the Terror itself—in the sense of mass executions—took place in a very restrained area. Of the eighty-seven departments in existence in 1793–1794, thirteen accounted for 89 percent of the executions. Areas that had extensive counterrevolutionary activity tended to have substantial support for the Terror. Political opponents fought each other in an intense civil war in places like the Rhône valley.[34] Places such as Dijon were far more typical: city authorities arrested five hundred eighty people, a third of them women, but merely confined many of them to their houses. Only ten locals died under the blade at Dijon, while seventy more citizens from Dijon's department died in Paris's Terror.

Most of France had a very different experience of the Terror from that of Toulon or Nantes. Six departments had no executions at all, and sixty-one of them had fifty or fewer. Even a center of Federalism as important as Calvados was little touched. It had only seven executions. Most areas used the Terror to enforce specific governmental policies. The committees of surveillance, especially in towns, did not flag in their efforts to arrest suspects: some seventy thousand people suffered detention. Once again, there were substantial geographic variances. In some cases, that meant economic policy—grain requisition or price-fixing—but far more often it meant enforcement de-Christianization, the Convention's greatest blunder. (See the following text.)

The Terror killed far more people in the Vendée or the southeast than died in Paris, but the events in the capital captured people's imaginations, then and afterwards. Guittard's journal makes special reference to only a few fall 1793 executions:

the Girondins, Marie-Antoinette, and a few other notables. Although the theme of executions is absent in Guittard's journal, the deaths of the Girondin leaders certainly affected public opinion. Ruault wrote to his brother, in December 1793:

> What would you have me say, my dear friend? What side can I take now in all that is happening? To the sorrows that consume our home [Ruault's son had just died] are joined the horrors, the stupidities, the public follies. . . . Adieu, my dear friend, I cover my eyes so that I do not have to see any more.

Guittard's journal changes dramatically in March 1794, when the violent intra-Left war finally came to a head. The various parties had been slandering each other with ever-increasing vituperation in January and February. The Cordeliers went so far as to drape black crepe around the copy of the Declaration of the Rights of Man hanging in their meeting room. On 4 March, their evening meeting called for an insurrection in Paris, to put an end to the Terror. Robespierre and his allies on the Committee of Public Safety struck back suddenly. In mid-March, the government arrested the Parisian radical leaders, some of whom had only recently been released from prison, and put them on trial.

The fight on the Left had begun in the fall of 1793, when the Montagnards arrested Roux, Varlet, Léon, and Lacombe. This fighting on the Left had created three separate factions: the Jacobin Club, led by Robespierre and his allies; the Cordeliers Club, now the stronghold of the *enragés;* and the Indulgents, consisting primarily of those who had split from the Cordeliers. The Indulgents were led by Danton and by Camille Desmoulins, a journalist who began issuing a new newspaper, the *Vieux Cordelier,* in December 1793. Desmoulins roundly attacked the Committee of Public Safety and Robespierre for their policies, above all for the continuation of a Terror that Danton and Desmoulins believed had outlived its usefulness.

The Jacobins sought, from December 1793 to April 1794, to destroy both of the other factions. They arrested the leaders of the *sans-culottes* in January, released them in February, and then struck again in mid-March. On 24 March, Guittard provides details of the death of the main conspirators: Hébert, Anarchasis Cloots, Rousin (commander of the Revolutionary Army), Momoro (chief administrator of the department of Paris), Vincent (chief administrator of the ministry of war), and thirteen others. He claims that 300,000 spectators watched the guillotine fall. These men, called the *enragés,* had provided the leadership to the *sans-culottes* in Paris, tying together the power of the Paris sections and the Commune. The Convention further cut the power base of this faction by eliminating the Revolutionary Armies, which they had dominated. In May, they even outlawed sectional political clubs.

The Convention had already (January 1794) arrested a prominent former Cordelier, Fabre d'Eglantine, because of his profiteering in the dissolution of the Company of the Indies. On 29 March, they arrested the other leading Indulgents, such as Danton and Desmoulins. Guittard mentions this conspiracy on 5 April, when Desmoulins, Danton, Fabre d'Eglantine, General Westermann, and Hérault de Séchelles, a former member of the Committee of Public Safety, joined ten others on the block. They stood accused of collaborating with the duke of Orléans (and

Robespierre giving a speech to the Jacobin Club. The artist provides us with vivid testimony of Robespierre's rigid, almost puritanical demeanor.

SOURCE: Bibliothèque Nationale.

his agent, the traitorous General Dumouriez) to place him on the throne. Another twenty-one people, including the wives of Desmoulins and Hébert, Godot, the archbishop of Paris, and the *procureur syndic* of Paris, Chaumette, went to the block on 13 April. These executions show the Byzantine politics of the time. Fabre d'Eglantine and Hérault de Séchelles had been violent opponents in December 1793; one recent study finds the latter at first an ally of the *enragés* and then an associate of the Indulgents. Desmoulins and Hébert spent much of January and February denouncing each other, yet their wives joined each other in execution. Godel and Chaumette had led the Committee's de-Christianization campaign and had nothing in common with the Indulgents. Robespierre and his allies merely tied them to convenient villains in order to distance themselves from the unpopular excesses of de-Christianization.

THE SINNER AND THE PRINCE OF DARKNESS

Andrzej Wajda's brilliant film, *Danton,* has a dramatic scene in which Danton invites Robespierre to a one-on-one meeting to patch over their differences. Danton, a lover of life and of its many pleasures, has a leading restaurant lay out a sumptuous dinner for the two of them; Robespierre, when he arrives, refuses to eat. He looks with contempt on Danton, who has commanded such a repast in a Paris teeming with the hungry. When Robespierre walks out, Danton trashes the dining room in frustration.

Georges Danton came from the tiny bourg of Arcis-sur-Aube, received a legal education, and took up practice before the Parlement of Paris. In July 1789, he became one of the many street-corner orators inciting the Parisian crowds to militant action. His skills as an orator led to a rapid rise in local politics: he became head of the section of the Cordeliers. Mona Ozouf, noting his imposing physical figure, compares him to a sectional Mirabeau, while Michelet thought him a "lion who descends into a bull, even a wild boar," darkened by his "wild sensuality." Mme Roland (wife of his main enemy) found him "repugnant and atrocious," yet having an "air of great joviality." Ozouf writes that he was "a massacrer without ferocity, a gambler without avidity, a terrorist without maxims, a parvenu without avarice, a frantic lazybones, a tender colossus."[35]

Ruault, whose earlier letters had criticized Danton, wrote more sympathetically about him on the day of his arrest:

Because Danton and Desmoulins wanted to stop the movement of the guillotine, they passed under it themselves; those good sentiments were stifled along with their lives. . . . The misfortune of Danton was to have regained credit with the good patriots and even the men of the world, since he had associated himself with Desmoulins at the *Vieux Cordelier* in an effort to stop the massacres of the Revolutionary Tribunal. These two men, chiefs of a too-famous party, had kept something human and wanted to make others forget their follies, even their

cruelties, by an honorable return to sound principles. The credit of Danton gave umbrage to Robespierre, who is today the king of the revolution, the pontiff of the Eternal, the apostle of that doctrine of the immortality of the soul that he has had pasted up on the pediment of all the churches. . . .

[Danton had told his friends three months ago] 'As long as they say *Robespierre and Danton,* things will go well; I will have nothing to fear; but if they ever say, *Danton and Robespierre,* I am a lost man.' In effect, Danton had begun to be named first. Confidence in him rose each day; tomorrow he will be at the Tribunal; the day after he will be killed with his friends. Such is the fate of patriots enraged and unenraged; such are the effects of anarchy; it devours its own children; it kills its brothers; it eats its own innards; in the end, it is the most horrible and cruelest of all monsters. This frightening monster is today among us in its greatest vigor. None of use can be sure of escaping it, because it strikes wrongly and faultily. Milton forgot to depict it in his hellish scenes."

[Letter of 10 April] "Danton is no more. Robespierre triumphs. The tiger has beaten the lion. But this triumph will be short-lived, if we can believe the prediction of Danton, as he walked to his death; and that man knows about revolution. You are perhaps curious to know of the last minutes of this proud revolutionary. He gaily put up with the interrogation of the Tribunal and mocked his judges and jury throughout; he went to the scaffold laughing at death. He was the only one of the band of the accused to keep a good countenance; when he appeared for the first time before the judges and they asked his name, age, and residence, he replied: 'My name is sufficiently known, you can find it in the Pantheon of history; as for my residence, it will soon be in the void.' . . . [On the way to the scaffold] Danton laughed . . . and argued with Lacroix and Hérault . . . 'that which vexes me is to die six weeks before Robespierre.'

'Danton was the last; when he saw the executioner coming to get him at the bottom of the scaffold, he cried out with a loud voice, *My turn!* and quickly mounted the fatal stairway. . . . Only the head of Danton was shown to the people,

(CONTINUED)

who cried "Vive la République! The eyelids of that head thrashed about, the eyes were lively and full of light, while the executioner promenaded it around the scaffold; the body that the head had just left had been so robust and vigorous, that the head seemed still to look and to breathe, and to hear the cries of the multitude."[36]

Robespierre, born in 1758, came, like Danton, from a provincial town (Arras), where he, too, practiced law. His contemporaries called him the "Incorruptible" for his austere personal life and his inflexible principles. Throughout the Revolution, this leader of the *sans-culottes*

continued to wear culottes; in a Paris where Revolutionary manners demanded he remove it, he sported a powdered wig. The German playwright, Büchner, in his work *Danton's Death,* called Robespierre "insupportably honest," while the American historian Robert Palmer suggested that he "had the fault of a self-righteous and introverted man. Disagreement with himself he regarded simply as error . . . He was quick to charge others with the selfish interests of which he felt himself to be free. . . . A lover of mankind, he could not enter with sympathy into the minds of his own

Georges Danton, a sketch by Jan Georg Wille, as Danton made his way to execution.
SOURCE: © Gianni Dagli Orti/Corbis.

(CONTINUED)

---

neighbors."[37] Michelet rightly called his ascendancy the "Papacy of Robespierre," while Ruault described him as "the prince of revolutionary darkness, who, in dying, saw his party buried with him and the Jacobins defeated, and watched all his projects and friends die with him on the scaffold."

After the imprisonment of Camille Desmoulins, Lucille Desmoulins tried to write to Robespierre, to remind him of his old friendship for her husband:

> Camille saw your pride growing, he felt early on the path you wanted to follow, but he recalled your old friendship, and as far from the insensibilities as from the low jealousies of your Saint-Just, he recoiled from the idea of accusing an old school friend, a fellow artisan of his work. . . . And you, you send him to his death! . . . For you know it yourself, we do not merit the fate that they prepare for us; and you can change it. If it strikes us, it's you who will have ordered it.[38]

Robespierre had great success as an orator, although his style differed greatly from Danton's. Where the latter overwhelmed the audience with his physical presence and his rolling cadences, with his remarkable knack for the memorable phrase ("l'audace, encore de l'audace, toujours de l'audace"), Robespierre spellbound listeners with his implacable moral intensity and ruthless logic. Where Danton relied on the spontaneous, Robespierre was an inveterate plotter and planner; ironically, his best speeches invariably accused others of precisely these faults.

Robespierre had the good fortune to be consistently ahead of the revolutionary curve: an early and ardent republican and a steadfast

---

An issue of the anti-Hébertiste newspaper, *Le Sappeur Sans-Culotte,* subsidized by the government, gives the general tenor of the propaganda of the time. As he writes, there is "Great Anger of the People against the infamous Père Duchesne and his accomplices, who wanted to free the [royal children in the Temple prison], open the doors to all conspirators held in Paris, cut the throats of the members of the Convention, and proclaim the son of the tyrant Capet (Louis XVI) as king." Guittard, like many others, seems to have bought into these charges. His journal entry for 13 April, the day of the execution of Chaumette *et alia,* reads as follows:

> All eighteen accused of having, in complicity with the infamous Hébert, Clootz, etc. . . . who had their heads cut off on March 24th, conspired against liberty and the security of the French people, in wanting to trouble the state by a civil war, in the aftermath of which the conspirators wanted, in March and April, to dissolve the Convention, assassinate its members and the patriots, destroy the republican Government, make off with the Sovereignty of the people and give a tyrant to the state: little Capet.

Guittard then begins a morbid daily body count. There were thirty-one on 20 April, many of them leaders of the Parlement of Paris; thirteen on 22 April, including such men as Le Chapelier, a leader of the Constituent Assembly; Malesherbes, former censor and counsel for Louis XVI at his trial; and the baron of Châteaubriand, father of the famous nineteenth-century writer. Then on 24 April,

---

(CONTINUED)

---

critic of Louis XVI. Louis's flight in June 1791 and the steady move toward republicanism in 1791–1792 seemed to bear out virtually every one of Robespierre's positions. In a February 1794 speech on the principles of the Revolution, he spelled out his view of the new political morality:

> We would wish to substitute in our country morality for egotism, probity for honor, principles for usages, duties for good manners, the empire of reason for the tyranny of fashion, contempt for vice for contempt for misfortune, pride for insolence, grandeur of the soul for vanity, the love of glory for the love of money, good people for good company, merit for éclat, the charm of happiness for the boredom of sensuality, the grandeur of man for the pettiness of the *grands,* a magnanimous, powerful, and happy people for a likeable, frivolous, and mis-

erable one; in a word, all the virtues and miracles of a republic for all the vices and absurdities of a monarchy.[39]

In a political system in which many important leaders had been compromised by efforts to reach some sort of accommodation with the king and the aristocrats—starting with Mirabeau and running up through Barnave and Danton (who had been an ally of Philippe d'Orléans), Robespierre's uncompromising attitude toward the old order gave him tremendous moral authority. Just as Danton's sinning humanity, which so endeared him to his contemporaries and to posterity, gave his enemies the weapons to defeat him, so, too, Robespierre's saintly, uncompromising moralism, which paved the way for his triumphs, in the end led to his death.

---

there were thirty-five executions and as many again on 28 April; twenty-four on 6 May, including thirteen leaders of the Parlement of Burgundy and eleven former administrators of the department of the Moselle. On 8 May, the executions followed with twenty-eight former Farmers General; and on 10 May, twenty-five people, among them Madame Elisabeth, sister of Louis XVI.[40] On 14 June, it was the turn of the Parlement of Toulouse, twenty-six of whose judges went to the scaffold; on 17 June, sixty-one more, accused of a plot against Robespierre and Collot d'Herbois (who had, in fact, survived an assassination attempt in late May), lost their heads. July's tally included a group of sixteen Carmelites from Compiègne on 17 June and peaked at fifty-five people on 23 June, a group that included the prince of Rohan and the famous Magon brothers, merchant–nobles of Saint-Malo, aged eighty and eighty-one!

Throughout his journal, Guittard dutifully reports the official line about all these executions. The condemned "sought the annihilation of the Republic," or they carried out a "plot against the Republic" or one to "restore the Monarchy" or "against the surety and liberty of the people." He seems never to question the existence of the plots or the guilt of the condemned, although he made a special point of making a drawing of a few of the executions: those of the Girondins, in fall 1793, and of the sixteen Carmelites in July 1794. To read his journal for the months from April to July 1794 is to enter a world gone mad.

Few historical moments have captured the collective imagination so much as the Reign of Terror. Charles Dickens, the great nineteenth-century English novelist,

THE TRIAL

Paris newspapers published the proceedings of some of the famous trials that took place in front of the Revolutionary Tribunal. The English novelist Helen Maria Williams, in Paris for the first half of the 1790s, provides the following translation of the trial of Louis XVI's sister, Madame Elisabeth, who died on 10 May 1794.

President of the Revolutionary Tribunal: When the tyrant, your brother, fled to Varennes, did you not accompany him?

Madame Elizabeth: Every consideration led me to follow my brother; and I made it a duty then, as I should have done on any other occasion.

Court: Did you not appear at the infamous and scandalous orgies of the bodyguard; and did you not walk round the table with Marie Antoinette, to induce each of the guests to repeat the horrid oath which they had sworn to exterminate every patriot . . . ?

Madame Elizabeth: Such orgies I believe never took place; but I declare that I was no manner whatever informed of their having happened, and never had any concern in them.

Court: You do not speak truth and your denial can be of no use to you, when it is contradicted on one side by public notoriety, and on the other by the likelihood which there must be in every sensible man's opinion, that a woman so intimately connected as you were with Marie Antoinette, both by the ties of blood and those of the strictest friendship, could not but be a sharer in her machinations. . . .

[Further accusations and denials]

Court: Were you not yourself anxious in dressing the wounds of the assassins sent to the Champs Elysées by your brother against the brave Marseillais?

[The Court here uses the term assassins to describe the defenders of the Tuileries Palace on 10 August 1792.]

Madame Elizabeth: I never knew that my brother had sent assassins against anyone whatever. If I have ever chanced to assist in dressing the wounded, it was humanity only that could have influenced me; it was not necessary for me to be informed what was the cause of their misfortune to hesitate whether I should afford them relief; and if I make no merit of this, I do not imagine that you can impute it to me as a crime.

Court: It is difficult to reconcile these sentiments of humanity to which you pretend, with that barbarous joy which you discovered, when you saw streams of blood flowing on the 10th of August. Everything leads us to believe you were humane only towards the assassins of the people, and that you have all the savageness of the most bloodthirsty beasts towards the defenders of liberty.[41]

---

captured its terrible dichotomy in the opening lines of *A Tale of Two Cities*: "It was the best of times. It was the worst of times." The Jacobin dictatorship accomplished many extraordinary goals. It organized the first modern army and used it to defeat a coalition of the other European powers in war; it tamed short-term inflation and provided affordable food for France's people; it crushed the Federalist revolt in the south and west and the counterrevolution in the Vendée; it encouraged popular participation in government, particularly by the lower classes; it abolished slavery and the last vestiges of feudalism; it wrote (but did not enact) a constitution that rested on universal manhood suffrage and that enshrined subsistence and public education as human rights. It accomplished these goals in most of France by means of widespread arrests, but with relatively little actual bloodshed. The Jacobins also inspired a remarkable patriotic ardor in their supporters, as even their severest enemies had to admit.

That Terror worked pretty effectively to accomplish its goals. Carnot, as the countless street signs claim, was indeed "the organizer of the victory"; by 1794, the French armies, larger than those of their opponents and now properly armed and supplied, swept all before them. The mobilization of the entire country, a mobilization enforced by Terror but also strongly supported by some elements of the population, worked. The Terror also had short-term success on the economic front. The revolutionary armies forcibly and effectively requisitioned grain from the countryside for the cities. By December, Paris had no more bread lines, using henceforth a system of bread ration cards.[42] Municipalities everywhere subsidized grain for the poor. At Grenoble, by April 1794, nearly ten percent of the city's families received bread directly from the hospital.

These short-term successes notwithstanding, we must not mince words about the Terror. It derailed the French Revolution, debased French political culture, and failed utterly, miserably, and completely as a form of government. Even the short-term successes, like the increased provision of grain, bred long-term failure. Forced requisition of grain supplies in the countryside worked but it inevitably produced resentment and resistance among the peasantry. The horrible grain shortages of 1795 can be traced back directly to the forced requisitions of 1794.

Moreover, in the ten percent of France in which it resorted to violence, the government did so on an unprecedented scale. The Jacobins murdered tens of thousands of their fellow citizens, many of them helpless victims, such as children. They trampled on the legal rights of their opponents by such means as declaring someone "outside the law," and thus subject to immediate arrest, conviction, and execution without normal due process. They removed rights of political participation—in clubs, in sectional assemblies, as petitioners to the Convention—from women. They executed Olympe de Gouges (Marie Gouze), author of the "Declaration of the Rights of Women and the Female Citizen," imprisoned Claire Lacombe and Pauline Léon, and drove the feminist writer Etta Palm d'Aelders into exile. They introduced such odious phrases as "enemies of the people" and "enemies of the Revolution," so grotesquely abused not only in their day but in more recent times.

Leaders such as Saint-Just urged the Convention to confiscate the property of all "enemies of the Revolution," (*Ventôse Decrees*, February–March 1794). They spoke in terms of virtue and justice:

> I do not know how to express my thought by halves. I am without indulgence for the enemies of my country; I know only justice. . . . Those who demand liberty for the aristocrats do not want the Republic, and fear for them. It is a glaring sign of treason, the pity that is shown for crime in a Republic than can be founded only on inflexibility.

They bequeathed to modern political discourse the odious connection between virtue and infallibility. Here they borrowed from Rousseau, who suggested that the general will of the people was sometimes misled, but never wrong. Rousseau never clearly delineates who will articulate the general will, but Saint-Just, Robespierre, and the other Jacobins grew steadily surer: they would. They made sure to silence all other voices who might make similar claims. They therefore executed the radical leaders like Hébert, the feminist leaders like de Gouges, and other major voices of the Left, like Danton and Desmoulins. They saved a special level of rage for those who claimed a similar monopoly on the voice of virtue, the priests.

❧ De-Christianization and Revolution: The War of the Priesthoods

> *Priests are to morality what charlatans are to medicine.*
>
> Robespierre, June 1794

Robespierre, in his speech about "Religious and Moral Ideas and Republican Principles," given in May 1794, as part of his campaign against atheism and on behalf of a new, civil religion dedicated to the Supreme Being and reason, emphasized the one way, the shining path:

> Everything has changed in the physical order; everything must change in the moral and political order. Half the revolution of the world is already accomplished; the other half must be achieved. . . . What conclusion should be drawn from what I have just said? That immorality is the basis of despotism, as virtue is the essence of the republic. . . . Consult only the good of the *patrie* and the interests of mankind. Every institution, every doctrine which consoles and which elevates souls should be welcomed; reject all those which tend to degrade and corrupt them.

He concluded that "the idea of the Supreme Being and the immortality of the soul is a continual recall to justice; it is therefore social and republican." He thus sought to position the Revolution between the excesses of atheism, which he feared would alienate the masses, especially the peasants, and the "darkness," "ignorance," and "superstition" of "fanaticism" (that is, Catholicism). He spoke out especially against the latter:

> Fanatics, expect nothing from us! To recall men to the pure cult of the Supreme Being is to strike a mortal blow at fanaticism. . . . You are your own assassins, and men do not come back to life morally any more than they do physically.[43]

Robespierre's words alert us to one of the Convention's most enduring legacies: de-Christianization. The Republic of the Year II (1793–1794) declared war to the death on religion; ever afterwards, not only in France but in Europe as a whole, republicanism and organized religion—especially, but not exclusively, Catholicism—remained sworn enemies. Each claimed a monopoly on virtue. The republicans claimed virtue emanated from the will of the people, expressed through their elected leaders. The Church claimed virtue emanated from God, revealed to His people by the clergy. The two priesthoods fought, (indeed, still fight), for the souls of the people.

The Jacobin leadership left two related and decisive legacies to nineteenth-century France: the memory of the Terror and aftermath of de-Christianization. The memory of the Terror polarized people's opinions on the political participation of the mass of the working poor and created a severe division between Paris and the provinces. The de-Christianization policy adopted in the fall of 1793 permanently alienated the Catholic Church and its congregations from the revolutionary tradition. The fundamental issue of Left–Right politics in France until the eve of World War I remained the relationship of Church and State. The French republican Left, particularly after 1848, was staunchly anticlerical; the French Catholic Church, well into the twentieth century, identified republicanism with de-Christianization.

The Revolution had had problems with the Catholic Church from the start. The confiscation of Church property in the fall of 1789, the Civil Constitution of the Clergy, and the absorption of the papal properties of Avignon and the Comtat into France (1791) provided a backdrop of hostility to the events of 1793–1801. Non-juring priests did play prominent roles in counterrevolutionary activity, whether among the Chouans in Brittany, the rural rebels in the Midi, or the Vendeans. Thousands of non-juring priests said clandestine masses every Sunday in many parts of France. Throughout the south, excluding the Rhône valley, the main purpose of the Terror was to root out non-juring priests and their allies. In regions outside of the great centers of Terrorist violence, a quarter of those executed were priests.[44]

De-Christianization added a new dimension to this conflict. It targeted the Constitutional church, which had possession of the churches in the fall of 1793, when the campaign began. The Jacobins, by aggressively destroying the Constitutional church, ironically assured that, when the Catholic Church revived, it would be dominated by its most conservative element. Little wonder that the Church would be the implacable foe of republicanism for more than century.

The Constitutional church had struggled in 1792 and 1793, particularly in the countryside. The more radical Jacobin deputies and their allies gradually came to see the two churches as one and the same. As one official near Macon wrote:

> Since the beginning of the Revolution, the Catholic cult has been the cause of many troubles. Under the cloak of religion, the progress of civic-mindedness has been much hampered. Disastrous wars have taken place. Would it not be appropriate to authorize only the cult of the Revolution?[45]

The strong impetus toward de-Christianization began in September and October 1793. In part, as Donald Sutherland suggests, it arose because of the immediate connection between priests (admittedly non-juring ones) and Counterrevolution. That motivation seems clear in the work of deputies on mission like Couthon and Fouché, each of whom pursued aggressive de-Christianization policies, and in the rhetoric of the Parisian *procureur syndic*, Anaxagoras Chaumette, who gave voice to demands from the *sans-culottes* that the churches be shut down. Ménétra's *Journal* shows how much Parisian artisans had come to view the Church as a bastion of superstition and bigotry before the Revolution. Once the Revolution broke out, they supported ever more vigorous action against the Church:

> these immoral men who constituted a second authority by means of all the chimeras invented by lies and sustained by ignorance backed up by fanaticism and superstition these creatures preferred to see the Nation fall into adversity through decrepitude rather than make the slightest sacrifice.[46]

De-Christianization really began on 5 October 1793, when the Convention changed the calendar. Denouncing the traditional calendar as a testimony to superstition and the Ancien Régime, the Convention decreed that 21 September 1792, the date of the declaration of the French Republic, would henceforth be day one of the Year I. The Convention further decreed that the calendar would have twelve months of thirty days each; each month would have three ten-day weeks; each week would have one day of rest, the *décadi*. Months now took names like Brumaire and Thermidor and days simply took their numerical name (first day, second day).[47] The following day, an unnamed Jacobin leader preached a "republican speech" from the pulpit of Saint-Sulpice. On 11 October, at Saint-Sulpice, the two orders co-existed. In honor of the first *décadi,* the section authorities organized a procession and the planting of an Italian poplar in the square in front of the church; they followed those festivities with a mass in honor of the troops and a brief speech. Two days later, the priests said the normal Sunday masses at Saint-Sulpice, but shops no longer closed. Henceforth, they would close only on the *décadi*. The authorities took the final step the following Tuesday, banning the celebration of the mass.

The climate of hunger and revolutionary fervor in fall 1793 led directly to the stepped-up de-Christianization of November. Under pressure from the Convention, archbishop Godel of Paris tore up his letters of ordination in front of the assembly. The parish priests of Paris followed suit, and those of Saint-Sulpice acted on 10 November. Guittard reports that they made a brief speech to the effect that "theology is to religion as chicanery is to justice, and that they had never believed a word of what they had taught, that they had only done it to fool the people." Two of the three priests had already married. That same day, at Notre Dame, the Commune of Paris organized a festival of Liberty, hiring an actress to portray the goddess of Liberty.

Paris authorities made every parish church turn in its ornaments, to be melted down by the Mint, and demanded all religious books be turned over to them for burning. All priests had to surrender their letters of ordination and abjure Catholicism in favor of the Cult of Reason and Liberty. Every *décadi*, authorities now undertook festivals in honor of Reason and Liberty, complete with moral instruction for the young in republican values. To facilitate this change, the authorities promised to make new instruction books. They took over some of the churches, such as Notre Dame, and made them into Temples of Reason. The more radical elements, like Chaumette, preached atheism.

On the next *décadi,* Guittard's section organized a huge festival, complete with a two-hour procession. The festivities began with a public burning of a pyre made up

De-Christianization. The artisans put on a mock religious procession; French towns had many such processions in 1793 and 1794, as the artisans and others expressed their profound anticlericalism.

Source: Bibliothèque Nationale, Estampes, coll. Hennin n. 11, 702.

of a Papal tiara, a bishop's miter, various religious vestments, and the statue of Saint Peter that had graced the baptistery of Saint-Sulpice, followed by a procession to the church and a ceremony at a new altar. The ceremony had two goddesses (presumably Reason and Liberty, although Guittard does not say so), surrounded by "cavaliers," with the National Guard ranged on one side and ranks of white-clad girls on the other. A "philosopher" gave a speech to the effect that "there was no more religion and no more God, that everything comes from Nature. . . . Thus the new Religion or rather cult is established today in all the churches of Paris." Not long afterward, the inhabitants, led by their school children, marched on the Convention, demanding that it fulfil its promises about new textbooks. All over France, local authorities removed the word "Saint" from place and street names and good republicans began to use names such as Brutus or Bêche (Hoe) or Pissenlit (Dandelion) in place of the discredited saints' names like Pierre or Jean or Marie. The unfortunate daughter of the foreign minister, P.-H. Lebrun, had to go through life known as Civilisation-Jémappes-République.

The Convention backtracked a little in early December, allowing religious ceremonies (Catholic, Protestant, or Jewish) to take place in private; the churches remained closed.[48] Ruault wrote that Robespierre himself "was frightened. He gave a report against this mania which will make of France a country of madmen, atheists, an ungovernable people." Chaumette and Godel played leading roles in the excesses of de-Christianization. Guittard even accused Chaumette of arguing that there "was

STRANGE BEDFELLOWS

Helen Maria Williams offers the following account of the last moments of Chaumette, Godel, and Madame Desmoulins.

It was one of the singular chances of these revolutionary moments that Camille Desmoulins, who with the pointed shafts of his wit had overthrown the idol of the populace, Hébert, perished himself but a fortnight later; and this own wife and the wife of Hébert, seated on the same stone in the Conciergerie, deplored their mutual loss, and were led together to the scaffold. The people, as Madame Desmoulins passed along the streets to execution, could not resist uttering exclamations of pity and admiration:

'How beautiful she is! how mild she looks! what a pity she should perish!' At the foot of the scaffold she embraced the wife of Hébert, bade her companions in the cart farewell, and resigned herself to the executioner with the serenity of an angel. . . . Far different from the meek and placid resignation with which Madame Desmoulins made the sacrifice of life in all its bloom and freshness, was the behaviour of Chaumette the procureur of the commune, and Godel the archbishop of Paris, who perished at the same time. Their aspect testified that death appeared to their perturbed spirits, not in the form he wears to suffering innocence, but armed with all his stings, and clad in all his terrors.[49]

no God and that man has no soul" and forcing priests to preach the same thing. Robespierre and his allies conveniently blamed Chaumette and Godel for the excesses, and sent them to the executioner's block in April 1794. Guittard wrote approvingly: "God discovered their projects and that is always the end of conspirators." By June, Robespierre himself would take part in a Festival of the Supreme Being. The Revolution thus rejected atheism for the deism of such Enlightenment figures as Voltaire.

Outside of Paris, de-Christianization spread slowly. The revolutionary army sent to Lyon in November 1793 carried out iconoclastic destruction along its line of march, which led through such important religious centers as Sens and Auxerre. The soldiers decapitated statues, burned crosses, destroyed ornaments, and looted churches. Such incursions aside, de-Christianization emanated from towns that supported the Jacobins. Areas like Lyon or Marseille in which deputies on mission played an important role in local administration, particularly local repression, had the highest numbers of priests who resigned in response to de-Christianization, but even cities like Limoges came over to the new "faith."

Out in the countryside, de-Christianization was an unmitigated disaster. Everywhere, women led the resistance. The typical chronology can be seen in two villages in the Burgundian department of the Yonne (Auxerre). In Taingy, the district commissioner seized the ornaments in November 1793 and closed the church in March. The following month, the village celebrated a festival of Reason but clandestine Catholic ceremonies took place constantly. In Courgis, the mayor noted that the inhabitants fled into the woods on Easter 1794. Scarcely ten men bothered to listen to the Revolutionary speeches made that day in the church. A crowd of women stoned the men sent to remove the local crosses. In the Yonne, in village after village, the peasants simply broke into the churches on Christmas 1794, to celebrate as they sought fit.

In the department of Haute-Loire, the town of Montpigié gave the authorities a lesson in civil disobedience. Ordered to take an oath to the new government, the local lay religious teachers refused (February 1795). When the mayor sought to arrest the teachers, the rest of the women rioted. He did manage to arrest both the teachers and about one hundred women, but the men soon rioted to get their wives back. The mayor released the married women, who reorganized, returned to the jail, released the teachers, and pummeled the mayor. Another local official, in Saint-Vincent, called upon to lead the celebration on behalf of the Supreme Being in June 1794, had an even more embarrassing failure:

> The unlucky celebrant began his patriotic oration when, at a sign from an old woman, the entire female audience rose, turned their backs on the altar of liberty, and raised their skirts to expose their bare buttocks and to express their feelings to the new deity. Confronted by the spectacle of serried rows of naked female backsides the celebrant was reduced to gibberish.[50]

The fall of Robespierre (July 1794) and the end of the Terror soon afterwards led to a gradual reduction in de-Christianization pressure. By February 1795, the Convention decided to create freedom of religion. Guittard tells us 21 February 1795 was "a remarkable day in the history of France." The decree allowed all religions to have services, provided they did so in specific locales only. The state would furnish neither locales nor salaries for clergy. On Sunday, 8 March 1795, priests openly said mass in Paris for the first time since November 1793; they did so in private homes, rented rooms, and convent chapels, not in the regular churches, which remained closed. Demand was so high that some priests had to say mass continuously from 6 A.M. until midnight. A little over two months later, on 31 May, the Convention returned all churches to the communes and allowed them to be used for religious services. Each commune (or *arrondissement* in large cities) was to have only one church, made equally available to all faiths. As Guittard wrote that day, "it's now a question of knowing if we will observe Sundays and if they will suppress the republican calendar."

In much of France, people organized passive resistance to the republican calendar. They could do little to prevent the changing of market days—the police simply confiscated goods brought to market on the wrong day—but they could subvert the *décadi* and civil marriage ceremonies, and continue to celebrate Sundays and church weddings. The government sought in 1797 to enforce the ban on work on the *décadi*, but that ban extended only to work done in public. Artisans therefore shut their doors and continued to work. Even those who could not work obstinately wore everyday clothes; they turned out in the best clothes only on Sundays, as before. As for weddings, people wore simple clothes to the city hall and elaborate finery to the church. One celebrant, Gabriel Guy, who showed up at a town hall wearing "improper clothing" was asked, given his appearance, if "he wanted the citizeness Marie Forest for his legitimate wife?" He responded "ironically and with insolence, that if he had not wanted her, he would not have presented himself here." His response elicited "immoderate and scandalous laughter."[51]

The Sunday issue had more importance in towns—where municipal governments and section assemblies enforced the new calendar—than in villages, where it
was far more common for the villagers to enforce Sundays and to ignore the *décadi*.
At the end of 1793, the committee of surveillance of the small Burgundian village of
Bèze wrote to their superiors:

> [most of the villagers] like the Republic, or appear to like it. However, we
> must not dissimulate about it, there is one point on which our fellow citi-
> zens are behind the Revolution's course: that of general Reason which it is
> so necessary to substitute for the Empire of superstition because they have
> not abstained from working on a single *décadi*; all of the feasts of the Roman
> cult continue to be celebrated with the same exactitude as before, and per-
> haps this exactitude is the true cause of the neglect of the *décadi,* which
> would be a further reduction of work days if they interwove it with the
> saints days of the old calendar.[52]

They blamed the persistence of such practices on the continued importance of the
clergy in their region. Because of their superior ability to read and write, many local
curés served as the chief civil administrator of their commune. The committee of
surveillance of Bèze suggested that the Convention look into the matter and purge
local administrations. The Convention followed this suggestion, which had echoes
in reports from many deputies on mission.

Here we must remember the centrality of the religious calendar to everyday life.
The Church mandated large numbers of festivals and work-free days, not merely the
fifty-two Sundays, but nearly as many feast days. Eliminating all those days of leisure
and substituting forty-one off days (the thirty-six *décadi* and the five *sans-culottides*
that brought the Revolutionary year up to three hundred sixty-five days) for the
roughly one hundred of the Ancien Régime was not likely to be a popular measure,
for secular as well as religious reasons. Combining the new holidays with the old, as
the committee from Bèze suggested, was similarly impractical.

Two conveniently overlapping objectives motivated the Jacobins in their campaign against the Church. First, as Jean Bart has suggested, the Jacobins desperately
needed to remove rural priests from their role in communal administration. Allowing a Fifth Column to persist within the ranks of the basic level of government made
no political sense. Second, the de-Christianization movement pitted two priesthoods
against one another. The new priesthood, the acolytes of the state, understood the
fundamental need to destroy the Church's hold on the most important elements of
everyday life: birth, marriage, death, subsistence, security, and education (taken in its
broadest possible meaning). The state had long had control of security, but the
Church in France dominated the other five. Its records—copies of which, admittedly, had to be given to state authorities after 1667—registered births, marriages,
and deaths. Its priests performed the rites central to all three. The Church shared
with the state the obligation for poor relief, but it dominated education. The
Jacobins, recognizing the need for the state to take control of real life from the
Church, acted vigorously on each of these fronts. They mandated civil registers of

birth, marriage, and death, as well as the obligation for civil marriage; they secularized poor relief and hospitals; they voted for a national, state-run education system. The Jacobins believed the state should have control of everyday life, and thus of the moral system embedded in it. Practical and philosophical considerations thus mandated the elimination of the priests, especially in rural areas.

9–10 Thermidor: The Fall of Robespierre and the Jacobins

28 July 1794 [10 Thermidor II]: "temperature—29 degrees Centigrade, the hottest day of the year. In the evening, there was a great thunderstorm." / 29 July "a cooler and more refreshing day."

Paris weather, 28–29 July 1794, as reported in Guittard's *Journal*

The policy of Terror had made some sense in the crisis situation of the fall of 1793 and winter of 1793 to 1794. The considerable amelioration of the situation everywhere, from the battlefields of Belgium to the killing fields of the Vendée to the bread markets of Paris, lessened people's sense of urgency. Robespierre and his allies sought, in part, to maintain a sense of urgency in the spring of 1794 by means of the Terror itself. The spectacular series of "conspiracies" discovered from February to July gave them the excuse to step up repression and executions. Few people had a closer identification with the Revolution than Hébert and Danton. Executing them as conspirators and traitors captured the popular imagination as nothing else could have.

The execution of fellow deputies made those sitting in the Convention quite nervous. Robespierre's constant warnings about new conspiracies and his threats to root out the traitors disturbed many. He launched a new campaign of this nature in mid-July 1794, leading his recent allies Collot d'Herbois, Billaud-Varenne, and Barère to organize the Convention against him. The timing was right for them. The spectacular success of French armies, especially in Belgium, where they defeated the Austrians at Fleurus (26 June) and then occupied Brussels and Antwerp, encouraged people to think the Terror should end. Given that Robespierre and his allies had just pushed through the infamous law of 22 Prairial (10 June 1794) that eliminated judicial rights for those accused of treason or conspiracy, and had used that law to implement a massive increase in executions, those opposed to the Terror had reason to act at once. Robespierre, Saint-Just, and Couthon quarreled sharply with Lindet, Carnot, Billaud-Varenne, and Collot d'Herbois in late June 1794. On 29 June, Robespierre walked out of the Committee of Public Safety, not to return until 23 July.

Billaud-Varenne and Collot d'Herbois were certainly as well inclined to Terror as anyone else, but they had personal scores to settle with Robespierre. Carnot, Lindet, and Prieur de la Côte-d'Or, who had the main administrative responsibilities, seem to have argued for a relaxation of the Terror in order to facilitate their own work. Many deputies in the Convention echoed the sentiments of Danton's friend, Thouet, who, after listening to Robespierre's speeches on morality, observed: "It's not enough for the bugger to be master, he has to be God."[53]

Events moved rapidly in late July. Robespierre had long ago alienated the members of the Committee of General Security, who objected to loss of jurisdiction to the Committee of Public Safety. His enemies were legion: Dantonists, friends of the executed radicals, personal rivals, and the functionary wing. Having purged Paris of the *enragés,* the Cordeliers, and the Indulgents, and having brought the sections to heel by eliminating nightly meetings and making their officers beholden to the Convention, Robespierre had a pretty weak base of support. Even mayor Pache, whose support had been so helpful in March, could no longer be counted upon. When some suggested Pache be arrested with the Hébertistes, the Convention had arrested him in May.

Robespierre turned to the Jacobin Club, denouncing Collot d'Herbois and Billaud-Varenne in an incendiary speech on the night of 26 July. They fled the premises and set to work organizing the deputies at the Convention, many of whom had been terrified by Robespierre's vague calls for more arrests in a speech earlier in the day. On 27 July (9 Thermidor of the Year II, in the Revolutionary calendar), on the floor of the Convention, Billaud-Varenne and his allies called for Robespierre's arrest. When Robespierre sought to speak in reply, the deputies drowned him out with cries of "Down with the tyrant!" and ordered his arrest and that of his supporters: Saint-Just; Couthon, Hanriot, commander of the Paris National Guard; and, on his own demand, Augustin Robespierre, brother of Maximilien.

Robespierre looked to his obvious allies, the Paris Commune. When the prisoners went to the Luxembourg prison, the jailers refused to accept them and sent them on to the Hôtel de Ville. There the Commune, who supported Robespierre, released the prisoners and appealed to the sections for support. Guittard says that Hanriot rode through the city, shouting "close your shops" and ordering his men to turn out. He returned to City Hall and tried to get his cannoneers—roughly two-thirds of the gunners reported for duty—to march on the Convention. They hesitated. Meanwhile, the members of the Commune spread throughout the city, trying to rouse the sections; deputies from the Convention did the same, trying to encourage their supporters. Guittard tells us that by 8 or 9 P.M., everyone in the city was in arms and mustered at the sections. "No one knew which side to take." His journal suggests the situation was touch and go. Robespierre had a strong party but citizens were reluctant to go against the Convention itself.

The Convention acted to place Robespierre and his allies, including the entire Commune, "outside the law." That is, they would, following a law moved by Saint-Just himself, lose all legal rights and be subject to arrest and immediate execution. Ruault's letter of 31 July to his brother strongly emphasizes the critical role of this step in mobilizing public opinion against Robespierre and his allies. The Convention sent deputies and mounted constabulary throughout the city to announce the news; Ruault claims these speeches led the pro-Commune crowds to break up and go home. Guittard reports: "All of the sections decided for the Convention, which was only natural." Detailed studies of the sections show that thirty-nine of the forty-eight did meet that night; of these, thirty-five voted to support the Convention rather than the Commune.

The roughly one-third of the National Guard units who supported Robespierre and the Commune began to lose faith as the night wore on. The workers had a strong

THE ARREST OF CATILINE-ROBESPIERRE [54]

Guittard's journal criticizes Robespierre for being an "ambitious criminal" and suggests, of his death, that it "is where your pride has led you." What ambition had Robespierre had? Here we find out a critical element in Robespierre's failure to gain sufficient support in the city. Guittard tells us what those deputies from the Convention, riding through the city, may have said to their fellow citizens:

> They say he wanted to have himself recognized as king at Lyon and in other departments and to marry the daughter of Capet [i.e., Louis XVI] . . . How can a simple individual get such an idea into his head!

This false rumor, as Bronislaw Baczko has suggested, reveals much about Guittard and his fellow Parisians.

> it seems a rumour that deserves to be taken seriously. Not in order to examine its validity; on the contrary, it is because it is so obviously false that it holds our attention. . . . a false rumour is a real social fact; in that it conceals a portion of historical truth—not about the news that it spreads, but about the conditions that make its emergence and circulation possible, about the state of mind, the *mentalités* and imagination of those who accepted it as true.[55]

Baczko set out to determine when and how it arose.

He suggests that it spread on the evening of 27 July (9 Thermidor), because none of the documents of earlier in the day, such as the

denunciations of Robespierre at the Convention, mention it. Several of the sectional assemblies of that evening seem to have discussed it, or a version of it. Some of the deputies from the Convention made specific mention of a fleur-de-lis seal found at Robespierre's house and Barère, in his official report to the Convention on 28 July, picked up that tale. The Committee of General Security took seriously the rumored release of the young royals: they sent troops to the Temple prison, to reinforce the guards there. In the Convention's session on the 28 July to discuss the fate of Robespierre, Thuriot, leading the charge, repeated virtually verbatim the claim made by Guittard, that Robespierre had sought to make himself king.[56] Other documents indicate that "workers" lining the route to his execution insulted him with cries of "Isn't he a handsome king?"[57]

Wild rumors, insecurity, extreme fluctuations of political loyalty—such was the madness of Paris in the summer of 1794. Yet these rumors had some relationship to reality. Ruault's letters see Robespierre's death as the revenge of Danton's old friends but he also accuses Robespierre of having sought, on 8 Thermidor, the support of the Jacobins for making himself "the sole head of the Republic." He openly accuses Robespierre of seeking dictatorial powers, an accusation that naturally found public expression as a desire to be "king."

recent grievance against the Commune, which had published a new wage control law on 23 July. The afternoon of 27 July (9 Thermidor), workers had protested the new wage limits in front of the Hôtel de Ville. The evening summons had produced about three thousand men, but their numbers had fallen to a mere two hundred by 1:30 A.M., when the last group left. Thirty minutes later, authorities arrived to arrest Robespierre and his supporters. The two brothers attempted suicide. Maximilien shot himself in the head and Augustin jumped from a window; both survived.

The next day, the Convention executed them all: the Robespierres, Saint-Just, Couthon, Hanriot, and seventeen others. Ruault says that they rode in three carts, draped with the tricolor flag, waved by an executioner as the column proceeded to the place de la Concorde: "It was a holiday, all of high society was at the windows to watch them pass; they applauded and clapped all along the rue Saint-Honoré." He tells us of the victims:

> Only Robespierre showed courage, in thus going to his death, and indignation in hearing these exclamations of joy. His head was wrapped in a cloth, his porcelain eyes, usually so dull, shined with life and animation in these final moments. The other condemned remained motionless; they seemed overcome with shame and sadness. Almost all were covered with blood and mud; Hanriot's eye hung from his head; one would have taken them for a troop of bandits captured in the woods after a violent combat. At 7 in the evening they were dead; an enormous people of men and women had come from all parts of the city to the place Louis XV to watch them be decapitated.[58]

On 29 July, the Convention sent the entire remaining membership of the Commune—seventy-one men—to the scaffold; on 30 July, another dozen lost their heads, all of them former members of the Commune. That same day, Guittard joined the members of his section and marched to the Convention, to offer their congratulations and promises of support: "All of the sections . . . congratulated [the Convention] for having discovered the plot of the criminals who wanted to slit the throat of the Convention and make civil war in Paris." Guittard would later record individual executions, but 30 July is the last day for which he records mass killing.

Robespierre and his allies had followed suicidal tactics. When the Left took power, in June and July 1793, it first purged the deputies of the Center–Left, the Girondins, and then purged itself, killing the Parisian radicals and the Dantonists. Although a further struggle within the radical Left itself led to the immediate events of 9–10 Thermidor, the deaths of the leading Jacobins and of the entire Paris Commune left the remainder of the radical Left without sufficient weight to sustain power. The Revolution's progressive shift to the Left shuddered to a halt; its course shifted back immediately to the Center–Left and then, inexorably, back toward the Right, toward the constitutional monarchy envisioned by the men of 1789. The Jacobins gave democracy a bad name among the middle and upper classes not merely in France but throughout the Europeanized world. Their vision of a Republic based on universal manhood suffrage did not die with them, but three generations would pass before it again became a reality.

Danton died a martyr, punished not for his sins but for his humanity; Robespierre died not only for his sins but for those of Danton and all the others. Where Danton joked in prison, telling the poet Fabre d'Eglantine, one of his fellow victims, "Eh bien, nous deviendrons tous poêtes, nous allons tous faire des vers" ("Well, we are all becoming poets, we are all going to make 'vers,'" the French word both for verses and for worms), Robespierre went glumly to his death, a bullet in his jaw. As Helen Maria Williams put it,

> A proof of the horrible oppression under which we groaned, was, that we lamented the fate of Danton—of Danton, the minister of justice on the 2d

of September, and one of the murderers of liberty on the 31st of May! Yet with all these crimes upon his head, Danton still possessed some human affections; his mind was still awake to some of the sensibilities of our nature; his temper was frank and social, and humanity in despair leant upon him as a sort of refuge from its worst oppressor.[59]

This Danton provided France with a convenient figure to lionize for the positive elements of the Republic of the Year II. Indeed Michelet states openly that the Dantonists created the Republic and tried to create a real justice to sustain it. Every French city has a rue Danton, often one of its most important streets. Paris honors Danton not only with a street but with a prominent statue on the Left Bank, on which are inscribed words from one of his most famous speeches: "After bread, education is the greatest need of the people." In early 1794, Danton was arguing for an end to the Terror: he wanted to stop virtually all of the executions. In later years, he thus became a symbol of what might have been, had not the Jacobins misguidedly descended into Hell in the spring of 1794.

In executing Robespierre, and in expunging his memory from public view whenever possible, France sought, and still seeks, to purify its republican tradition from the evil excesses of its birth. Carnot can stand for the stunning achievements of the republican armies; Danton can represent a republic for all the people, where education is a natural right: let their statues grace public squares and their names adorn the avenues of the chic. Robespierre, as Ruault rightly said, must remain the prince of revolutionary darkness, whose "name will long remain attached to the anarchic terrible splendors of the revolution," and thus dare not be spoken, or acknowledged, in public.[60]

Notes

1. The day of the creation of the Republic, 21 September 1792, was the first day of the Year I. See the following text for details.

2. Lyon, a center of Federalist activity, revolted against the Convention in the spring of 1793. A Revolutionary Army laid siege to the city and captured it in October 1793.

3. R. Cobb, *Paris and its Provinces, 1792–1802* (Oxford: Oxford University Press, 1975), 129.

4. "Universal" manhood suffrage meant all men over twenty-one, who had been domiciled in the same place for a year, and who did not work as servants.

5. The Mountain took its name from the fact that its deputies sat in the upper left hand side of the Salle du Manège in the Tuileries Palace, where the Convention met. Contemporaries called the uncommitted deputies who sat in the lower seats, the Plain. Later, those seeking to polarize the Convention called the uncommitted group the Marais, or Marsh.

6. Here we must distinguish between areas in which the peasants themselves led the counterrevolutionary forces—like the Vendée, in which the Jacobin clubs

did not take root, and those, like part of the Rhône valley, in which the nobility or urban oligarchies led the opposition. The strength of counterrevolutionaries in Arles and Avignon led to extreme politicization of the surrounding countryside: between 50 and 90 percent of the communes in the six departments of the region had Jacobin clubs, a percentage far in excess of that seen anywhere else.

7. *Journal de Célestin Guittard de Floriban, Bourgeois de Paris sous la Révolution,* ed. R. Aubert (Paris: Éditions France-Empire, 1974). Readers can simply refer to the date in question. Guittard was a *rentier,* a man who lived off his investments, such as government annuities. He violently opposed de-Christianization, but the *Journal* suggests he belonged the large uncommitted Center on other political matters.

8. The Left focuses on the birth of liberty (fall of the Bastille) and on the Jacobin rescue of France in its darkest hour; the Right focuses on blood and terror.

9. The district councils—administratively, socially, and politically—stood between the other two. They played a particularly important role in the sale of nationalized lands. I. Guégan, *Inventaire des Enquêtes administratives et statistiques, 1789–1795* (Paris, 1991), shows the Executive Council sent four times as many orders to departmental as against district councils. The Convention sent 70 percent of its requests to districts and municipalities.

10. Their strangest choice was the last man elected, Philippe Égalité, the new name of Philip, duke of Orléans, cousin of Louis XVI.

11. Many historians, following the lead of the great German sociologist Jürgen Habermas, have recently examined the evolving and expanding public sphere that often discussed, in salon conversation or in print, broad policies of reform and even political theory. But these people had very little experience of practical, everyday politics.

12. The Alien and Sedition Acts of 1798 are a classic American example of the equation of party opposition with treason in the 1790s.

13. The United States, of course, offered the unedifying spectacle of the vice-president, Aaron Burr, killing a former secretary of the treasury, Alexander Hamilton, in a duel (1804).

14. One document suggests central government expenses of 3.9 billion *livres,* excluding reimbursements of state debt, between 1 July 1791 and 1 September 1793. Feeding the armies consumed just under 20 percent of total government expenses, and total military costs about two-thirds of all receipts. Taxes produced only 368 million *livres;* the state used *assignats* to cover the rest. Roughly one-third of the *assignats* issued between 1790 and 1795 had been used to buy nationalized lands. When an *assignat* had been used for this purpose, the government burned it.

15. Guittard's journal shows us the state of affairs even in Paris: he did not receive his assessment for the military tax of 1791 until October 1792! He paid promptly (in December) but later tells us he paid one of his 1792 taxes in March 1793 and the other in October.

16. The American ambassador, Morris, wrote to George Washington on 28 December 1792, that he was sure a majority of the deputies would vote to appeal to the people. He informed Washington that Brissot and Roland worked out the details with Tom Paine, who would move in the Convention that Louis and his family be exiled to the United States.

17. Speeches of 8 and 13 Ventôse Year II (26 February and 3 March 1794), reproduced in P. Beik, ed., *The French Revolution* (New York: Walker and Co., 1970), citation on 291.

18. We see again here the close connections of French and American events; the famous Anglo-American pamphleteerist Tom Payne sat on the Convention's Constitutional Committee.

19. This draft did produce 150,000 conscripts.

20. Some historians have been reticent to make this specific connection, but two details in Guittard's testimony suggest its legitimacy. First, the number of women is precisely that organized by the CRRC. Second, Guittard notes that the crowd of two hundred or three hundred women wore "cockades in their bonnets." In September, the leaders of the CRRC got the Convention to decree that all women wear such cockades. I would take the emphasis on cockades in May, and again in September, to the be the calling card of the CRRC.

21. Artisans traditionally operated on a piecework system. They took it easy early in the week—often taking an unofficial holiday on "Holy Monday"—and then worked feverishly to finish their piece quota on Friday and on Saturday morning.

22. The first citation comes from G. Rudé's *The Crowd in the French Revolution* (Oxford, 1959), 121; the second and third are from O. Hufton, *Women and the Limits of Citizenship in the French Revolution* (Toronto, 1992), 30.

23. In homage to R.R. Palmer's indispensable work, published in 1941 by Princeton University Press, reissued in 1965 by Atheneum Publishers in New York.

24. Contemporaries added the names of their home departments to each of the (unrelated) Prieurs who sat on the Committee: Marne is the area around Châlons-sur-Marne, in the old province of Champagne. The Côte d'Or is the department for Dijon, capital of Burgundy.

25. Lindet has a small street named for him.

26. Brest, site of a great navy yard, long had a large working-class electorate, who supported the Communist Party. In the twentieth century, Robespierre has been a hero of the Communists, so they named the main street after him when they got control of the local government. The Paris Métro now has a stop named for him, naturally in one of the suburbs that form part of the "Red Belt" around the city.

27. Caen harbored several of the proscribed twenty-nine, who had fled Paris. The former mayor Pétion, now fallen from grace, was among them.

28. Guittard's journal here offers important evidence that relatively open democracy still operated in the spring and summer of 1793. His entry of 18 April tells us of the Montagnard petition calling for the expulsion of the Girondins that

"anyone who wanted could sign or not sign this petition; they did not force anyone." In July, he records the strong debates over the Constitution in his section. Guittard disliked the Jacobins, so he would have had no reason to gloss over their attempts to stifle democracy.

29. Ruault, *Gazette,* 341.

30. Ruault, *Gazette,* letter of 22 Brumaire, Year II, extract from torn-up letter. 342–343.

31. Ruault, *Gazette,* 343, letter of 1 December 1793.

32. Let us remember, in Louis's case, the foreign plots were quite real.

33. The fall of the Jacobins made Carrier a fine scapegoat; the Convention executed him in December 1794.

34. Among the nine districts of the department of Var (around Toulon) that had twenty or more incidents of revolutionary violence between 1790 and 1793, five had sixteen or more incidents of *counter*revolutionary violence, and three others had more than eleven such incidents each. By way of contrast, twenty of the twenty-two districts that had five or fewer incidents of revolutionary violence, similarly had five or fewer counterrevolutionary incidents.

35. Furet and Ozouf, *Dictionnaire,* 247–248. Ozouf's excellent portrait of Danton appears on pages 247–257.

36. Ruault, *Gazette,* letters of 2 April and 10 April 1794, pp. 347–351.

37. Palmer, *Twelve Who Ruled,* 6–7.

38. *Oeuvres de Camille Desmoulins* (Paris: Ebrard, 1838; reprinted in New York: AMS, 1972), v. II, 217–218. Robespierre never received the letter, which Mme Desmoulins did not finish.

39. Cited in M. Sonenscher, *Work and Wages. Natural law, politics and the eighteenth-century French trades* (Cambridge: Cambridge University Press, 1989), 360. Beik, *French Revolution,* 278, contains a translation, which I have modified slightly.

40. Robespierre opposed her execution but his colleagues on the Committee over-ruled him.

41. J. Fruchtman, Jr., ed., *An Eye-Witness Account of the French Revolution by Helen Maria Williams. Letters Containing a Sketch of the Politics of France* (New York: Peter Lang, 1997), 156–159. The excerpt here contains about half of the transcript provided by Williams.

42. The Commune based the cards on a house-to-house census conducted in November: all households reported the number of people, their need in bread, and the name of the baker from whom they got bread. They merely brought their card to him and he gave them their ration, at a set price.

43. I have used the translations of Beik, *The French Revolution;* the two speeches are found on pp. 288–312.

44. In contrast, in the three great centers of Terrorist violence, fewer than 7 percent of those killed were priests. By late 1793, non-jurors included two groups: those

who initially refused to swear the oath and those who had initially sworn, but later retracted to protest state policies.

45. Sutherland, *France, 1789–1815,* 211. Sutherland has excellent discussion of these issues on pages 208–217.

46. Ménétra, *Journal of My Life,* 217–218.

47. See appendix for the Revolutionary calendar.

48. Although most places of worship in France were, of course, Catholic churches, there were some Protestant "temples" and Jewish synagogues. The general attitude of the Revolutionaries toward religion is well illustrated by their attitude toward Jews. The Sephardic communities of the western ports (Nantes, Bordeaux), who were quite assimilated and who had had to practice Judaism in secret until 1789, suffered little discrimination. The Ashkenazic communities of the east—Metz and Nancy above all—practiced traditional Judaism in the open. Local communities there attacked religious Jews; the town government of Nancy even sought permission to expel Jews from the city. To their credit, the Paris authorities refused.

49. *An Eye-Witness Account of the French Revolution by Helen Maria Williams,* 150–151. Williams, it should be noted, was herself held prisoner and nearly executed, so she is a strongly anti-Jacobin witness.

50. Hufton, *Women and the Limits of Citizenship in the French Revolution,* 118.

51. A story told by I. Woloch, "'Republican Institutions,' 1797–1799," in *The French Revolution and the Creation of Modern Political Culture. Volume 2: The Political Culture of the French Revolution,* ed. C. Lucas (Oxford, New York, 1988), 378.

52. Bart, *La Révolution en Bourgogne,* 266–267. My translation.

53. Cited in Doyle, *French Revolution,* 277.

54. Helen Maria Williams, who was in prison under sentence of death at the time, claims that she could hear the newspaper hawkers shout this headline on the night of 9 Thermidor. *An Eye-Witness Account,* 187. Catiline was a famous Roman traitor, whose name was often invoked to slur those accused of treason during the French Revolution.

55. B. Baczko, *Ending the Terror. The French Revolution after Robespierre,* trans. M. Petheran. (Cambridge, 1994), 2–3.

56. Guittard may well have repeated in his entry for 27 July what he learned from his newspapers on the 28th or 29th, which would have reported what was said in the Convention. It should be noted that Thuriot made no mention of the marriage.

57. We can note in passing here that Ruault's description of those lining the rue Saint-Honoré as the well-to-do makes much more sense, because the street, then as now, lay in a very fashionable part of town.

58. Ruault, *Gazette,* letter of 30 July 1794 (12 Thermidor), 357–364.

59. *An Eye-Witness Account of the French Revolution by Helen Maria Williams,* 149.

60. Ruault, *Gazette,* 361–362, letter of 12 Thermidor II. In the original, the phrase reads "les fastes anarchiques de la révolution." The word *fastes,* literally "splendors," usually refers to great feasts or balls, such as those given at Versailles. In the context of the letter, I believe Ruault uses it ironically, hence the addition of "terrible."

Chapter Five

Revolutionary Legacies

*There are those who let the dead bury
the dead, and there are those who are forever
digging them up to finish them off.[1]*

J. Baudrillard, *The Illusion of the Dead*

The French Revolution is over.

François Furet, 1978

THE THERMIDORIAN REACTION

CHRONOLOGY	October 1794–October 1795
October 1794	French victories in the German Rhineland
12 November	Convention closes Paris Jacobin Club
8 December	Banned Girondin deputies restored to Convention
24 December	Wage and price controls (General Maximum) relaxed
27 December	Barère, Billaud-Varenne, Collot d'Herbois, and Vadier impeached
January 1795	French troops enter Amsterdam; Dutch renounce the House of Orange and create the Batavian Republic
8 February	Marat's remains removed from Panthéon
8 March	Federalists pardoned; Federalist deputies restored to their seats

C H R O N O L O G Y	(continued)
1 April	*Sans-culottes* demonstration (Germinal) in Paris; artisans invade the floor of the Convention but movement fails; Billaud-Varenne, Collot d'Herbois, and Vadier sent to French Guiana
5 April	Treaty of Basel: Prussia officially recognizes the French Republic
20–24 May	Prairial uprising in Paris; *sans-culottes* again invade the Convention, again are defeated and disarmed (24 May)
8 June	Death of Louis XVI's son; Count of Provence becomes heir to the throne
22 August	Adoption of Constitution of 1795
1 October	Annexation of Belgium
5 October	Royalist uprising in Paris is crushed; General Bonaparte distinguishes himself in the fighting
16–21 October	Legislative elections under the "two-thirds" decree

The Parisian thunderstorm of 28 July 1794 broke France's fever and created a new political climate. For all intents and purposes, the French Revolution ended that hot July evening, when Robespierre and the Montagnards went to their deaths. The phrase "Thermidorian Reaction" has ever afterward meant a sharp shift rightward in a revolutionary movement and, by implication, an end to the revolution.

> Revolutions age relatively quickly. They age badly, if only because they cannot themselves accept, nor be accepted, except through their symbolism: that of a new departure in History, of a radical rupture in time, of a work scarcely begun, in short, of a perpetual youth. The French Revolution certainly did not age less gracefully than those which succeeded it and were inspired by it. Yet none of them, for good reason, has wished to recognize itself in Thermidor: like a magic mirror, the Thermidorian moment brings back to each newborn revolution the image of usury and of decrepitude that lies in wait for it.[2]

In the revolutionary canon, "Thermidor" ends the youthful love affair with a revolution. That love invariably leads to emotional excesses, to violent swings of mood, to rash actions lamented later in the cool of reasoned reflection. Even those happy to be rid of the violence called forth by strong emotions, however, lament the passing of the ardor that sustains the great deeds of the revolution. The Jacobins, for all their faults, inspired in ordinary Frenchmen, such as the soldiers of the Revolu-

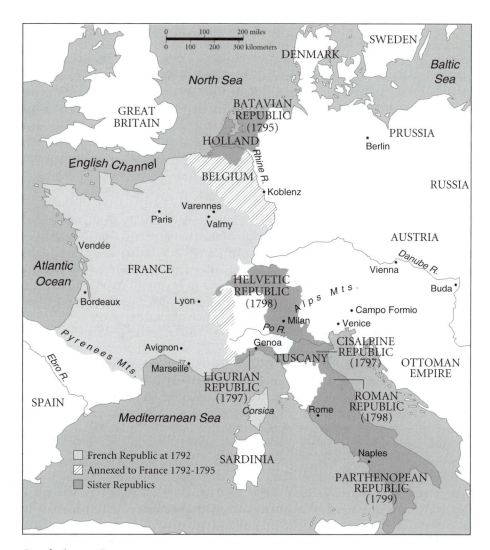

Revolutionary France.

tionary armies, an astonishing degree of such Revolutionary ardor. In contrast, the Thermidorians of 1794 initiated a dispiriting period of French history: their contemporaries lamented the moral turpitude of the government and its failure to create a stable political system in France. Their failure led directly to Napoleon Bonaparte's *coup d'état* of 18 Brumaire (9–10 November 1799), which inaugurated nearly seventy-five years of empires and monarchies on French territory.

Yet matters were not so simple; the men who overthrew Robespierre, even aside from the Terrorists like Collot d'Herbois and Billaud-Varenne still sitting as members of the Committee of Public Safety, hardly belonged to the Right in the politics of the France of 1794. Most of the men in the Convention, and many of those in the two Councils of the Directory, had voted for the death of Louis XVI. Those who overthrew Robespierre wanted to preserve much of what the Mountain had done, but also to eliminate its excesses and what they viewed as the tyrannical power vested in the Committee of Public Safety. Indeed, the Convention asked Robert Lindet, a member of the Committee, to draft its annual report for the Year II, presented in September 1794. Lindet stressed the need to avoid revenge and extremism and to recognize the difference between "errors and abuses" and "crimes." His language continued to emphasize the centrality of the sovereign and free "people," a classic Jacobin phrase, and to tie the overthrow of the Girondins (31 May–2 June 1793) to the appropriate course of the Revolution begun in 1789.

Thermidor had started an irresistible momentum toward the Right; Lindet's report marked one of the final spasms of Jacobinism in the rump of the Convention. Having executed Robespierre and his allies primarily because of the excesses of the Terror, the Convention faced the embarrassing situation of having hard-core Terrorists like Billaud-Varenne and Collot d'Herbois in its midst. Many agreed with Ruault, that these men "merited the same recompense" as Robespierre. In the fall of 1794, the Convention gradually came to believe that repudiating the Jacobin ascendancy would preserve the Republic. The Convention slowly stripped the Committee of Public Safety of its power, forcing a quarter of the membership to step down every six weeks. They closed the Jacobin Club of Paris, restored the banned Girondin deputies to the Convention, and expelled the "Terrorists." In 1795, they drew up a new Constitution, creating the government known as the Directory, which brought the Revolution back to a central ground more amenable to most French people. This center failed to hold in the face of the passionate intensity of the Left and Right.

Even after the return of the Girondin deputies (December 1794), the Convention stood well to the left of center in the general French political spectrum. Many *conventionnels,* as the members were called, had supported the Terror; others were comrades in arms of radicals such as Danton. Thermidor did bring the Convention back right of where it had been, but it did not, by any stretch of the imagination, give power to the Right. France's 1794 political spectrum included many counterrevolutionaries, as well as constitutional monarchists. These people, not those who carried out Thermidor, represented the Right. The Thermidorians moved the Convention itself back to a Center–Left position.

The political affiliations of the Thermidorian leaders notwithstanding, the Right benefitted enormously from the changed political climate of 1794–1795. New rules about sales of national land again favored the rich; the Catholic Church returned; Right-wing dandies (the *muscadins*) formed street gangs and terrorized the Left; conservative landowners took over local politics in many regions; the White Terror took bloody revenge on former Jacobins in the southeast. The last days of the Convention (August 1794–October 1795) and the Directory (1795–1799) undid many of the democratic changes wrought between 1789 and 1794, paving the way for the old Montagnard Napoleon Bonaparte to seize power and strangle French democracy after 1799. Revolutionary culture gave way to new outpourings of excess. Ostentation, a lethal vice under the Jacobins, became again the order of the day. Jacques David, the greatest Revolutionary artist, would soon be memorializing Napoleon's self-coronation, an affair whose garish excess equaled Versailles's decadence at its worst.

Settling Scores, 1794

Public opinion now floats uncertainly on many things and many people. Must we love or betray Jacobinism? Was Jacobinism useful or harmful for the establishment of the Republic? There is the timely discussion that ferments all heads from one end of France to the other.[3]

Nicolas Ruault, 8 October 1794

The fall of Robespierre and his allies led inexorably to a shift to the Center. In his journal entry of 31 July 1794, the bourgeois bond holder Célestin Guittard expressed surprise that the Jacobins reopened and continued their meetings. In August, the Convention overturned the law of 22 Prairial (which had stripped legal rights from all accused of treason) and decreed that the Paris sections could meet only once a week, on the *décadi*. The decree also ended the practice of paying citizens 40 shillings to attend: this measure reportedly saved one million *livres* a year.[4]

The political in-fighting hardly ended with the fall of Robespierre. In early September, a deputy denounced Billaud-Varenne, Collot d'Herbois, Barère, Vadier, and David on the floor of the Convention, and called for their arrest. The deputies, after a violent debate, declared his accusations to be calumnious, but he had set the tone for what was to come. Jean-Lambert Tallien and two of his allies, who had led the charge against Robespierre in the Convention, were expelled from the Jacobin Club on 5 September. Four days later, someone attempted to assassinate Tallien. That attempt led to a "tumultuous" meeting of the Convention about the Jacobin Clubs on 10 September. Less than two weeks later, the Convention abolished the forty-eight sectional committees of surveillance, creating twelve new committees in their place, each with jurisdiction over four sections. They kept up the offensive in October, banning popular societies and sectional committees from affiliating or corresponding with each other and mandating that all such societies provide the government with complete lists of membership: names, ages, addresses, professions, places of birth.

Everyone saw these rules for what they were: an attack on the Jacobins. In early November, in response to an attack on the Paris Jacobin Club by some sixty to eighty rock-throwing *muscadins,* the Convention decided to close the Club and seize its papers. Many sections responded ten days later by marching to the Convention to congratulate it for getting rid of an organization that had wished to take its place. The Convention took the final full step on 8 December, recalling the roughly seventy-five deputies expelled by the Mountain. These deputies had opposed the execution of Louis XVI, but they had all voted him guilty of treason; they solidified the Center-Left coalition in charge of the government. In late November and early December, the Convention put Carrier, the butcher of Nantes, on trial: they executed him on 16 December. At the end of the December, in a dramatic demonstration of how much political opinion had shifted since September, the Convention impeached Barère, Billaud-Varenne, and Collot d'Herbois and later placed them under arrest.

The collapse of the Jacobins had immediate repercussions in the provinces. As in Paris, the fall of Robespierre led to an immediate release of thousands of prisoners, most of whom had an understandable hatred of Jacobinism. The Thermidorians quickly eliminated the pro-Jacobin district councils and restored the pro-Girondin departmental councils. They sent out new agents into the communes and departments, to get better control of the actual administration; these agents helped purge countless local officials, from municipalities on up. Such changes took time to implement but their cumulative effect emboldened all enemies of the Jacobins, from the Girondins to the counterrevolutionaries. The deputies on mission soon assaulted the local Jacobin clubs, arresting leaders and purging memberships. Finally, in August 1795, the Convention closed all political clubs and seized their papers.

The worst situation took place in the southeast. In an episode known as the White Terror, local officials purged governing councils and sectional assemblies of all Jacobin sympathizers.[5] In cities such as Marseille and Lyon, where the Jacobins and their enemies had traded power in 1793, this led to more settling of scores. Authorities either encouraged or ignored mobs who assaulted the prisons holding the radicals. At Lyon, the rioters set fire to the prisons "to force the Jacobins on to the roof where they were hacked to death."[6] The mob at Aix, like the one at Lyon, released ordinary criminals and slaughtered the thirty Jacobins in custody. The anti-Jacobins marched an army against Marseille, but it was defeated in battle outside the city. A few weeks later, local anti-Jacobins stormed the prisons of the city and dismembered ninety-seven Jacobins. All over the southeast mobs assaulted local Jacobins. At Avignon, they threw a judge from the local Revolutionary Tribunal into the Rhône river and harpooned him. Many others fell to armed bands in the countryside.

Armed bands of peasants in the Midi and in the west supported a return to the monarchy. The southern bands kept up a low level of guerrilla warfare but those of the Vendée and Brittany posed greater threats. The Bretons sought to link up with a landing of émigré nobles, abetted by the British. An expedition of three thousand debarked on the Rhuys peninsula (June 1795), near Vannes, where it met up with ten thousand Chouans. General Lazare Hoche marched ten thousand regulars to meet them a few days later and, after a brief fight, captured six thousand men. He shot six hundred forty of the émigrés and over one hundred peasants. Three months later, the British tried again, this time sending arms and a fleet to link up with the Vendéan leader Charette, on the coast of Poitou. This expedition carried with it the Count of Artois.

Artois's older brother, the Count of Provence, had become the royal Pretender on 8 June 1795, when Louis XVI's son died in a Paris prison. Provence had issued a foolish proclamation upon becoming the royalist hope, saying that he would restore the Ancien Régime were he to return. His *Proclamation of Verona* (June 1795) made it impossible for all but the most ardent royalists to support his return. Artois and the Vendéans had little luck against Hoche and his regulars. The royal pretender ignominiously left Poitou in November. In the ensuing months Hoche and his men hunted down the main Vendéan leaders, Stofflet and Charette, and executed them (February–March 1796). The Thermidorians, acting first as the Convention (to October 1795) and then as the Directory, decisively defeated the military counter-revolution both in the south and the west. Royalist forces had other avenues of attack, however, and the Directory proved more susceptible to them.

The Constitution of 1795 (Constitution of the Year III)

> *Civil equality, in fact, is all that a reasonable man can claim. Absolute equality is a chimera; for it to exist, there would have to be absolute equality in intelligence, virtue, physical strength, education, and fortune for all men.*[7]

François Antoine Boissy d'Anglas, defending the
Constitution of 1795, 23 June 1795

The Center–Left coalition running the Convention in early August lost power within a month. After the recall of the purged deputies in December 1794, the Convention had a solid Girondin majority. They had a fairly clear idea of what they wanted to do to bring French politics back into line with what they believed the country needed: repudiation of the Terror but salvation of the Revolution. That meant getting rid of those most associated with the Terror, like Billaud-Varenne, and making sure that the urban workers could not effectively influence politics. This first goal naturally led the old Girondins to ally with the Right, many of whom were monarchists.

The deputies clearly set forth their ideas in a new Constitution (1795). The *conventionnels* had three sets of principles on which to draw:

1. Those of the summer of 1789.

2. The Constitution of 1791.

3. The failed Constitution drafted by Condorcet's committee in 1793.

France theoretically lived under the Constitution of 1793, rapidly drafted by Hérault de Sechelles (executed with Danton in April 1794), and adopted by the Convention with scarcely any debate. That Constitution had been suspended before it took effect. The very deputies who had voted for its remarkable principles—universal manhood suffrage, rights of all to·education, sustenance, and employment—repudiated their own handiwork. The deputies specifically rejected universal manhood suffrage and its Constitution of 1793. The chief spokesman of the 1795 Constitution, François Boissy d'Anglas, violently attacked the earlier document. In his words, "that constitution, conceived by ambitious men, drafted by schemers, dictated by tyranny, and accepted through terror, is nothing other than the express preservation of all the elements of disorder, the instrument designed to serve the avidity of greedy men, the interest of turbulent men, the pride of the ignorant, and the ambition of usurpers."

The Convention did not completely reject the principle of male democracy, which still had powerful resonance in the France of 1795. They learned from the American experience, borrowing from many American state constitutions the principle that only male property owners would sit in the legislative body. The deputies here harkened back to the mainstream principles of the Enlightenment. As the Physiocrat (and royal minister) Turgot had written:

> Mobile wealth is as fugitive as talent, and unfortunately those who possess no land have a country only through their hearts, through their opinions, through the happy prejudices of childhood. . . . [the ownership of land constitutes] the true and solid link between the proprietor of houses and the fatherland, his true means of providing subsistence for his children, his true citizenship.[8]

The Constitution of 1795 combined many of the principles of the Constitution of 1791 with ideas that had been put forward by the constitutional monarchists in the summer and fall of 1789, only to be rejected. The deputies reversed one of the initial votes taken by the Constituent Assembly when they shifted to a bicameral legislature, with a lower Council of 500 and an upper Council of 250.[9] The new Constitution compromised between the eligibility rules of 1791 and 1793 for the primary elections. Men over twenty-one, paying a given tax, and domiciled in their commune for a full year, could vote. The breadth of this initial suffrage dwarfed the pathetic electorate of Great Britain (well under 50,000) or even of most of the United States.[10] At least 5 million men could vote in the primary process.[11]

Once again, the electoral colleges chosen on the first go-round would meet to select the actual deputies to the Councils. Here the new Constitution reached back to the last-minute, elevated property standard for electors voted, but not enforced, in 1791. Even the elevated standards for electors and deputies left about 500,000 people eligible to serve. Every year, some 30,000 of them were supposed to do so, because the Constitution set a standard of one elector per two hundred eligible voters.[12] Whatever the legal system, local officials seem to have followed established local procedures. How else can we explain the fact that 6.3 percent of the electors of Toulon in 1797 were sailors, who surely did not pay one hundred days' wages in taxes? In the department of the Seine, surrounding Paris, the largest or second largest social group among the electors remained artisans and shopkeepers: about a quarter in 1797 and 1799, and 37 percent in 1798. The most prominent trade was that of grocer (sixteen in 1798, seventeen in 1799); most of the shopkeepers dealt in relative luxury goods (books, jewels, gold), but the 1798 assembly had a large contingent of carpenters (twelve). These men held eligibility, in most cases, because they rented a dwelling/shop assessed at 150 *livres* a year or more. The main group excluded from the electoral assemblies was farmers. Only the richest "cultivators," as they now called themselves, surely less than 5 percent of rural taxpayers, held eligibility.

The Constitution strongly tightened the bonds between land ownership and the offices of elector and deputy. As Ruault put it, in a letter of 28 June 1795,

> According to the spirit of our new Constitution, one must have learned some mechanical craft to be a simple citizen; and to be eligible for certain public functions, one must be an owner of a few morsels of land. One is obliged to have one's ass in the soil, as the peasants of our province would

say, to be something in the new France and to leave the ranks of the vile proletarians.[13]

Boissy d'Anglas put the matter quite bluntly in the final debates:

> . . . We must be governed by the best; the best are those who are best edu-
> cated and most interested in the maintenance of the laws; now, with few ex-
> ceptions, you find such men only among those who, owning a piece of
> property, are devoted to the country that contains it, to the laws that pro-
> tect it, and to the tranquility that maintains it. . . A country governed by
> property owners is an organized society; one governed by the propertyless
> is in a state of nature.[14]

His reference to the "state of nature" was clear to his fellow deputies. He meant the state of nature of the seventeenth-century English philosopher Thomas Hobbes, which Hobbes defined as a state of war "of every man, against every man." Hobbes went on: "To this war of every man, against every man, this also is consequent; that nothing can be unjust. The notions of right and wrong, justice and injustice, have there no place." Boissy d'Anglas and the other *conventionnels* accepted Hobbes's de-scription as accurate because they believed they had just lived through it. They wanted to enshrine the control of property owners in a new constitution, in the be-lief that only those with property have a sufficient stake in society to preserve it.[15]

The Last Hurrah of the *Sans-Culottes*

> *Everyone murmurs and is very discontent. . . . when people are hungry and
> there is no bread, there is no more reason, all the pretty speeches no longer
> tempt the ear.*
>
> Journal of Célestin Guittard, entry of 31 March 1795

The Parisian workers disliked intensely the political evolution of the fall of 1794. Ménétra certainly expressed the sentiments of many artisans in showing relief at the "end of the murders," but he went on: "but people were still unhappy. This National Convention in which everyone had the greatest confidence was and one can say so nothing but a nest of slanderers of vindictive men seeking to slaughter one party so as to replace it with another one."[16] They soon realized that matters had shifted dra-matically, when the Convention removed (8 February 1795) Marat's remains from the Panthéon. Several sections demonstrated against this "sacrilege."

Miserable weather and high prices fueled popular discontent. A desperate short-age of firewood intensified a brutal January freeze, which bottomed out on the night of January 22–23, when the lowest temperature in the memory of man (0° F) froze "everything in the houses." The cold snap ended in a thaw so rapid it led to a flash flood on the Seine (29 January). The bread situation alarmed everyone. In March, the government had to ration bread: one pound a day per inhabitant, except for workers, who got a pound-and-a-half. On 20–23 March, the sections called out their companies to stand guard, because the bread rationing had led to "discontentment." Fighting broke out again between the Jacobin supporters and the *muscadins*. On 28 March, a crowd of some five hundred women marched to the Convention demanding bread. The government postponed the elections (putting "water in its [Paris's] wine," as Guittard put it), and banned evening assemblies. On the 31 March, they cut the bread ration to half a pound, and even that amount rarely got to consumers. The next day, ten thousand working poor marched on the Convention, demanding bread, and occupying the assembly hall for four hours. The (unarmed) Germinal Uprising fizzled out in the face of the National Guard. It led to the arrest of sixteen deputies and to the deportation of Billaud-Varenne, Collot d'Herbois, and Vadier, whom the demonstrators had sought to free.

The bread situation worsened, with rations dropping to two ounces a day by early May. This time, the workers arrived armed at the Convention. The Prairial Rising (20 May), was led, Guittard suggests, by women, who demanded "bread and the Constitution of 1793." On the floor of the Convention, the situation got out of hand. The workers murdered a deputy. This time, the deputies from the rump of the old Mountain, who had stood aloof during the Germinal rising, joined the rebels. Under the eyes of armed workers the Convention voted to release Jacobin deputies, to provide bread, and to restore the Constitution of 1793. The initial success did not last, as the loyal National Guard forcibly ejected the demonstrators. The Convention then rescinded its earlier votes and arrested the deputies who had proposed the motions.

The confrontation continued the next day, when a force estimated at forty thousand in support of the Convention faced down a group half its size taken primarily from the *sans-culottes* faubourgs of Saint-Antoine and Saint-Marcel. Many of those supporting the Convention came from National Guard units in Paris; Ménétra, old Jacobin though he was, marched with his section in support of the Convention. On the 23 May, thirty thousand troops surrounded the faubourg Saint-Antoine. Sweeping through it street by street, they disarmed the entire faubourg and arrested between twelve hundred and sixteen hundred. "*Septembriseurs,* massacrers, men of blood," as Guittard called them. The authorities captured those responsible for Féraud's murder and quickly executed them. In the coming weeks, the government arrested another three thousand "suspects," that is, those sympathetic to the Jacobins. In sharp contrast to earlier round-ups and to events going on in the provinces at the same time, these people were not executed. Authorities later released them, although many would be re-arrested during subsequent crackdowns.

Ruault captured the essence of the problem in a letter to his brother on 6 May, in which he described the desperate risings of Germinal and Florial as simple "convulsions of hunger." Yet he did not stop with such an analysis, he continued:

> That which is more unfortunate . . . that which makes the evil almost incurable, is that the government no longer walks with the people. It has against it a frightening majority. Now, a government which walks against and not with the people must necessarily break against that indestructible mass. The former Committee of Public Safety only saw the *sans-culottes,* had eyes only for the poor people; it was more demagogic than democratic. It had all

the rich, all the proprietors against it; it perished. Today, it's the opposite. They only value the proprietors and the rich; they have contempt for the poor, whom they trample under their feet. . . . The great art of founding a Republic in the center of our old Europe is to make the poor and the rich walk together freely, of a common accord.[17]

There would be one more rising in Paris (October 1795), but it was the Right-wing sections that carried it out. Once again, troops stood firm, led by the newly promoted General Napoleon Bonaparte, who turned his cannons on the roughly twenty-five thousand rebels. Ruault told his brother that the troops of the line fired up and down the streets until midnight, when the local prostitutes fanned out to lift the valuables of the fallen. He greatly exaggerates the casualties, estimating the dead at eight thousand (a few hundred would be closer), but his testimony gives us some sense of how seriously contemporaries viewed this uprising.[18]

Some sections, such as that of Bonconseil, sent people to both sides; others supported the Convention. In the end, the troops cleared the bridges over the Seine. The Convention abolished sectional assemblies and the section-dominated National Guard, replacing the latter with a body under its direct control. This rising demonstrated the effectiveness of the measures taken to disarm Paris in May 1795. All the reports suggest that two key factors prevented the rebels, who outnumbered the Convention's supporters by 4 to 1, from winning:

1. They had no cannon.

2. Those who did have firearms, lacked ammunition.

Three weeks later, the Convention officially ended, to be replaced by the new bicameral assembly and an executive consisting of a Directory of five men, who would serve as the executive.

THE DIRECTORY, 1795–1799

In general, we are finally tired of revolutions and we sigh only for a rest bought by six years of sacrifices, of patience, of calamities, and of glory . . . being as much enemies of anarchy as of despotism, we believe that liberty reposes only in a happy medium.[19]

Vivant Carion, Burgundian journalist, October 1795

CHRONOLOGY	November 1795–November 1799
3 November 1795	Directory officially takes power[20]
10 May 1796	Arrest of members of the Conspiracy of the Equals

CHRONOLOGY	(continued)
March–April 1797	Royalist success in legislative elections
26–27 May	Trial of the "Equals" ends; execution of Gracchus Babeuf
15 July	Decrees against refractory clergy repealed
4 September	Elections invalidated, royalist deputies removed from Legislature; local elections overturned, Carnot and Barthélémy removed (18 Fructidor)
5 September	Draconian laws against refractory clergy reinstated
April 1798	Jacobins successful in legislative elections
11 May	Election results again invalidated, new deputies removed
July 1799	Jacobin Club reopens
13 August	Jacobin Club closed again
9–10 November	*Coup d'état* of 18 Brumaire; Napoleon becomes effective ruler of France

What seems clear today is that between the royalists and the terrorists there is a third party which wants one no more than the other and which will combat them both with an equal intrepidity.[21]

L.–S. Mercier, 1795

The repression of the risings of 1795 removed the Parisian masses from their key role in national politics. Power shifted back to the elites who had real economic and social prestige in the country, above all landowners and lawyers. The sales of nationalized land conducted under the Directory auctioned off much larger lots. Guittard mentions that the priory of Evergnicourt (his home village), accounting for 70 percent of the total land sold in the village during the Revolution, went to a society of eleven men in November 1795. The shift from the more balanced land sales of the early 1790s—still dominated by larger buyers, but involving many small ones too—to the large-lot sales of 1796–1799 stands as a clear indication of the nature of the Directory regime and of those who profited from it. The figures for the district of Avallon, in northern Burgundy, tell the tale. The urban middle class bought 80 percent of the land sold there between 1791–1793, only 60 percent of that sold between 1793–1795—when the Jacobins deliberately sold land in smaller plots—and more than 90 percent sold after 1795.

The situation got worse when the Directory eliminated the *assignats* (by then worthless) and replaced them with the *territorial mandates,* in essence, a new form of *assignat.* These notes could be directly redeemed for land, without the formality

The departure of the Thermidorians. This caricature suggests that the deputies leaving office in 1799 had enriched themselves at the public expense.

SOURCE: Bibliothèque Nationale, Estampes, coll. Hennin n. 12516.

of a sale at auction. One recent examination of this mechanism shows that half of the *mandates* issued—1.1 billion *livres*—went to large-scale military suppliers, who immediately turned them into enormous landed holdings. The rich merchant-bankers who supplied the army used this paper money to buy up the land of émigré nobles that came on the market in these years. They obtained bargain prices because the *mandates* depreciated so rapidly in value, becoming worthless by the summer. As the Burgundian farmer Paquelin noted, "people only use paper money to pay their taxes." The government was reduced to the humiliating expedient of collecting taxes partly in kind: even the five Directors received part of their salaries that way.

The Directory suffers in the historiography for its many failures. One might more fairly split its impact into two parts. On the one hand, the Directory failed completely to create a viable political system in France. On the other hand, the Directory supervised the effective creation of what Isser Woloch has called the New Regime, which established the broad outlines of French administration, solidified by Napoleon and calcified by successor regimes in the nineteenth century.[22] The Directory reintroduced bullion coinage (1797), repudiated the government's debt (1797), and put the tax system on a firm footing (1798). Local studies suggest that authorities began systematically to collect the *patente* in 1797; overall records show that receipts from taxation, which had fallen as low as 35 million *livres* in 1794–1795, reached 341 million *livres* in 1798–1799. The Directory even reintroduced excise

TERROR AND TAXES

The government had terrible problems collecting its taxes. Only when the Jacobins introduced draconian controls on a wide range of financial transactions, such as payment of government bond annuities, did things start to get better. In 1791 or 1792, Guittard, the Parisian bond holder, simply collected his bond interest from local government officials and paid no attention to his tax assessments; indeed, it is extremely unclear that he even received proper notice of his obligations. In 1793–1794, however, he found he had to produce tax documents to get his annuity payments: he had to pay the *impôt mobilier* (108 *livres*) and contribute to a forced loan (January 1794, for 237 *livres*) before he could collect what the government owed him. The forced loan proved to be quite effective, producing something like 228 million *livres,* almost all of it actually coming from the rich. Those assessed for 10,000 *livres* or more made up only 7 percent of the taxpayers, but contributed 65 percent of the money.[23]

Guittard gave more money for small special taxes, such as the levy to outfit volunteers for the front (January 1794), monthly payments of from 2 to 6 *livres* to find a substitute for his guard duty or the 44 livres he spent on shirts for two "brothers in arms" going to the front (November 1793). Guittard tells us of the confiscation of all Church ornaments (November 1793), which the government melted down for their gold and silver. The looting of the churches did not enjoy popular support in the countryside but many in the cities, such as the Parisian *sans-culottes,* strongly urged this course of action.

Even after the Jacobins fell from power, Guittard found that the more rigorous procedures they had established lingered on. Under the Directory, these practices became routinized: the government no longer had to rely on raw terror to collect taxes. Written tax rolls and timely collection and disbursement of money became again a normal function of everyday life. In that sense, the Directory provided a New Regime that finally gave France the sort of functional state that people had taken for granted before 1789.

taxes: first on tobacco, then on transit of goods, finally on goods imported into towns—even Paris—in 1798.

The initial steps in the creation of this administration took place in an atmosphere of chaotic dishonesty. Whether it is the letters of Helen Maria Williams or those of Nicolas Ruault, everyone commented upon the appalling corruption. For Ruault, the entire country had been given over to "brigandage, murder, and pillage." He rebuked:

The agents of the government, which calls itself republican, do not profess any of the principles which must constitute a republican government. Probity, virtue, a certain austerity of mores, which have always existed in infant Republics, and without which they cannot subsist, cannot be found in ours. One does not see in the offices of these men *French* citizens but only corrupt men who sell for *gold* the positions, employments, and functions at the disposition of the ministers; one bargains with them as one would over goods at a market . . . The deputies themselves carry out exchange, shamefully trafficking with exchange agents . . . This infamous selling corrupts the public spirit at Paris and in all of the departments.[24]

Politically, the Directory lurched from one expedient to the next. No regime born of such blatant moral turpitude could long survive. Mercier wrote, in 1798: "There is not a single day when one does not say: That's immoral!"[25] The August 1795 referendum overwhelmingly approved the new Constitution, yet this support masked underlying discontent with the so-called laws of 5 and 13 Fructidor (August 1795), which mandated that two-thirds of the new deputies had to come from the Convention's ranks. Guittard claimed that his section, which approved the Constitution 1,820 to 6, strongly opposed the Convention's efforts to co-opt its own members into the new body.[26] The available evidence suggests no one else liked them either: the Vendémiaire rebellion was partly a response to the two-thirds decree. Three hundred ninety *conventionnels* obtained seats in the rigged portion of the October 1795 elections, as against only four elected in the open, unrestricted voting.[27] The re-elected deputies selected an additional ninety-four of their fellow *conventionnels* to bring the total returned to five hundred eleven.

The five hundred eleven returning *conventionnels* came overwhelmingly from the old Girondin faction and from the Right wing of the Convention. All of the Girondin deputies outlawed in 1792 who sought re-election were chosen and those who had opposed Louis XVI's execution outnumbered those who had favored it by almost two to one. The overall political make-up of the two Councils leaned much more to the Right than had the Convention. Most estimates suggest three hundred five confirmed republicans, two hundred twenty-six deputies in the middle, and one hundred fifty-eight royalists. The Directory's efforts to maintain a middle-of-the-road approach, however, can be seen in the Councils' choice of the five Directors of the executive council, regicides all: Paul Barras, Louis Marie de La Révellière-Lépreaux, Étienne Letourneur, Jean-François Reubell, and the famous Abbé Sieyès. Sieyès refused to serve, in part because the Convention had rejected some of his ideas about the Constitution. In his place, the Council of 250 chose another regicide, the Montagnard Lazare Carnot. Barras, a former viscount and a firm Jacobin, was the most politically adroit of the group, but the five had no clear direction. The Constitution also required that one of the five be replaced each year, based on a drawing of lots.

The Directory stumbled along in 1796, concerned above all with the foreign war (see the following text), with the subsistence crisis, and with making sure that the radicals did not revive. The Directors had a minor scare in the spring of 1796, the Conspiracy of the Equals. The leader of this group, Gracchus Babeuf, coined its most memorable phrase: "Real equality, the common happiness, or death!" Unfortunately for him and his fellow conspirators, they ended up with the latter. Babeuf proposed a social model that closely resembled modern communism, with social ownership of property. Few of his contemporaries supported such ideas. Even hard-core Jacobins blanched at the abolition of private property. Babeuf's most famous co-defendant, Philippe-Michel Buonarroti, later would become the author of one of the founding texts of modern penal codes. He got off with a jail sentence; Babeuf went to the block in May 1797.

The repression of this comic opera conspiracy formed part of a larger attack on the Jacobins and their allies. Considerable evidence suggests that local authorities deliberately sought to exclude the poor from voting rolls. In some areas, officials arbitrarily set the figure for a day's wages (the minimum tax contribution for a voter) at triple its real level. In others, they manufactured other objections to potential Jacobin voters. The situation varied sharply from department to department. In a sample of eight departments compiled by Malcolm Crook, three had more eligible voters in 1797 than in 1795, three had fewer, and two about the same. The department of Aveyron (Rodez) had the largest increase, up from 18,773 to 32,105, while the Orne (Alençon) had the biggest decline, from 24,435 to 5,154. In the eight departments as a whole, votes cast rose roughly 50 percent. The wild levels of voting volatility between 1795 and 1799 very strongly illustrate the extremely unstable political system. The extremes could range from the department of the Orne, which rose from 5,000 eligibles in 1797 to over 35,000 in 1799; to that of Haute-Garonne (Toulouse, a Jacobin stronghold), where eligibility declined from 32,468 in 1797 to only 12,453 in 1798. Given the obvious chicanery involved in such fluctuations, it is little wonder that French society finally lost respect for the Directory and its elections. Turnouts could be quite respectable in 1798, but this diminished respect became glaringly apparent in 1799, when many departments reported voter turnouts under 10 percent.[28]

The new constitution required elections every year, starting in 1797. The first elections took place in March 1797, immediately after one of the directors, Letourneur, had to step down in favor of François Barthélémy, a member of the Clichy Club, political nexus of the Councils' moderate deputies. These elections accentuated the rightward drift, in part because many potentially Left-leaning voters had not been allowed to cast ballots. Of the two hundred sixty deputies up for replacement, two hundred sixteen were *conventionnels:* only eleven of them won reelection. The royalists won one hundred eighty seats, bringing their contingent in the two councils to about three hundred thirty. General Jean-Charles Pichegru, who had been secretly negotiating with the émigrés, not only became a deputy but was elected president of the Council of 500. Two months of the new assembly proved too much for the more leftist Directors. Barras, Reubell, and La Révellière surrounded Paris with General Hoche's troops, named the general minister of war, and gave the ministry of foreign affairs to Talleyrand, an unscrupulous opportunist.

A few weeks later, on 4 September (18 Fructidor), using troops sent by General Bonaparte, Reubell, La Révellière, and Barras struck again. They had documentary evidence (provided by Bonaparte) of Pichegru's treachery, and used that evidence of conspiracy—and the known royalism of many deputies—to conduct a *coup d'état.* They purged Carnot and Barthélémy and conducted a rump meeting of the Councils to displace one hundred seventy-seven deputies elected in 1797, voting to deport fifty-three of them.[29] Seventeen actually faced deportation, although eight of them, among them Pichegru, escaped. The meeting annulled the elections of forty-nine departments, from the top to the bottom. In the department of the Sarthe, for example, they replaced five hundred ninety-nine of the eight hundred seven elected officials; in the Pas-de-Calais, seventy-three of eighty-seven municipalities were deposed.[30] The Councils closed newspapers, arrested editors, and placed all publications under government supervision for a year. Special military commissions tried and shot one hundred sixty people, and criminal commissions dispatched others. The Councils then enacted new laws against émigré nobles and refractory clergy, demanded that all priests and government officials swear that they "hated monarchy," and arrested thousands of priests.

The following year, the Left revived in the elections, perhaps in part because of the successful efforts of provincial Jacobins to restore the eligibility of low-income voters in places like the Orne.[31] In a broader sense, however, the old Jacobin activists achieved better results because of their revived political activity, in arenas such as the press. Once again, the Directors carried out a purge. This time they eliminated one hundred twenty-seven deputies, eighty-six of them Jacobin sympathizers. The Councils often sided with secessionist electoral assemblies: in nineteen departments, minority groups of electors held separate meetings and chose different deputies, who were then ratified by the Councils. The Councils also invalidated local election results. Predictably, the Councils clamped down on anything that smacked of Jacobinism. In the final elections of the Directory, spring 1799, the government lost again: only sixty-six of its one hundred eighty-seven endorsed candidates won. This time the Councils did follow the law more closely by repudiating twenty-five of the twenty-seven secessionist electoral assemblies. These new elections brought in about fifty Jacobin sympathizers, raising the total to perhaps two hundred fifty in the two Councils.

These election results left the Directory stuck in the middle, year after year. Mercier suggests they sought to create a third "party" (his word), one that rejected monarchy, on the one hand, and "anarchy" (i.e., Jacobinism), on the other. Given that close to two-thirds of the members of the two Councils supported one of these two parties, the Directory had no reasonable chance of survival. The elections of 1797, 1798, and 1799 all demonstrated the overwhelming national rejection of the then-current government. Government candidates lost decisively in 1797 and 1799; they had mixed results in 1798. The electoral campaigns suggest that a significant group of French people wanted to maintain a Republic, but that another large group wanted to return to some elements of pre-republican France. Quite apart from nostalgia for cheaper times (Mercier castigates those who wanted to return to the days of "café au lait" for 6 shillings), a very strong desire to return to the Catholic Church motivated many, especially in the countryside. Given that the urban middle class had obtained most of the land confiscated from the Church, we can have little wonder that they, especially, feared its return.

Many of them certainly wanted a Catholic Church to return, because they believed strongly in the moral usefulness of religion for the masses, but they did not want the Ancien Régime Catholic Church. The devastating impact of de-Christianization on the Constitutional clergy, however, made the return of a compromise Church, one willing to accommodate the Revolution, impossible. In fact, when Napoleon signed the Concordat of 1801 with the Pope, he brought back the non-juring clergy, those most opposed to the republican legacy.

The shift to the Right in 1794–1795 initially gave the Church a chance to come out of hiding. The Paris churches reopened on 21 June 1795, when a bishop led a High Mass at Saint-Germain-l'Auxerrois. Guittard, who claimed that Parisians wanted to take up Sundays and return to the old calendar, says that on 21 June shops were closed and workers idle, even though it was not a *décadi*. Despite the return of the Church, the Constitution of 1795 meant that the new calendar remained the legal one until 1806.[32]

In the countryside, peasants adopted the new calendar only if obliged to do so by overwhelming force. Nor did they turn to Constitutional clergy to restore their services, which had often been conducted clandestinely in any case. They welcomed back the old, "good" priests: those who had refused the Oath. The Councils initially elected in 1797, with their strong contingent of royalists, naturally encouraged the return of the non-juring clergy; they even rescinded the legislation against them (July 1797). The 18 Fructidor coup (September 1797) naturally restored the anticlericals in the Councils. The next day, they overturned the July decree and re-instituted the death penalty for non-juring priests. For the next several months, government officials stepped up persecution of the refractory priests, arresting nearly two thousand of them in France and ten thousand in Belgium. Initial plans to deport them had to be cancelled due to the blockade by the British Navy, so the poor priests had to rot away in prisons on the southwestern coast. The Directory never reached an accommodation with the Church, leaving that task to its successor, the Consulate of Napoleon Bonaparte (Concordat of 1801).

The Economy: Chaos and Renewal

> *Luxury is like a spirituous liquor that intoxicates the spirit.[33]*
>
> L.-S. Mercier, writing of the revival of luxury
> in the Paris of the Directory, 1798

The Directory failed utterly in most of its policies. Its initial economic policies, such as the relaxation of price controls, would seem to be another such failure. The end of the Terror accelerated inflation: the *assignats* fell to 20 percent of face value by December 1794. Yet a longer-term view of the Directory's economic and fiscal policies should count them as its greatest success. The post-Thermidor Convention endorsed economic freedom, abolishing wage and price controls in December 1794.[34] The abolition of the Maximum really did little more than recognize what was already happening. Grain prices remained controlled, although forced grain requisition, obviously not a viable long-term solution, gradually ended.

The government could not prevent the catastrophic decline of paper money, first the *assignats* and then the *territorial mandates*. Hyperinflation set in during 1795, when the prices of goods rose from one hour to the next; as Guittard said in April, "one price today, another tomorrow." People like him, who lived on annuities, lost all purchasing power. In February 1796, the government exchanged its old bond for new ones on a 10 to 1 basis, up to 10,000 *livres*, but a month later a 100-*livre* *assignat* was worth only 40 centimes.

In Paris, a measure of grain that had sold for 15 *livres* in May 1792 cost 5,000 *livres* by October 1795. Bread that sold for 20 *livres* a pound on 12 November cost 50 the next day! A sack of potatoes that had cost 2.5 *livres* in March brought 160 *livres* in November. In town after town, bakers followed the example of those of Rochefort, who made an official declaration of quitting their profession because they could not find sufficient grain to bake their bread. Well might the Burgundian historian Jean Bart call it the "time of empty bellies."

THE HUNGRY BOURGEOIS

The change did not help those seeking to buy bread. Although historians have frequently noted the bad harvest of 1794, Guittard's brother wrote from Champagne that they would have "wine and grain in full beauty" that year. The wine harvest was so full that the "winegrowers did not know what to do with their *assignats*." Guittard's brother Jean, wrote (April 1795) to his unfortunate Parisian sibling that he should come back to their village of Evergnicourt, where they had bread, butter, eggs, a little lard, and wine; he even sent a 12-pound loaf of bread as proof. Guittard's friend M. La Motte, just back from the country, told him the same thing. *Laboureurs* were "the best off, because they have at home milk, butter, cheese, eggs, vegetables, poultry, goats, pigs, fruits, lard." Guittard soon became dependent on the bread from his brother and sister, who continued to send loaves until January 1796. Without these loaves, he would have been in serious difficulty. On August 18, 1795, his cook left him; later in that entry, we perhaps find out why: "Today, for the first time, I had to get bread from the Section" (that is, from the relief committee). His new cook lasted only two weeks.

The Directory made it legal to trade in silverplate for coinage and to use coins again in January 1796; the following month, it abolished the *assignats*—burning the presses in a public demonstration—but markets did not know how to react. The *louis d'or* (an actual gold coin) sold on 23 February for prices ranging from 7,850 to 8,600 *livres*. The madness did not end until 1797, when the government returned to metal currency. Even that took some time, as France did not have enough specie to meet demand. Much of what it did have came from loot sent home by its conquering armies in Italy and the Low Countries. The restoration of a real metal currency began to take effect by the fall of 1797. Stable money, abetted by the good harvests of 1796 to 1798, led to stable prices. The last two years of the Directory did not have the wild fluctuations of earlier times.

The restoration of a real currency in 1797 took place in an economy that lay in shambles. The failure to provide a stable currency, the inability to collect regular taxation, the incessant demands of the national government, the violent requisitions of the Jacobins: all of these policies struck hard blows at every sector. The textile industry had begun its slump in the middle of the 1780s, when overproduction and (after 1786) rising English competition led to widespread decline and to massive unemployment in cities such as Troyes or Reims or in the textile villages of Normandy or Picardy. Production seems to have bottomed out during the Jacobin period and to have started a slow recovery in 1796–1797. Silk cloth production, focused on Lyon, naturally suffered from the Terror and counter-Terror that racked the city for several years.

The coal mines, above all those of Anzin, regained over 80 percent of their Ancien Régime production level (300,000 tons in 1788), after falling as low as 63,000 tons in 1794. As for the colonies, their trade simply disappeared: Saint-Domingue's slave rebellion (see the following text) ended its sugar production, and unrest on Martinique and Guadeloupe undermined their trade, too. In 1793, after the open declaration of war between France and Great Britain, the British seized both Martinique and

Guadeloupe. Although a local insurgency restored the latter to nominal French authority, the British navy's control of the Atlantic eliminated what was left of colonial trade. Many displaced planters fled to New Orleans, where they reinforced that city's French elements. Even that bastion soon gave out: Napoleon sold the city, and the entire Louisiana Territory, to the United States in 1803 for $10 million.

That the Revolutionary period had evil effects on the urban economy is certain: the populations of most major cities declined. Paris lost 100,000 people. The nadir came in 1794–1795, when the death rate rose 50 percent, due largely to malnutrition. Port cities, such as Bordeaux, suffered from the loss of the West Indies and from the British blockade. Bordeaux's population declined from 110,000 in 1790 to only 93,000 in 1801. People left because businesses failed. The forty sugar refineries of 1789 had been reduced to ten by 1800. The local rope and tobacco manufactories that had employed twenty-two hundred people in 1789 gave work to only four hundred in 1801. In France as a whole, industrial output declined by about 40 percent from 1789–1799.

This dismal picture did improve somewhat in the last two years of the Directory. The return to sound money (at least, relatively speaking) and decent grain harvests helped reestablish some economic stability. Farmers with produce to sell did well. Those who supplied the armies did even better. Cotton manufacturing witnessed a sharp upturn in the late Directory period, in part due to army demand. French producers began to introduce new technology, above all the water frame and the new spinning mills, just before 1800. Arms manufacturers did a thriving business, yet the metal sector, which should have prospered in a wartime economy, had its failures. The factories of Le Creusot, for example, lost more than 2 million francs between 1796 and 1801. The islands of economic prosperity, such as certain bankers and investors, stood out in a sea of misery. They helped create the startling disparities of wealth commented upon by all observers in the Paris of the late 1790s.

As Mercier suggests, the luxury trades recovered well under the Directory. The drastic fall-off in production of expensive wines, such as champagne, reversed. Champagne traders like the house of Clicquot began to ship more wine, a precursor to the rapid expansion of the first decade of the nineteenth century. Clicquot shipped 16,000 bottles of champagne in 1790, 32,000 bottles in 1802, and 93,000 bottles a year between 1805–1810. Wigmakers, jewelers, restauranteurs—all those associated with luxury—did well. Mercier tells the amusing story of one such enterprising entrepreneur, who had an unusual path to riches:

> He thought that all the turkeys stuffed with truffles, all the salmons, all the Mayence hams, so many wild boar stews, so many Bologna sausages, so many patés, so many wines, liqueurs, sorbets, ice creams, lemonades had to find there, in the final analysis, their common reservoir, and making it very spacious and above all very commodious for so many people who engage in all manner of voluptuousness, the residue (*caput mortum*) of the surrounding kitchens would become a gold mine for him. . . .
> This man did as the Emperor Vespasian, who leased out the latrines of Rome. His son mockingly reproached him for it, so the Emperor took a

gold coin, put it under the nose of his son, and said to him: "Well, does that smell bad?"

It's in the Palais-Égalité [Palais Royal] that in all ways the gold that comes from that which is most foul, leaves no trace of bad odor.[35]

The Coup of 18 Brumaire

The republican system is so gangrenous in all its branches that it seems impossible to honest people, to those who have not drunk every shame and lost all modest decency, that it can last longer than this year.

Nicolas Ruault, 9 May 1796

War Against Europe: The Rise of Napoleon Bonaparte

Every peasant that I met in the fields, the vineyards or the woods approached me to ask if there were any news of General Bonaparte, and why did he not come back to France; never once did anyone enquire about the Directory.[36]

Joseph Fiévée

C H R O N O L O G Y	1796–1799
April 1796–July 1797	Bonaparte pummels Austrians and their allies in Italy; creates Cispadane Republic (October 1796), then Cisalpine Republic (July 1797) and Ligurian Republic
December 1796–January 1797	Expedition to Ireland fails; United Irishmen later (spring 1797); crushed by England
18 April 1797	Leoben agreement between Bonaparte and Austrians, ratified as Peace of Campo Formio in October
January 1798	French troops intervene against the Pope; Roman Republic declared; annexation of Mulhouse; *de facto* annexation of left bank of the Rhine[37]
March 1798	Declaration of Helvetian (Swiss) Republic
May–July 1798	Napoleon's victories in Egypt (Battle of the Pyramids, July 1798)
1 August 1798	Admiral Nelson annihilates the French fleet at Aboukir; European war. Fighting in Germany, Italy, and Switzerland; France against the Second Coalition: Great Britain, Austria, Spain, Italian states, and Russia

CHRONOLOGY	(continued)
January 1799	French defeat Neapolitan troops; occupy mainland portion of Kingdom of Naples; declare the Republic of Naples
April 1799	French evacuate Milan; Cisalpine Republic collapses
May 1799	Royalist forces retake Naples; Neapolitan Republic disintegrates
June–August 1799	French defeats in Italy; withdrawal of French troops; end of Roman Republic
23 August 1799	Napoleon abandons his troops in Egypt, secretly sails for France
9 October 1799	Napoleon arrives in France
9–10 November 1799	*Coup d'état* of 18 Brumaire; Napoleon becomes effective ruler of France

The wars of 1794–1799 were a messy business. At the time of Thermidor, France faced a coalition that included Great Britain, Austria, Prussia, and Spain. In 1794, the Revolutionary armies swept to victory in Belgium, where General Jourdan defeated the Austrians (Fleurus, 26 June), and in the Rhineland. Jourdan's victory paved the way for an invasion of the Netherlands (December), where the monarchy, lacking popular support, quickly collapsed. Local "patriots," heirs of the failed revolutionaries of 1787, allied with the French and proclaimed the Batavian Republic. The French soon signed a treaty with this "sister" republic, which left a French force of occupation/protection in place and provided for a huge Dutch indemnity. French forces also occupied the left bank of the Rhine, south and west of Cologne and Luxembourg. Great Britain remained unwavering in its hostility, but France signed peace agreements with Prussia (at Basle, the first European diplomatic recognition of the new government, 1795), Spain (1795), and Austria (1797). Spain even allied with France against Great Britain in 1796, although it would change sides again in 1799.

French military successes relied on three key elements:

1. The sheer size of the armies, which invariably outnumbered their opponents.

2. The revolutionary ardor of the soldiers, a factor commented upon by all observers at the time.

3. The ability of the generals.

The first element derived from France's introduction (1793) of mass conscription, which gave it a substantial advantage over opponents that relied on traditional means of recruitment. The second advantage flowed naturally from the circumstances of the initial fighting. The allies had invaded France, which allowed the French government to rally its people to save "the fatherland in danger." The Jacobin mass conscription of fall 1793 raised about 300,000 men. Each canton received its quota of soldiers, who were usually chosen by lot. The "levée en masse" differed fundamentally from earlier efforts to raise troops in that it fell equally on all men: no longer could the rich buy exemption. Detailed studies of local recruitment show that the well-to-do did, in fact, provide a significant portion of the soldiers, in direct contrast to the situation of earlier conscriptions (1792 and February 1793) that had allowed the rich to buy exemption. Perhaps not coincidentally, those conscriptions had touched off widespread violence (most famously the Vendée rebellion) and led to massive desertions.

Many of the men drafted in 1793 ended up as lifelong soldiers. Men unlucky enough to be of draftable age (eighteen to twenty-five) in the fall of 1793 provided the core of the French armies for the next six years, until the draft of 1799. By late 1794, France had the astounding total of 750,000 men under arms, yet the government raised only 70,000 more soldiers from 1794–1797. This limited recruitment meant that the soldiers inspired by revolutionary ardor in 1793 remained in place as late as 1797 (indeed, many of them even afterward). It also meant that France had a remarkably veteran army in the fighting of 1796–1797.

The failure to recruit sufficient replacements led to a steady decline in the size of the army, which bottomed out at about 325,000 men in 1798. In response to this decline, the Directory instituted the Jourdan Law of 19 Fructidor VI (5 September 1798), the first law of universal conscription in any state. All men aged twenty to twenty-five had to sign up for the draft. In theory, the state would first take the men aged twenty and twenty-one, and then the others, by year, as necessary. In practice, the extraordinary military effort of 1798–1799, which included severe French losses, upset all these careful provisions. The army needed so many replacements that it took men from each of the five classes, which touched off some armed resistance in traditional antidraft regions.

Government officials attached to the armies, often deputies on mission from the Convention, constantly bombarded French troops with propaganda designed to make them committed republicans, yet obedient soldiers. The authorities encouraged the troops to sing Revolutionary songs, like the *Marseillaise* or *Ça ira;* they hosted Revolutionary festivals; they encouraged troops to read pro-government newspapers. French generals believed their men to possess a moral superiority over their opponents, a factor which had something to do with the extensive reliance of the French armies on the bayonet charge.[38]

The third element, the capacity of the generals, can also be tied directly to revolutionary change. In the Ancien Régime, only men from the highest ranks of the aristocracy commanded armies. Sometimes these men could be commanders of talent, like Maurice de Saxe, illegitimate son of the King of Poland; often, they were blundering idiots. The Revolution paved the way for men of moderate social status to rise up in the army. The list of successful generals of 1794–1799—Hoche, Jourdan, Moreau, Bonaparte, and the others—contains not a single member of the great aristocracy. Napoleon liked to say that every soldier in his army carried a marshal's baton in his knapsack, because men rose up due to their bravery and military ability.

Ordinary soldiers, taken from a peasant or artisan family, had little realistic hope of becoming generals, even in the Revolutionary armies, but those from middle-class or petty noble families, like Napoleon himself, proved once again the immemorial advantage of selecting quality leaders from the largest possible pool of candidates. Hoche, who had worked in the royal stables as a boy, and who enlisted as an ordinary soldier in 1783 (he reached the rank of sergeant in 1789), was a rare example of someone rising from the ranks to command.

The French used two different strategies in the areas they conquered. In regions contiguous to France, they usually annexed the territory. France annexed Belgium and the left bank of the Rhine in 1793, lost them in 1794, and re-annexed them in 1795. It later annexed Geneva and Mulhouse, as well as the county of Nice and French Savoy. In the Netherlands and most of Switzerland, however, France encouraged the creation of "sister" republics, which then provided large indemnities to France. In 1796, in the wake of several victories by Napoleon Bonaparte's army, Italian republicans in cities such as Modena created a Cispadane Republic, for which they drew up a constitution. In 1797, Napoleon took more control of this process. He co-opted local Italian republicans at Milan (Cisalpine Republic, 1797) and Genoa (Ligurian Republic, 1797); his successors in Italy followed the same technique at Rome (1798), and Naples (January 1799). Napoleon directly appointed the governments of his two "republics" and left their constitutions in abeyance.

The two different systems of occupation naturally led to distinct fiscal relationships with France. French armies had to pay for themselves. In a place like Belgium, incorporated into France, that meant taxes—over 50 millions francs in 1794 alone. The new "sister" republics, like the Batavians (Dutch), often had to pay indemnities to cover the costs of the French troops stationed on their soil. The Dutch faced an initial payment of 200 million francs, of which they paid three-fourths. The Dutch then had to pay for an army of twenty-five thousand men, although France kept as few as ten thousand men in Holland. French armies became notorious for their systematic looting and pillaging. The duchy of Luxembourg sent deputies to the Convention to complain that "the French remove everything, right down to the doors and windows; they ceaselessly ransom the inhabitants and break everything they cannot carry off."[39] The government sent out artists to select the finest paintings and sculptures of occupied areas: canvases by Rubens and Van Dyck left Belgium in 1794–1795, just as those by great Italian masters made their way from Milan or Venice to Paris in 1797. The Directory even organized a special parade of stolen artworks from Italy on the fourth anniversary of the fall of Robespierre.

In 1796, given the drastic circumstances of the French economy, the armies in the Netherlands and Italy provided the money to keep France afloat. In Italy, the most successful French general was the Corsican Napoleon Bonaparte, who conquered most of north–central Italy in 1796–1797. Bonaparte paid his army in cash and even forwarded some 45 million *livres* worth of coinage back to France in 1796. Bonaparte and the Austrians, without the approval of the Directory government, drew up an agreement that gave Venice to Austria, ending the city's centuries-old independence, and confirmed French gains in the Low Countries, Rhineland, and northern Italy (initial agreement at Leoben, June 1797, confirmed at Campo Formio, October 1797). In separate agreements, Napoleon got the Pope to renounce his rights to Avignon and

YOUNG NAPOLEON

Napoleon Bonaparte seems slowly to be losing his place as a towering figure of the collective imagination, at least in the Anglophone world. Throughout the nineteenth and early twentieth centuries, every successful businessman hoped to be called a "Napoleon of industry," just as every general dreamed of Napoleonic battlefield successes. Wellington, Waterloo, Napoleon, the Old Guard—every school child knew these heroic names and places of memory. Lenin fulminated against the dangers of Bonapartism when he and his colleagues seized power in Russia in 1917. Hitler's empire drew comparisons to that of Napoleon, just as his disaster in Russia in 1941 evoked memories of the ruin of Napoleon's Grand Army of 1812. Orwell called *Animal Farm's* dictator–pig, Napoleon.

Napoleon's image lingers on in France: Paris remains covered in landmarks that sing his praises—the Arc de Triomphe, the column in the place Vendôme—as well as with avenues and streets that bring to mind his great victories or the names of his famous generals. Even French cookbooks contain recipes for the legendary chicken Marengo (his meal before that great victory of 1800) or for the pastries known as "napoleons."

Born in Corsica in 1769, member of a middling noble family, Napoleon grew up speaking Corsican, not French. He went to one of the new royal military schools established for boys from middling noble families and became a lieutenant in the royal artillery. He did little during the first three years of the Revolution, rising to the rank of captain by early 1793. At first uninvolved in Revolutionary politics, he became an avid supporter of the Robespierrist wing of the Jacobins in 1793. His great break came at the siege of Toulon, when his deft placement of cannon and sound tactical advice led to the defeat of the British and the recapture of the city. He earned an immediate promotion to brigadier general.

Robespierre's fall led to Napoleon's brief arrest in the fall of 1794, but he quickly obtained release. Moving to Paris, he became a client of Barras, elected as one of the first five Directors. The Right-wing *vendémiaire* uprising (5 October 1795) gave Bonaparte another chance to show his facility for using cannon. He commanded the artillery, and the troops, who crushed the rebellion. Naturally, such service to a powerful patron like Barras led to military command: Bonaparte took over the army in Italy. His lightning campaign of early 1797 routed the Savoyards; he defeated their Austrian allies in the fall. Master of northern Italy, able to provide the Directory with substantial Italian specie, Bonaparte became, like other leading generals, an important political figure. The death of the most important such rival, Lazare Hoche (19 September 1797), gave Napoleon, scarcely twenty-eight at the time, the hopes of dominating the situation.

The military events of 1798–1799 enhanced Napoleon's standing. His successful campaign in Egypt captured the popular imagination in 1798. His main military rivals—Joubert, Moreau, and Jourdan—suffered defeats in Germany, Italy, and Switzerland between March and August 1799. Joubert conveniently died at the battle of Novi on 15 August. Little wonder that those plotting the overthrow of the Directory looked to Bonaparte for their military support, expecting to use this young general to implement their political agenda.

Yet the young Napoleon had no intention of allowing himself to be used. During his successful first stay in Italy, he reportedly told a friend:[40]

> What I have done so far is nothing. I am only at the debut of the career that I must carry through. Do you think that it is for the glory of the lawyers of the Directory, of Carnot, of Barras, that I triumph in Italy? Do you think it is also to found a Republic? What an idea! A Republic of 30 million men! With our mores, our vices! Where is the possibility of that? It's a chimera that has besotted the French, but which will pass like so many others. They need glory, the satisfactions of vanity. But of liberty, they understand nothing by it.

the Comtat (March 1797) and the king of Sardinia–duke of Savoy to accept French possession of Nice and Savoy (occupied in 1792–1793, and officially ceded in 1797).

With France's Continental opponents all beaten by late 1797, Bonaparte convinced the Directors to allow him to invade Egypt in 1798, to cut off English access to India. He first captured Malta, where he abolished the Crusading order of St. John of Jerusalem that ruled the island. His troops quickly took Alexandria and defeated the Mamelukes at the Battle of the Pyramids (21 July 1798), but his navy was annihilated by the British under Admiral Horatio Nelson, at the Battle of the Nile (1 August). Bonaparte marched an army toward Syria in February 1799 but failed to take Acre (May 1799) and withdrew.

The foolish Egyptian expedition, whose only positive effect was the discovery of the Rosetta Stone (which enabled scholars to decipher ancient Egyptian hieroglyphics), had momentous diplomatic consequences. In the aftermath of Nelson's victory, the Ottoman Empire, to which Egypt owed nominal fealty, declared war on France. The Kingdom of Naples followed suit, sending an army to retake Rome from the French. The Neapolitans succeeded at first but were quickly thrown back by General Championnet, who captured Naples and proclaimed a Republic (December 1798–January 1799). The Republic lasted little more than a month. The Directory cashiered Championnet for exceeding his orders and withdrew most of its troops from Naples. The Neapolitan Republic was quickly overthrown by a peasant rebellion begun in Calabria by Cardinal Ruffo and his "invasion" force of eight men!

Napoleon's Mediterranean adventure had also infuriated Russian Tsar Paul I, who claimed to be the protector of the Knights of Malta. Paul objected as well to his exclusion from the Rastadt talks about the future of the Holy Roman Empire. Soon Russia had allied with Naples against France. The Ottomans allowed the Russians to send a fleet through the Dardanelles and the Austrians permitted Russian troops to winter in their territory. Little wonder that by March 1799 Austria and France were again at war. In the fighting of 1799, Russian armies had great success early in the campaign, driving the French from much of Italy and Switzerland. In the end, poor Allied coordination allowed the French to recover Switzerland, but they were driven from Italy. Meanwhile, Bonaparte abandoned his army of 35,000 in Egypt and secretly returned to France, landing at Fréjus, in southern France, on 9 October.[41]

The Coup

> *It is a great tragedy for a nation of thirty million inhabitants in the eighteenth century to have to call on bayonets to save the state.*

> General Napoleon Bonaparte to Foreign Minister Talleyrand,
> November 1799

Fighting continued in the north as well. The French suffered losses in the Rhineland and the Low Countries early in 1799, but quickly reversed those trends. By late 1799, they had driven across the Rhine again, and had expelled the invading Anglo–Russian force from the Netherlands. The military problems of the early fall of 1799 exacerbated tensions inside of France. The Directory could not really call upon public support from any group. The *sans-culottes* detested it, both for political and economic reasons; the Jacobin bourgeoisie resented the stolen election of 1798 and the constant measures taken against the Left; the royalist landowners and bourgeoisie felt robbed of their political rights in 1797.

In the summer of 1799, all of these disgruntled groups began to undermine the Directory's authority. The key blow came in late spring 1799, when Reubell had to step down. The Councils replaced him with Sieyès, a vocal opponent of current policies. In short order another director, Treilhard, resigned, to be replaced by an ally of Sieyès, Louis Gohier. Sieyès and Gohier formed an alliance with Barras, and forced out La Révellière and Merlin de Douai. The incoming directors, Roger Ducos (a regicide) and General Jean Moulin, lined up behind Sieyès. The opposition had now taken control of the executive branch of government.

The topsy-turvy world of Parisian politics spun wildly in July 1799. On 6 July, a new political club opened in the Salle de Manège at the Tuileries: the room in which the Convention had met. The Manège Club quickly attracted over three thousand members, among them two hundred fifty of the deputies to the two Councils. Three weeks after it opened, however, the Directory forced the club to move to the Left Bank. On 13 August, the minister of police, the ex-Terrorist Joseph Fouché, closed it entirely. This anti-Jacobin blow, taken by an ex-Jacobin leader, took place at virtually the same moment as some apparently pro-Jacobin moves. On 1 August, the Directory ended press controls, allowed Jacobin papers to reopen, and named Robert Lindet, one of the members of the Committee of Public Safety of the Year II, as finance minister. These various moves made sense, given that the government needed to ally either with elements of the monarchists or of the Jacobins in order to have a working majority in the Councils. The government thus naturally made overtures to each side, yet those overtures often involved repressive measures against the opponents of those being wooed.

Instability in Paris was matched by instability in the provinces. A peasant uprising in the Toulouse region led to a siege of the city—a Jacobin stronghold—and to a battle in which four thousand peasants lost their lives. The Chouans rose again in the west, this time sacking Le Mans (October). Troops quelled the disturbances, but people everywhere feared the rising level of anarchy. In this climate of uncertainty, Napoleon Bonaparte made a triumphant procession from Provence to Paris. In Paris, his brother Lucien, now a member of the Council of 500, held secret negotiations with key political figures such as Sieyès, Roger Ducos, the minister of justice Cambacérès, foreign minister Talleyrand, and some of Bonaparte's old corps commanders. On 9 November, the pro-Bonaparte forces convinced the Councils to pass a motion, made by Lucien himself, to move their meetings to the old palace of Saint-Cloud, on the outskirts of Paris, to forestall action by the Parisian masses. They named Napoleon Bonaparte commander of all troops around Paris. The five Directors then resigned, although Moulin and Gohier did so only under duress.

The next day, 18 Brumaire (10 November 1799), Napoleon Bonaparte came to the chambers of the two Councils. The Elders received him somewhat coldly; the Council of 500 hooted at him, demanded that he be placed outside the law, and finally jostled and cut him. Lucien responded by haranguing the loyal troops outside, telling them the deputies sought to assassinate Napoleon. The troops stormed into the chambers, sweeping aside the small guard, and cleared the hall. A few hours later, rump meetings of the two bodies voted the constitutional changes the Bonapartes had demanded. They excluded sixty-one deputies from their meetings and gave full authority to a new triumvirate of Consuls: Sieyès, Roger Ducos, and Napoleon Bonaparte. So died the Directory and with it the First French Republic.

⤳ The Republican Legacy

> *. . . the most persistent ghost of the French Revolution was not the woman of the revolutionary crowds but the counter-revolutionary woman of 1795–1796. . . . she succeeded in becoming the basis of a troubling legend. Her putative control of the family . . . threatened the full flowering of the rational state, the other Eden. Once again, hysterical, perverse, irrational, unreliable Eve was constructed to explain why man was kept from earthly paradise.*

> Olwen Hufton, Creighton Lecture, 1989

The republican experiment of 1792–1799 revolutionized not merely politics but all of life. The Republic created an expanded France, new law codes, new administrative structures, new cultural mores, and a changed artistic climate. It destroyed the hegemony of Catholicism, rearranged urban–rural relations, established political divisions that would last into the twentieth century, embroiled all of Europe in a series of bloody wars, and provided Europeans with a political vocabulary for their future: some of it perhaps benign, "Right" and "Left," and some of it more sinister, "enemies of the people" and "enemies of the Revolution."

The Revolution, in its all-encompassing magnitude, left a cultural legacy everywhere in the European-influenced world. Just as the Revolution spawned two violently opposed political movements—republicanism and monarchism—so, too, it encouraged two strongly divergent artistic currents—Classicism and Romanticism. The most famous of the Revolutionary artists was Jacques-Louis David, an avowed Jacobin and Robespierrist. Helen Maria Williams even went so far as to call him Robespierre's lackey.

David had achieved considerable fame before the Revolution; his *Oath of the Horatii* (1785) provides an outstanding example of the revival of Classical themes and the cult of the fatherland. His canvases recorded many of the Revolution's highest and lowest moments. Among the most famous of these paintings are his portrayal of the *Tennis Court Oath* (1791), with its deliberately mythologizing techniques; the stark portrait of Marat (1793), lying dead in his bathtub; and a simple sketch of Marie-Antoinette on her way to the guillotine. *The Assassination of Marat,* which, despite its title, does not show the actual deed, presents the viewer with the bleeding martyr clutching his pen, the murder weapon lying beside the tub. It hung in the meeting room of the Convention, to remind all of their Revolutionary duty.

David played a central role in the Jacobin period, not only as a Parisian deputy to the Convention but as the chief decorator of the great Revolutionary festivals. In August 1793, he masterminded a massive festival in honor of the fall of the monarchy.

Its centerpiece was a new figure in the iconography of the Revolution: Hercules, known as the "French people," slaying the Hydra of Federalism. During the Jacobin ascendancy, David spearheaded the movement to replace the previously dominant figure of Revolutionary iconography—Liberty, always presented as a woman (and, as Guittard's journal tells us, often a live woman, rather than a statue)—with the super-masculine one of Hercules.[42] All of David's work for the festivals relied heavily on Classical models and on those of the greatest earlier movement of Classical revival, the Italian Renaissance. The festivities for the June 1794 Festival of the Supreme Being included a statue modeled on Michelangelo's *David,* as well as many Classical allegories. The fall of the Jacobins led to the fall of Hercules. Marianne, the symbol of Liberty, returned to preeminence. David, along with the other leading Terrorists, faced removal from the Convention and arrest in the fall of 1794, but he survived the purge.

David continued to work in accordance with the political dictates of his times. Under the Directory, he went back to historical paintings, offering the *Rape of the Sabine Women* at the exhibition of 1799. He also early tied his star to that of the young Bonaparte, starting (but not finishing) a portrait of him in the late 1790s. Soon, David would provide Bonaparte with great masterpieces to record his triumphs, such as *Napoleon Crossing the Alps,* in which the young and masterful leader, astride a magnificent white horse, leads his troops through the mountains in the most difficult of conditions. (See Plate.) In time, David would record coronations for his new master.

Different approaches flourished in the 1790s in all the arts. Painters such as Greuze and Fragonard continued the traditions of the eighteenth century. The great sculptor Houdon still flourished, doing busts of many of the greatest figures of the day, both French and foreign. Houdon's busts often provide tantalizing clues to the fates of his subjects. The bust of Barnave, now in the Carnavelet Museum in Paris, shows a handsome, proud, indeed haughty young man. (Does the contemptuous glance of the brilliant young lawyer help us to understand why he fell from grace with his colleagues?) A nearby room holds a bust of Mirabeau, his monstrous head dominating the room, his fury warm even in cold stone.

Musicians, too, felt the Revolutionary ferment. In France, composers such as Rouget de Lisle, whose *La Marseillaise* became the anthem of republicanism (and, late in the nineteenth century, under the Third Republic, the national anthem), or Méhul, whose *Chant du départ,* with its words by the poet Marie-Joseph Chénier, rivalled Rouget de Lisle's work in popularity in the 1790s, competed with composers who produced purely traditional operas. Outside of France, whether we look at composers such as Beethoven; writers, such as Schiller; or philosophers, such as Kant, all had to come to terms with the Revolutionary world, even if they rejected it. Here the Revolutionary armies left a fatally mixed legacy. Many intellectuals and artists responded positively to the Revolution. The execution of Louis XVI and the Terror appalled European opinion, but the republican experiment inspired ardor outside of France as well as within. Urban elites agitated for representative, sometimes even republican government. These movements looked to France for an example, and often borrowed French nationalist terminology as a means to oppose ruling monarchs. When the Revolutionary armies began to invade surrounding countries and to impose "republican" governments, however, public opinion began to shift. In Germany especially, but in Italy to some degree as well, nationalism grew as a reaction against the French.

Napoleon, too, elicited such responses. Beethoven first dedicated a symphony to the charismatic republican general, but then angrily rejected the imperial conqueror.

In England, the Revolution touched off a tremendous debate. Opposition focused around the greatest denunciation of the Revolution, Edmund Burke's *Reflections on the Revolution in France* (1790), which ridiculed the idea of a Revolution on behalf of natural rights. Burke had many opponents, most prominent among them Tom Paine, *The Rights of Man* (1791), and Mary Wollstonecraft. She published an attack on Burke, *A Vindication of the Rights of Man,* and then shifted to a broader assault in her most famous book, *A Vindication of the Rights of Woman* (1792). In it, she encouraged men to treat women as equals, and women to act as the reasoned beings they were. She supported equal education for girls and boys and rights for women, based on their capacity to reason. *Vindication* is the foundation text of modern feminism, a classic example of how revolutions have unintended consequences. Wollstonecraft in England, just like Toussaint L'Ouverture in Saint-Domingue, took up the cudgels for liberty for all: in her case for women, in his case for African slaves.

Most of the men who made the French Revolution had no intention of granting greater freedom to either group. The events in France touched off unrest in French West Indian colonies. The complex societies of blacks, mulattos, and whites had great difficulty reaching an agreement about the new political rights. In Saint-Domingue, for example, mulattos owned many plantations and slaves: if political rights were to be based on property, they would get them. Whites, many of whom owned no property, insisted on the primacy of skin color over property. In France, some supported one group, some the other; a few enlightened souls, such as Condorcet, even supported freedom for the slaves. The various legislative bodies went back and forth on this issue. At first blacks and mulattos got no satisfaction, but then the Constituent Assembly decreed (May 1791) that free-born blacks and mulattos should have the same political rights as whites. Later in 1791, blacks took matters into their own hands; one of Guittard's correspondants, a M. Clausson living in Saint-Domingue, wrote him that the rebellion had done 2 billion *livres* of damage.

The Convention abolished slavery (February 1794) but, in reality, the action of the mulattos and slaves themselves had resolved the issue. Led by Toussaint L'Ouverture, the slaves defeated the local whites and mulattos, to say nothing of expeditionary forces sent by the French and the British (1794). All the expeditions of Europeans eventually fell victim to disease. The final French expedition of 1802–1803 actually captured L'Ouverture, but the force soon melted away, its commander among those carried off by yellow fever. L'Ouverture's successor, Jacques Dessalines, then established an independent Haiti. The British captured the other French West Indian islands and held most of them for some time, but these islands reverted to France in the end. The Convention's abolition of slavery, widely praised in France and elsewhere, did not prove permanent. Once he had consolidated power, Bonaparte reestablished both the slave trade and slavery itself on the remaining French islands.

Women fared little better than blacks. The preceding narrative makes clear the important role of women in the great Revolutionary events: the October Days of 1789, the risings of 1793 and 1795. They participated effectively in the ordinary political life of France as well. Individual women, like Madame Roland or Claire

The Conservative Response: Burke and Revolution

No one in the Anglophone world can escape Edmund Burke's views of the French Revolution. Burke's *Reflections on the Revolution in France* (1790) profoundly affected the great Anglophone historian of the Revolution, Thomas Carlisle, just as it influenced Charles Dickens. Dickens's work, in turn, has resonated widely in modern Anglophone culture, not only in such venues as the Hollywood version of *A Tale of Two Cities,* but even in films such as D.W. Griffith's silent classic, *Orphans of the Storm.* Griffith presents us with the entirely fanciful scene of Robespierre and Danton walking the streets of Paris together in spring 1789: the printed descriptions tell us that the sinister, sniveling Robespierre is a "pussy-footer if ever there was one," but that Danton is "the Abraham Lincoln of France"!

Burke, who supported the American Revolutionaries because he believed they fought for their legitimate rights as Englishmen, rejected the French Revolution because of its reliance on abstract principles. Burke's ideas remain Holy Writ for contemporary American conservative writers such as George Will. Let us briefly sample Burke's masterwork.

> I flatter myself that I love a manly, moral, regulated liberty as well as any gentleman of that society [the Revolutionary Society of England, which supported the French Revolution], be he who he will; and perhaps I have given as good proofs of my attachment to that cause, in the whole course of my public conduct. I think I envy liberty as little as they do, to any other nation. But I cannot stand forward, and give praise or blame to any thing which relates to human actions, and human concerns, on a simple view of the object, as it stands stripped of every relation, in all the nakedness and solitude of metaphysical abstraction. Circumstances . . . give in reality to every political principle its distinguishing colour, and discriminating effect. The circumstances are what render every civil and political scheme beneficial or noxious to mankind. Abstractly speaking, government, as well as liberty, is good; yet could I, in common sense, ten years ago have felicitated France on her enjoyment of a government (for she had then a government) without enquiry what the nature of that government was, or how it was administered? Can I now congratulate the same nation upon its freedom? Is it because liberty in the abstract may be classed amongst the blessings of mankind, that I am seriously to felicitate a madman, who has escaped from the protecting restraint and wholesome darkness of his cell, on his restoration to the enjoyment of light and liberty? . . .
>
> I should therefore suspend my congratulations on the new liberty of France, until I was informed how it had been combined with government; with public force; with the discipline and obedience of armies; with the collection of an effective and well-distributed revenue; with morality and religion; with the solidity of property; with peace and order; with civil and social manners. All these (in their way) are good things too; and, without them, liberty is not a benefit whilst it lasts, and is not likely to continue long. The effect of liberty to individuals is, that they may do what they please; We ought to see what it will please them to do, before we risque congratulations, which may be soon turned into complaints. Prudence would dictate this in the case of separate insulated private men; but liberty, when men act in bodies, is *power.* Considerate people, before they declare themselves, will observe the use which is made of *power,* and particularly of so trying a thing as *new* power in *new* persons, of whose principles, tempers, and dispositions, they have little or no experience . . . [43]

Lacombe, provided leadership to political movements of all kinds. The Girondins rallied around Madame Roland, while Lacombe seems to have played a key role in the May 31–June 2, 1793 events that led to their fall. In a speech denouncing female participation in politics, Chaumette, procurator general of Paris, singled out Madame

Equality for blacks. In this 1791 engraving, reason establishes legal equality between whites and blacks. The measure applied to free blacks only; the vast majority of blacks in French colonies legally remained slaves until the Convention abolished slavery on 4 February 1794.

SOURCE: © Giraudon/Art Resource, New York.

Roland and Olympe de Gouges as examples of "denatured women" who wanted to "renounce their sex" in order to be men, that is, in order to participate in public life. In Paris, women attended sectional assemblies and presented petitions to the various legislative bodies. They even voted in certain places. At Laon, for example, they cast their ballots for the Constitution of 1793.

Many French women, such as those in the Roman-law regions of the south, obtained important property rights from the new law codes, fully promulgated by 1793. The law now imposed equal inheritance and forbade favoritism toward one child, such as the oldest male. Married women got greater control of their property and the right to use and enjoy more of the joint family property after the death of their husbands. Under the Ancien Régime, women in some provinces, such as Brittany, had enjoyed extensive property rights, but women in other areas, notably the Roman law regions of the south, suffered from considerable legal discrimination. The new law gave these women a level of legal equality their mothers could never have imagined and contributed mightily to their struggle for greater authority within their families.

The Revolutionaries also legalized divorce (Constitution of 1791). Urban households, in particular, started to take advantage of the new law. Although rural communities had divorce rates of only 1 or 2 percent in the 1790s, large cities such as

Lyon had rates as high as 25 percent (1793; the rate fell to 12 percent the following year). Divorce reform, initially presented as a boon to women either mistreated by their husbands and/or forced into marriages by their families, did not necessarily have its intended consequences. The relaxation of the old ban on divorce made it legally easier for men to abandon their families, a problem that became particularly severe in times of famine, such as 1795. Women's legal gains did not survive the Republic, as Napoleon imbedded profoundly misogynist principles into his legal code.

For most women, the Revolution revolved around the same issues that were critical to men. As women bought and prepared the food, they naturally played key roles in the food riots resulting from subsistence issues. Women artisans, like male ones, also demonstrated about work-related matters: the laundresses who demanded cheaper soap in 1793 provide the best-known but hardly a unique example. Women did not generally act together out of a spirit of cooperation on the basis of gender: the key group opposing the Club of Republican Revolutionary Citizenesses in the fall of 1793 was the market women of Les Halles. The conflict between these two groups of women involved, above all, their relationship to groups of male allies, and to economic grievances (of the market women) not specifically related to gender. That male authorities relished the opportunity to get women out of politics seems beyond question. One Jacobin wrote in September 1793: "It is these counter-revolutionary sluts who cause all the riotous outbreaks, above all over bread. They made a revolution over coffee and sugar, and they will make others if we don't watch out."[44]

The revolutionaries bequeathed to posterity a society built, in theory, around individual rights. They went to great lengths to make sure that the individuals in question were men only, because they (most of them) believed that women lacked reason. In the West Indies, many whites (seconded by allies in France itself) similarly sought to exclude mulatto and black men from full civil rights.

The Revolution also constructed the enduring foundations of the modern French state. Here the Directory deserves some credit. The continuities between 1792 and 1797 are much stronger than we sometimes think. After all, until the elections of 1797, well over half of the men ruling France had been in the legislative body since September 1792. As late as 1799, a third or more of the men in the two Councils had been legislators since the beginning of the Republic. We should not be misled by the political instability of the Directory, because the New Regime took firm root, in virtually every sector, precisely during this period.

To carry out these governmental activities, the bureaucracy expanded constantly in the 1790s. Mercier wrote of these men: "Never has bureaucracy been brought to so exaggerated a point . . . Never has business so languished since the creation of this army of clerks who are to work what valets are to service." He claims this mob of clerks not only "troubled the civic order but demoralized the administration." For him, all these men produced was a mountain of paper:

An Indian recently come to Paris, whose affairs brought him to a minister's office, struck by these pyramids of circulars which overwhelm the bureaux, did not hesitate to affirm that a single secretary general of the ministry uses more paper in one day than his country uses in an entire year.[45]

THE RIGHTS OF WOMAN

Mary Wollstonecraft's *A Vindication of the Rights of Woman* (1792) laid out the foundation for modern feminism—the belief, as Betty Friedan once put it, that a woman is a human being. Wollstonecraft belonged to radical political circles in England; she had already published an attack on Edmund Burke's *Reflections*, titled *A Vindication of The Rights of Man*. That she took her inspiration from the Revolutionary moment is abundantly clear; *The Rights of Woman* begins with a letter sent to Charles Maurice de Talleyrand, former bishop of Autun, who headed the educational sub-committee of the Constitutional Committee of the Constituent Assembly. Talleyrand had recommended universal state-run education for boys. Wollstonecraft begins by questioning the exclusion of girls from serious education and moves from that opening premise to a ringing avowal of equal rights for women. Before turning to a brief passage from her letter to Talleyrand, it should be noted that several of the male Revolutionary leaders supported rights for women. Condorcet believed women should vote and have full civic rights; Tom Paine, the great Anglo-American pamphleteerist, and a deputy to the Convention, agreed. Even though Condorcet and Paine both sat on the Constitutional Committee of the Convention (the former effectively chaired it), they could not get their principles incorporated into the text they reported out.

To M. Talleyrand-Périgord,

Having read with great pleasure a pamphlet which you have lately published [on compulsory education in France], I dedicate this volume to you, to induce you to reconsider the subject, and maturely weigh what I have advanced respecting the rights of woman and national education: and I call with the firm tone of humanity; for my arguments, Sir, are dictated by a disinterested

---

The Jacobin dictatorship and the Directory combined to make the key innovations. The Jacobins introduced widespread use of centrally appointed agents to help locally elected administrators in their work. The Directory cleared up the confusion in local administration by eliminating the district councils, who had played a key role under the Jacobins, and by standardizing the use of cantonal level municipalities in the countryside. The enormous demands on local administration throughout the 1790s—central governments sent out hundreds of orders for inquests on population, agriculture, poor relief, industry, conscription, etc.—forced people to develop a much more intimate relationship with the central state. The state now knew much more about each French woman or man than it had ever known before. Napoleon would give final form to many of these new institutions—like secondary schools, and departmental prefects (appointed by the central government to administer the department)—but they developed in earnest in the republican years. The negative side of these local reforms, a side grossly exacerbated by Napoleon, was that they vitiated local democracy.[46]

Liberty, Equality, Property: A Cultural Battle

All of us are equal, but some of us are more equal than others.

Napoleon the pig

(CONTINUED)

spirit—I plead for my sex—not for myself. Independence I have long considered as the grand blessing of life, the basis of every virtue—and independence I will ever secure by contracting my wants, though I were to live on a barren heath.

It is then an affection for the whole human race that makes my pen dart rapidly along to support what I believe to be the cause of virtue: and the same motive leads me earnestly to wish to see woman placed in a station in which she would advance, instead of retarding, the progress of those glorious principles that give a substance to morality. My opinion, indeed, respecting the rights and duties of woman, seems to flow so naturally from these simple principles, that I think it scarcely possible, but that some of the enlarged minds who formed your admirable constitution, will coincide with me....

Contending for the rights of woman, my main argument is built on this simple principle, that if she be not prepared by education to become the companion of man, she will stop the progress of knowledge and virtue, for truth must be common to all, or it will be inefficacious with respect to its influence on general practice....

Consider, I address you as a legislator, whether, when men contend for their freedom, and to be allowed to judge for themselves respecting their own happiness, it be not inconsistent and unjust to subjugate women, even though you firmly believe that you are acting in the manner best calculated to promote their happiness? Who made man the exclusive judge, if woman partake with him the gift of reason? ...

But, if women are to be excluded, without having a voice, from a participation of the natural rights of mankind, prove first, to ward off the charge of injustice and inconsistency, that they want reason—else this flaw in your New Constitution will ever shew that man must, in some shape, act like a tyrant, and tyranny, in whatever part of society it rears its brazen front, will ever undermine morality.[47]

Since the time of the French Revolution, all states of the Europeanized world have struggled with the conflict between liberty and property. For many years the Paris Métro had first- and second-class cars, clear recognition of the Orwellian principle of unequal equality.[48] As Boissy d'Anglas's remarks (cited previously) make clear, those who wrote the Constitution of 1795 would certainly have agreed with Napoleon the pig. Much as we dislike admitting it, our contemporary societies essentially agree. Even today, those with property have effective rights that those without much property lack, as they have had in virtually all human societies.

That sad fact, however, should not hide the remarkable reality of the first half of the statement: that all of us are equal. The French Revolution enshrined that principle forever in the hearts of France's people. As the spread of France's tri-colored flag has subsequently proven, the principle spread eventually throughout the Europeanized world.[49] Even Napoleon, when he wanted to change the constitution of France, held a plebiscite to do so. The Directory repudiated the "anarchic" democracy of the Jacobin ascendancy and restored the severe social divisions of earlier times, but it could not completely destroy the democratic impulse.

The revival of trade led to a revival of many other aspects of Parisian life. People could now seek out luxury goods again. Wigmakers, put out of work by the fashion shift of the radical period, could now get out of politics and get back to work. Jewelers, clothiers—everyone involved in furnishing goods to the upscale population—

had a tremendous revival of business. Even the gambling tables made a comeback in the Palais Royal. Yet they, too, felt the democratic impulse. In sharp contrast to the profile of arrested Ancien Régime gamblers, more than a quarter of those arrested at the gambling dens during the Directory came from the artisan world: shoemakers, coachmen, gardeners, clerks, and many other lower-class men.

One group initially serving only the rich, but soon providing for a more democratic clientele, sparked a revival that has echoes in our own day: restauranteurs. The outbreak of Revolution coincided with the rise of the restaurant in Paris. In the 1780s, *restaurateurs* had begun to shift from their traditional craft—providing restorative soups to customers—to making full meals. Gouverneur Morris's diary speaks constantly of going to the restaurants, and he lists establishments of quite varied quality. The deputies and those with business to do with them provided a steady clientele for the establishments that quickly sprung up around the Palais Royal. Chefs of the great princes, whose patrons had fled France, opened up fashionable restaurants inside the Palais Royal or on adjoining streets. Antoine Beauvilliers, author of *The Art of the Chef* (1814), former chef of the count of Provence (Louis XVI's brother), started the trend before the Revolution. Once it broke out, he was joined in the Palais Royal district by Méot, the ex-chef of the prince of Condé; Robert, who had also worked for Condé; and the so-called Provençal Brothers, who had worked for the prince of Conti. They introduced the cooking of their native Provence to Paris: *brandade* and *bouillabaise* soon became all the rage.[50] If you did not want Provençal fare, then cooking from other regions of France was available. Those inclined to international cuisine could choose from English beefsteak, German sauerkraut, Spanish garbanzos or peppered ham from Xerica, Italian macaroni, polenta, or ices, Russian caviar and smoked eel, Indian rice or curry, American potatoes, chocolate, and pineapples, to cite only a few choices. Mercier describes one of the more outrageous establishments:

> There, one dines Oriental style; but the greedy never enter there. These pleasures are only for the prodigal, but he will find there on certain days all the pomp and bizarreness of the feast of Trimalcion [a Roman hedonist]. At a certain signal, the ceiling opens up and columned floats, guided by a Venus, descend from the sky; sometimes it's Aurora [goddess of the dawn], sometime it's Diana [goddess of the hunt] who comes to seek her dear Endymion. All of them are dressed as goddesses. The connoisseurs make their pick and the divinities, not of Olympus but of the ceiling, join up with their mortals.[51]

Beauvilliers trained the greatest chef of the age, the man who would, more than any other, be responsible for the rise of French *haute cuisine* in the nineteenth century: Antonin Carême. He began as a pastry chef for Beauvilliers but later developed into the most famous chef in the world, working for Tsar Alexander; George IV of England; Talleyrand; and the richest banker of the age, the baron Rothschild.

Carême would later publish several key books of modern cookery; his manuals on pastry became the bible of the new breed of pastrymakers who sprang up in nineteenth-century Paris. He belonged to that world of the Palais Royal under the Directory that reestablished Paris as a luxury capital of the world. The dozen or so famous restaurants of that enclave are all gone, save one. Today, the wealthy tourist can still eat at the Grand Vefour, in the Galerie de Beaujolais of the Palais Royal. With luck, he or she can reserve the table often occupied by a famous eighteenth-century customer, that same Napoleon Bonaparte who brought the Republic, and the Revolution, to a close. The rest of us, like the vast majority of Paris's population under the Directory, have to be satisfied with looking in the window.

New Definitions

The French language has conquered the esteem of Europe and for more than a century has been the classic language there. . . . But that idiom, admitted in political transactions, used in several cities of Germany, Italy, the Low Countries, in a part of the pays of Liège, of Luxembourg, and of Switzerland, even in Canada and on the banks of the Mississippi, by what fate is it still ignored by the great part of the French people?[52]

Report on Public Instruction, made to the Convention (1794)

The French Revolution redefined the meaning of ordinary words and created new words of its own, to describe a world unlike any that had existed before. "Monsieur" and "Madame," once reserved for the nobility, became the property of all urban dwellers, from the humblest artisan to the richest banker. Common names had to be abandoned. Six thousand French towns and villages tried to change their names under the First Republic; Parisians renamed fourteen hundred streets.[53] The more radical militants, such as the *sans-culottes* of Paris, wanted to abolish the use of the polite form of you (*vous*), which traditionally expressed unequal relationships: the powerful addressed the weak as *tu,* the latter responded with *vous.* Even in contemporary France, one's attitude toward the *vous/tu* distinction invariably reflects one's political leanings (the Left prefers *tu*). Most critically, as the *Report on Public Instruction* makes evident, the French language itself became the symbol of freedom. Local languages—dialects, regional variations of French, and distinct languages (Breton, Basque, etc.)—became *de facto* symbols of ignorance, backwardness, and reaction. French republicanism stood for the French language, and its culture. That sense of cultural superiority provided an important impetus both to the homogenization of the cultures of French territory and to later imperialism.

The democratic culture of the Revolution extended into many aspects of daily life. As the modern business suit attests, the clothing of working men (those without culottes) became the model for the clothing of all men at work. Women's fashions rejected the excesses of the final days of Versailles: out went the outrageous wigs, the deeply cut necklines, the wild hoop skirts; in came simple dresses, flattened hairdos, and demure bonnets. The Directory led fashion back in the direction of the scandalous and the excessive, but women's clothing, like men's, gradually became more utilitarian.[54]

Les Tricoteuses Jacobines, ou de Robespierre.

JACOBIN vociférant une Motion à la Tribune.

LE BONET ROUGE.

Patriotic Jacobin supporters, dressed in the style of 1793 to 1794: simple trousers or dress, and the red bonnet of the Revolution.

Source: Musée Carnavalet.

Women kept other disabilities, too. They did not get real legal equality from the Revolution, although the First Republic treated them far better than Napoleon or his nineteenth-century successors would do. Women bring us back to our original questions: Who are the French? What is France? How did the Revolution change the answers to those questions? No one could deny that a woman, "born and domiciled in France" (to use the constitutional phrase describing male citizens), was "French." She was, after a fashion, a citizen. In many instances, she received the same legal rights and protections as a man. Yet she was not really a citizen, as she had no right to vote or to participate in political life. The state would rely on her to raise good citizens (her sons) and to be a good republican mother, but she had no role in public politics.

As Wollstonecraft suggested, "tyranny, in whatever part of society it rears its brazen front, will ever undermine morality." The Republic, to its credit, never retreated from the Jacobin abolition of slavery, but public opinion still tolerated slavery, which Napoleon reintroduced soon after he took power. The Republic encouraged a tremendous exchange of populations within Europe. Something like 200,000 people fled France. Many nobles, of course, left between 1789 and 1792, but most of the emigrants came from the ordinary mass of the population. Tens of thousands of others moved into France: some of them, like Anarchasis Cloots (from Germany) or Tom Paine or Benjamin Constant (a Swiss), played important roles in French political and intellectual life. Napoleon Bonaparte, soon to be Emperor, came from Corsica, which had been annexed by France only a few years before his birth. Culturally, Corsica, and Bonaparte, had much closer ties to Italy than to France.

The Palais Royal under the Directory. Fashions have not returned to the excesses of the 1780s, but the simple clothing of the Jacobins had given way to much more stylish, and expensive garb. The Palais Royal was filled with restaurants and other forms of entertainment.

SOURCE: Bibliothèque Nationale, Estampes, coll. Destailleur, n. 1012.

Bonaparte offers a superb example of the Revolutionary transformation. He became French, through the schools of the Ancien Régime, because he accepted French culture. The Ancien Régime long followed such a policy, although its application lacked consistency. The Revolution made explicit what had long been implicit: those who accepted French culture could be French citizens. No group better illustrates this principle than the Jews. The Constituent Assembly immediately offered citizenship to the assimilated Jews of Bordeaux and the great ports; they hesitated to allow the Ashkenazic Jews of eastern France, who had not assimilated, the full rights of citizens. In the end, the decoupling of the Church and the State made it possible to allow Alsatian Jews to remain religious Jews, yet to become French citizens. Like all privileged groups, they had merely to "swear the civic oath which will be regarded as a renunciation of all the privileges and exceptions introduced previously in their favor" (Decree of 27 September 1791).

The occupation of areas near France—Belgium, the left bank of the Rhine, parts of Savoy, the county of Nice, Geneva, Mulhouse, Luxembourg—raised thorny questions about what was France and who were the French. The various French governments treated all these regions as part of France: they got their own departments, elected representatives to the legislature, paid regular French taxes. Their citizens were "French." Yet many contemporaries took a dim view of some of the annexations: Carnot strongly opposed the incorporation of the left bank of the Rhine, on the grounds that the German population rejected a direct tie to France. France had already done precisely the same thing in Alsace and the German-speaking parts of Lorraine, but the Revolution changed the meaning of such boundary alteration. The Constituent Assembly had specifically renounced wars of conquest, yet the Convention conveniently circumvented this legality by harkening back to the boundaries of Roman Gaul as the "natural" frontiers of France.

Already in January 1793, Danton declared: "The limits of France are marked out by nature. We shall reach them at their four points: at the Ocean, at the Rhine, at the Alps, at the Pyrenees."[55] Danton's "France" thus brought back the lands of the Salian Franks, around Cologne, the ancient capital of Charlemagne, at Aachen, and even Xanten, which the *Song of Roland* had marked out as the boundary of Francia in the twelfth century. Popular culture had long tied the French to ancient Gaul, and thus adopted the Rhine as France's "natural" frontier. The Revolutionary government, in this as in so many other matters, responded to a genuine public opinion when it annexed these territories and declared their inhabitants "French."

Their inhabitants had other ideas, which the Revolution strengthened. By giving such strong stimulus to the idea of the "nation," the Revolution abetted the resistance of the non-Francophone areas it tried to take over. The citizens of Koblenz or Cologne felt themselves to be German, not French, and no amount of force or French propaganda was likely to change such feelings, so deeply rooted in the local German culture and so watered by the rising tide of German nationalism.

The Revolution, above all the Jacobin government, also created a new strain of French nationalism. Mme de Staël rightly predicted (1798) that the Revolutionaries had proclaimed a Republic "fifty years before the people's minds were ready for it." Even that Republic (founded in the Revolution of 1848) lasted but four years, not to become permanent until 1879. People's minds *were* ready for the French nation forged in the Revolutionary fires. The hottest fire, that of the Jacobins, democratized society to an extent that demolished all preconceptions of the social order, of social identity, and of national identity. Michelet, nationalist and republican, closed his six-volume history of the Revolution (which ends with Thermidor) with a paean to the Jacobins, because these "great hearts, with their blood, made for us the Fatherland."[56]

Just as the Roman world, in collapsing, allowed a new world to take shape, so, too, the end of the Ancien Régime ushered in a new world. The French Revolution did not stand alone in the earth-shattering events of the late eighteenth century. The creation of the American colossus, the unbinding of the industrial Prometheus, the rise of individualism, of which the Revolution was both a cause and an effect: all fundamentally altered the old world. The new world would move much faster. The Revolution, in that sense, was well ahead of its time, because it moved too fast. In French politics, the nineteenth century largely repeated the Revolution, but took one hundred years instead of ten to do its work.

The Revolution transcends French history, has a beginning but no end, because its fundamental goal, the democratization of human society—through liberty, equality, and fraternity—remains unachieved. Furet, rejecting the Marxist interpretation of the Revolution, felt that it had come to an end, that the journey was over. In a certain way, he thus became the heir of Robespierre, for whom the Revolution was a destination, that same shining city on a hill that has inspired so many revolutionaries and which invariably turns from Emerald City into a watered-down version of the London of *1984's* Oceania.

For Danton, the Revolution never ends, because it is a journey. He makes mistakes, repudiates them, becomes the hero of those who want human society bettered, but human. Just as Nicolas Ruault praised Danton's humanity in the days after his death, so, too, the national secretary of the French Socialist Party, Marcel Debarge, recently commented that "I like Danton because I have always had a weakness for people who live, who screw."[57] So, too, do the French, that ever-changing people who name their streets for the old Terrorist. They believe themselves to be the people made by the Revolution: to be those "born and domiciled in France," in whose nation of equal citizens the sovereignty resides; to be those whose fraternal unity grew out of Jacobin democracy; and to be those whose liberty demands the skepticism of Danton, rather than the certainty of Robespierre. They have learned that unified sovereignty, combined with such certainty, provides as great a threat to liberty as the old tyrannies. They have learned that the exclusionist principle, imbedded even in the word "fraternity," with its implicit exclusion of women, invariably destroys the greatness of a nation. Their heroes, like Danton or Henry IV, are lovers of life, in all its messiness, in all its contradictions.

France of the eight hundred-year Capetian monarchy, France of the Revolution, France of human rights and human wrongs, "a hundred, a thousand different Frances of long ago, yesterday or today": all of them live on, their places of memory haunting the human landscape, reminding us that every people, like the French, creates itself, and that the boundaries of every human space, of every France, are a human creation. In defining the "heroes of yesteryear," human societies define their present by means of their past. They name their streets, buildings, public spaces for those heroes, hoping thus, by means of fixing names to seemingly permanent structures, to use the past to define a future when all that will be left of our physical world, as of that of our ancestors, will be such structures.

The Ancien Régime and the Revolution reveal to us the illusion of such thinking. All over France, the physical evidence of the Ancien Régime survives—in churches, palaces, castles, even in place names. The Revolution's legacy lives on in another way, in the hearts and minds of the French people, for whom the revolutionary ideals of liberty, equality, fraternity have become the defining qualities of their human society. They have become, in a word, France.

Notes

1. Cited in M.-H. Huet, *Mourning Glory. The Will of the French Revolution* (Philadelphia: University of Pennsylvania Press, 1997), 149.

2. B. Baczko, "L'expérience thermidorienne," in *The French Revolution and the Creation of Modern Political Culture. V. 2: The Political Culture of the French Revolution,* ed. C. Lucas (Oxford, New York: Permamon Press, 1987), 367. My translation.

3. N. Ruault, *Gazette d'un parisien sous la Révolution. Lettres à son frère. 1783–1796,* ed. A. Vassal and C. Rimbaud (Paris: Librairie Académique Perrin, 1976), 368.

4. This figure, if accurate, suggests that about five thousand people got paid to attend each evening session, if the sessions met (as officially authorized) three times every ten days. The sectional militants, who had met nightly until forbidden to do so in September 1793, often continued relatively permanent sessions in sectional societies, but these had neither government sanction nor subsidy.

5. White was the color of the royalists, hence the name. Let it be noted that the officials who carried out the White Terror were *not* royalists, but republicans, often Girondins.

6. Sutherland, *France 1789–1815,* 266.

7. P. Beik, ed., *The French Revolution* (New York: Walker, 1970), 317–318.

8. Cited in W. Sewell, Jr., *Work and Revolution in France. The language of labor from the Old Regime to 1848* (Cambridge, New York: Cambridge University Press, 1980), 129–130.

9. The Council of 250s members had to be over forty, those of the Council of 500 over thirty. The initial Council of 250 was chosen by lot from among the over-forty deputies elected in 1795.

10. Only one of the original thirteen states had universal manhood suffrage in 1787.

11. Malcolm Crook, *Elections in the French Revolution. An apprenticeship in democracy, 1789–1799* (Cambridge: Cambridge University Press, 1996), estimates that the new rules set the electorate at about 5 million men, perhaps 15 to 20 percent higher than in 1791.

12. D. Woronoff, *The Thermidorian Regime and the Directory 1794–1799,* tr. J. Jackson (Cambridge: Cambridge University Press, 1983; Paris: Editions du Seuil, 1972), and many other surveys suggest a total number of electors of about thirty thousand. Here, as in the earlier discussions on eligible electors in 1791, I am relying on the recent work of two historians, Malcolm Crook and Mel Edelstein, which has conclusively demonstrated that the disenfranchisement clauses eliminated far fewer people than we had thought.

13. Ruault, *Gazette,* 382. Ruault suggests to his brother that they buy a little piece of land and "find a little retreat . . . in this very turbulent Republic."

14. Text of Boissy d'Anglas's speech in Beik, *French Revolution,* 313–324. I have modified his translation of the final phrase.

15. Virtually all members of elite society accepted this principle, whether in France, Great Britain, or the United States. Different systems used different mechanisms to achieve the same end: some American state legislatures, for example, did not give their deputies a salary, making sure that only those of independent means could serve.

16. Ménétra, *Journal of My Life,* 222–223. The translator has here chosen the word "slanderers" where a literal translation would be denunciators.

17. Ruault, *Gazette,* 378–339, letter of 6 May 1795 (16 Floréal) Year III.

18. Ménétra's *Journal* (232–233) recounts his participation, and that of many armed Guardsmen from his section.

19. Cited in J. Bart, *La Révolution française en Bourgogne* (Clermont-Ferrand: La Française d'Édition et d'Imprimerie, 1996), 277.

20. The chronology of military and diplomatic events appears in the following text.

21. Mercier, *Le nouveau Paris,* 467.

22. I. Woloch, *The New Regime. Transformations of the French Civic Order, 1789–1820s* (New York: Norton, 1994).

23. Guittard's contribution of 237 *livres* would place him slightly above the median: roughly 30 percent of those imposed paid 100 *livres* or less, 39 percent between 100 and 999 *livres,* and the final 31 percent more than 1,000 *livres.* The forced loan gave a personal exemption as well as exemptions for each family member, so that the poor rarely had to pay.

24. Ruault, *Gazette,* 395.

25. Mercier, *Le nouveau Paris,* 471.

26. These decrees also made the Convention's deputies eligible to serve again as legislators, except for sixty-five Jacobin deputies, who were banned from re-election. Neither Guittard nor any other source known to me mentions opposition to these clauses.

27. In addition, the government named nineteen *conventionnels* to represent Corsica, then occupied by the English.

28. Crook's statistics suggest remarkable local variations: percentage turnout declined overall, but it ranged from 46 percent in the Doubs down to 6 percent in Charente-Inférieur.

29. The two new Directors were Philippe Merlin de Douai and François de Neufchâteau, who took over primary responsibility for the economy.

30. Here I am relying on the figures cited by Sutherland, *France 1789–1815,* 305.

31. As noted above, these fluctuations varied sharply from area to area: the number of eligibles dropped sharply in the departments around Toulouse and Châlons-sur-Marne.

32. Guittard's pro-Church views, which permeate his *Journal,* make him a somewhat biased witness on this issue, but a majority of French people certainly shared his views on the calendar and the rhythm of everyday life.

33. Mercier, *Le nouveau Paris,* 381.

34. Saint-Just and other Jacobin leaders had supported the free market in 1793.

35. Mercier, *Le nouveau Paris,* 465. He refers both to the latrines and to the prostitution, gambling, and government corruption taking place in the Palais Royal.

36. Cited in F. Furet, *Revolutionary France, 1770–1880,* trans. A. Nevill (Oxford: Basil Blackwell, 1992; Paris: Hachette, 1988), 208.

37. Negotiators from France and the Holy Roman Empire did not create a legal basis for annexation until April 1798, at the Congress of Rastadt, but the French government created four departments in the Rhineland in January 1798 and afterwards treated the area as part of France.

38. Even Napoleon, who began as an artillery officer and usually made effective use of his cannons, believed in the bayonet. This tactical commitment to the bayonet partly explains the extraordinarily high level of casualties in Napoleonic battles.

39. Cited in J. Godechot, "Le 'drainage' des ressources des pays occupés," in *L'État de la France pendant la Révolution (1789–1799)*, ed. M. Vovelle (Paris: Éditions la Découverte, 1988), 317.

40. F. Furet, "Bonaparte," in Furet and Ozouf, *Dictionnaire Critique*, 219–220.

41. Bonaparte returned to Italy in 1800, defeating the Austrians at Marengo. Other French successes led to a new treaty, at Lunéville, essentially the same as Campo Formio.

42. Lynn Hunt has dissected the implications of this substitution of Hercules for Marianne within the larger context of Jacobin misogyny. See *Politics, Culture, and Class in the French Revolution* (Berkeley: University of California Press, 1984), esp. Chap. 3.

43. E. Burke and T. Paine, *Reflections on the Revolution in France and The Rights of Man* (Garden City, NY: Anchor Books, 1973), 19–20. This useful paperback, now out of print, contains the full texts of these two fundamental reactions to the French Revolution.

44. Hufton, *Women and Citizenship*, 35.

45. Mercier, *Le Nouveau Paris*, 453 on paper; 469 on *bureaucratie*—a word actually created in 1793 and made widespread by Mercier himself.

46. In that sense, I would argue that they went against a trend already clear at the end of the Ancien Régime. Village communities seem to have revived their own democratic traditions in the eighteenth century, developing powerful village assemblies. Such assemblies existed in late medieval times and in the sixteenth century, but seem to have become disoriented by the transition to the more powerful central state in the seventeenth century. In the eighteenth century, I believe they revived as an effective mechanism mediating village relations with that state. Alas, for the moment such opinions are mere speculation; we lack systematic research on this vital topic that would enable one to offer stronger conclusions.

47. M. Wollstonecraft, *A Vindication of the Rights of Woman*, ed. C. Poston (New York: Norton, 1975, 1988), 3–5, selections.

48. The RER segment of the Métro just abolished this distinction in December 1999. I would see a difference between such means of long-range transportation as trains and planes and mass transit, provided as a public service.

49. The democratic principle, of course, existed in these other regions long before anyone had heard of the French Revolution. The Atlantic Revolutions—in the

United States, the Netherlands, France, Haiti, and Poland, to cite the most prominent—gave new impulse to such principles in many areas.

50. *Brandade* is creamed cod; *bouillabaise* is a fish stew.

51. Mercier, *Le nouveau Paris*, 431. Endymion was the handsome shepherd whom Diana (also goddess of the moon) observed asleep one night. Taken by his beauty, she descended to Earth to kiss him in his sleep. Endymion has been the subject of many poems, perhaps most famously that of John Keats.

52. B. Deloche and J.-M Leniaud, *La Culture des Sans-Culottes* (Paris: Editions de Paris, Presses de Languedoc, 1989), 259–260.

53. Most of these names reverted back later on.

54. Here one must allow for much wider swings of fashion than in men's clothing. Women's clothing, as the annual Paris fashion shows amply attest, still contains significant elements of the extreme, the ridiculous, and the impractical.

55. Doyle, *Oxford History*, 200.

56. Michelet, *Histoire de France*, v. XVII (Lausanne: Editions Rencontre, 1967), 438.

57. Cited in Huet, *Morning Glory*, 163.

A P P E N D I X

The following documents are provided to help readers get a little flavor of the debates of the time, and to offer them the chance to draw some of their own conclusions from original sources. All translations are my own. For further documents in English, I would particularly recommend two collections, the first of them, alas, long out of print.

P. Beik, ed., *The French Revolution.* New York: Walker, 1970.

L. Hunt, *The French Revolution and Human Rights. A Brief Documentary History.* Boston and New York: Bedford Books of St. Martin's Press, 1996.

The *Cahiers* of 1789

Montigny-Montfort, cahier drawn up on 14 March 1789

This serf village had one hundred taxable hearths in 1789, holding six hundred twenty people. About eighty of them showed up for the meeting, most of them peasants. There were eight ploughmen (sometimes calling themselves ploughman-merchant), twenty-one "cultivators," thirty-one cottagers, and a half dozen artisans; only one woman attended. The richest person in the village was the "farmer" of the seigneur, whose tax assessment of 218.3 *livres* was more than double that of the second highest taxpayer and about ten times the assessment of the average cottager.

His Majesty having decided that the representatives of the Third Estate shall equal in number those of the two leading orders combined, it remains only to decide on the manner of voting, which decision he left to the nation assembled.

The main part of the communities demonstrated their wish in this regard and declared for voting by head. . . .

1. Our intention is that our deputies cannot vote on any proposition unless the assembly is composed of deputies, like them, freely elected; unless the deputies of the Third Estate are in equal number to the representatives of the other two combined; unless the deliberations are done by the three orders meeting together; and unless votes are counted by head.

2. We estimate that it is necessary to assure in an invariable manner the periodic meetings of the Estates General, and of provincial estates.

3. The nation cannot be subject to any law that it has not consented, or to the payment of any subsidy it has not accorded.

4. All general laws will be formed and promulgated in general assemblies of the Nation.

5. All taxes and public charges, present and to come, without distinction, will be assessed equally on all citizens in just proportion to their properties and faculties.

6. The individual liberty of all citizens must be assured in an inviolable manner.

9. The suppression the tax of *franc-fief** and the salt tax, or at least the reduction of the price of salt to no more than one half of what it is today, must be a principal objective of the deputies.

10. The land tax seems to be the most just, but as it might be insufficient, it would be agreeable to levy taxes on luxury, on liveried servants, on carriages, on all horses other than those used for ploughing, and on all dogs other than those owned by shepherds and ploughmen.

12. The *banalités, mainmortes, corvées,** tolls, and all other charges and servitudes onerous to the people, must be abolished, with payment to the owners after verification of their titles of ownership.

* The *cahier* refers to several traditional levies related to feudalism: the *franc-fief* was the tax paid by a commoner who owned a fief; *banalités* were seigneurial monopolies, such as mills and wine presses; *corvées* were forced labor services, owed initially to the seigneur but, in the eighteenth century, also to the state, for the upkeep of roads. *Mainmorte* had two meanings: in most of France, it meant property whose owner (usually a religious institution) could not bequeath property to an heir, thus inalienable property. Here, in Burgundy, it referred to one of the obligations of serfs. The inhabitants tried to put their complaints about serfdom into the cahier, but the presiding officer of the meeting, Jean Andoche Guiod, judge of the local seigneur, refused to allow them to do so on the grounds that "private interests" could not be discussed in the meeting. He finally agreed to append a special document about their "private" grievances, which listed the many seigneurial duties they paid. The second article explains two key burdens of serfs: "The inhabitants are additionally charged each year to carry out (*corvées*) four ploughings and two hoeings for each ploughman and three hoeings for each cottager, and with the payment of *mainmorte:* when one of a married childless couple dies, the Seigneur gets half the estate, and gets the rest when the other dies, which is unjust, given that the property should revert to the relatives."

Clergy of the diocese of Béziers, cahier drawn up 6 April 1789. The village priests and the bishop quarreled sharply at the assembly

The clergy of the seneschalsy of Béziers asks His Majesty:

1. The maintenance of the Roman Catholic religion as the sole public worship, and to see to the Christian education of the youth by the establishment of one or two bodies of regular clergy (monks or friars) to provide that schooling . . .

2. The execution of the ordinances of the Church and the State for the abstinence prescribed for the holy time of Lent and the sanctification of Sundays

and holy days and to that end that magistrates be enjoined to look to their execution and to the maintenance of good order and of respect for Holy Places.

3. That it be forbidden to non-Catholics to avoid going to priests to declare births, marriages, and deaths, and that civil judges cannot receive declarations from Protestants without a certificate from the (Catholic) parish priest attesting that they are not Catholic.

6. The Clergy offers to contribute to all taxes of whatever kind in proportion to its faculties . . .

8. They demand the periodic meeting of the Estates General, in which the Ministers of His Majesty will have to give account of their administration.

9. They demand the abolition of arbitrary letters of arrests (*lettres de cachet*).

10. They demand the suppression of the salt tax, sales taxes, and import-export duties and that salt be sold for a free market price.

13. They demand the reformation of the civil and criminal codes. . . .

Excerpts from the cahier adopted 26 March 1789 by the nobility of the bailiwick of Longuyon

The Court (Assembly) full of respect and devotion for its Sovereign who has deigned today to call to his august person all the orders of the State not only to bring to him without fear their Wishes but to make use of their enlightenment to attain, and make sure of, the Happiness of all his Subjects. Penetrated by recognition for the well-intentioned views of His Majesty, and animated by a patriotic zeal, the nobility, after maturely deliberating about the abuses that have slipped into all branches of the bodies of the States and of the indispensable reforms to be carried out, puts at the foot of the Throne its wishes and grievances . . .

1. His Majesty is humbly beseeched to accord local estates to the province of Lorraine and Barrois. . . .

2. That it is of great importance to allow the Nobility to keep its honorific distinctions which place it above the people and give it an influence over them, by the respect and the deference that it always has for those it sees honored, distinguished by public opinion, and by the proper authority that is confided to it [the nobility] to maintain internal order in the countryside, on which depends the tranquility and felicity of the public.

3. Take away all considerations from the nobles and the seigneurs in their lands and you will see the people arrogant, undisciplined, and contemptuous of the same orders they have respected. . . . the Nobility and the Seigneurs, after reflections made by a sincere desire for the public good, demand that no attack be made against their prosperity, fiefs, rents, and other rights, and that local justice (i.e., seigneurial courts) be allowed to judge without appeal all cases between private individuals involving less than 50

livres. . . . and that all rights that Seigneurs had held or hold that have been altered or lost by time and circumstance be reestablished . . .

4. That all laws be proposed, deliberated, and sanctioned by the Estates General to be promulgated afterwards in the name of the Monarch and that the Estates General meet at fixed intervals . . .

5. That no Citizen can be judged except by the law and by magistrates and that all arbitrary letters of arrest be suppressed.

6. That the Ministers be accountable to the Estates General . . .

7. That all pecuniary privileges be abolished and that no future subsidies be created that are not equally divided among all the orders without distinction.

17. That there be established in the province a heraldic tribunal composed of gentlemen to judge definitively all proofs of nobility.

18. That the Deputies first occupy themselves in determining the national debt and that they cannot consent to any subsidies before a Constitution is first established . . .

Excerpts from the cahiers of the town of Alençon, drawn up 28 February 1789

The commune of Alençon, penetrated by the necessity to see to the good of the State, to repair the numberless evils caused by abuses that have slipped into all parts of the administration, recommends to its deputies that they distance themselves from anything that may serve as a pretext of disunion among the three orders of the State.

They must regard France as an immense family whom common interests bring together; it is by the reunion of all its forces and all the knowledge of each individual that the general good must be carried out. Children of the same father, we must all have only one heart and one soul, and if some of us have private rights to claim, it must be the case that the common interest ties us one to the other so strongly that it can even resolve questions of private interest. . . .

They should occupy themselves first with that which might interest the three orders.

It is important to one and all that the rights of the Nation be recognized and restated.

These rights touch upon personal security and on security of property; they were established by a general convention that cannot have any other goal than the interest of all and of each in particular.

It is to avoid the evils of arbitrary authority that the Nation must recover the right to make law concurrently with the monarch. This law must be the principle of the sovereign power, as well as that of the obedience of the people; it is to this law that the executive power must ceaselessly subordinate itself; it is this law that must be the rule for the power of the magistrate established to oversee its strict observance; once established, neither the monarch nor the magistrate can have the right to change or modify it.

If the legislative power belongs to the Nation, the Nation must exercise it in all ways possible; it is the Nation that establishes civil and criminal law and taxes. . . . [they go on to call for regular meetings of the Estates General].

A law is vicious if it does not guarantee the surety of the citizen. This surety must extend to the person and property of the citizen. . . .

Personal liberty depends on the absolute liberty that all citizens must have; it must be general and undefined and allow him to entirely follow his will, in everything that is not contrary to the law. . . .

The surety of citizens requires too that the judge be established by the suffrage of all citizens. Confidence cannot be commanded; it is a chimera if based on constraint.

. . . It is necessary that the Nation have the right to consent to all taxes and to fix the contribution of each citizen; it is the Nation that must see to the assessment and recovery of all taxes (they go on to call for the abolition of all tax farms and monopolies).

Third Estate of Longuyon, preamble to cahier of 26 March 1789

Everything the French have always wanted with the greatest ardor receives today its entire accomplishment, we desire a King who only wishes to govern by Laws, a Sovereign passionate with an extreme love of justice, desirous of procuring for us days of tranquility, of sweetness and peace, we possess it, the Nation assembles, happy day for us! A day of even more consolation for our Sovereign, who will know in it even more the Love of his people, all will tell him that if the Throne were elective, it would be he whom our Wishes would call to it, and that we have always loved him and cherished him, that in the midst of the evils and the multiple attacks against public and private liberty that draw from us tears of despair, we have kept him in our Hearts, we admire him in silence.

It is to remedy these evils to recompense our love that good will as well as justice permits us to present to him our grievances and our reclamations. The Third Estate of the bailiwick of Longuyon presents its grievances with the confidence that children have in their Father, consequently the Lord King is very humbly supplicated to agree: first, that the general assembly, before listening to anything, before according any tax, before taking any action on the public debt, pronounce and decide definitively that the Votes will be counted by head . . .

That afterwards the assembly solicit from his good will and his justice a law under the name of contract or social act between the Sovereign and his people, which would become for the future the Safeguard of the personal liberty of all citizens, of the general and private prosperity, the buttress of the Throne, and above all the protection against the return of these disastrous events that oppress at this time the King and the Nation.

Selection of comments from the cahiers of Paris

All selections from C.-L. Chassin, *Les Élections et les cahiers de Paris en 1789* (Paris: Jouast et Sigaux: Paris, 1888; reprint edition of 1967), 4 vols. Volume number and page numbers in parentheses for each entry.

General cahier of the Clergy (III, 305–317)

The clergy of Paris, *intra muros*, penetrated by gratefulness to the King, and impressed by the desire to aid, as much as it might depend on them, to the views of justice and good will that led His Majesty to bring his Nation to him to assure the happiness of his peoples and the prosperity of his empire . . . in these sentiments of love and confidence, which establish between the Nation and its King the essential rapport, that Religion commands and the interest of the State requires, that the Clergy of Paris charges its deputies to the Estates General to demand:

1. That the Apostolic Roman Catholic religion, the only true one, the only religion of the State, of which the principles are so intimately tied to the maintenance of authority and to the happiness of peoples, be conserved in all of its integrity, and that to it alone, to the exclusion of all others, belong public exercise of religion.

2. That, in consequence, His Majesty be supplicated to order the revision of the edict of September 1787 concerning non-Catholics; the Clergy cannot dissimulate the lively alarm this edict inspires in them. (This edict allowed non–Catholics to baptize their children, get married, and bury the dead in their own churches and to declare births, marriages, and deaths only to state clerks, rather than to their parish Catholic priest, as had been the case before.)

8. That religious orders be conserved and protected as useful, not only to Religion but even to the State. . .

17. . . . the Clergy of Paris demands that education be confided in all provinces to the different religious orders . . .

20. That there be established and founded in each parish, in proportion to their size, free schools, but distinct and separate for the one and the other sex.

Section on constitution and civil administration

But, before continuing with its grievances, and making known its views on political and civil administration, the Clergy of Paris, inviolably attached to the constant doctrine of the Church of France, as well as to the ancient principles of the French Constitution, and justly alarmed by the sort of revolution that dangerous and foreign opinions have made in spirits, rushes to declare:

That the French government is a purely monarchic government

That the sovereign and legislative power resides in the sole person of the King

But that, in the exercise of his authority, the monarch is tied by fundamental and constitutional laws, and that forms exist which must necessarily precede and prepare the execution of these laws.

That it regards as belonging essentially to the Constitution the right that the French Nation has not to pay any taxes or subsidies except those freely consented and determined, in form, size, and duration

the inviolable right that all Orders, all corporations, all private individuals have to be conserved and maintained in all their properties

the right that every individual has not be deprived of his personal liberty, except in cases, and by forms determined by the law

the existence, the distinction and the reciprocal independence of the three Orders; independence such that none of the Orders can be deprived of its right to vote separately, nor obliged by the deliberations of the two others . . .

That the act of humanity and justice of which our august monarch has solemnly given the example, be imitated everywhere in France, and that one make disappear the last vestiges of personal serfdom, indemnifying the seigneurs when need be.

That the slave trade be itself totally suppressed, if it is possible, or at least that one assure, by good laws, to all Blacks in our colonies a gentle and moderate treatment, and all the aid of religion and humanity.

Clergy of the parish of St-Paul, cahier (I, 50–54)

Objects relative to the good of the three Orders:

1. The will of the Assembly is that it belongs essentially to the Nation to rule on the Constitution, to set up its bases, and to itself make its laws, with the assistance of the Sovereign.

2. That the executive power resides essentially and uniquely in the person of the Monarch.

3. That liberty of the press be accorded and wisely tempered by the responsibility of the author and the printer of the work.

4. That the Ministers and all administrators be responsible for their administration to the Estates General.

5. That all properties founded on real (legal) titles be respected.

6. That the Estates General be convoked at regular, fixed intervals.

7. That no citizen can be arrested in virtue of an arbitrary letter of arrest ...

8. That no tax be established, no loan be considered legitimate unless it has been consented by the Estates General.

9. That votes by taken by head at the upcoming Estates for the creation of articles that must establish the Constitution, and then, once the Constitution is established, that they deliberate by Order; the first means being more fitting to find out the general will, the second for conserving common and respective interests.

16. That all humiliating forms to which the men and deputies of the Third Estate have been subject be abolished, no man must be at the knees of another man.

22. That all little spectacles (theaters, etc.) of the capital, fecund source of all corruption, be suppressed.

General cahier of the Nobility (II, 320–323)

The wish of the noble Citizens of Paris is that opinion be given by Order at the Estates General, that, on this question itself, the Estates only deliberate by Order ... nonetheless, the Estates General will advise in their wisdom the means to prevent the veto of one Order being able to oppose the confection of laws that interest the general happiness of the Nation....

[handwritten margin note: Rule ≠ majority vote]

The deputies will demand before all else that there be made an explicit Declaration of the rights that belong to all men, and that it set forth their liberty, their property, their surety.

Immediately after this Declaration, they will demand that it be recognized as the first principle of the Constitution, that the throne is hereditary in the August reigning family, from male to male, following the order of primogeniture, to the exclusion of women and of the female line....

They will then demand that it be made statute:

That all laws can only be made by the agreement of the Estates General and the King.

That the executive power belong in its entirety to the King alone.

That individual liberty be assured by a law against all arbitrary attacks.

That the press be free, and that a special law clearly and precisely define what will be the crimes in such matters (as libel), and by what penalties they will be repressed and punished.

That property will be sacred ...

That the Estates General alone can accord subsidies, determine their nature, their means, their length; that no loan will be opened or extended, that no creation of offices, no levy of money will be made without their consent ...

That the Estates General have regular meetings, convoked at least every three years ...

That the Estates General, having always been the only ones competent to vote subsidies, declare all those that exist today suppressed by right, that nonetheless they reestablish them for the moment, solely for the time of their meeting, so that no necessary expense remain suspended ...

[handwritten note: Nobility demanding permanent representative body]

Cahier of the Third Estate, district of Filles-Saint-Thomas, article 4 (II, 411)

Attest that all French people are born free and equal, in rights, and that all power derives from the Nation.

Cahier of the Third Estate, district of the Mathurins (II, 426–430)

Liberty, property—that's what constitutes a real monarchy.

Liberty cannot be reconciled with arbitrary orders; property cannot exist if the faculty to tax does not reside uniquely in the Nation assembled.

It is to these two essential and fundamental principles that the principal objects to be demanded must refer back.

1. That the Estates General of the kingdom be assembled at least every three years . . .

2. That no public act be reputed law, if it has not been consented or demanded by the Estates General.

4. That the Bastille be demolished, and that there be raised in its place a monument with the statue of the King, with the inscription at its base: To Louis XVI, King of a free people.

[handwritten: July 14, 1789.]

*[handwritten: *Storming of Bastille not Spontaneous]*

Cahier of the Third Estate, district of St-Germain-des-Prés (II, 430–431)

1. That it be ruled that to the Nation assembled, reunited with the King, belongs the right to make the laws of the kingdom.

2. That to the Nation alone belongs the right to accord the subsidies necessary for the needs of the State.

3. That no contribution be consented by the Estates General until the national Constitution is recognized.

[handwritten: want constitution b/c want constitutional monarchy]

[handwritten margin note: educated & free]

Cahier of the Third Estate, district of Théatins (II, 433–437)

3. That there be made a formal law by which in the future deputies from the Third Estate can in no case be chosen other than from that order alone . . .

6. The legislative power be forever separated from the executive power and put into the hands of the Nation.

It is easy to demonstrate that it cannot be otherwise except in a country under submission to despotism.

14. All arbitrary taxes be suppressed and replaced by others equally distributed. (Article 16 demands the abolition of the salt taxes, sales taxes, entry duties, etc.)

25. That it be permitted to priests to marry, because marriage is not incompatible with their functions and is not forbidden to them by any divine law.

26. That divorce similarly be permitted, because an indissoluble contract is contrary to the inconstant character of man.

29. That it be finally recognized that toleration is one of the most essential virtues in the state of society, and that it does not belong to man to decide on that which does not belong to man. All religions are permitted in the most polite Nation in the world. They can there worship in public and these religions will no longer be a motive of exclusion to any of the privileges heretofore enjoyed by Roman Catholics.

30. That religious professions (monks, nuns, etc.) in the future be generally extinguished and suppressed, as contrary to the social will and to the good of the fatherland, whose population they diminish . . . and their goods, acquired by the Nation, will serve for the payment of the national debt and a multitude of purposes of general utility. This article is one of the most important of this *Cahier*.

31. That the revenues of bishops, abbots, priors, vicars, curates . . . be distributed in a less unequal and less revolting proportion . . . so that no vicar should have less than 1,200 *livres* or revenue.

41. That one destroy forever this shameful prejudice that punishes bastards, and that they be admitted indistinctly to all public or private functions.

Article 6 of the Cahier of the Third Estate, district of Saint-Joseph, in the Halles quarter (II, 449)

roots of radicalism 3-4 yrs later

working ex

6. That the Bastille crumble and rot, that this same soil, watered by the tears of the victims of arbitrary power, be henceforth watered only by tears of lightness and appreciation; that the place, scourged by the continued existence of this living sepulcher, be henceforth ennobled by a national monument, raised to the glory of our good King, and which will preserve for posterity the memory of his virtues and his love for the French, of whom he is the father, that the demolitions of this vast tomb themselves serve to lay the foundations of a temple to Liberty by a monument to the Estates General, and like the brave Americans, who transformed into defensive weapons the statue of their oppressor, we will transform this refuge of tyranny and of tears into a refuge of liberty and concord: let us be French, in a word, that is to say free, and the buttresses of the Throne and of the Fatherland.

Citizenship

Declaration of the Rights of Man and of the Citizen, 26 August 1789

By the National Assembly of France
The representatives of the people of France, formed into a National Assembly, considering that ignorance, neglect, or contempt of human rights, are the sole causes of public misfortunes and corruptions of government, have resolved to set forth in a solemn declaration, these natural, imprescriptible, and unalienable rights: that this declaration, being constantly present to the minds of the members of the body social, they may be ever kept attentive to their rights and their duties: that the acts of the leg-

islative and executive powers of government, being capable of being every moment compared with the end of political institutions, may be more respected: and also, that the future claims of the citizens, being directed by simple and incontestible principles, may always tend to the maintenance of the Constitution, and the general happiness.

"For these reasons the National Assembly doth recognize and declare, in the presence of the Supreme Being, and with the hope of His blessing and favor, the following sacred rights of men and of citizens:

I. Men are born, and always continue, free, and equal in respect of their rights. Civil distinctions, therefore, can be founded only on public utility.

II. The end of all political associations, is, the preservation of the natural and imprescriptible rights of men; and these rights are liberty, property, security, and resistance of oppression.

III. The nation is essentially the source of all sovereignty; nor can any individual, or any body of men, be entitled to any authority which is not expressly derived from it.

IV. Political liberty consists in the power of doing whatever does not injure another. The exercise of the natural rights of every man has no other limits than those which are necessary to secure to every other man the free exercise of the same rights; and these limits are determinable only by the law.

V. The law ought to prohibit only actions hurtful to society. What is not prohibited by the law, should not be hindered; should any one be compelled to that which the law does not require.

VI. The law is an expression of the will of the community. All citizens have a right to concur, either personally, or by their representatives, in its formation. It should be the same to all, whether it protects or punishes; and all being equal in its sight, are equally eligible to all honors, places, and employments, according to their different abilities, without any other distinction than that created by their virtues and talents.

VII. No man should be accused, arrested, or held in confinement, except in cases determined by the law, and according to the forms which it has prescribed. All who promote, solicit, execute, or cause to be executed, arbitrary orders, ought to be punished; and every citizen called upon or apprehended by virtue of the law, ought immediately to obey, and renders himself culpable by resistance.

VIII. The law ought to impose no other penalties but such as are absolutely and evidently necessary: and no one ought to be punished, but in virtue of a law promulgated before the offense, and legally applied.

IX. Every man being presumed innocent till he had been convicted, whenever his detention becomes indispensable, all rigor to him, more than is necessary to secure his person, ought to be provided against by the law.

X. No man ought to be molested on account of his opinions, not even on account of his religious opinions, provided his avowal of them does not disturb the public order established by the law.

XI. The unrestrained communication of thoughts and opinions being one of the most precious rights of man, every citizen may speak, write, and publish freely, provided he is responsible for the abuse of this liberty in cases determined by the law.

XII. A public force being necessary to give security to the rights of men and of citizens, that force is instituted for the benefit of the community, and not for the particular benefit of the persons with whom it is intrusted.

XIII. A common contribution being necessary for the support of the public force, and for defraying the other expenses of government, it ought to be divided equally among the members of the community, according to their abilities.

XIV. Every citizen has a right, either by himself or his representative, to a free voice in determining the necessity of public contributions, the appropriation of them, and their amount, mode of assessment, and duration.

XV. Every community has a right to demand of all its agents, an account of their conduct.

XVI. Every community in which a separation of powers and a security of rights is not provided for, wants a constitution.

XVII. The rights to property being inviolable and sacred, no one ought to be deprived of it, except in cases of evident public necessity, legally ascertained, and on condition of a previous just indemnity.

Speeches by Robespierre and Barnave on the suffrage, 1791

Maximilien Robespierre was unable to give this speech to the National Assembly, so he had it printed in March–April 1791. He speaks here against a property qualification for voters. He lost the debate in 1791, but the Constitution of the Year II enacted universal manhood suffrage. That constitution collapsed with the Jacobins; the Constitution of 1795 returned to a property qualification. Translation from Beik, *The French Revolution,* pp. 14–35, selections.

Messieurs, I questioned, for a moment, whether I should propose to you my ideas concerning the provisions you appear to have adopted. But I saw that it was a question of defending the cause of the nation and of liberty, or of betraying it by my silence; and I wavered no longer. I have even undertaken this task with a confidence all the more firm in that the imperious passion for justice and the public welfare which imposed it on me were common to us both and it is your own principles and authority that I invoke in their favor.

Why are we gathered in this temple of the laws? Without doubt, to give to the French nation the exercise of the imprescriptible rights which belong to all men.

This is the purpose of every political constitution. If it fulfills this aim, it is just and free; if it opposes this aim, it is nothing but a conspiracy against mankind.

You recognized this truth yourselves, in a striking manner, when you decided, before beginning your great work, that a solemn declaration must be made of the sacred rights that serve as the immutable foundations upon which that work must rest.

"All men are born and remain free, and are equal before the law."

"Sovereignty resides essentially in the nation."

"The law is the expression of the general will. All citizens have the right to concur in its making, either by themselves or through their freely elected representatives."

"All citizens are eligible to all public offices, without any other distinction than that of their virtues and talents."

These are the principles that you have consecrated: it will now be readily seen which are the measures that I wish to combat; it will be sufficient to test them against these immutable laws of human society.

Now,

1. Is the law the expression of the general will when the greater number of those for whom it is made can have no hand whatever in its making? No. And yet to deny such men as do not pay a tax equal to three days' waged the right even to choose the electors whose task it is to name the members of the legislative assembly—what is this but to deprive a majority of the French completely of the right to make the laws? This provision is therefore essentially unconstitutional and antisocial.

2. Are men equal in rights when some are endowed with the exclusive faculty of eligibility to the legislative body or to other public institutions, and others merely with that of electing them, while the rest are deprived of all these rights at once? No. Yet such are the monstrous distinctions drawn between them by the decrees that make a man active or passive, or half active and half passive, according to the varying degrees of fortune that permit him to pay three weeks' wages, ten days' wages in direct taxes, or a silver mark. All these provisions are, then, essentially unconstitutional and antisocial.

3. Are men admissible to all public employments, with no other distinctions than virtues and talents, when inability to pay the required tax excludes them from every public office without regard for the virtues and talents that they possess? No. All these provisions are therefore essentially unconstitutional and antisocial.

4. And again, is the nation sovereign when the majority of the persons composing it is deprived of the political rights which constitute sovereignty? No. And yet you have just seen that these same decrees deny them to the majority of the French. What, then, would your Declaration of Rights amount to if these decrees were allowed to continue? An empty formula. What would the nation become? A slave; for liberty consists of obeying laws one has given oneself, and slavery of having to submit to the will of another. What would your constitution become? A veritable aristocracy. For aristocracy is the condition in

which one part of the citizens is sovereign and the rest subjects. And what an aristocracy! The most intolerable of all: that of the rich.

All men born and domiciled in France are members of the political society called the French nation; that is to say, they are French citizens. They are so by the nature of things and by the first principle of the law of nations. The rights attached to this title do not depend on the fortune that each man possesses, nor on the portion of the taxes to which he is subject, because it is not taxes that make us citizens; it is citizenship that obliges one to contribute to public expenditure in proportion to one's means. Now, you may give laws to citizens—but you may not annihilate them as citizens.

All the good that you have done was a duty of the most serious kind. Failure to do all the good that you can would be a breach of trust; the harm that you would be doing would be a crime against the nation and against humanity. And more: if you do not do everything for liberty, you will have done nothing. There are not two ways of being free: one must be so entirely or become a slave again. The least resource left to despotism will soon restore its power. Yes, already it surrounds you with its seductive influences; soon it will overwhelm you with its power. Oh, you who are proud to have attached your names to a great change and are not too concerned whether it is sufficient to assure the happiness of mankind, do not be deceived; the din of praise that novelty and superficiality have produced will soon die away; posterity, comparing the greatness of your obligations and the immensity of your resources with the fundamental vices of your work, will say of you, with indignation: "They could have made men happy and free, but they did not wish to; they were unworthy."

But, you will say, the people! Those who have nothing to lose! They will be able, like us, to exercise all the rights of citizenship.

People who have nothing to lose! How unjust, how false is this proud, crazy language in the sight of truth!

These men of whom you speak are apparently men who live, who subsist in the heart of society, with no means of living or subsisting. For if they have such means, they have, it seems to me, something to lose of to preserve. Yes, the rough clothing that covers me, the humble retreat where I buy the right to withdraw and to live in peace; the modest wage with which I nourish my wife, my children; these are not, I admit, lands, ch,treaux, or coaches-and-pairs; all that is called nothing, perhaps, by luxury and opulence; but it is something to humanity; it is a sacred property—as sacred, no doubt, as the brilliant possessions of the rich.

I will say more! My liberty, my life, the right to obtain protection or vengeance for myself and for those who are dear to me, the right to repel oppression and to exercise freely all the faculties of my mind and heart; all these so good belongings, the first that nature has bestowed on man—are they not placed, like your own, under the protection of the laws? And yet you say that I have not interest in these laws; and you wish to deprive me of the share that I must have, as you must, in the administration of public affairs, and for no other reason than that you are richer than I! Ah! If the balance should cease to be equal, should it not favor the citizens of lesser fortune? Have not the laws been framed and the public authority been established to protect the weak against injustice and oppression? To place the public authority entirely in the hands of the rich is therefore to flour all the principles that govern society. . . .

Authority cannot retreat without compromising itself, it was said, although in fact it had sometimes been forced to draw back. This maxim was actually good for despotism, whose oppressive power could be sustained only by illusions and terror; but the tutelary authority of the nation's representatives, based both on the general interest and on the strength of the nation itself, can repair a disastrous error without running any risk other than of awakening the sentiments of confidence and admiration which encompass it; it can be compromised only by an invincible perseverance in measures contrary to liberty and rejected by public opinion. There are some decrees, however, which you cannot repeal, namely those to be found in the Declaration of the Rights of Man, because it was not you who made these laws; you only announced them. It is to the immutable decrees of the eternal legislator placed in the reason and hearts of all men before you ever inscribed them in your code that I appeal against the dispositions which infringe them and must disappear before them. . . .

Antoine Barnave, speaking to the National Assembly on 11 August 1791, here opposes raising the property qualification for electors, but defends the principle of property qualifications for voters (active citizens) and for electors. The Constitution of 1791 did have such qualifications. Translation from Beik, *The French Revolution*, pp. 169–176, selections.

Representative Government and Social Order, National Assembly Session of Thursday, 11 August 1791

M. Barnave:

I maintain that the proposal put forth by M. Roederer [to close the discussion] is not a regular motion, but a means by which he intends to fight the committee's proposal, a proposal which I defend. The true means of upholding, in the integrity of its principles, the constitution that has been decreed is to set it on pure and unshakable foundations. It shows a poor understanding of the means to establish liberty to search for it in what destroys it. It is not enough to want to be free; it is still necessary to know how to be free. [Murmurs on the far left; applause everywhere else.]

All those who have opposed the opinion of the committee have shared this fundamental error in their means; they have confused democratic government and representative government. It is because of this that they have mistakenly identified the rights of the people with the position of elector, which is merely a public function to which no one has a right, and which society assigns as its interest prescribes.

In democratic countries, one can with seriousness examine from the point of view of the rights of man the question of the quota of property or of tax contribution necessary to constitute the citizen and give him the right to vote in pubic assemblies; but where the government is representative, and especially where there exists an intermediate degree of electors, because it is on behalf of the entire society that each elects, the society in whose name and for whose sake the election takes place has the basic right to determine the conditions under which it wishes the choices to be made on its account by certain individuals. If there exist individual rights among the political rights in your constitution, that of active citizen is such a right; your committees have not proposed that you alter it.

The function of the elector is not a right; once again, it is for everyone that any one person exercises it; it is for everyone that the active citizens name the electors; it is for the sake of the entire society that they exist; it is for society alone to determine the conditions under which one can be an elector . . .

I demand of those who come to us with comparisons of those governments (of ancient Athens and Sparta) with our own whether they wish to purchase liberty at such a price (slavery). I demand of those who ceaselessly profess here metaphysical ideas of liberty, because they have no real ideas of liberty, of those who ceaselessly plunge us into clouds of theory, because the essential, fundamental notions of governments are absolutely unknown to them; if, when they come before this assembly to set pure democracies against the representative government for whose sake I will shortly demonstrate that the decree which we propose to you is indispensably necessary; I demand of them once again whether they have forgotten that which experience proves, that the pure democracy of a part of the people can exist only through the civil, political, effective, and absolute slavery of the other part of the people.

Now I say that representative government, the first, the freest, the most noble of governments, has only one trap to avoid, has only one failure to fear: that is corruption. I say that for representative government to be eternally good, eternally free, there is only one anxiety, one care to consider when it is constituted, and that is the purity and so far as possible the incorruptibility of the electoral body. But, Gentlemen, if there lies the true base of representative government, it follows that every form which, for whoever has eyes to see, clearly tends to subject the election of representatives to the influence of the government itself or of rich citizens is by that very fact equivalent to the complete destruction of representative government.

You have been shown from different points of view the three advantages that should be found in electoral assemblies. First, enlightenment; and it is impossible to deny that, not in the case of any particular individual but in that of a large number of men, a certain amount of wealth, a certain tax contribution, is to a degree an indication of more extensive enlightenment. The second guarantee lies in the interest in public affairs on the part of the one whom society has charged with the making of its choices. And then the last guarantee lies in the independence of fortune which, in placing the individual above need, more or less places him beyond the reach of corruption.

These three means of achieving liberty, these three guarantees that the electoral assemblies can give to the nation in the persons of the electors who compose them—I do not look for them in the superior class, for it is there, without a doubt, that along with the independence of the enlightened one would find too easily motives that are personal and interests stemming from private ambitions that are removed from the public interest, and also means of corruption which, while different from those stemming from need, often are all the more alarming for liberty.

Gentlemen, you have established, at least through custom, that the electors would not be paid; and it is recognized, by each of us, that the very large number of members whom, for the maintenance of public liberty, you have introduced into the electoral assemblies would make very expensive, quite apart from other difficulties, the payment that would be accorded to them. Now I say, however, that from the moment the elector is without sufficient property to refrain from working for a certain period of time and to pay the expenses of his transportation to the place of the election, one of these three things must happen, that he forego the election, that he be paid by the state; or else, finally, that he be paid by the person who wishes to be elected. [Sharp applause.]

As soon as the government is determined, as soon as, by an established constitution, the rights of each individual are regulated and guaranteed (and that is the moment I hope we are going to reach), then there is no longer any difference of interest between men who live by their property and those who live by honest work. Then there remain in society only two opposed interests, the interest of those who want to preserve the existing state of affairs because they see in it well-being combined with property, existence with work; and the interest of those who wish to change the existing state of affairs because there is no resource for them except in a succession of revolutions; because they are beings who fatten and grow, as it were, in troubled times, like maggots in putridity. [Sharp applause.] Well, it is true that in an established constitution, all who are honest, all who want well-being and peace, have essentially the same interest. Everything depends on placing the common interest in the hands of those who, in that very extensive class, have enlightenment, somewhat more of a personal interest that deters them from corruption, and finally the necessary guarantee that will provide everyone with the certainty that their common interests will be well defended.

Therefore I want the electors to be taken from this general class, but from this same class I want chosen those who have, or show promise of having, a certain enlightenment, who are not easily deceived; those who, in this common interest that they share with everyone, find enough advantages, and who have a way of life to preserve that is important enough so that they would will not sacrifice it for the personal advantages of those who would pit against the common interest they have with society the particular interest of corruption: for it is necessary for the one who elects on behalf of society to be attached to the social interest by his property in such a way that it is not easy to offer him through corruption an interest greater than that which binds him to the common and general interest. To the extent that you stray from this principle you will fall, as I have assured you, into the only abuse of representative government: your elections will be corrupt. Does anyone flatter himself that there will always prevail this ardent and pure zeal for liberty that animates the least affluent citizens in a time of revolution? Is it not known that in peaceful times an alliance is always formed between the poorest class and the government or the opulence that is its source of livelihood? Poverty, extreme poverty, in the electoral corps, will have no other effect than to place wealth, extreme wealth, or corruption into the legislative corps; and you will see happen in France what occurs daily in England in borough elections where the electors are generally very poor: sometimes the election will not even be managed by means of money, a method which would at least limit corruption because of its very high cost, but will be purchased with pots of beer, as is done in England by a very great many members of Parliament.

Let us return, then, to the principal point, which is not to seek representation in either of the two extreme classes, neither among extremely rich men nor among extremely poor men, but in the middle class; and let us see whether that is where the committee has placed it.

They will not propose to you dispositions beyond those that they have presented to you, but I declare to you that what is here proposed is the view of all the members, the only real and direct guarantee of the conversation of France's liberty, tranquillity, and prosperity. [Applause]

Women's Rights and Revolution

Address of French Citizenesses to the National Assembly, 12 July 1791 Written by Etta Palm d'Aelders

The chains of the French have loudly fallen away, the Éclat of their fall turning despots pale and shaking their thrones; an astonished Europe has fixed an attentive eye on the star that illuminates France and on the august senate that represents a people who, to the wish to be free add the love of being just.

Yes, gentlemen, you have broken the cold bronze scepter to put it its place the olive branch, you have sworn to protect the weak, it is your duty, it is your happiness, it is in your interest to destroy at their source those Gothic laws that abandoned the weaker but more interesting half of humanity to a humiliating existence, to an eternal slavery.

In recognizing his rights, you have rendered to man the dignity of his being, you will not leave women to buckle under an arbitrary authority, for to do so would be to overthrow the fundamental principles on which repose the majestic edifice you have built with your indefatigable work for the happiness of the French; it is not longer time for tergivisations; philosophy has taken truth out of the shadows; the hour sounds; justice, sister of liberty, calls for the equality of rights of all individuals, without difference of sex, the laws of a free people must be equal for all beings, like the air and the sun! For too long, alas! the imprescriptible rights of nature have been misunderstood; for too long bizarre laws, worthy product of centuries of ignorance, have afflicted humanity; and finally, for too long the most odious tyranny has been consecrated by absurd laws. . . . (She demands the recission of article XIII of the new code of police, which gives husbands authority over their wives.)

Conjugal authority can only follow upon the social pact. It is part of the wisdom of legislation; it is in the general interest to establish a balance between despotism and license; but the power of the husband and wife must be equal and individual. The laws cannot establish any difference between these two authorities . . . Fathers of the fatherland, do not soil your immortal work by such a discordant stain; you must make a moral code, without question, but mores are the work of time and education; they cannot be commanded; . . .

Representatives of the nation, in the name of your honor, in the name of holy liberty, reject the unjust and impolitic code; it will be the apple of discord in families, the tomb of liberty; constraint flays the soul; the slave thinks only of breaking her/his chains, of revenge for servitude; without doubt the committee, to present this odious article, consulted theologians and not philosophers. Heh! Consult only your heart; it will instruct you better than the maxims of the jurisconsults of past centuries; these men immersed in despotism, who take the avidity of their souls for an effect of virtue. Nature forms us to be your equals, your companions, and your friends: we are the support of your childhood, the felicity of your maturity, and the consolation of your old age; sacred titles for you to recognize.

Declaration of the Rights of Women and of the Female Citizen, Olympe de Gouges (Marie Gouze), 1791

A fuller text of the document can be found in Hunt, *The French Revolution and Human Rights.* I have included a brief citation from a preliminary statement attached to the Declaration that Hunt does not translate.

Man, are you capable of being just? It's a woman who asks you the question; you will, at least, not deny her that right. [De Gouges uses the familiar "tu" form of you throughout.] Who gave you the sovereign empire to oppress my sex? Your force? Your talents? Observe the Creator in his/her wisdom; examine nature in all its grandeur, which you seem to wish to approach, and give me, if you dare, an example of this tyrannic empire. Go to the animals, consult the elements, study the plants, and finally glance at all the modification of organized matter . . . look, rummage through, and distinguish, if you can, the sexes in the workings of nature. Everywhere you will find them mixed together, everywhere they cooperate in a harmonious ensemble in this immortal masterpiece.

Only man has ridiculously clothed himself in a principle of exemption to this rule. Bizarre, blind, puffed up by sciences and degenerated, in this century of enlightenment and sagacity, by the most crass ignorance, he wishes to command as a despot over a sex that has received all intellectual faculties; he pretends to play at revolution, and to demand his rights to equality, to say nothing more.

Preamble

Mothers, daughters, sisters, the female representatives of the nation, demand to be constituted into a national assembly. Considering that ignorance, neglect, or contempt for the rights of woman are the sole causes of public unhappiness and the corruption of governments, they have resolved to set forth in a solemn declaration, the natural, inalienable, and sacred rights of woman, in order that this declaration, constantly before all members of the body social, will ceaselessly recall for them their rights and their duties . . .

In consequence, the sex superior in beauty as in courage, in maternal suffering, recognizes and declares, in the presence and under the auspices of the Supreme Being, the following Rights of Woman and the Citizeness:

1. Woman is born free and remains equal in rights to man. Social distinctions can only be founded on common utility.

2. The goal of all political association is the conservation of the natural and imprescriptible rights of Woman and of Man: these rights are liberty, property, security, and, above all, resistance to oppression.

3. The principle of all sovereignty resides essentially in the Nation, which is nothing more than the reunion of Woman and Man . . .

4. Liberty and justice consist in rendering to the other all that belongs to her or him; thus the exercise of the natural rights of woman has no other limits

than those opposed to it by the perpetual tyranny of man; these limits must be reformed by the laws of nature and reason.

6. The law must be the expression of the general will; all Citizenesses and Citizens must participate in its formation, either themselves or through their representatives; it must be the same for all; all citizenesses and citizens, being equal in its eyes, must be equally admissible, according to their abilities, to all public honors, positions, and employments, without other distinction than their virtues and talents.

Postscript

Woman, wake up! The tocsin of reason is making itself heard throughout the universe; recognize your rights. The powerful empire of nature is not longer surrounded by prejudices, fanaticism, superstition, and lies. The torch of liberty has dissipated all the clouds of besotted folly and usurpation. . . . Oh women! Women, when will you cease to be blind? What are the advantages you have harvested from the Revolution? A more marked contempt, a more signal disdain. In the centuries of corruption, you reigned only over the weakness of men. Your empire is destroyed; what remains to you? The conviction of the injustices of man. The insistent demand for your patrimony, founded on the wise decrees of nature: how can you fear for so beautiful an enterprise?

The Fall of the King

The following materials all come from the *Archives Parlementaires,* the chronological record of debates in French representative assemblies, beginning in 1787. The originals can be found in the records for the indicated days.

"The King's declaration addressed to all French people on his leaving Paris," 20 June 1791. The secretary of the National Constituent Assembly read the declaration to the deputies.

As long as the king could hope to see reborn the kingdom's order and happiness, through the means employed by the National Assembly and through his residence next to that Assembly in the capital of his kingdom, no personal sacrifice was too great; he would not even have complained against the nullity of all his efforts caused by his absolute lack of liberty since the month of October 1789, if this hope could be fulfilled; but today the sole recompense of so many sacrifices is to witness the destruction of royalty, to see all powers unrecognized, properties violated, the security of people everywhere placed in danger, crimes resting unpunished, and a complete anarchy establishing itself above the laws, without the appearance of authority given to them by the new Constitution being sufficient to remedy a single of the evils that afflict the kingdom: the king, after having solemnly protested against all the acts carried out in his name during his captivity, believes he must put before the eyes of the French and of all the universe the picture of his conduct, and that of the government that has been established in the kingdom.

We have seen His Majesty, during the month of July 1789, to distance any cause of defiance, send away the troops he had called close to his person; that after the first flares of revolt had already manifested themselves in Paris and even in the regiment of his guards, the king, strong in his conscience and the rightness of his intentions, did not fear to come alone among the citizens of his capital. . . . Everyone knows the events of the night of October 6th (1789), and the impunity that has covered them for more than two years. God alone prevented the execution of even greater crimes, and turned the French nation away from a stain that would have been inexpungible. . . .

But the more sacrifices the king made for the happiness of his peoples, the more the factions worked to misrepresent his actions, and to present royalty under the most false and most odious colors.

The convocation of the Estates General, the doubling of the Third, the pains the king took to level out all the difficulties that might retard the assembly of the Estates General, and those that were raised after their opening, all of the retrenching in his own expenses, all the sacrifices that he made for his peoples at the session of 23 June (1789); finally the union of the three orders, carried out by the king's will, a measure that His Majesty then judged indispensable for the activity of the Estates General: all of his efforts, all of his pains, all his generosity, all of his devotion to his people, all has been misunderstood, all has been denatured.

When the Estates General, having given itself the name of National Assembly, began to occupy itself with the Constitution of the kingdom, one recalls the memoirs that the factions took the initiative to have brought from several provinces, and there were movements in Paris tending to make the deputies fail to carry out one of the principal clauses in all of their cahiers, which stated that the making of the laws would be done in concert with the king. In contempt of this clause, the Assembly placed the king outside of the Constitutional process, refusing to grant him the right to agree to or to refuse his sanction . . .

Justice

The king has no participation in the making of the laws . . . Justice is rendered in the king's name, the letters of provision of judges are sent by him, but it is only a matter of form . . .

Interior administration

It is entirely in the hands of the departments, the districts, and the municipalities, overly numerous jurisdictions that gum up the machinery of government and often work at cross purposes. . . .

What becomes of an army when it has neither leaders nor discipline? Instead of being the force and safeguard of a State, it then becomes its terror and scourge. How many French soldiers, when their eyes have been unclouded will not blush at their conduct, and will not look with horror on those who have perverted the good spirit that reigned in the French army and navy? What disastrous dispositions encourage soldiers and sailors to frequent political clubs! The king has always thought that the law must be equal for all: officers who are in the wrong must be punished; but they, like subalterns, must be punished according to dispositions fixed by laws and regulations; all doors must be open so that merit can show itself and can advance; all the welfare that one can give to soldiers is just and necessary, but there cannot be an army without officers and without discipline, and there will never be officers or discipline so long as the soldiers believe they have the right to judge the conduct of their leaders. . . .

Finances

The king had declared, well before the convocation of the Estates General, that he recognized that the assemblies of the nation had the right to accord subsidies, and that he did not wish to tax his peoples without their consent. All of the *cahiers* of the deputies to the Estates General agreed in putting the reestablishment of the finances in the first rank of the matters with which the Assembly should occupy itself. . . . The 4 of February 1790 the king himself pressed the Assembly to deal effectively with so important a task; it did not do so until too late, and in an imperfect manner. . . . The Assembly hurried to replace taxes the weight of which, in truth, lay too heavily on the people, but which did provide assured resources . . . The ordinary taxes are now greatly in arrears and the extraordinary resource of the 1200 million *(livres)* of *assignats* is practically all used up. . . .

But the more we see the Assembly approach the end of its labors, the more we see wise men losing their credit, the more we see increase each day dispositions that can only cause difficulty and even impossibility in the conduct of government, and inspire for it mistrust and disfavor: the other regulations, instead of applying healing balm to the wounds that still bleed in several provinces, instead only increase disquiet and make the discontented more bitter. The spirit of political clubs dominates and invades everything; the thousand calumnious and incendiary newspapers and pamphlets that are daily circulated are only their echoes, and prepare spirits for the direction in which they wish to lead them. The National Assembly has never dared to remedy this license, so far from a true liberty; it has lost its credit, and even the force of which it has need to retrace its footsteps and change that which seems to it proper to correct. One sees in the spirit that reigns in the political clubs, and the manner in which they have taken over the new primary assemblies, what one can expect of them; and if they give an inkling of any disposition to come back for any change, it is to destroy the remainder of royalty and establish a metaphysical and philosophical government, impossible to carry out.

People of France, is this what you meant in sending your representatives to the National Assembly? Do you desire that the anarchy and the despotism of the political clubs replace the monarchical government under which the nation has prospered for fourteen hundred years? Do you desire to see your king covered with insults and deprived of his liberty, while he concerns himself only with establishing yours?

Given all these reasons, and the impossibility in which the king finds himself to work for the good and to prevent the bad being committed, is it astonishing that the king has sought to recover his freedom and to put he and his family in security?

People of France, above all you Parisians, inhabitants of a city that the ancestors of His Majesty like to call the good town of Paris, beware of the suggestions and the lies of your false friends; come back to your king; he will always be your father, your best friend. What pleasure would he not have in forgetting all the personal injuries and to find himself once again among you, when a Constitution, which he will have freely accepted, by which our holy religion will be respected, and by which the government will be established on a stable footing and be useful in its actions, when the goods and the estate of each will not be troubled, when the laws will not be violated with impunity, and, finally, in which liberty will be laid atop firm and unbreakable foundations.

The reading of the declaration led to a tumultuous debate. Abbé Grégoire spoke first, moving that a copy of the declaration be sent to the constitutional committee; that motion passed without debate. Antoine Barnave then insisted that the declaration was too important a document merely to be passed to a single committee; he further suggested that all military officers in the Paris region swear an oath to carry out the orders of the Assembly. Robespierre took a much more militant line.

M. Robespierre: I can only say that I am astonished that in such circumstances we only propose such insignificant and illusory measures, and that we offer to the nation only a new oath, after so many others. The other measures already taken by the National Assembly seem to me equally weak and insufficient; but I believe at the same time that this moment is not ripe for preparing men; that we must know more specifically the circumstances that led to the great event that concerns us; and that we must first think profoundly. What the National Assembly must do in order not to mislead the nation is to warn all good citizens to look out for traitors and to protect the health of the common wealth (*chose publicque*).

Danton's speech of 2 September 1792

This speech comes from Georges Danton, at that time Minister of Justice, speaking to the Legislative Assembly on 2 September 1792, requesting support for decrees setting up house-to-house searches for arms in Paris, and punishment for "enemies of the fatherland" who do not cooperate. Reports of the speech helped inflame the crowds carrying out the September Massacres. I have left the last sentence in the original French because it is Danton's most famous phrase, and gives a sense of the flavor of his rhetorical flourishes.

It's quite satisfying, Gentlemen, for the ministers of a free people to be able to announce to them that the fatherland has been saved. (Applause.) Everyone rises up, everyone trembles, everyone burns to fight.

You know that Verdun is no longer in the power of our enemies. You know that the garrison has sworn to immolate the first man who suggests surrender. A part of the people has headed to the frontier, another digs entrenchments, a third, armed with pikes, defends the interior of our cities.

Paris seconds this great efforts. The commissioners of the Commune (town government) have solemnly proclaimed an invitation to the citizens to arm themselves and march for the defense of the fatherland. It is in this moment, Gentlemen, that you can declare that the capital has proved itself worthy to all of France. It is in this moment that the National Assembly has become a veritable committee of war.

We ask that you work with us to lead this sublime movement of the people, by naming commissioners who will assist us in this great measures.

We ask that who refuses to serve in person or to provide his arms, be punished with death. (Applause.)

We ask that instructions be provided to citizens to lead their movements. We ask that couriers be sent to all the departments to let them know about the decrees that you will have issued.

The tocsin that has sounded is not an alarm signal, it's the signal to attack the enemies of the fatherland. (Lively applause.)

Pour les vaincre, Messieurs, il nous faut de l'audace, encore de l'audace, toujours de l'audace, et la France est sauvée. (Redoubled applause). (To defeat them, Gentlemen, we need audacity, still more audacity, always audacity, and France will be saved.)

Voting for the death of Louis XVI (15–16 January 1793)

Each deputy at the Convention had to give his opinion on the question of the sentence for Louis XVI. He had been unanimously found guilty of treason, but the question of the sentence—death or imprisonment, followed by banishment—sharply divided the Convention. The deputies could take three positions: death; death, with a later consideration of a suspended sentence and exile; imprisonment for the duration of the war, followed by exile. Those voting death achieved a majority, but that majority required the votes of the group expecting a subsequent suspension of the sentence. When that issue came to vote later on, however, the Convention rejected it by a clear majority and condemned the king to immediate death; he went to the guillotine a few days later. Herewith a sample of some of the brief speeches deputies gave when announcing their vote in favor of death.

Robespierre (Paris): I don't like long speeches on obvious questions: they are a sinister presaging for liberty; they cannot add to the love of the truth and to patriotism, which renders them superfluous. . . . All that I know is that we are the representatives of the people, sent to cement public liberty by the condemnation of the tyrant, and that's enough. I do not know how to offend outrageously reason and justice in regarding the life of a despot as more worthy than those of simple citizens, and torturing my spirit to let the greatest of the guilty escape from the penalty that the law pronounces against crimes much less serious, and which have already been inflicted on his accomplices. I am inflexible toward oppressors because I am compassionate toward the oppressed; I do not know a humanity that rips out the throat of the people and which pardons despots. . . . I do not know how to oppose words devoid of sense and unintelligible distinctions to certain principles and imperative obligations. I vote for death.

Danton (Paris): I am not among that mob of statesmen who ignore that one does not deal with tyrants, who ignore that one only strikes kings in the head, who ignore that one cannot expect anything from Europe except through the force of our arms. I vote for the death of the tyrant.

Lavicomterie (Paris): As long as the tyrant breathes, liberty is in peril; the blood of citizens cries out for vengeance; I vote for death.

Raffron du Trouillet (Paris): I vote for the death of the tyrant within twenty-four hours. We must purge the soil of the fatherland as quickly as possible of this odious monster.

Panis (Paris): Imprisonment or banishment could rip out the throat of new-born liberty. The law, justice, the fatherland, those are my motives; I vote for death.

Robert (Paris): I condemn the tyrant to death, and in pronouncing that decree, I have only one regret: that my jurisdiction does not extend to all tyrants, to condemn them all to the same fate.

Garrau (Gironde): Citizens, I do not examine whether we must bring a judgment against Louis, or take a measure for general security. Louis is convicted of having conspired against (public) security; I open the book of the law, I find that it carries the penalty of death against all conspirators; I vote for death.

Deleyre (Gironde): To frighten tyrants and those who would succeed Louis; to maintain the Republic; for the health of the people; for the instruction of the human species, I vote death.

Notes

1. Original found in R. Robin, *La société française en 1789*. Semur-en-Auxois. (Paris: Plon, 1970), 410–415.

2. Original found in B. Hyslop, *A guide to the general cahiers with the texts of unedited cahiers* (New York: Octagon, 1936, 1968), 221–223.

3. Original found in Hyslop, *A guide to the general cahiers,* 316–318.

4. I have used the word deference to translate in the phrase "les differences qu'il a toujours pour ceux qu'il voit honorer"; differences in this sense clearly means those distinctions based on the higher status of the nobility, for which I think the English word deference is the closest translation.

5. Original in R. Jouanne, *Cahiers de doléances des corps et corporations de la ville d'Alençon.* (Alençon: Imprimerie alençonnaise, 1929), 100–105.

6. Original in Hyslop, *Guide,* 319.

7. In French modifiers agree with the gender of the noun modified, thus the original French makes it impossible to know if de Gouges might have thought that God was a woman.

8. The king is being disingenuous about his enthusiasm for representative bodies voting taxation prior to 1789; the Assemblies of Notables of 1787 and 1788 collapsed because Louis refused to grant this principle. His other comments about finances, however, are well taken.

9. The phrase "chose publicque" literally means the public thing; all of Robespierre's listeners would have known its long association with the Latin *res publica,* which would have had the English translation commonwealth or, in the late eighteenth century, republic. In calling for the protection of the "chose publicque," therefore, Robespierre here makes an oblique, yet clear reference to the republic. Immediately after the king's forced return, he and the Jacobins clamored for the abolition of the monarchy and the creation of a republic, in the modern sense of the term.

BIBLIOGRAPHY

Primary Sources

The following list of primary sources merely scratches the surface of what is available for the late eighteenth century. Interested readers will want to read the great thinkers of the time, such as Rousseau and Voltaire. I have also listed below only those memoirs that I have used extensively; the list of memoirs available would run on far too long.

P. de Beaumarchais, *The Barber of Seville and the Marriage of Figaro,* trans. J. Wood. Harmondsworth: Penguin Books, 1964.

P. Beik, ed., *The French Revolution.* New York: Walker, 1970.

E. Burke and T. Paine, *Reflections on the Revolution in France and The Rights of Man.* Garden City, NY: Anchor Books, 1973.

Ch.-L. Chassin, *Les Élections et les Cahiers de Paris en 1789.* Paris: Jouast et Sigaux, 1888, four vols., Geneva reprint edition of 1967.

G. Chinard, ed., *The Letters of Lafayette and Jefferson.* Baltimore and Paris: The Johns Hopkins University Press and Les Belles Lettres, 1929.

C. Desmoulins, *Œuvres de Camille Desmoulins.* Paris: Ebrard, 1838; reprinted in New York: AMS, 1972.

The Despatches of Earl Gower, ed. O. Browning. Cambridge: Cambridge University Press, 1885.

O. Equiano, "The Interesting Life of Olaudah Equiano," in *Classic Slave Narratives,* ed. H. L. Gates. New York: Mentor, 1987. A new edition of this classic has just appeared, edited by W. Sollors, *The Interesting Narrative of the Life of Olaudah Equiano.* New York: Norton, 2001.

C. Guittard de Floriban, *Journal de Célestin Guittard de Floriban, Bourgeois de Paris sous la Révolution,* ed. R. Aubert. Paris: Éditions France-Empire, 1974.

L. Gottschalk, ed., *The Letters of Lafayette to Washington, 1777–1799,* ed. Philadelphia: American Philosophical Society, 1976.

M. Lhéritier, ed., *Les débuts de la Révolution à Bordeaux d'après les Tablettes manuscrites de Pierre Bernadau.* Paris: Société d'histoire de la Révolution Française, 1919.

J. de Maistre, *Considerations on France,* trans. and ed. R. Lebrun. Cambridge: Cambridge University Press, 1994.

J.-P. Marat, *Œuvres Politiques,* ed. J. De Cock and C. Goëtz. Brussels: Pole Nord, 1989–1993, 5 vols.

J. Ménétra, *Journal of My Life,* intro. D. Roche, trans. A. Goldhammer. New York: Columbia University Press, 1986.

G. Morris, *A Diary of the French Revolution,* ed. B. Cary Davenport. Boston: Houghton Mifflin, 1939, two vols.

N. Retif de la Bretonne, *Les Nuits Révolutionnaires, 1789–1793,* ed. M. Dorigny. Paris: Les Éditions de Paris, 1989. Excerpts taken from Les Nuits de Paris.

N. Ruault, *Gazette d'un Parisien sous la Révolution. Lettres à son frère, 1783–1796,* ed. A. Vassal and C. Rimbaud. Paris: Librairie Académique, 1976.

L. de Tourzel, *Mémoires de Madame la duchesse de Tourzel, gouvernante des enfants de France de 1789 à 1795,* J. Chalon, ed. Paris: Mercure de France, 1969.

G. Washington, *Writings,* ed. John Rhodehamel. New York: Literary Classics of the United States, 1997.

H. M. Williams, *An Eye-Witness Account of the French Revolution* by Helen Maria Williams. *Letters Containing a Sketch of the Politics of France,* J. Fruchtman, Jr., ed. New York: Peter Lang, 1997.

Witness to the Revolution: American and British Commentators in France, 1788–94. ed. P. Burley. London: Weidenfeld & Nicolson, 1989.

M. Wollstonecraft, *A Vindication of the Rights of Woman,* ed. C. Poston. New York: Norton, 1975, 1988.

A. Young, *Travels during the Years 1787, 1788 and 1789.* London: W. Richardson, 1794, three vols.

General Works

There are many multivolume histories of the Revolution. The classic ones are by Alphonse Aulard, Thomas Carlisle, Jean Jaurès, Georges Lefebvre, and Albert Mathiez. To them one must add Alexis de Tocqueville's *The Old Regime and the French Revolution,* more of an essay than a detailed look at the Revolution, but a book fundamental to any understanding of the historiography of the Revolution.

M. Bouloiseau, *The Jacobin Republic 1792–1794,* trans. J. Mandelbaum. Cambridge: Cambridge University Press, 1983.

A. Cobban, *The Social Interpretation of the French Revolution.* Cambridge: Cambridge University Press, 1964. See also volume I of Cobban's three-volume *History of Modern France.*

W. Doyle, *The Origins of the French Revolution.* Oxford and New York: Oxford University Press, 1980.

_____, *The Oxford History of the French Revolution.* Oxford and New York: Oxford University Press, 1989.

F. Furet, *Revolutionary France, 1770–1880,* trans. A. Nevill Oxford: Basil Blackwell, 1992; Paris: Hachette, 1988.

F. Furet and M. Ozouf, *Dictionnaire Critique de la Révolution Française.* Paris: Flammarion, 1988.

G. Lefebvre, *The Coming of the French Revolution,* trans. R. R. Palmer. Princeton: Princeton University Press, 1947, 1989.

A. Soboul, *The French Revolution, 1787–1799,* trans. A. Forrest and C. Jones. New York: Random House, 1974.

D. Sutherland, *France 1789–1815, Revolution and Counter-Revolution.* New York: Oxford University Press, 1986.

M. Vovelle, *The Fall of the French Monarchy, 1787–1792,* trans. S. Burke. Cambridge: Cambridge University Press, 1983.

D. Woronoff, *The Thermidorian Regime and the Directory 1794–1799,* trans. J. Jackson. Cambridge: Cambridge University Press, 1983.

Chapters 1-5

The following select bibliography focuses on works written in English. Readers interested in more detailed bibliography can consult the works cited here.

R. Andrews, *Law, Magistracy, and Crime in Old Regime Paris, 1735–1789.* Cambridge: Cambridge University Press, 1994.

K. Baker, Condorcet, from *Natural Philosophy to Social Mathematics.* Chicago: University of Chicago Press, 1975.

_____, ed., *The French Revolution and the Creation of Modern Political Culture.* Oxford and New York: Pergamon Press, 1987–89, four vols.

B. Barry, *Senegambia and the Atlantic Slave Trade,* trans. A. Armah. Cambridge: Cambridge University Press, 1998.

D. Bell, *Lawyers and Citizens: The Making of a Political Elite in Eighteenth-Century France.* Oxford and New York: Oxford University Press, 1994.

L. Berlanstein, *The Barristers of Toulouse in the Eighteenth Century.* Baltimore and London: Johns Hopkins University Press, 1975.

G. Bossenga, *The Politics of Privilege. Old Regime and Revolution in Lille.* Cambridge: Cambridge University Press, 1991.

T. Brennan, *Burgundy to Champagne, the Wine Trade in Early Modern France.* Baltimore: Johns Hopkins University Press, 1997.

_____, *Public Drinking and Popular Culture in Eighteenth Century Paris.* Princeton: Princeton University Press, 1988.

D. Brewer, *The Discourse of Enlightenment in Eighteenth-Century France.* Cambridge: Cambridge University Press, 1993.

R. Brubaker, *Citizenship and Nationhood in France and Germany.* Cambridge, MA: Harvard University Press, 1992.

J. Censer, ed., *The French Revolution and Intellectual History.* Chicago: Dorsey Press, 1989. This work offers a superb collection of articles that summarizes key arguments of such important historians as Furet, Hunt, Lucas, Tackett, and others.

R. Chartier, *The Cultural Origins of the French Revolution,* trans. L. Cochrane. Durham: Duke University Press, 1991.

G. Chaussinand-Nogaret, *The French Nobility in the Eighteenth Century,* trans. W. Doyle. Cambridge and New York: Cambridge University Press, 1985.

L. Chevalier, *Laboring Classes and Dangerous Classes in Paris during the First Half of the Nineteenth Century,* trans. F. Jellinek. Princeton: Princeton University Press, 1973.

R. Cobb, *Paris and Its Provinces, 1792–1802.* Oxford: Oxford University Press, 1975.

_____, *The Police and the People: French Popular Protest, 1789–1820.* Oxford: Clarendon Press, 1970. Cobb wrote many iconoclastic books on the Revolution; his work on the Revolutionary armies of 1793 to 1794 is well worth a look, too.

A. Cooper, *Slavery and the French Revolutionists (1788–1805),* trans. F. Keller. Lewiston, NY: Edwin Mellen Press, 1988.

R. Darnton, *The Forbidden Best-Sellers of Pre-Revolutionary France.* New York: Norton, 1996. Darnton has several other books on Enlightenment publishing and other topics in eighteenth-century cultural history; all are important contributions.

_____, *The Kiss of Lamourette.* New York: Norton, 1990. I particularly recommend the essay, "What was so revolutionary about the French Revolution?" in this collection. It appeared first in the New York Review of Books.

B. Deloche and J.-M Leniaud, *La Culture des Sans-Culottes.* Paris: Editions de Paris, Presses de Languedoc, 1989.

W. Doyle, *Venality: The Sale of Offices in Eighteenth-Century France.* Oxford: Clarendon Press, 1996. Doyle has also authored an important book on the Parlement of Bordeaux.

J. Duguet et alia, *La Révolution Français 1789–1799 à Rochefort.* Projets Editions: Poitiers, 1989.

C. Fairchilds, *Domestic Enemies. Servants & Their Masters in Old Regime France.* Baltimore and London: Johns Hopkins University Press, 1984. See also the books by S. Maza and J.-P. Guitton on servants.

C. Fick, *The Making of Haiti: The Saint Domingue Revolution from Below.* Knoxville, TN: University of Tennessee Press, 1990.

S. Fiette, *La noblesse française des Lumières à la Belle Époque.* Paris: Perrin, 1997.

F. Furet, *Interpreting the French Revolution,* trans. E. Forster. Cambridge and New York: Cambridge University Press, 1981.

D. Garrioch, *Neighbourhood and Community in Paris 1740–1790.* Cambridge and New York: Cambridge University Press, 1986.

P. Gay, *The Enlightenment.* New York: Norton, 1969, 1977, two vols.

D. Gordon, *Citizens without Sovereignty. Equality and Sociability in French Thought, 1670-1789.* Princeton: Princeton University Press, 1994.

J. Grieder, *Anglomania in France, 1740–1789.* Geneva: Droz, 1985.

N. Hampson, *Danton.* New York: Holmes & Meier, 1978.

O. Hufton, *The Poor of Eighteenth-Century France, 1750–1789.* Oxford: Clarendon Press, 1974.

L. Hunt, *Politics, Culture, and Class in the French Revolution.* Berkeley: University of California Press, 1984.

_____, *Revolution and Urban Politics in Provincial France, Troyes and Reims, 1786–1790.* Stanford: Stanford University Press, 1978.

R. Isherwood, *Farce and Fantasy. Popular Entertainment in Eighteenth-Century Paris.* New York: Oxford University Press, 1986.

C. L. R. James, *The Black Jacobins: Toussaint Louverture and the San Domino Revolution.* London: Allison & Busby, 1936, 1980.

H. C. Johnson, *The Midi in Revolution. A Study of Regional Political Diversity, 1789–1793.* Princeton: Princeton University Press, 1986.

J. H. Johnson, *Listening in Paris: A Cultural History.* Berkeley: University of California Press, 1995.

P. Jones, *The Peasantry in the French Revolution.* Cambridge: Cambridge University Press, 1988.

S. Kaplan, *The Bakers of Paris and the Bread Question, 1700–1775.* Durham: Duke University Press, 1998. Kaplan's earlier works on the grain trade are also must reading for understanding the trade in this most critical of commodities. His delightful work on the historians' quarrel at the time of the Bicentennial (1989), *Farewell Revolution,* offers unmatched insights into the politics of Revolution historiography.

E. Kennedy, *Cultural History of the French Revolution.* New Haven: Yale University Press, 1989.

M. Kennedy, *The Jacobin Club of Marseilles.* Ithaca: Cornell University Press, 1973. Kennedy has also published three books on the history of the Jacobin clubs during the Revolution.

G. Lefebvre, *The Great Fear of 1789,* trans. J. White. New York: Pantheon, 1973. Lefebvre dominated the scholarship of the Revolution from the 1930s through the late 1950s; his thesis on the peasants of northern France during the Revolution, one of the last books he published, is of particular importance. Readers will want to compare his presentation of that issue with the one of Liana Vardi, also listed in this bibliography.

C. Lucas, *The Structure of the Terror, the Example of Javogues and the Loire.* Oxford and London: Oxford University Press, 1973.

F. Lyons, *France under the Directory.* Cambridge: Cambridge University Press, 1975.

F. Malino, *A Jew in the French Revolution: The Life of Zalkind Hourwitz.* Oxford: Blackwell, 1996.

_____, *The Sephardic Jews of Bordeaux: Assimilation and Emancipation in Revolutionary and Napoleonic France.* University, AL: The University of Alabama Press, 1978.

H. Mason, ed., *The Darnton Debate. Books and Revolution in the Eighteenth Century. Studies on Voltaire and the Eighteenth Century, 39.* Oxford: Voltaire Foundation, 1998.

A. Mathiez, *Études sur Robespierre.* Paris: Éditions sociales, 1973. Mathiez wrote many books on the Jacobin period, on topics ranging from famine to Danton.

S. Maza, *Private Lives and Public Affairs.* Berkeley: University of California Press, 1993. See also Maza's fine book on servants (*Domestic Enemies*).

M. Ozouf, *Festivals and the French Revolution,* trans. A. Sheridan. Cambridge, MA: Harvard University Press, 1988.

R.R. Palmer, *Twelve Who Ruled.* Princeton: Princeton University Press, 1941; New York: Atheneum Publishers, 1965. Palmer's study of Alexis de Tocqueville and his father (*The Two Tocquevilles*) makes for an interesting new look at the son.

J.-R. Pitte, *Gastronomie française. Histoire et géographie d'une passion.* Paris: Fayard, 1991.

M. Price, *Preserving the Monarchy. The comte de Vergennes, 1774–1787.* Cambridge: Cambridge University Press, 1995.

D. Roche, *The People of Paris,* trans. M. Evans and G. Lewis. Berkeley: University of California Press, 1987.

G. Rudé, *The Crowd in the French Revolution.* Oxford: Oxford University Press, 1959. Rudé published many fine books on the Revolution, above all on its crowds.

R. Schneider, *The Ceremonial City. Toulouse Observed 1738–1790.* Princeton: Princeton University Press, 1995.

W. Sewell, *Work and Revolution in France: The Language of Labor from the Old Regime to 1848.* Cambridge and New York: Cambridge University Press, 1980. Sewell also has an interesting book on the Abbé Sièyes.

J. Sirich, *The Revolutionary Committees in the Departments of France, 1793–94.* New York: Howard Fertig, 1971; Harvard Historical Studies, 1943.

M. Slavin, *The Hébertistes to the Guillotine. Anatomy of a "Conspiracy" in Revolutionary France.* Baton Rouge, LA: Louisiana State University Press, 1994.

M. Sonenscher, *Work and Wages. Natural Law, Politics and the Eighteenth-Century French Trades.* Cambridge: Cambridge University Press, 1989. Sonenscher's book on the hatters of eighteenth-century France provides a rare in-depth look at one craft.

J. Swann, *Politics and the Parlement of Paris under Louis XV, 1754–1774.* Cambridge: Cambridge University Press, 1995. J. Rogister's book on the same subject offers a directly contrary view to one set out by Swann.

T. Tackett, *Priest and Parish in Eighteenth-Century France.* Princeton: Princeton University Press, 1977.

_____, *Religion, Revolution, and Regional Culture in Eighteenth-Century France: The Ecclesiastical Oath of 1791.* Princeton: Princeton University Press, 1986.

J. M. Thompson, *Robespierre.* Oxford, New York: Basil Blackwell, 1988. Thompson has also written a one-volume general history of the Revolution.

D. Troyansky, *Old Age in the Old Regime.* Ithaca, NY: Cornell University Press, 1989.

L. Vardi, *The Land and the Loom: Peasants and Profit in Northern France 1680–1800.* Durham: Duke University Press, 1993.

R. Waldinger, P. Dawson, and I. Woloch, eds., *The French Revolution and the Meaning of Citizenship.* Westport: Greenwood Press, 1993.

A. Williams, *The Police of Paris, 1718–1789.* Baton Rouge, LA: Louisiana State University Press, 1979.

Selected Recent Historiography on the French Revolution

SEQ Chapter 1

The historiographical debates on the French Revolution have moved in new directions since the Bicentennial, so I have created a special sub-section for a selection of the most important recent works that focus directly on the Revolution.

F. Aftalion, *The French Revolution, an Economic Interpretation,* trans. M Thom. Cambridge: Cambridge University Press, 1990.

D. Andress, *Massacre at the Champs de Mars. Popular Dissent and Political Culture in the French Revolution.* Woodbridge, Suffolk: Royal Historical Society, Boydell Press, 2000.

H. Applewhite, *Political Alignment in the French National Assembly, 1789–1791.* Baton Rouge and London: Louisiana State University Press, 1993.

B. Baczko, *Ending the Terror. The French Revolution after Robespierre,* trans. M. Petheran. Cambridge: Cambridge University Press, 1994.

K. Baker, *Inventing the French Revolution.* Cambridge and New York: Cambridge University Press, 1990.

J. Bart, *La Révolution française en Bourgogne.* Dijon: La Française d'Édition et d'Imprimerie, 1996.

S. Bernard-Griffiths, M.-C. Chemin, and J. Ehrard, eds., *Revolution Francaise et "Vandalisme Revolutionnaire."* Paris: Universitas, 1992.

P. Bourdin, *Le Noir et le Rouge, itinéraire social, culturel et politique d'un prLtre patriote (1736–1799).* Clermont-Ferrand: Presses Universitaires Blaise-Pascal, 2000.

M. Crook, *Elections in the French Revolution. An Apprenticeship in Democracy, 1789–1799.* Cambridge: Cambridge University Press, 1996.

A. de Baecque, *The Body Politic. Corporeal Metaphor in Revolutionary France, 1770–1800.* Trans. C. Mandell. Stanford: Stanford University Press, 1997.

S. Desan, *Reclaiming the Sacred. Lay Religion and Popular Politics in Revolutionary France.* Ithaca, NY: Cornell University Press, 1990.

A. Forrest, *Soldiers of the French Revolution.* Durham: Duke University Press, 1990. Those interested in military matters will also want to read the works of French scholar J.-P. Bertaud.

M. Fitzsimmons, *The Remaking of France. The National Assembly and the Constitution of 1791.* Cambridge: Cambridge University Press, 1994.

D. Godineau, *The Women of Paris and Their French Revolution,* trans. K. Streip. Berkeley: University of California Press, 1998.

P. Higonnet, *Goodness beyond Virtue: Jacobins during the French Revolution.* Cambridge, Ma.: Harvard University Press, 1998.

P. Gueniffey, *La politique de la Terreur.* Paris: Fayard, 2000.

O. Hufton, *Women and the Limits of Citizenship in the French Revolution.* Toronto: University of Toronto Press, 1992.

M.-H. Huet, *Mourning Glory. The Will of the French Revolution.* Philadelphia: University of Pennsylvania Press, 1997.

L. Hunt, *The Family Romance of the French Revolution.* Berkeley: University of California Press, 1992.

J. Markoff, *The Abolition of Feudalism.* University Park, PA: Pennsylvania State University Press, 1996.

J. Markoff and G. Shapiro, *Revolutionary Demands: A Content Analysis of the Cahiers de Doléances of 1789.* Stanford: Stanford University Press, 1998.

A. Mayer, *The Furies. Violence and Terror in the French and Russian Revolutions.* Princeton: Princeton University Press, 2000.

S. E. Melzer and L. Rabine, *Rebel Daughters. Women and the French Revolution.* New York, Oxford: Oxford University Press, 1992.

J. Popkin, *Revolutionary News: The Press in France 1789–1799.* Durham: Duke University Press, 1990.

D. Roche, *A History of Everyday Things: The Birth of Consumption in France, 1600–1800,* trans. B. Pearce. Cambridge: Cambridge University Press, 2000. Roche has also written a fine book on the history of clothing in this period.

T. Tackett, *Becoming a Revolutionary. The Deputies of the French National Assembly and the Emergence of a Revolutionary Culture (1789–1790).* Princeton: Princeton University Press, 1996.

J. Tulard, *Les temps des passions. Espérances, Tragédies et Mythes sous la Révolution et l'Empire.* Paris: Bartillat, 1996.

J.-M. Varaut, *La Terreur judiciaire. La Révolution contre les droits de l'homme.* Paris: Perrin, 1993.

M. Vovelle, *Revolution against the Church,* trans. A. José. Columbus, OH: Ohio State University Press, 1991. Vovelle has many other important books on the Revolution and the eighteenth century, above all his writings on the history of mentalités.

S. Wahnich, *L'impossible citoyen. L'étranger dans le discours de la Révolution française.* Paris: Albin Michel, 1997.

I. Woloch, *The New Regime. Transformations of the French Civic Order, 1789–1820s.* New York: Norton, 1994. Woloch has written other fine books on the Jacobin clubs after Robespierre and on French veterans.

INDEX